Great Smoky Mountains National Park

Amy C Balfour, Kevin Raub, Regis St Louis, Greg Ward

PLAN YOUR TRIP

Welcome to the Great Smoky Mountains National Park 4
Great Smoky Mountains National Park Map 6
Great Smoky Mountains National Park's Top 10 ... 8
Need to Know 14
What's New 16
If You Like... 17
Month by Month 19
Itineraries 22
Outdoor Activities 26
Travel with Children ... 32

ON THE ROAD

GREAT SMOKY MOUNTAINS NATIONAL PARK ... 38
Day Hikes 39
Newfound Gap Road 39
Roaring Fork Motor Nature Trail, Greenbrier & Around Cosby 50
Cades Cove 52
Cataloochee Valley...... 56
Additional Hikes 58
Overnight Hikes 59
Newfound Gap Road 60
Around Cosby 62
Fontana Dam & Western North Carolina 63
Sights & Activities 65
Newfound Gap Road 65
Cades Cove & Foothills Parkway 68
Cataloochee Valley 70
Fontana Dam & Western North Carolina 71
Courses 72
Sleeping 72
Newfound Gap Road 73
Cosby & Big Creek...... 73

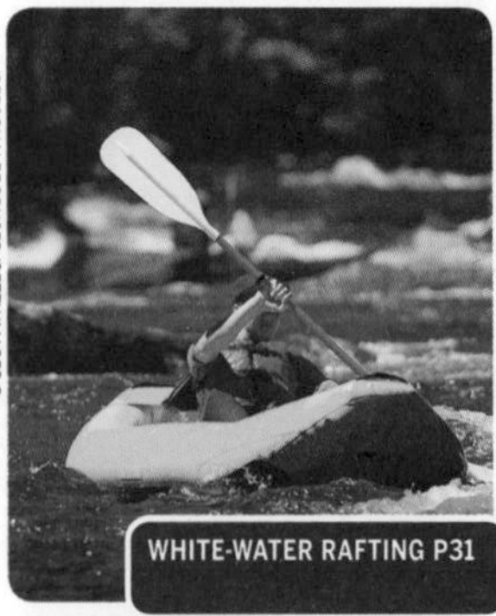
PERSONALPRODUCER/GETTY IMAGES ©
WHITE-WATER RAFTING P31

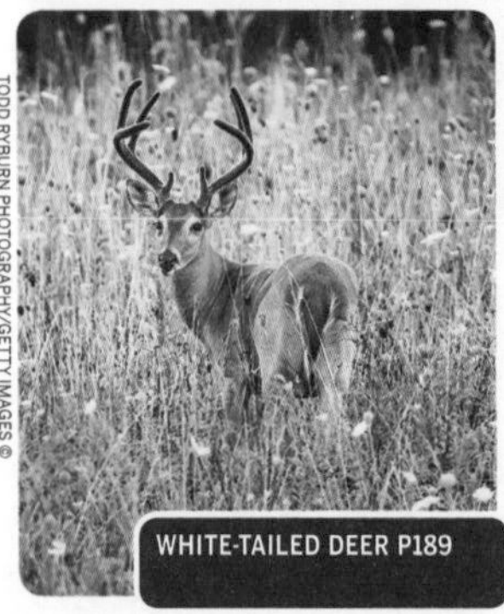
TODD RYBURN PHOTOGRAPHY/GETTY IMAGES ©
WHITE-TAILED DEER P189

KIP STAHL/500PX ©

Contents

Cades Cove, Abrams Creek & Foothills Parkway 76
Cataloochee Valley & Balsam Mountain 76
Fontana Dam & Western North Carolina 76
Eating 77

EAST TENNESSEE ... 79
Knoxville 82
Pigeon Forge 88
Gatlinburg 92
Chattanooga 97
Cherokee National Forest 104

NORTH CAROLINA MOUNTAINS 109
High Country 112
Blowing Rock 112
Boone 115
Asheville 117
Western North Carolina 127
Cherokee 127
Bryson City 129
Pisgah National Forest .. 130
Brevard 131
Nantahala National Forest 133

ATLANTA & NORTH GEORGIA ... 134
Atlanta 135
North Georgia 154
Athens 154
Dahlonega 159
Amicalola Falls State Park 161
Blue Ridge 162
Helen 164
Clayton 168
Tallulah Gorge State Park 169

UNDERSTAND

Great Smoky Mountains National Park Today 174
History 176
Wildlife 185
People of the Smoky Mountains ... 190
Forests of the Smoky Mountains ... 194

SURVIVAL GUIDE

Clothing & Equipment 198
Directory A–Z 202
Transportation 208
Health & Safety 211
Index 217
Map Legend 223

OGLE FARMSTEAD, NOAH OGLE NATURE TRAIL P48

COVID-19

We have re-checked every business in this book before publication to ensure that it is still open after 2020's COVID-19 outbreak. However, the economic and social impacts of COVID-19 will continue to be felt long after the outbreak has been contained, and many businesses, services and events referenced in this guide may experience ongoing restrictions. Some businesses may be temporarily closed, have changed their opening hours and services, or require bookings; some unfortunately could have closed permanently. We suggest you check with venues before visiting for the latest information.

Welcome to Great Smoky Mountains National Park

Get back to nature among mist-shrouded peaks, shimmering waterfalls and lush forests in the great American wilderness.

Forested Landscapes

The sun-dappled forests of the Great Smoky Mountains are a four-season wonderland. Rich blooms of springtime wildflowers come in all colors and sizes, while flame azaleas light up the high-elevation meadows in summer. Autumn brings its own fiery rewards with quilted hues of orange, burgundy and saffron blanketing the mountain slopes. In winter, snow-covered fields and ice-fringed cascades transform the Smokies into a serene, cold-weather retreat. This mesmerizing backdrop is also a World Heritage Site, harboring more biodiversity than any other national park in America.

Echoes of the Past

In small mountain communities around the Smokies, early settlers built log cabins, one-room schoolhouses, stream-fed gristmills and single-steeple churches amid the fertile forest valleys. The park has preserved many of these vestiges of the past, which make up one of the largest collections of log structures in the nation. You can glimpse the lives of these homesteaders while exploring photogenic open-air museums sprinkled across the park. You can walk bridges built by the Civilian Conservation Corps during the Great Depression and explore abandoned resort villages from the lumber days.

Mountain High

The Smokies are part of the vast Appalachian chain, among the oldest mountains on the planet. Formed more than 200 million years ago, these ancient peaks were once much higher – perhaps as high as the Himalayas – but have been worn down by the ages. You can contemplate that remote past while huffing up to the top of a 6000ft peak overlooking the seemingly endless expanses of undulating ridges. There are mesmerizing viewpoints across the park, as well as one mountaintop lodge that can only be reached by foot.

Reconnecting with Nature

The Smokies are a magical place to unplug from modern life and reconnect with nature – indeed you'll be forced to, given the lack of mobile-phone service within the park. Days here are spent hiking past shimmering waterfalls and picnicking beside boulder-filled mountain streams, followed by evenings around the campfire as stars glimmer above the forest. Abundant plant and animal species create memorable opportunities for wildlife-watching, whether seeing elk grazing in Cataloochee, watching turkeys strut near Oconaluftee, or perhaps spying a bear in Cades Cove.

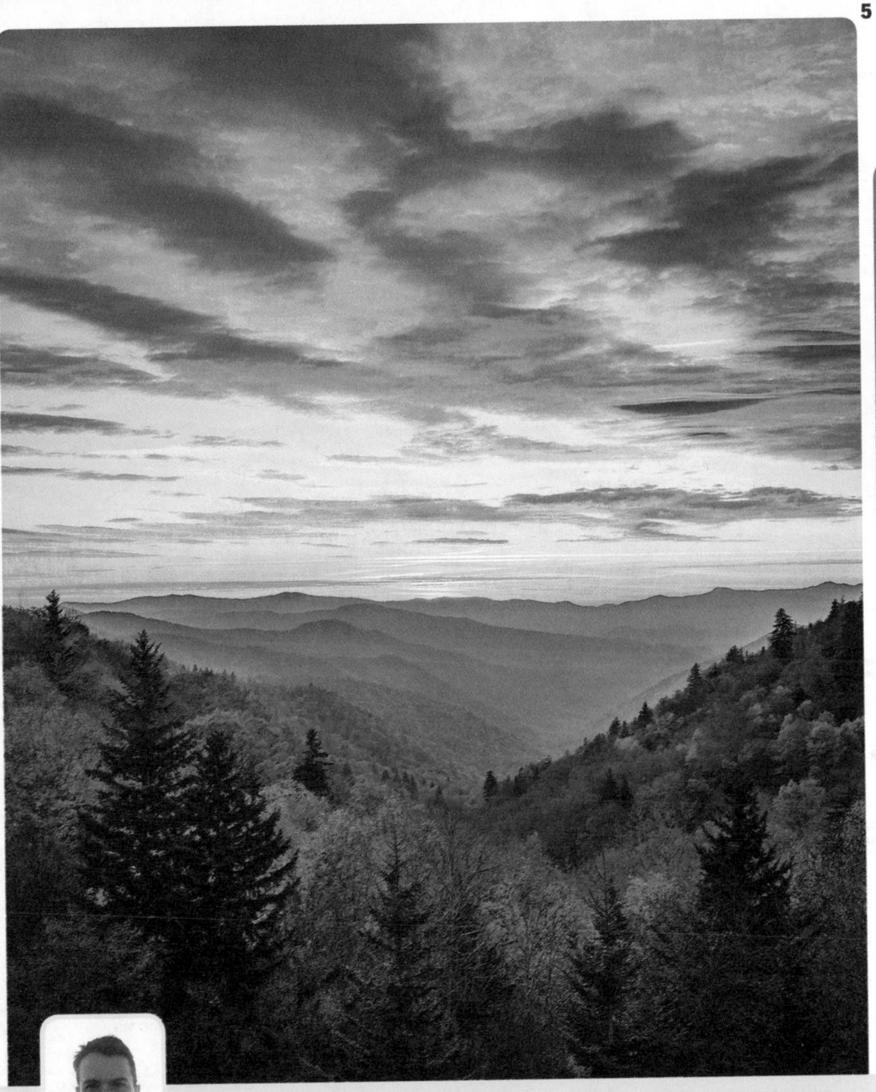

Why I Love Great Smoky Mountains National Park

By Regis St Louis, Writer

I have fond memories of coming to the park as a young boy and experiencing the wonderment of nature for the first time: thundering waterfalls, towering trees that reached high into the sky and fern-lined streams full of salamanders. Years later, after returning with my own children, I realized these biologically rich forests have lost none of their magic. The Smokies have so many different facets – from the hundreds of miles of hiking trails to the myriad cascades and breathtaking mountaintop views – it's hard not to be filled with wonder after a trip here.

For more about our writers, see p224

Above: View from the Oconaluftee Valley Overlook (p47)

Great Smoky Mountains National Park

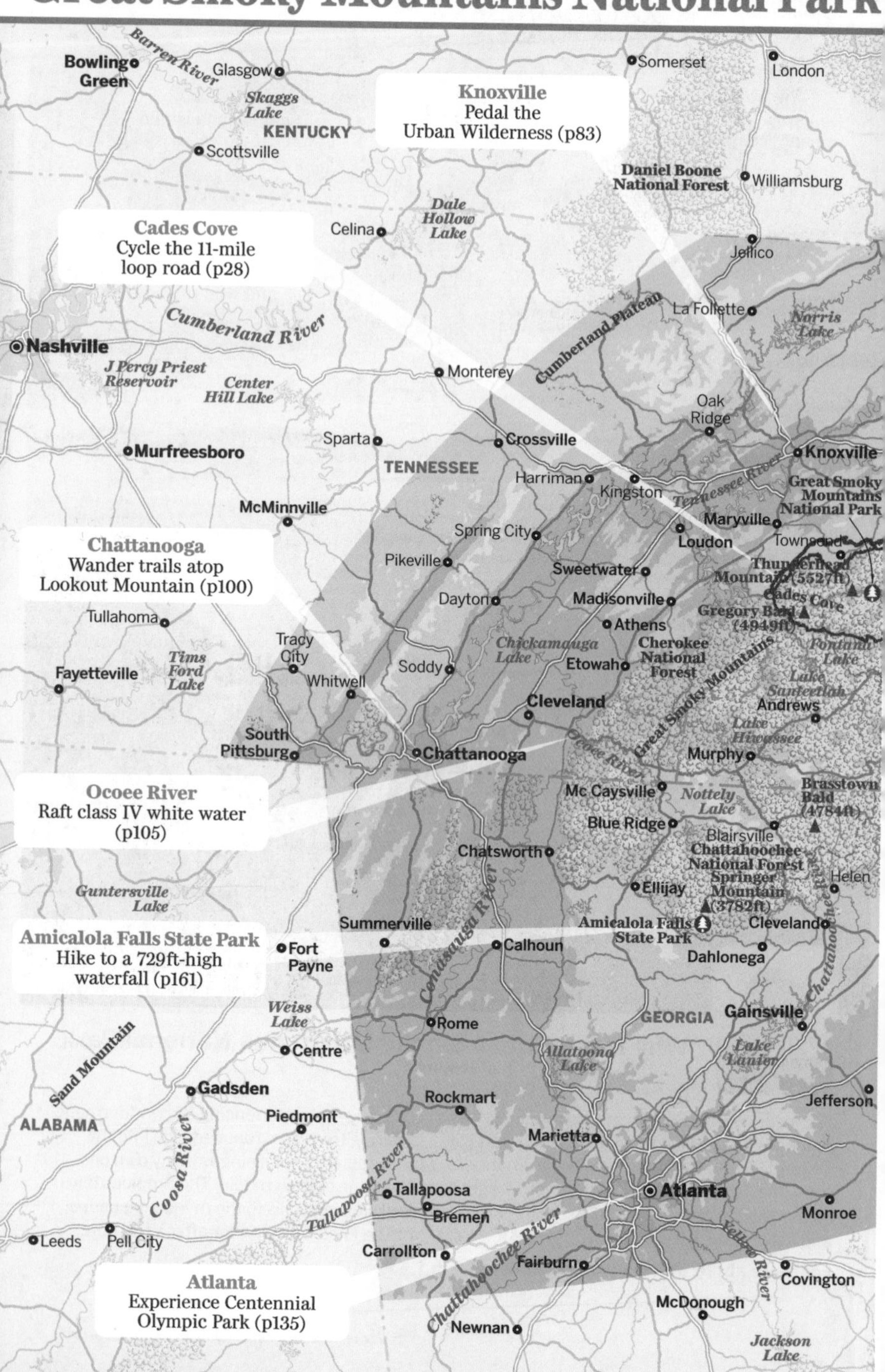

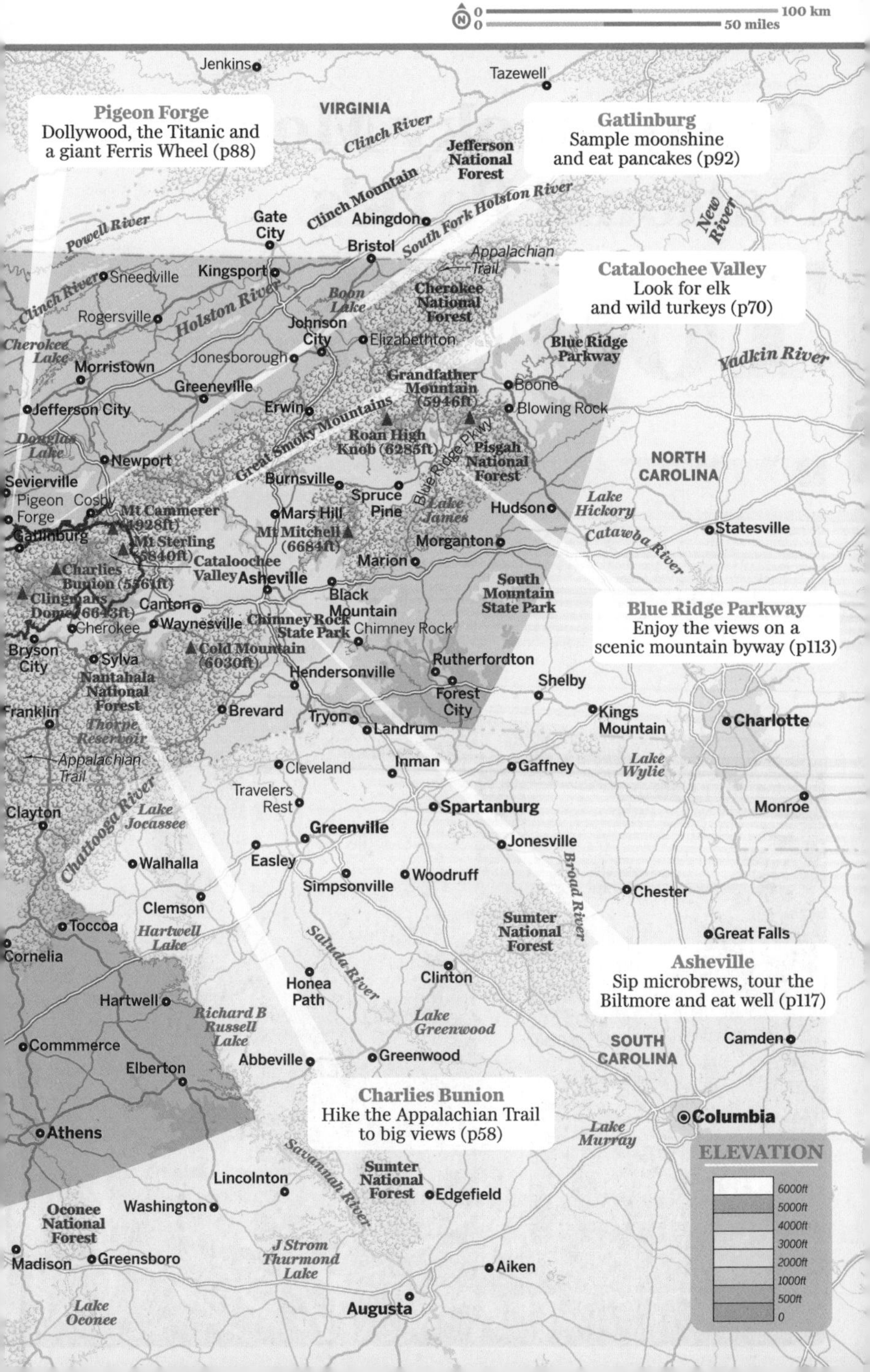

0 — 100 km
0 — 50 miles

Pigeon Forge
Dollywood, the Titanic and a giant Ferris Wheel (p88)

Gatlinburg
Sample moonshine and eat pancakes (p92)

Cataloochee Valley
Look for elk and wild turkeys (p70)

Blue Ridge Parkway
Enjoy the views on a scenic mountain byway (p113)

Asheville
Sip microbrews, tour the Biltmore and eat well (p117)

Charlies Bunion
Hike the Appalachian Trail to big views (p58)

Jenkins
Tazewell
VIRGINIA
Clinch River
Jefferson National Forest
Clinch Mountain
South Fork Holston River
New River
Powell River
Gate City
Abingdon
Bristol
Appalachian Trail
Sneedville
Kingsport
Clinch River
Holston River
Boon Lake
Cherokee National Forest
Rogersville
Johnson City
Elizabethton
Cherokee Lake
Jonesborough
Blue Ridge Parkway
Yadkin River
Morristown
Greeneville
Grandfather Mountain (5946ft)
Boone
Jefferson City
Erwin
Great Smoky Mountains
Blowing Rock
Douglas Lake
Roan High Knob (6285ft)
Pisgah National Forest
NORTH CAROLINA
Newport
Blue Ridge Pkwy
Sevierville
Burnsville
Pigeon Forge
Cosby
Spruce Pine
Lake James
Hudson
Lake Hickory
Gatlinburg
Mt Cammerer (4928ft)
Mars Hill
Mt Mitchell (6684ft)
Statesville
Mt Sterling (5840ft)
Morganton
Catawba River
Charlies Bunion (5561ft)
Cataloochee Valley
Asheville
Marion
South Mountain State Park
Clingmans Dome (6643ft)
Canton
Black Mountain
Cherokee
Waynesville
Chimney Rock State Park
Chimney Rock
Bryson City
Sylva
Cold Mountain (6030ft)
Rutherfordton
Nantahala National Forest
Hendersonville
Shelby
Forest City
Franklin
Brevard
Kings Mountain
Charlotte
Thorpe Reservoir
Tryon
Landrum
Appalachian Trail
Cleveland
Inman
Gaffney
Lake Wylie
Travelers Rest
Spartanburg
Monroe
Clayton
Chattooga River
Lake Jocassee
Greenville
Jonesville
Easley
Walhalla
Woodruff
Broad River
Simpsonville
Chester
Clemson
Sumter National Forest
Toccoa
Hartwell Lake
Great Falls
Cornelia
Saluda River
Honea Path
Clinton
Hartwell
Richard B Russell Lake
Lake Greenwood
Commmerce
SOUTH CAROLINA
Camden
Abbeville
Greenwood
Elberton
Columbia
Athens
Lake Murray
Savannah River
Sumter National Forest
Lincolnton
Edgefield
Washington
Oconee National Forest
J Strom Thurmond Lake
Madison
Greensboro
Aiken
Augusta
Lake Oconee

ELEVATION
6000ft
5000ft
4000ft
3000ft
2000ft
1000ft
500ft
0

Great Smoky Mountains National Park's Top 10

1

Clingmans Dome

1 No matter when you visit, the highest peak (p66) in the national park offers dazzling views. From the circular, flying-saucer-like viewing platform, you'll have a sweeping 360-degree panorama of the undulating waves of forested peaks that stretch off into the distance. While it's an easy but steep uphill walk along the paved half-mile path to the observation tower, there are many outstanding trails that cross through here – including the Appalachian Trail. And if you come in winter, when the access road is closed, you'll have those grand views all to yourself. Clingmans Dome observation tower (p66)

Appalachian Trail

2 America's most fabled walk in the woods (p31) stretches for nearly 2200 miles across 14 states. Some 71 miles of the challenging trail runs along the spine of the Smoky Mountains, taking you to soaring overlooks, through misty coniferous forests and past old-fashioned fire towers offering staggering views over the park's verdant expanse. Even if you don't have a week to spare (much less six months to hike the whole thing), you can still enjoy some marvelous day or overnight hikes along this legendary trail.

SEAN PAVONE/ALAMY STOCK PHOTO ©

2

JCARILLET/GETTY IMAGES ©

Mt LeConte

3 Mt LeConte is the third-highest peak in the Smokies, and can be seen from practically every viewpoint. Several trails including Alum Cave Bluffs (p39) and the Trillium Gap Trail to Grotto Falls (p51) wind their way up, passing rushing rivers, waterfalls, log bridges and precipitous views before reaching the summit at 6593ft. At the top, you can pay a visit to the rustic lodge (p73) that's been in operation since before the creation of the national park in 1934. Book a cabin (well in advance) to make the most of this extraordinary Smoky Mountain experience. LeConte Lodge

Newfound Gap Road

4 The only paved route that bisects the park, the Newfound Gap Road (p47) offers fabulous mountain forest scenery as it curves its way for 33 miles between Cherokee, NC, and Gatlinburg, TN. While you could make the north–south traverse in an hour or two, it's well worth taking it slow, stopping at scenic overlooks, having a picnic lunch beside a rushing mountain stream and going for a hike or two along one of the many memorable trails that intersect this iconic motorway.

3

4

5

Waterfalls

5 Abundant rainfall and steep elevation provide the perfect ingredients for one of the park's great attractions: its picturesque waterfalls. Thundering cascades are dotted all around the Smoky Mountains, and some of the most popular hiking trails follow the creeks and mountain streams up to waterfalls, often surrounded by lush forest. To escape the crowds, head to waterfall trails in the far corners of the park. And if time is limited, focus on one of the cascades near Gatlinburg. Stunning 80ft-high Rainbow Falls (p50) lives up to its name, with rainbows visible in the mist on sunny days. Rainbow Falls

CAROLYN FRANKS/SHUTTERSTOCK ©

Cades Cove

6 Surrounded by mountains, the lush valley of Cades Cove (p52) is one of the most popular destinations in the national park. The draw: great opportunities for wildlife-watching, access to some fantastic hiking trails, and remnants of buildings from the 19th and early 20th centuries. In fact, on an easy tour of the area, you can visit old churches, barns, log houses and a working gristmill, most of which date back to the first European settlement in the 1820s. Cable Mill Historic Area (p69)

Roaring Fork Motor Nature Trail

7 Although it's just 5.5 miles long, this scenic road (p48) holds a treasure chest of natural wonders. Named after the fast-flowing mountain stream that courses beside it, the Roaring Fork takes you to lookouts with panoramic views, past pockets of old-growth forest and right beside shimmering waterfalls. You'll also see vestiges of human settlement in the area, including an old farmstead that sheds light on the area's early inhabitants. Several excellent hiking trails start from this road, including to the lovely Grotto Falls.

Alum Cave Bluffs

8 Home to hundreds of miles of trails spread across 500,000 acres, the Smoky Mountains do not lack when it comes to hiking. The Alum Cave Bluffs trail (p39), however, merits special attention for its outstanding scenery and sweeping views the higher up you go. You'll also see wildflowers and old-growth forest, cross mountain streams on photogenic log bridges and perhaps get a glimpse of wildlife along the way. The multihued cliffs provide a mesmerizing vantage point over the surrounding green forests.

Cataloochee

9 Tucked into the eastern reaches of the national park, Cataloochee (p70) is one of the top wildlife-watching spots in the Smokies. You can watch massive elk grazing, see wild turkeys strutting about and perhaps even spy a bear or two. Hiking paths crisscross the valley, including the Boogerman Trail, which leads through old-growth forest. Cataloochee was also home to one of the largest settlements in the Smokies, and you wander through log cabins, a one-room schoolhouse and a photogenic church, all dating back to the early 1900s. Bull (male) elks

Rafting the Pigeon River

10 Many winding creaks and crystal-clear streams rushing through the Smokies find their way into the Big Pigeon River. When they converge, they create a fantastic setting for white-water adventures (p31) on churning rapids amid a gorgeous forest backdrop. Families with small kids can enjoy a peaceful paddle on the Little Pigeon, while those seeking a bit more adventure should opt for the Upper Pigeon with its class III and IV rapids. It all makes for a fun day's outing with some of the best rafting in the southeast. Little Pigeon River

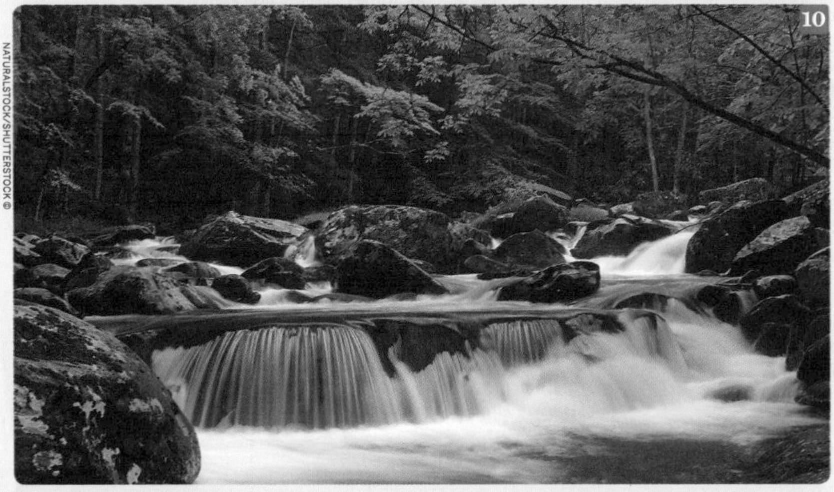

Need to Know

For more information, see Survival Guide (p197)

Entrance Fees
None

Number of Visitors
11.3 million (2017)

Year Founded
1934

Money
ATMs are common in Gatlinburg. If camping in the off-season, bring small bills (dollars, fives, 10s) to pay at the self-pay kiosks.

Cell Phones
Cell-phone coverage is generally unavailable in the park. At some high points near the edge of the park, you might get a signal, but don't count on it.

Driving
Newfound Gap Rd is the only paved road crossing the mountains within the park. It is narrow. Watch for people standing on the edge of the road looking at wildlife.

When to Go

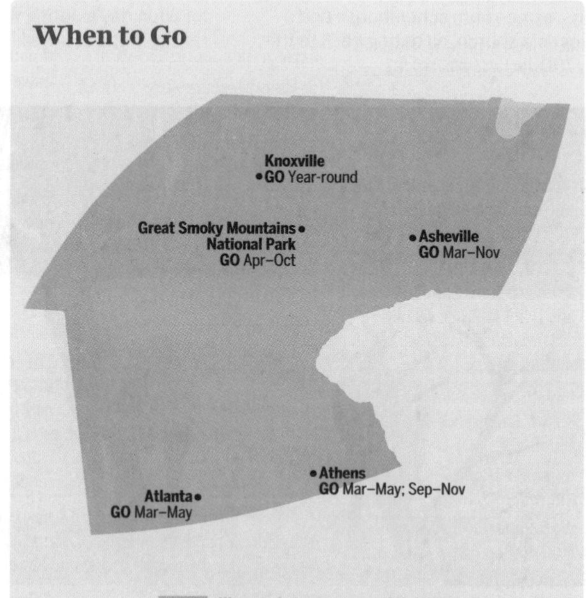

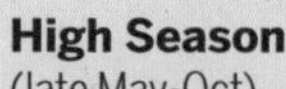

High Season
(late May-Oct)

- Synchronous fireflies draw crowds in late spring.
- Women's Work Festival spotlights rural Appalachian home life in June.
- Park is lush and green in summer.
- In fall, mountain forests blaze with color.

Shoulder
(Mar-late May)

- Wildflowers begin to bloom.
- The Wildflower Pilgrimage draws crowds with guided hikes and natured focused activities.
- Wildlife becomes active.
- Campgrounds are crowd-free.

Low Season
(Nov-Feb)

- Clear views through leafless trees.
- Roads may close due to snow.
- Some facilities close.
- Holiday shows in nearby towns.

Useful Websites

Great Smoky Mountains National Park (www.nps.gov/grsm) Hiking, camping and park activities, backcountry permits and reservations, useful links and park alerts.

Lonely Planet (www.lonelyplanet.com) Destination information, hotel bookings, traveler forums and more.

Smoky Mountains (www.smokymountains.com) Detailed info on hikes, historic sites and gateway towns outside the park.

Important Numbers

If you have an emergency in the park and you have cell service, dial 911; be sure you note your location (trail, campground etc).

For long-distance and toll-free calls, dial 1 followed by three-digit area code and seven-digit local number.

Park Headquarters & Park Emergency Number	☎865-436-9171
General Park Information	☎865-436-1200
Backcountry Information	☎865-436-1297
Gatlinburg Police	☎865-436-5181
Cherokee Police	☎828-497-4131

Exchange Rates

Australia	A$1	$0.71
Canada	C$1	$0.76
China	CNY10	$1.43
Euro zone	€1	$1.13
Japan	¥100	$0.88
Mexico	MXN$10	$0.49
New Zealand	NZ$1	$0.65
UK	£1	$1.28

For current exchange rates see www.xe.com.

Daily Costs

Budget: Less than $50

- Campsite in the national park: $18–27 per night
- Entrance to the national park: free
- Pint of beer at the Smoky Mountain Brewery: $4

Midrange: $50–150

- Double room in a midrange hotel in Gatlinburg: $75–120
- Half-day white-water rafting on the Big Pigeon River: $50
- Lunch for two at Three Jimmy's: $35–45

Top End: More than $150

- Overnight lodging and meals for two people at the LeConte Lodge: $296
- Four-hour horseback ride: $140
- Dinner for two at St John's Meeting place in Chattanooga: $80–140

Opening Dates

The park is open 24 hours a day, year-round. However, many secondary roads maintain seasonal closures, and only two of the park's campgrounds are open year-round. Backcountry campsites are open year-round, but some close periodically owing to bear activity. Visitor centers are open year-round (closing only on Christmas Day), but the hours change seasonally. Other park sites, such as LeConte Lodge and the Mingus Mill, open seasonally (typically mid-March to mid-November).

Park Policies & Regulations

Wildlife Visitors are required to stay at least 50yd from any wildlife – particularly elk, which are often spotted in Cataloochee and near the Oconaluftee Visitor Center. Feeding wildlife is prohibited (fines are up to $5000).

Alcohol Consumption of alcoholic drinks is not permitted in the park except in designated campgrounds, picnic areas and shelters.

Bicycles Not permitted on park trails except for the Oconaluftee River Trail, the Gatlinburg Trail and a small section of trail beginning at the Deep Creek trailhead up to the end of the gravel on the Indian Creek Trail.

Flora Picking plants or removing them from the park is prohibited.

Drones These are not allowed to be used within the boundaries of the park.

Getting There & Around

The majority of visitors arrive at the park by car. Buses serve nearby gateway cities, but you'll still need to hire a car from one of these cities to reach the park.

Knoxville, TN 40 miles northwest of Sugarlands Visitor Center

Asheville, NC 55 miles east of Oconaluftee Visitor Center

Chattanooga, TN 150 miles southwest of Sugarlands Visitor Center

Atlanta, GA 170 miles southwest of Oconaluftee Visitor Center

Charlotte, NC 170 miles southeast of Oconaluftee Visitor Center

Nashville, TN 230 miles northwest of Sugarlands Visitor Center

For much more on **getting around**, see p209

What's New

Foothills Parkway

After years of construction and tens of millions of dollars in investment, the new 16-mile stretch of the Foothills Parkway opened in November 2018. Visitors can now enjoy a 33-mile stretch of magnificent views on the newly extended parkway. (p67)

Firefly Lottery

Watching the synchronous fireflies in late May or early June at Elkmont remains a highly popular activity, and the park runs a lottery for limited spaces to gain access to the event. The lottery is free to enter and happens over one weekend in late April. (p77)

Wildflower Pilgrimage

The big wildflower pilgrimage in April keeps getting better with more guided walks, night-time wildlife-watching, nature sketching classes and wilderness tutorials. It always sells out. (p19)

Chimney Tops Trail

One of the park's most popular trails has reopened following the devastating fires of 2016. The views are memorable, but the summit remains closed for the long-term. (p46)

Campsite Reservations

Visitors can now book more campsites online (or by phone). You can reserve ahead at all campgrounds except Deep Creek. Look Rock campground remains closed owing to major repairs required. (p72)

Trail Upgrade

Repairs on the scenic Rainbow Falls trails continue through 2019. During this time, the trail is closed from Monday to Thursday and opens only on weekends. The nearby Bull Head Trail remains closed for the long-term. (p50)

Great Smoky Mountains Institute at Tremont

This excellent learning center has expanded its offerings, with a wide range of adult classes as well as camps for kids and backpacking trips for teens. (p72)

Mountain Biking

Parson Branch Rd remains closed to traffic; this is good news for cyclists who can take to this scenic (but hilly!) road without worrying about motor vehicles. (p28)

Gatlinburg

The lively Tennessee town of Gatlinburg at the northern entrance to the national park is back in action after the 2016 fires, with newly opened hotels and resorts, including Anakeesta, with its ziplines and canopy walks through the trees. (p92)

Elkmont Upgrades

Work continues on the Elkmont Historic District, as crews rehabilitate the century-old cottages that were once part of 'Daisy Town'. In coming years, you'll be able to explore more homes in this once-vibrant summertime village. (p66)

For more recommendations and reviews, see lonelyplanet.com/usa/the-south/north-carolina/great-smoky-mountains-national-park

If You Like...

Hiking

Home to more than 800 miles of walking trails, the national park has no shortage of great hikes, from short waterfall jaunts to multiday treks across the mountains.

Appalachian Trail The legendary trail runs for 71 miles through the Smokies; hike a short segment or its entire length. (p31)

Alum Cave Bluffs Walk past streams, through lush forest growth and ascend rock ledges on this challenging but rewarding hike off Newfound Gap Rd. (p39)

Grotto Falls One of the park's loveliest falls, with a trail that leads behind its cascades. (p51)

Ramsey Cascades Take in massive old-growth trees and puff your way up to a rewarding view of the park's highest falls. (p50)

Gregory Bald Climb to this high-elevation meadow offering jaw-dropping views over the surrounding forests and rolling ridges. (p52)

Laurel Falls A short but steep hike to a lovely cascade. Go early in the morning to beat the crowds. (p44)

Rainbow Falls Watch the sprays of mist create tiny arcing rainbows as water plunges from steep slopes fringed by greenery. (p50)

Scenic Views

Panoramic views are one of the great draws of this mountain park.

Mt LeConte Watch out for llamas as you hike your way up to the Smokies' third-highest peak. (p27)

Clingmans Dome The best view in the park is at the 360-degree, open-air observation platform atop the park's highest mountain. (p66)

Charlies Bunion A craggy promontory that offers windswept views over the northern swath of the park. (p58)

Shuckstack Tower A historic fire tower, just off the Appalachian Trail, with grand views of Fontana Lake and the surrounding mountains. (p71)

Look Rock Tower Just off the Foothills Pkwy there's an easy hike up to this weather-monitoring station with 360-degree views. (p69)

Andrews Bald Escape the Clingmans Dome crowds by heading out to this high-elevation meadow reachable on a 3.6-mile (round-trip) hike. (p45)

Gregory Bald Walk through azaleas while admiring the grand mountain views. (p52)

Outdoor Adventures

Hiking aside, the Great Smoky Mountains offer a plethora of adventures.

Smokemont Riding Stables Go horseback riding across streams and along hilly forested paths. (p31)

Tsali Recreation Area Blaze over rugged trails in the Nantahala National Forest, home to some of the best mountain biking on the east coast. (p133)

CLIMB Works Zipline through the treetops at this adventure spot east of Gatlinburg. (p93)

Big Creek Watch the light of the moon dance on the mountain stream below as you sit fireside at this peaceful campground in the park's eastern reaches. (p73)

Nantahala Outdoor Center Feel the adrenaline rush on a white-water rafting trip down the Nantahala River. (p129)

Fontana Lake Hire a kayak and head off for a paddle among lovely waterside scenery at the southern edge of the park. (p31)

History

You can peer into the past by visiting the well-preserved buildings from early settlers. Log cabins, gristmills, churches and farmsteads all attest to the industriousness of the pioneering inhabitants who scratched out a living amid the wilderness.

Mountain Farm Museum Discover how people survived and thrived in this fascinating open-air museum near the Oconaluftee River. (p65)

Cataloochee Valley Visit an old schoolhouse, a Baptist church and a log-cabin post office in this far-flung corner of the park. (p70)

Elkmont Historic District Wander through abandoned cabins that were part of an exclusive resort community in the 1910s and 1920s. (p66)

Kephart Prong Trail See the ruins of an old Civilian Conservation Corps camp on a lush forest-lined trail. (p45)

Cable Mill Historic Area A highlight of Cades Cove, this working 1870s mill once served the area's 700-plus residents. (p69)

Mingus Mill Learn about clever 19th-century engineering strategies at this picturesque structure just off Newfound Gap Rd. (p65)

LeConte Lodge Peruse photos dating back to the 1930s, then spend the night in an old-fashioned cabin at this long-running, electricity-free lodge high in the mountains. (p202)

Tipton Place Visit a photogenic 1870 homestead, one of many historic buildings in the Cades Cove area. (p69)

Top: Grotto Falls (p51).

Bottom: Little Cataloochee Baptist Church (p57).

Month by Month

TOP EVENTS

Wildflower Pilgrimage, April

Synchronous Fireflies, June

Independence Day Midnight Parade, July

Mountain Life Festival, September

Festival of Christmas Past, December

January

It's a wintry wonderland in the Smoky Mountains, with plenty of snow and icy temperatures. It's a fine time for snowshoeing and seeing the park without the crowds.

February

Winter remains in full swing in the mountains. If the subzero temperatures don't deter you, it's worth visiting for cross-country skiing, frozen waterfalls and fireside evenings in a rental cabin.

March

Temperatures are on the rise during the last month of winter. Some campgrounds and mountain roads open towards the end of the month. Not a bad time for hiking, with excellent visibility through tree lines still bare of foliage.

April

Spring means wildflowers, bigger crowds (during spring break) and the reopening of most campgrounds and roads. Nights can still dip below freezing, but days can be delightfully sunny and warm.

Wildflower Pilgrimage

A must for nature lovers, this four-day event (www.wildflowerpilgrimage.org) features more than 160 events, including guided hikes, wildlife photography, bird-watching, edible-mushroom walks, nighttime bat or owl strolls, outdoor sketching and indigenous storytelling. Registration opens in February and it always sells out, so plan ahead.

May

One of the best months to see spring wildflowers and flowering trees such as dogwoods and redwoods in the forests. Warm days mix with rainfall (a year-round possibility), and lodging prices are still lower than peak summer rates.

Tour de Blount

One Saturday in mid-May you can join other cyclists on the Tour de Blount (www.tourdeblount.com), a 78-mile ride that includes a punishing stretch of the Foothills Pkwy with grades of up to 14%. Shorter routes (25, 42 and 54 miles) are also available.

June

With warm days and cool nights, June is a great month for camping, hiking and other outdoor activities. Mountain laurel begins to bloom. On the

downside, expect crowds and high lodging prices.

☆ Synchronous Fireflies

For two weeks in late May or early June each year, you can see the incredible display of Synchronous Fireflies, when thousands of fireflies blink in perfect harmony. Elkmont Campground is the best place to see it. Enter the lottery in late April to earn a spot. (p187)

Women's Work Festival

One Saturday in mid-June, the Mountain Farm Museum showcases the many skills employed by rural women in the mountains. Learn about hearth cooking, spinning, and doll- and craft-making with corn husks. There's also live music. (p65)

July

The peak summer season continues with traffic-filled park roads and mobbed hiking trails. Prices are high and accommodation options are scarce (book well ahead). Ample ranger-led activities offer plenty of amusement for families.

Independence Day Midnight Parade

Proudly claiming to host the first Independence parade each year, Gatlinburg kicks off its festivities on the evening of July 3 with floats, marching bands and costumed performers setting out at the stroke of midnight. The festivities continue through the next

Top: Mountain laurel blooms in the warmer months, and can be found throughout the park.
Bottom: Synchronous fireflies (p187).

day, ending at 10pm with fireworks over downtown.

August

Expect hot, steamy days and nights, and high lodging prices if you visit in August – though the crowds do thin out a bit towards the end of August (when many children are back in school).

September

Cooler temperatures and thinner crowds make September a fine month to take advantage of the Smokies' outdoor attractions. Regular ranger-led talks and several big festivals happen as well.

Music of the Mountains

In early September you can hear traditional Appalachian rhythms at this two-day festival held at Sugarlands Visitor Center and in the settlement of Townsend, TN. Expect quality old-time bands and plenty of toe-tapping tunes at this family-friendly gathering. (p203)

Mountain Life Festival

Held over one weekend in mid-September at the Mountain Farm Museum, this festival celebrates the fall harvest. See old-time skills come alive in the making of hominy, apple cider, sorghum molasses and lye soap. There's also a music jam to keep things lively! (p65)

October

One of the busiest months in the Smoky Mountains owing to the fiery fall colors lighting up the forests. Avoid coming on weekends, and expect higher prices and car-filled roads at peak hours (11am to 4pm).

November

The crowds of leaf-peepers thin as the blazing autumn colors now litter the floor (rather than the treetops). Some roads and campgrounds close for the season. You can score good deals on lodging.

December

Holiday shows happen in towns near the Smokies (such as Pigeon Forge) and Christmas decorations cover the storefronts of Gatlinburg and Bryson City. As long as you bundle up, it's a fine time for park hikes without the crowds.

Festival of Christmas Past

Celebrate Christmas in the Smokies with live bands, storytelling, harp singing and traditional craft demonstrations (quilting, weaving, basket-making, spinning). There are plenty of hands-on kid's activities to keep small ones amused. Held at the Sugarlands Visitor Center in early December. (p203)

Holiday Homecoming

In mid-December, the Oconaluftee Visitor Center hosts a holiday shindig with a jam session of mountain music, traditional craft-making, and apple cider and cookies on the porch. A roaring fire in the fireplace adds to the good cheer. (p205)

Itineraries

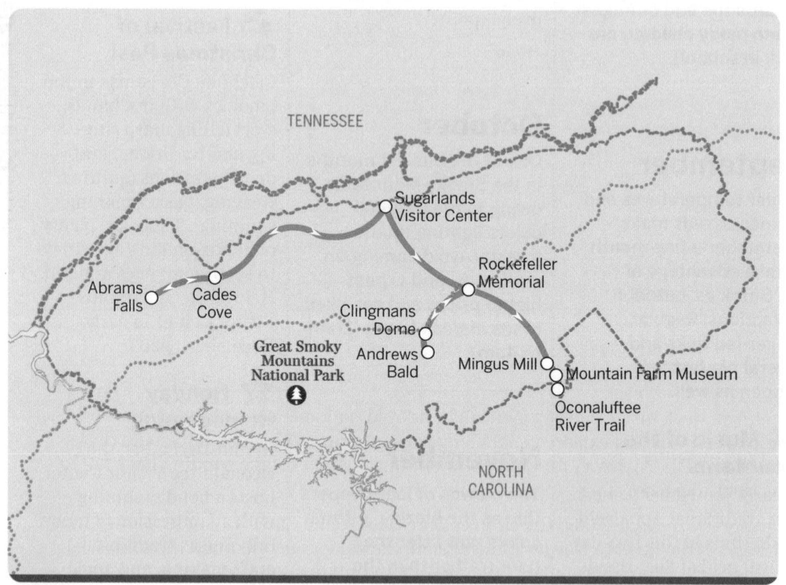

Park Highlights

Exploring the Great Smoky Mountains National Park over two days gives you ample time to take in some of the park's highlights, including historical sights, great views and pretty waterfalls.

Start off at the **Sugarlands Visitor Center** and check out its small museum of wildlife exhibits. Next head to **Cades Cove**, where you can explore austere farmers' cottages and dilapidated family cemeteries on the 11-mile driving loop surrounding the historic 19th-century mountain settlement. Cap the day with a hike to **Abrams Falls**, a lovely cascade that spills into a scenic natural pool.

The next morning, drive to the top of the park's highest peak, **Clingmans Dome**, where an observation tower offers jaw-dropping, 360-degree views of the mist-shrouded mountains. Before returning to your car, make a hike out to the mountain meadow of **Andrews Bald** for yet more magnificent views. Afterwards, drive back down and make a stop at the **Rockefeller Memorial**, which straddles two states. From there, head towards the Cherokee entrance and stop at the **Mingus Mill** and the **Mountain Farm Museum** for a bit of 19th-century history. Finish with a stroll along the picturesque and easy **Oconaluftee River Trail**.

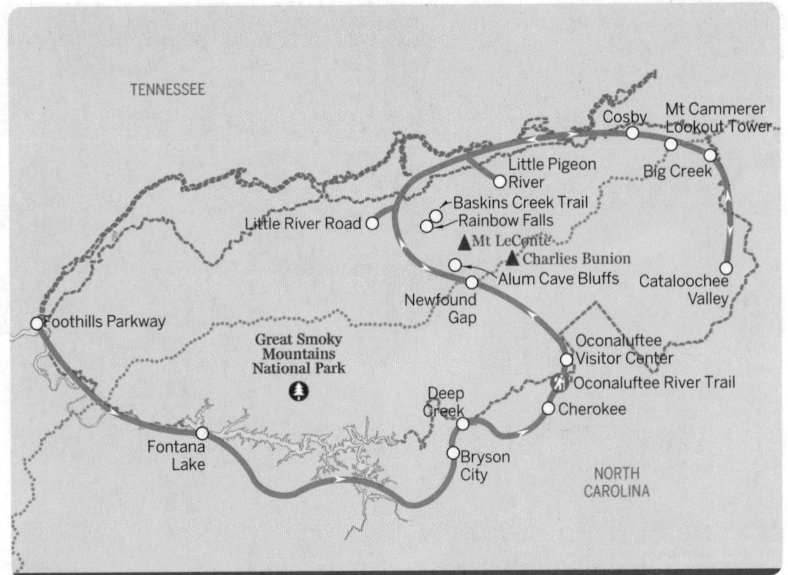

The Complete Smoky Mountains

Spending a week inside one of America's best-loved national parks gives you time to escape the crowds and explore its far-flung corners. Start with a north-to-south drive on the **Foothills Parkway** for an overview of the park. Next take winding Hwy 129 to **Fontana Lake** to kayak.

On day two, head to **Deep Creek** to explore photogenic waterfalls. Afterwards, drive to the end of the Road to Nowhere and explore the wild scenery beyond the tunnel. Alternatively, ride the old-fashioned Great Smoky Mountains Railroad. End with a meal and microbrew at Nantahala Brewing Company in **Bryson City**.

Day three starts in **Cherokee** at the excellent Museum of the Cherokee Indian. Continue into the park and stop in the **Oconaluftee Visitor Center**, which has exhibitions on the early settlers. Afterwards, visit the Mountain Farm Museum for the log structures. End with a stroll along the **Oconaluftee River Trail**.

On day four, hit the trails for the rewarding hike up to **Alum Cave Bluffs**. If you've arranged far in advance, spend the night at the lodge atop **Mt LeConte**. If not, descend for a drive along the **Little River Road**.

For your fifth day, hike to popular **Rainbow Falls** or the less crowded **Baskins Creek Trail**. Afterwards drive to **Cataloochee Valley** to explore historic structures and look for elk.

On day six, hike up **Big Creek**, one of the loveliest streams in the Smokies. Great picnic spots overlook rushing falls, massive boulders and deep pools. Afterwards, raft the **Little Pigeon River**.

On your last day, make one last mountaintop hike and get a taste of the legendary Appalachian Trail. Head to **Cosby**, where you can climb to the **Mt Cammerer Lookout Tower**, or further on to **Newfound Gap**, for the hike to the rocky outcropping of Charlies Bunion.

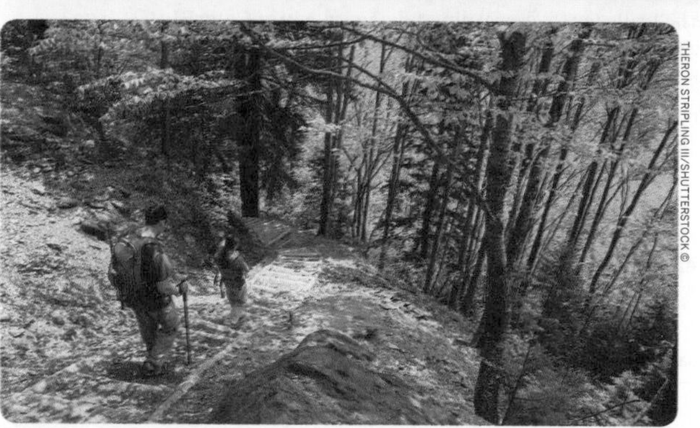

Top: Newfound Gap Road (Hwy 441; p58)

Bottom: Alum Cave Bluffs trail (p39)

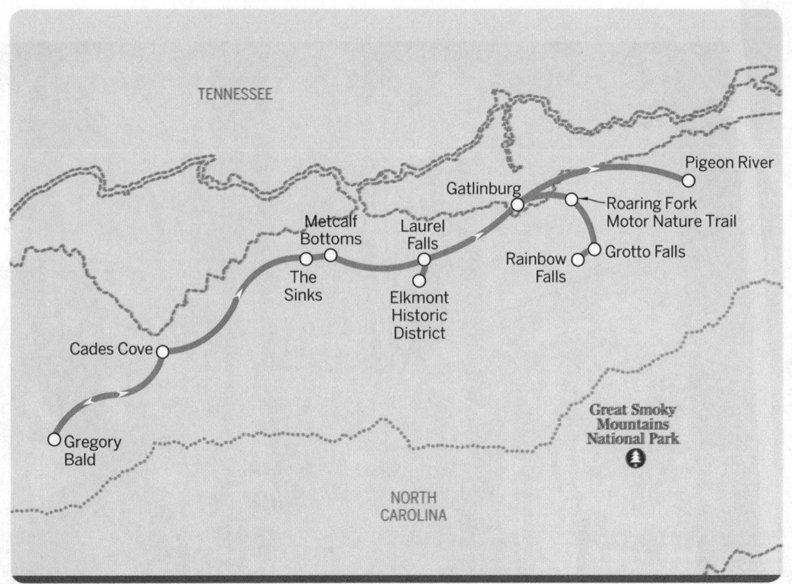

Northern Explorer

The north side of the park has some of the Great Smoky Mountains' most famous sites, with picturesque drives, rushing rivers, enchanting hikes and settler-era homesteads.

Go early to **Cades Cove** for the best chance to spy wildlife. If it's Wednesday or Saturday hop on a bike and cycle the loop road, which closes to traffic before 10am. Alternatively, spend the day making the challenging hike up **Gregory Bald** for a stunning panorama.

On day two, follow the scenic park road west, stopping for waterfall views at **The Sinks**, and picnicking at **Metcalf Bottoms**. Afterwards, stroll the abandoned resort village at **Elkmont Historic District**. In the late afternoon, hike up to **Laurel Falls**, one of the park's most popular waterfalls.

The next day head off for another great waterfall hike, either **Rainbow Falls** or the less challenging **Grotto Falls**. Afterwards, enjoy the beautiful scenery and historic attractions along the **Roaring Fork Motor Nature Trail**.

For your last day, head out for some waterside adventure. The **Pigeon River** is a fantastic spot for white-water rafting. Cap the day with souvenir shopping in **Gatlinburg**, followed by a meal of mountain trout in the atmospheric Peddler Steakhouse.

Hiking in the fall

Plan Your Trip

Outdoor Activities

Hiking the trails and driving scenic roads through the park are by far the most popular activities in the Smokies. But if you're here for more than a few days, you can tack on other outdoor adventures, including horseback riding, kayaking and white-water rafting.

Best Activities

Appalachian Trail (p31)

Hike a piece of the legendary trail, which travels for 71 miles across the Smokies before continuing up to Maine.

White-water rafting (p31)

Feeling the power of the Pigeon River as you churn along class III and IV rapids.

Fontana Lake (p31)

Taking in a unique perspective of the Smokies from a canoe or kayak.

Mt LeConte

No matter which trail you take, it's a great achievement making it to the top. Several trails including Alum Cave Bluffs (p39) and the Trillium Gap Trail to Grotto Falls (p51) wind their way up before reaching the summit at 6593ft.

Hiking

Whether you have an irrepressible urge to climb a mountain or just want to get some fresh air, hiking in Great Smoky Mountains National Park is the single best way to experience the sublime beauty of this area. Even if you're only here for a short visit, be sure to include at least one hike in your itinerary. Trails range from flat, easy and short paths to longer, more strenuous endeavors. Many are excellent for families and there's even one wheelchair-accessible trail. No matter what your physical ability or endurance level, there's a hike out there for you.

Day Hikes

The Great Smoky Mountains features some great day hikes, ranging from the short and flat, to the advanced and challenging. Always try to head out as early as possible, as you'll beat the worst of the crowds, and have the best opportunities for wildlife-watching.

Overnight Hikes

There are many overnight hike options. You can make two-day trips that include park highlights, or hike to less-visited corners of the mountains along routes. There's also the famed Appalachian Trail (p31), parts of which you can include in many itineraries (see p59 for overnight hike options and more information on permits and reservations).

Quiet Walkways

In addition to hiking trails, the national park also has 14 quiet walkways scattered around the park. These are maintained paths that generally attract fewer people than the better known trails. Most run from about 400yd to a half-mile in length along fairly easy terrain, and are meant to provide a fine place to enjoy nature without the crowds. Small, inconspicuous signs mark their location, with parking for just one or two cars. Eight of these quiet walkways are sprinkled along Newfound Gap Rd. Several others are located west of Sugarlands Visitor Center on Fighting Creek Gap Rd; there's even one hidden away on the Road to Nowhere (p129), about 7 miles northwest of Bryson City.

Hiking Essentials in the Smoky Mountains

Weather

➡ Check the forecast before setting out. Always carry rain gear, just in case. Bring a winter hat, gloves and other warm-weather gear from October to March.

What to Pack

➡ Good hiking boots, walking stick (or hiking poles), rain jacket, high-energy snacks, water (2 quarts per person on long hikes).

When to Go

➡ Mid-April to May for spring wildflowers, October for fall foliage, January and February for wintry landscapes.

Guides & Maps

➡ *Hiking Trails of the Smokies* for a detailed overview of every trail in the park.

➡ *Great Smoky Mountains National Park Trails Illustrated Topographic Map* (by National Geographic) 1:70,000 scale.

Best Hikes with a View

Charlies Bunion (p58) Magnificent views and the chance to hike a stretch of the Appalachian Trail.

Gregory Bald (p52) A sweeping panorama with mountains folding off into the distance.

Andrews Bald (p45) The highest grassy bald in the park.

Chimney Tops (p46) Contemplate the craggy clifftops and blackened skeletal tree trunks from the 2016 fires.

Clingmans Dome (p66) This observation tower marks the highest peak in the park.

Best Waterfall Hikes

Rainbow Falls (p50) A challenging but rewarding uphill hike to these dramatic cascades.

Abrams Falls (p52) Take amazing snapshots of the large natural pool facing these photogenic falls.

Grotto Falls (p51) Walk behind the falls for unique perspectives.

Ramsey Cascades (p50) You'll pass towering old-growth trees en route to these dramatic falls.

Cycling

Bicycles are welcome on most park roads, with the exception of the Roaring Fork Motor Nature Trail. However, it is important that you choose your road wisely. Because of steep terrain, narrow byways and heavy car traffic, many park roads are not well suited to safe or enjoyable riding. Great Smoky has no mountain-biking trails. Bicycles are allowed only on the Gatlinburg Trail (p49), the Oconaluftee River Trail (p58) and the Lower Deep Creek Trail. They are prohibited on all other park trails.

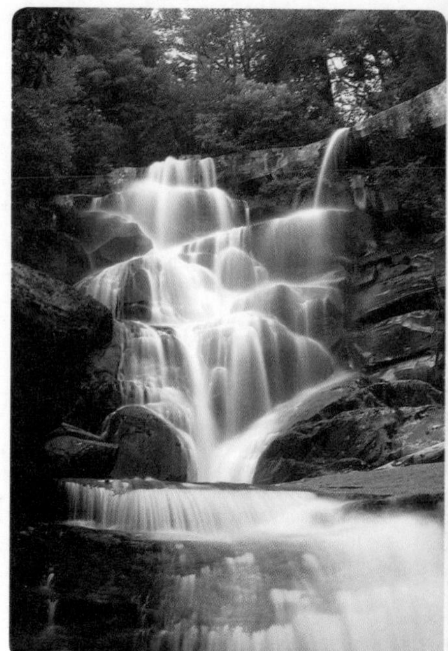

Ramsey Cascades (p50)

By far the best place for a carefree cycling tour is Cades Cove, particularly when the road is closed to cars (Wednesday and Sunday before 10am from mid-May to late September). In summer and fall, rent cycles from Cades Cove Campground Store (p203).

The 8-mile-long Parson Branch Rd (p28) is another option for riding, though it can be unsafe. This gravel and dirt road is closed to motor vehicles owing to hundreds of dead hemlock trees within striking distance of the road.

Cades Cove Trading (Map p70; ☎865-448-9034; www.cadescovetrading.com/bikes; adult per hr $7.50, child under 10yr $4.50; ⏲9am-9pm late May-Oct, to 5pm Mar-late May, Nov & last week of Dec, closed rest of the year) Rents cruisers and hybrid bicycles in a building beside the campground store. Opens at 6:30am on Wednesday and Saturday from late May through late September when the loop road is closed to automobile traffic until 10am – and is perfect for cycling!

Parson Branch Road This 8-mile-long road is permanently closed to motorized traffic, though it's open to mountain bikers and walkers, who can enjoy some serene forest views along its graveled

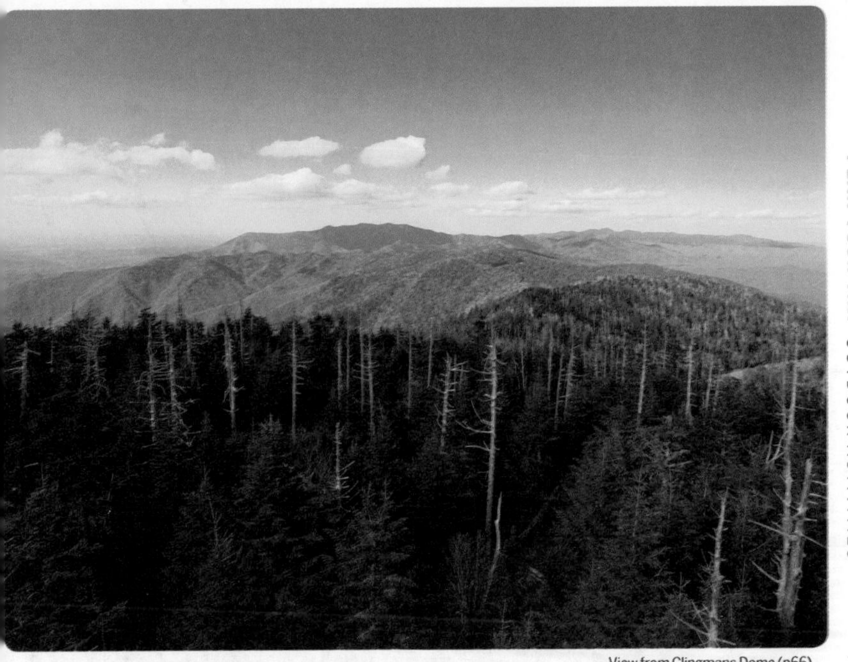

View from Clingmans Dome (p66)

length. Keep in mind, though, that the threat of falling trees is serious here. The road should definitely be avoided during high winds and after heavy rain, when loose soil can cause trunks to uproot themselves. You'll go through rhododendron tunnels and pass over creek crossings as you wind your way between Forge Creek Rd and Hwy 129 in the south.

If you don't have a bike, you can hire one from Cades Cove Campground (p76) and make the trip down – a ride best undertaken when the Cades Cove Loop Rd is closed to cars (before 10am on Wednesday and Saturday, from May through September).

Beyond the Park

You can find some decent mountain biking outside the national park if you know where to look. If you're staying on the northeast side of the park, it's worth checking out CLIMB Works (p93). This ziplining and mountain-biking site has a 2-mile loop trail that's fun for beginners, and bikes are available for hire on-site.

For a wider variety of trails, head to the Tsali Recreation Area (p133). Set on a peninsula jutting into Fontana Lake, Tsali is famed for its mountain biking. It has four loops (as well as various connector and extension trails) totaling some 40 miles of trails that are challenging but not overly technical and offer spectacular lake and mountain views. It's located about 15 miles southwest of Bryson City, just off Hwy 28.

Horseback Riding

A staggering – or should we say galloping – 550 miles of the park's hiking trails are open to horses and their humans. Assuming you're not towing your own horse, sign on for a trail ride at one of the park's three stables, all open between mid-March and mid-November. It's best to call ahead to make reservations.

One-hour trail rides cost about $35 per person. Those who want a bit more saddle time can sign up for longer rides, ranging from 2½ to four hours. The park no longer offers overnight trips.

MICHELE BURGESS/ALAMY STOCK PHOTO ©

Top: Kayaking Fontana Lake

Bottom: Horseback riding in Cades Cove (p29)

APPALACHIAN TRAIL

The storied Appalachian Trail (AT) is an irresistible draw for many hikers. For some it's the only reason they come to the Great Smokies. Around 71 of the AT's 2180 miles pass through the park, and many through-hikers consider these to be the highlight of the entire trail. For the most part, the trail follows the crest of the Great Smoky Mountains, shadowing the shared border between North Carolina and Tennessee.

An excellent time to make the hike is in September or October, when traffic on the trails has dissipated somewhat and autumn leaves are at their finest. In October, however, snow should be expected.

Hikers on the AT sleep in backcountry shelters spaced 3 to 8 miles apart; reservations are required. During the summer, you'll likely need to make the necessary consecutive reservations well in advance.

Check out the Appalachian Trail Conservancy's website (www.appalachiantrail.org) for more information.

Smokemont Riding Stables (828-497-2373; www.smokemontridingstable.com; 135 Smokemont Riding Stable Rd; 1/4hr ride $35/140, wagon ride $15; 9am-5pm mid-Mar–Oct) Offers one- and four-hour horseback rides as well as waterfall and wagon rides.

Sugarlands Riding Stables (865-436-3535; www.sugarlandsridingstables.com; 1/2hr ride $35/70; 9am-4pm Mar-May & Sep-Nov, to 5pm Jun-Aug, closed Dec-Feb) Get out on horseback at the nearest stables to Gatlinburg.

Cades Cove Riding Stables (Map p70; 865-448-9009; www.cadescovestables.com; 10018 Campground Dr, Townsend; 1hr guided trail ride adult $35, child 2-12yr $25, carriage & hay rides adult $15, child 2-12yr $10; 9am-4:30pm early Mar-Nov;) Offers guided trail, carriage and hayrides near Cades Cove.

Kayaking & Canoeing

Owing to the park's shallow, rock-filled streams, options are limited for kayaking or canoeing. One exception is **Fontana Lake** (off Fontana Rd) on the southern edge of the park, west of Bryson City. This picturesque lake is actually a reservoir impounded by Fontana Dam on the Little Tennessee River. Framed by forest-covered slopes, the 29-mile-long lake, with its deep blue waters, is a lovely spot for a paddle. You can hire kayaks, canoes and even stand-up paddleboards and pontoon boats at the **Fontana Marina** (828-498-2129; www.fontanavillage.com; off Fontana Rd; scenic boat tour adult/child $20/10, kayak or canoe hire per 1/4hr $10/25).

Swimming

The park discourages people from swimming or even wading in streams and natural pools around the park. The currents are strong and unseen obstacles can lead to bad falls, or getting your legs pinned while the water forces you under the surface. Drowning is one of the leading causes of death in the park.

White-water Rafting

One of the top spots in the southeast for white-water rafting is along the Pigeon River, just northeast of the park. Various outfitters run trips along the river, including **Rafting in the Smokies** (800-776-7238; www.raftinginthesmokies.com; Hartford Rd; rafting trip $35-42, zipline $39;), one of seven operators on this stretch of river. Most operators offer both adrenaline-fueled trips along the Upper Pigeon (for ages eight and up) and more easy-going paddles for families (ages three and up).

Trips typically last 1½ to two hours for a 6-mile trip, with prices around $45 to $50. Be sure to reserve ahead.

Hiking in the Great Smoky Mountain

Plan Your Trip

Travel with Children

The Smoky Mountains can be a wonderland for small travelers. There are adventures aplenty, with mesmerizing wildflower-filled hikes, horseback rides, rafting trips and star-filled nights gathered around the campfire. To make the most of your family holiday, it helps to plan ahead.

SILVIA FRIGERIO/EYEEM/GETTY IMAGES ©

Best Activities for Kids

Hiking

With hundreds of miles of trails, you won't lack for options. Easy trails such as the half-mile Sugarlands Valley Nature Trail or the Oconaluftee River Trail are good options for pint-sized visitors.

Wildlife-Watching

Watch herds of elk feeding at dawn or dusk near the Oconaluftee Visitor Center or in the Cataloochee Valley.

Horseback Riding

Take a short but fun one-hour ride through the forest after clomping through a river near Smokemont Riding Stables.

Fun on the Farm

Near the Oconaluftee River, you can check out the log cabins and the seasonal livestock (chickens and pigs) at the old-fashioned, open-air Mountain Farm Museum.

Bike Riding

Hire bikes and take a spin along the 11-mile-long Cades Cove Loop Rd – best on Wednesday and Saturday mornings when it's closed to automobile traffic.

Great Smoky Mountains for Kids

Welcome to one of the most family-friendly national parks in the US. There are loads of outdoor activities, including outstanding hikes (short and long alike), ample picnic areas, open spaces to run around and explore, and intriguing exhibitions with kids in mind.

That said, there are some challenges to keep in mind. Dining services are nonexistent in the park, so you'll need to load up on snacks and picnic fare before entering the wilds. Have plenty of water on hand (or a filtration device), as there are no water fountains at the trailheads.

Drives can be long within the park, so make sure you look at the map when planning the day's activities. The heavy crowds can also be a big turnoff in the summer. You can beat the worst of the holiday parade by heading out early, and avoiding the most popular areas during peak hours.

Lastly make sure everyone is properly outfitted with good shoes, warm clothes and rain gear. The weather can change in the mountains and can vary from one side of the park to the other.

Ranger Programs

Like some other national parks in the US, the Smoky Mountains has a junior ranger program, which is geared towards kids from ages five to 12. You can participate by picking up a junior ranger booklet ($2.50) at one of the visitor centers, then having the kids complete the activities in the book. Afterwards, present the book to a ranger at one of the visitor centers, and they'll be on their way to earning a junior ranger badge. While it might sound a bit hokey, it can be a fun way for young minds to get involved and learn about the park in a non-traditional setting.

During the summer, the park offers a number of free ranger-led programs. These cover a wide range of topics, with rangers describing mountain medicines people used in the past, what it was like to go to school in a log cabin in the 1880s, sleuthing strategies in the wilderness (in the ever popular 'Whose poop is this?' talk), wildlife in the park (beavers, bears, elk) and fun facts about geology and the park's formation. Ask at a visitor center or check the website for upcoming activities.

Children's Highlights

Family Hikes

Gatlinburg Trail (p49) Leave the carnivalesque atmosphere of Gatlinburg behind on this fairly flat 2-mile trail through forest along the West Prong of the Little Pigeon River.

Sugarlands Valley Nature Trail (p202) An easy, paved half-mile trail with the remnants of

100-year-old cabins and scenic spots along the river.

Oconaluftee River Trail (p58) A lovely gateway to the Smokies' wonders, this smooth 3-mile round-trip trail skirts the edge of the pretty Oconaluftee River.

Laurel Falls (p44) Check out the pretty waterfalls and hillside views on this popular 2.6-mile hike.

Children Age 12 & Under

Clingmans Dome (p66) Making the short but steep walk up to the flying-saucer-like tower, which has a magnificent 360-degree panorama.

Junior Ranger (p33) Learning about the park by completing the activity book for a badge.

Park Programs (p33) Touching a furry pelt and learning about baby bears during a hands-on ranger talk at a visitor center.

Mountain Farm Museum (p65) Peering inside log cabins and saying howdy to the chickens and pigs at this open-air spot.

Outdoor Adventures

Horseback Riding (p31) Heading off for a fun one-hour ride (or all-ages hay ride) at Cades Cove, or another of the park's stables.

White-water Rafting (p31) Feeling the cool spray as you paddle along churning class III rapids near Gatlinburg.

Camping (p76) Roasting marshmallows over a crackling fire as the sky fills with stars at Deep Creek Campground.

Picnicking Having lunch at Chimneys Picnic Area, followed by a bit of rock skipping along the West Prong River.

Beyond the Park

Families with children of all ages could spend several days enjoying the sites outside of the park. Gatlinburg is a wonderland for some (and hell on earth for others). Its people-packed main street is littered with attractions of all types – from haunted houses and mini-golf courses to fudge shops, candy stores and souvenir stands. Two open-sided chairlifts whisk you up a mountain for fine views.

If you prefer to avoid the circus-like atmosphere of Gatlinburg, you'll find other options. Bryson City, near the Deep Creek section of the national park, is the starting point for the Great Smoky Mountains Railroad, which offers scenic journeys aboard vintage steam- or diesel-powered trains.

Another kid-pleaser is Dollywood, a theme park and water park near Pigeon Forge offering endless days of amusement (it's also a resort with cabins, pools and plenty of kid activities, plus evening entertainment). Further afield to the west, you'll find Chattanooga, famed for its riverside trails, pedestrian bridges, outdoorsy activities and fun restaurant scene. East of the park, Asheville is another buzzing city offering ample rewards for young and old alike.

A white-tailed deer buck (p189)

Planning

While it's always a good idea to allow free time for some serendipitous discoveries, you'll definitely need to do some planning before hitting the road.

For all-round information and advice, check out Lonely Planet's *Travel with Children*.

Mountain Farm Museum (p65)

Accommodation

If your kids are good hikers, and you've reserved well in advance, you can overnight in the LeConte Lodge (p202), the only non-campground accommodation in the park. The lodge begins taking reservations in early October for the following year, and dates fill up quickly. Note that it closes from mid-November to mid-March.

Reservations for park campgrounds are accepted up to six months in advance. Plan as far ahead as possible if coming during the summer. Cancellations or date changes to a campsite reservation incur a $10 fee.

Outside the park there's a wealth of family-friendly options, including lodges, cabins and hotels, some of which have appealing extras such as swimming pools and play areas. Most accommodations outside the park do not charge extra for children under 12, though policies vary from place to place.

What to Pack

You'll be able to find just about anything you could need at major towns outside the park, but to avoid a long winding drive out of the park while you're enjoying the forest, it's best to be prepared.

Children's paracetemol and ibuprofen Always good to have on hand for the unexpected fever that arises in the middle of the night.

Fleece Even in the summer, nights can be chilly.

Rain jacket Precipitation is always a possibility in this wet region.

Hiking shoes Bring something sturdy that ties and covers the toes, and socks.

Sun hat A must at any time of year.

Sunscreen and bug repellent Mosquitos and ticks are the concern, and you'll want repellent during the warmer months (May through September).

Water bottles Keep everyone hydrated and happy throughout the trip. Consider buying a water purification device to avoid all the plastic by-products.

Beach towels For exploring creeks and streams throughout the park, and perfect for picnics.

Water sandals You'll want to splash in creeks without worrying about sharp rocks and stubbed toes.

Safety

It's easy to forget, as you're browsing the exhibits in the visitor center, that you're on the edge of a vast wilderness area. Trails can be narrow and slippery, with dangerous drop-offs. Rushing streams might look enticing for a wade, but can quickly knock a child (or even an adult) off his or her feet. There's also the threat of poison ivy, not to mention the wildlife – snakes, bears, elk, yellowjacket wasps (be sure to carry an EpiPen if your child is allergic to bee stings).

With all this in mind, it's best to lay down some ground rules before you arrive in the park. Young children will undoubtedly see other kids scrambling up loose rocks off the trail, trying to climb around slippery waterfalls and other risky activities and may want to do the same. Make sure you keep small children close on hikes. As an added precaution, it's wise to have all children carry a whistle in case they get lost.

The bigger threat than falls or drowning is of course the human threat – or rather vehicular one. Car accidents are the leading cause of injury and death in the park. Be particularly careful when parking at trailheads. Sometimes you'll have to park beside the road, without much room to maneuver, and other drivers don't always slow down for young families wandering across the road.

Local law requires that children under four years of age ride in a car seat, while kids aged five to eight must ride in a booster-seat system. Most car-rental agencies rent rear-facing car seats (for infants under one year of age), forward-facing seats and boosters for about $10 per day, but you must reserve them in advance.

Dining

Even the most upscale restaurants outside the park welcome families. Throughout the park you'll find plenty of picnic spots – many with grills for those who want to do a bit of daytime barbecuing. Since there are no traditional restaurants within the park itself, be sure to pack a cooler and load up at a grocery store first. The best places to procure supplies are Gatlinburg and Townsend for the north side of the park, and Cherokee and Bryson City for the south side of the park.

Cades Cove Campground has a small snack bar that sells sandwiches, soup, pizza, ice cream, drinks and other fare. Elkmont Campground has a smaller concession stand that doles out a few snacks. At either you can also buy ice and firewood.

On the Road

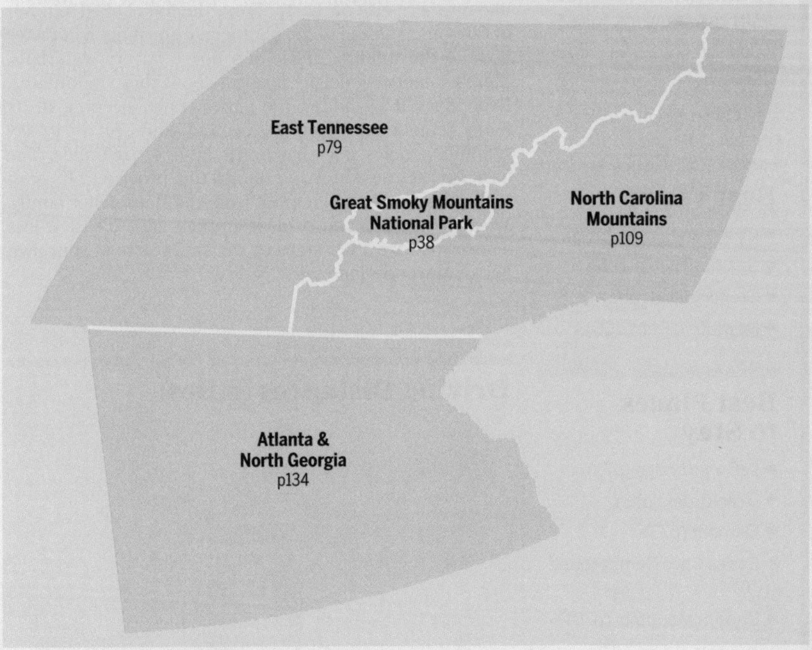

East Tennessee
p79

Great Smoky Mountains
National Park
p38

North Carolina
Mountains
p109

Atlanta &
North Georgia
p134

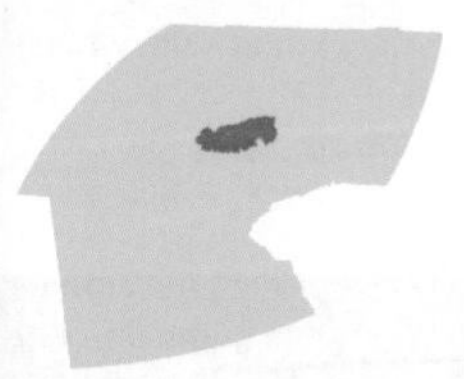

Great Smoky Mountains National Park

Includes ➡

Day Hikes 39
Additional Hikes........... 58
Overnight Hikes 59
Sights & Activities 65
Courses 72
Sleeping 72
Eating 77

Best Views

- ➡ Clingmans Dome (p66)
- ➡ Charlies Bunion (p58)
- ➡ Gregory Bald (p52)
- ➡ Newfound Gap (p66)

Best Places to Stay

- ➡ LeConte Lodge (p73)
- ➡ Deep Creek (p76)
- ➡ Elkmont (p73)
- ➡ Cades Cove Campground (p76)
- ➡ Balsam Mountain (p76)

Why Go?

Imagine watching the sky go from ink-black to periwinkle-blue as pink dawn clouds ripple across the endless, wrinkled chain of peaks stretching towards the horizon. It's like nowhere else on Earth. From the fog-choked summit of Clingmans Dome to the photogenic ghost town of Cades Cove to the tinkling music of a dozen silvery waterfalls, there's something deeply magical about these mountains. Experience it by hiking the park's trails, sleeping in its many remote campgrounds, cooling your feet in its icy swimming holes and driving its craggy backroads. The park charges no admission thanks to a proviso in its original charter as part of a grant from the Rockefeller family. Most visitors don't stray far from their cars. It's their loss – once you take a few steps on the trail you're in your own personal wonderland.

Driving Distances (miles)

	Asheville (NC)	Atlanta (GA)	Chattanooga (TN)	Knoxville (TN)
Atlanta (GA)	230			
Chattanooga (TN)	210	135		
Knoxville (TN)	110	200	120	
Sugarlands Visitor Center (TN)	90	220	150	40

DAY HIKES

The Great Smoky Mountains offers some fabulous day hikes. These range from short and flat riverside jaunts to challenging hikes to craggy overlooks with jaw-dropping views. Wherever you go it's best to set out early, as you'll beat the worst of the crowds, and have the best opportunities for wildlife-watching.

Newfound Gap Road

Trailheads along Newfound Gap, Little River Rd and Clingmans Dome Rd are included below. Little River Rd joins Newfound Gap Rd at Sugarlands Visitor Center. Clingmans Dome Rd rolls west from Newfound Gap, which straddles Tennessee and North Carolina.

Alum Cave Bluffs

Start/End Alum Cave Bluffs parking area

Duration 2½ to 3½ hours round-trip

Distance 4.6 miles

Difficulty Hard

Elevation Gain 2200ft

One of the 10 most popular trails in the Smoky Mountains, **Alum Cave Bluffs** (off Newfound Gap Rd) often draws a crowd. It's a fantastic walk crossing log bridges, spying old-growth forest and enjoying fine views, though you should try to be on the trail before 9am to enjoy the scenery without the maddening crowds.

From the trailhead along Newfound Gap Rd, you quickly leave the sounds of traffic behind as you cross a stout bridge over a mountain stream (the Walker Camp Prong) and enter a wilderness of rosebay rhododendrons and thick ferns, with American beech and yellow birch trees soaring overhead.

Soon you'll be following along the rushing waters of Alum Cave Creek, which offers many fine places to stop and enjoy a bit of leisurely stream time (indeed, many families don't make it farther than the first mile). Enjoy this fairly flat, scenic stretch as the climbing begins after mile 1.1.

At that point you'll cross the Styx Branch, named after the mythological river forming the boundary between the natural world and the underworld. From here it's about 600yd to Arch Rock, a picturesque natural tunnel, which you'll pass though along carved stone steps leading up the steep slope.

The tough ascent continues, leading past old-growth hardwoods as it winds up Peregrine Peak (keep an eye out for the falcons for which the mountain is named). Around mile 1.8 you'll reach a heath bald where the views begin to open up, amid mountain laurel and sand myrtle. A bit further (around mile 2), you'll reach the aptly named Inspiration Point, offering even more impressive views of the forested valley below. Stop here to catch your breath before pressing on the final 600yd to Alum Cave Bluffs. Despite the name, this is not a cave but rather an 80ft-high concave cliff. It provides fine views and dry shelter when the rains arrive.

Though most people turn around here, you can press on to Mt LeConte, another 2.7 miles uphill, if you still have plenty of energy left. The terrain on this stretch is particularly challenging, as the trail passes over narrow rock ledges – steel cables bolted into the mountain provide useful handholds. At the summit, hot chocolate and other snacks await. Otherwise, it's an easy downhill descent back to your starting point.

TRAIL DIFFICULTY

We've rated hikes in the Great Smoky Mountains by three levels of difficulty to help you choose the trail that's right for you.

Easy Manageable for nearly all walkers, an easy hike is less than 4 miles, with fairly even terrain and no significant elevation gain or loss.

Moderate Fine for fit hikers and active, older children, moderate hikes have a modest elevation gain – in the range of 500ft to 1000ft – and are usually less than 7 miles in length.

Hard Hikes have elevation gains of more than 1000ft, are mostly steep, may have tricky footing and are often more than 8 miles long. Being physically fit is paramount.

All hikes, from day hikes to backcountry treks, follow well-marked, established trails and, unless otherwise noted, the distance listed in each hike description is for a round-trip journey. The actual time spent hiking will vary with your ability. When in doubt, assume trails will be harder and take longer than you think.

Great Smoky Mountains National Park

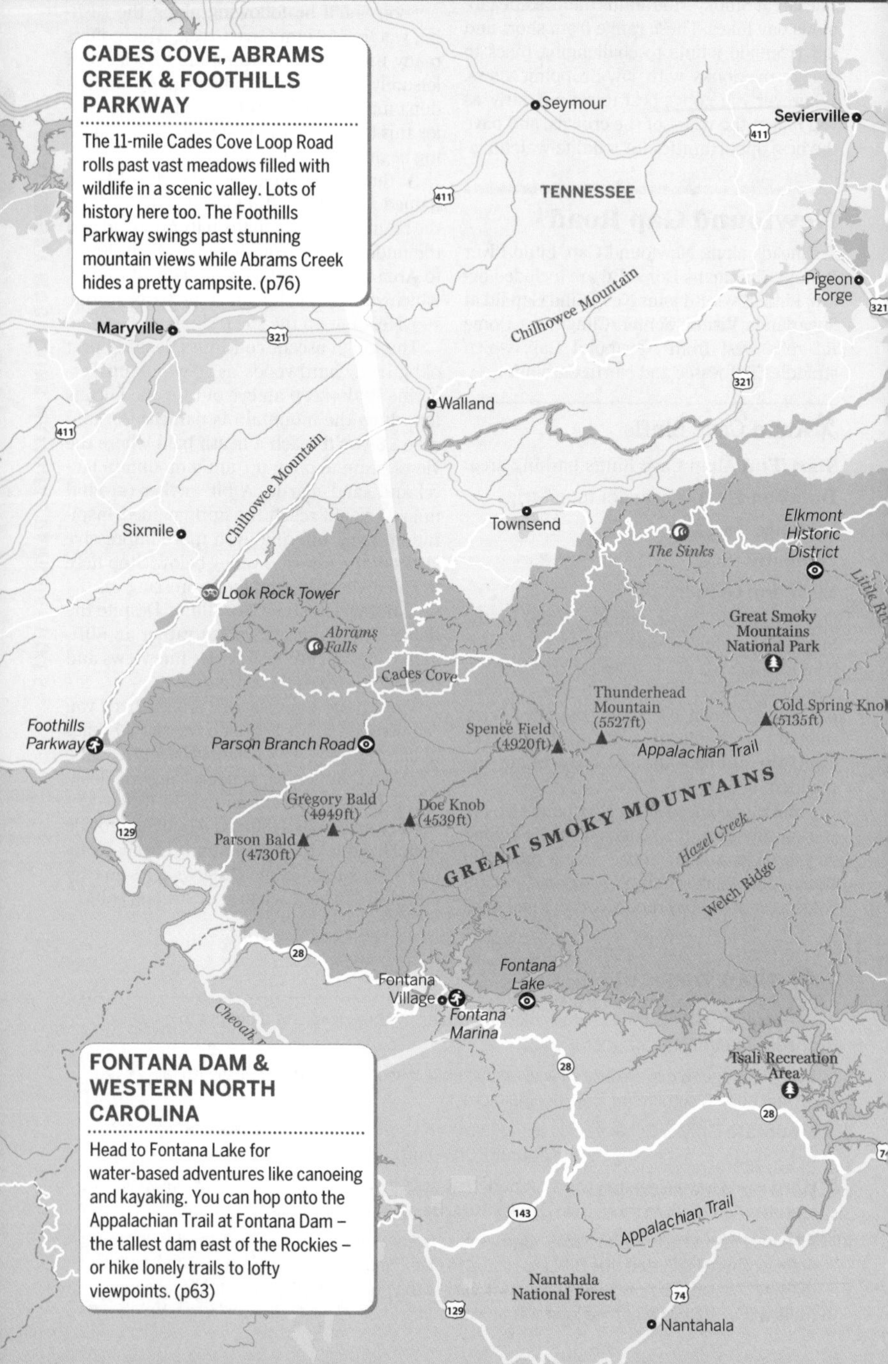

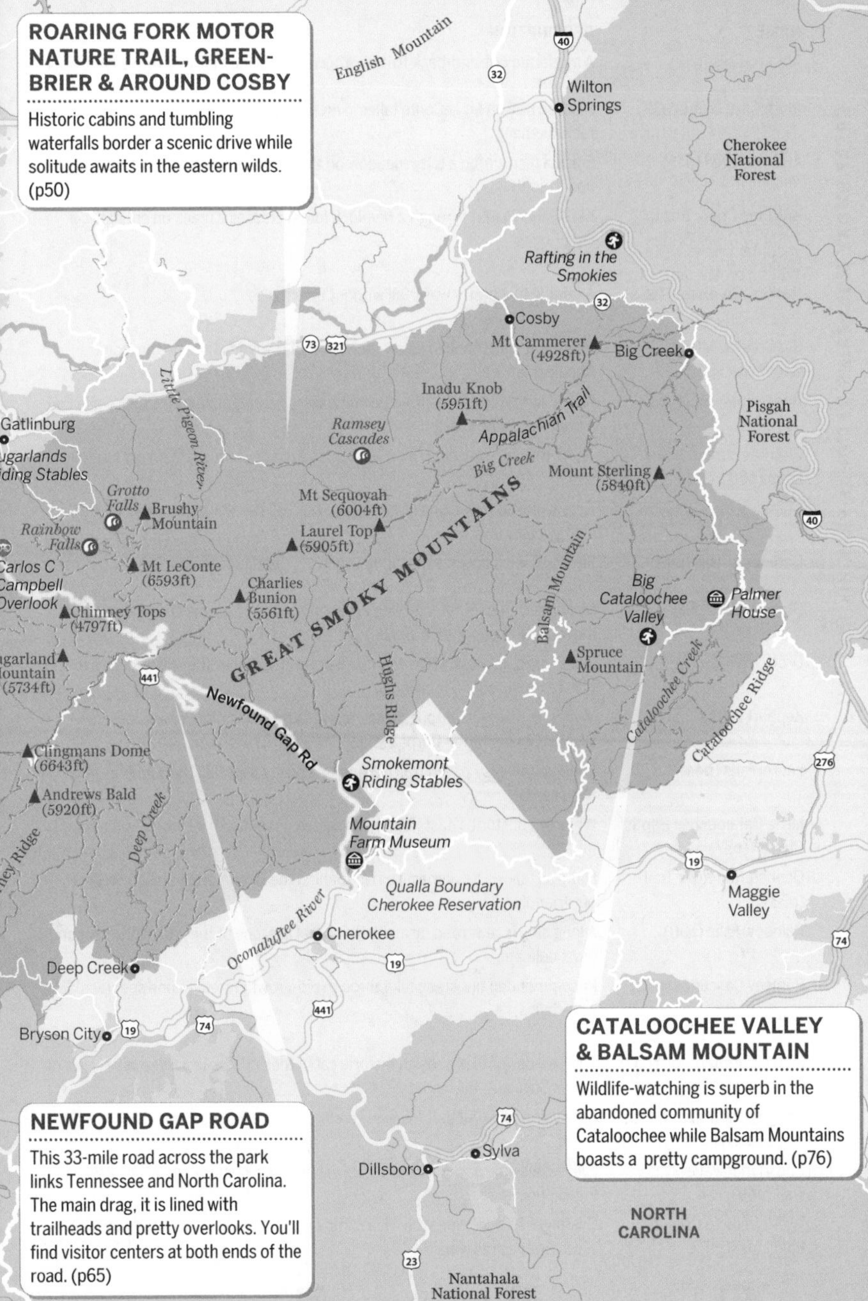

0
0
20 km
10 miles
ROARING FORK MOTOR NATURE TRAIL, GREENBRIER & AROUND COSBY
Historic cabins and tumbling waterfalls border a scenic drive while solitude awaits in the eastern wilds. (p50)
English Mountain
Wilton Springs
Cherokee National Forest
Rafting in the Smokies
Cosby
Mt Cammerer (4928ft)
Big Creek
Little Pigeon River
Inadu Knob (5951ft)
Appalachian Trail
Pisgah National Forest
Gatlinburg
Sugarlands Riding Stables
Ramsey Cascades
Big Creek
Mount Sterling (5840ft)
Grotto Falls
Brushy Mountain
Mt Sequoyah (6004ft)
Rainbow Falls
Laurel Top (5905ft)
Carlos C Campbell Overlook
Mt LeConte (6593ft)
GREAT SMOKY MOUNTAINS
Charlies Bunion (5561ft)
Chimney Tops (4797ft)
Balsam Mountain
Big Cataloochee Valley
Palmer House
Sugarland Mountain (5734ft)
Hughs Ridge
Spruce Mountain
Cataloochee Creek
Cataloochee Ridge
Newfound Gap Rd
Clingmans Dome (6643ft)
Smokemont Riding Stables
Andrews Bald (5920ft)
Deep Creek
Mountain Farm Museum
Qualla Boundary Cherokee Reservation
Maggie Valley
Oconaluftee River
Cherokee
Deep Creek
Bryson City
CATALOOCHEE VALLEY & BALSAM MOUNTAIN
Wildlife-watching is superb in the abandoned community of Cataloochee while Balsam Mountains boasts a pretty campground. (p76)
NEWFOUND GAP ROAD
This 33-mile road across the park links Tennessee and North Carolina. The main drag, it is lined with trailheads and pretty overlooks. You'll find visitor centers at both ends of the road. (p65)
Sylva
Dillsboro
NORTH CAROLINA
Nantahala National Forest

HIKING IN THE GREAT SMOKY MOUNTAINS NATIONAL PARK

NAME	DESCRIPTION
Abrams Falls (p52)	A moderate out-and-back to a photogenic waterfall tumbling into a large pool
Alum Cave Bluffs (p39)	Beloved trail up Mt LeConte takes in Arch Rock, Inspiration Point and a rock overhang
Andrews Bald (p45)	Enjoy a picnic atop a lofty meadow on this moderate hike, which ends with an uphill climb
Anthony Creek Trail to Anthony Creek Bridge (p55)	Kid-friendly jaunt through a hemlock forest crosses a creek on enticing log bridges
Baskins Creek Trail (p58)	A ramble to a pretty waterfall without the crowds
Big Creek & Mt Cammerer (p62)	Overnight hike that climbs a watchtower and spends time on the iconic Appalachian Trail
Boogerman Trail (p56)	Partial loop trail named for a hermit passes soaring tulip trees, rock walls and a bridge-busting creek
Charlies Bunion & Kephart Loop (p60)	A 14.1-mile hike passing Charlies Bunion then descending to an old lumber site
Chimney Tops (p46)	Fires wreaked havoc on the landscape but you can still enjoy views of the craggy chimneys
Gatlinburg Trail (p49)	Easy trail links downtown Gatlinburg with Sugarlands Visitor Center; pet-friendly
Gregory Bald (p52)	Strenuous hike with a tumbling creek, old-growth forest and a mountain-top meadow with panoramic views
Grotto Falls (p51)	Listen for black-and-white woodpeckers and squint at the salamanders to falls tumbling over a rock ledge
Kephart Prong Trail (p45)	Moderate hike rolls through thick forest to the ruins of a Depression-era Civilian Conservation Corps camp
Laurel Falls (p44)	Popular and easy paved trail leading to a pretty waterfall that tumbles into two separate pools
Little Cataloochee Baptist Church (p57)	Whispers of stories past float by on this remote hike to a 19th-century church
Oconaluftee River Trail (p58)	Flat trail follows its namesake river behind the Oconaluftee Visitor Center; pet-friendly
Rainbow Falls (p50)	A long slog is rewarded by misty Rainbow Falls, one of the park's prettiest and most delicate
Ramsey Cascades (p50)	Recommended but steep hike through old-growth forest to one spectacular waterfall
Rich Mountain Loop (p53)	This woodsy path passes an historic cabin then climbs to a ridge with views of Cades Cove and Townsend
Rough Fork Trail to Woody Place (p56)	Family-friendly trail that follows a creek to an old homestead
Sugarlands Valley Nature Trail (p49)	Fully accessible paved trail provides views of the West Prong of the Little Pigeon River
Twentymile to Gregory Bald Loop (p63)	Overnight hike includes the AT, a climb up a vintage fire tower and majestic views from a grassy bald

 *Views*  *Waterfalls*  *Wildlife-Watching*

START LOCATION	DIFFICULTY	DURATION	DISTANCE	ELEVATION GAIN	FEATURES
Cades Cove	Moderate	3-4hr	5 miles round-trip	under 800ft	
Newfound Gap Rd	Hard	2½-3½hr	4.6 miles	2200ft	
Clingmans Dome	Moderate	2½hr round-trip	3.6 miles	950ft	
Cades Cove	Easy	2hr	3.2 miles round-trip	495ft	
near Roaring Fork Motor Trail	Moderate	3-4hr	5.6 miles round-trip	about 1400ft	
Big Creek	Moderate to hard	2 days	16.7 miles	3568ft	
Big Cataloochee Valley	Moderate to hard	4hr	7.5 miles	about 1000ft	
Newfound Gap	Moderate	2 days	14.1 miles	4185ft	
Newfound Gap Rd	Moderate to hard	1½-3hr round-trip	3.5 miles	1460ft	
Newfound Gap Rd	Easy	1hr	2 miles one way	22ft	
Cades Cove	Hard	6-7hr	11 miles round-trip	3036ft	
Roaring Fork Motor Nature Trail	Easy to moderate	1½-2½hr round-trip	2.6 miles	380ft	
Newfound Gap Rd	Easy to moderate	2hr round-trip	4.2 miles	860ft	
Newfound Gap	Easy to moderate	1½-2hr round-trip	2.6 miles	310ft	
Little Cataloochee	Moderate	2-3hr	4 miles round-trip	719ft	
Newfound Gap	Easy	1-2hr	3 miles round-trip	minimal	
Roaring Fork Motor Nature Trail	Moderate to hard	3-4½hr round-trip	5.4 miles	1600ft	
East of Roaring Fork Motor Nature Trail	Moderate to hard	3-4½hr round-trip	8 miles	2280ft	
Cades Cove One	Hard	5-6hr	8.5 miles	1800ft	
Big Cataloochee	Easy	1hr	2 miles round-trip	144ft	
Newfound Gap Rd	Easy	30min round-trip	0.5 miles	2ft	
Western NC	Hard	2-3 days	18.3 miles	4500ft	

 *Picnic Spots*  *Great for Families*  *Bicyles Permitted*

Newfound Gap Road – Day Hikes

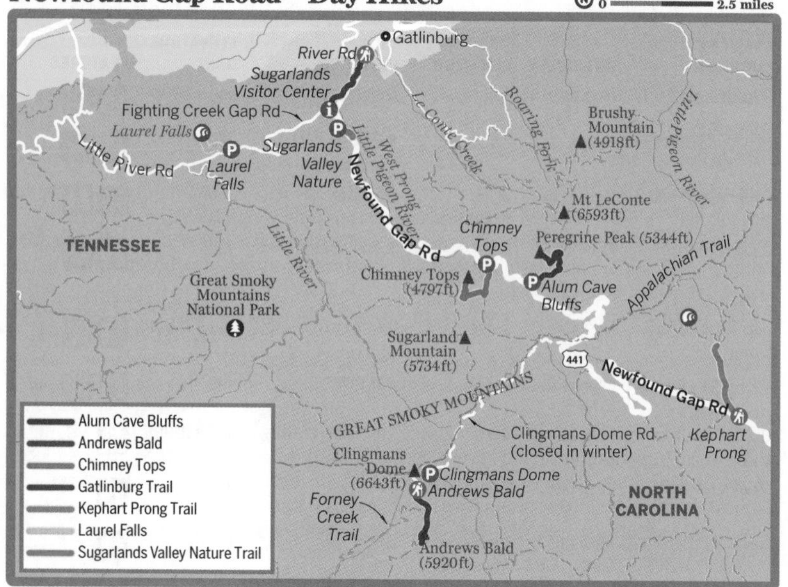

Laurel Falls

Start/End Laurel Falls parking area

Duration 1½ to two hours round-trip

Distance 2.6 miles

Difficulty Easy to moderate

Elevation Gain 310ft

The **Laurel Falls trail** (off Fighting Creek Gap Rd) is one of the most popular waterfall trails in the park. The falls are certainly impressive, but if you're coming in the summer, know that this trail gets frustratingly packed. Come very early or late in the day to beat the worst of the crowds.

The route is so popular, in fact, that the park service has paved the entire length of the trail (in part to prevent added erosion to the mountain). Although it's smooth going, the trail is a little too steep for it to be an easy trip for strollers and wheelchairs, though we have spotted both on the trail.

Apart from the scenic waterfall, this trail has a little of everything: wildflowers in springtime, fiery colors in autumn, wooded ridges and sweeping views over the forest.

From the parking area, the trail starts out with a short steep section, then continues along a steady uphill rise past small shrublike mountain laurels (which turn the hills pink and white in early summer) and stands of rhododendrons. Continuing uphill, you'll soon pass pines, maples and dogwoods before the view opens up to your left and reveals a fine outlook over the valley. Further ahead, you'll pass rocks on your left, which the Civilian Conservation Corps had to partially blast their way through to create the trail back in the 1930s.

The trail continues uphill, at times growing narrower. If in a group, you'll want to go single file, and watch your step in cold weather as it can be icy (a sign reminds hikers that falls have resulted in deaths here).

At mile 1.3 you have arrived. Powered by annual rainfall of 55in, the 75ft-high waterfall is a refreshing sight, though it's nearly always packed. After taking in the view, you can either make the return descent or leave the crowds behind and continue along the trail, which intersects with the Little Greenbrier Trail at mile 3.1.

Look for the trailhead (and many, many cars parked along the road) on the north side of Fighting Creek Gap Rd, about 3.8 miles west of the Sugarlands Visitor Center.

Andrews Bald

Start/End Parking area for Clingmans Dome

Duration 2½ hours round-trip

Distance 3.6 miles

Difficulty Moderate

Elevation Gain 950ft

Spectacular views await from this high-elevation grassy meadow near Clingmans Dome. While it's a fairly straightforward hike to get here, you'll need to save some energy for the return, which is nearly entirely uphill – unlike many other trails in the Smokies, the Forney Ridge Trail to **Andrews Bald** (off Clingmans Dome Rd) starts high and ends low(er).

The trail starts off along Forney Ridge and passes through forest of red spruce and Fraser fir. The latter is suffering from a devastating infestation of the non-native balsam woolly adelgid, a type of sap-sucking aphid, and you'll see lots of bare branches and fallen firs along the way.

Just after 1 mile, you'll reach a signboard indicating the Forney Creek Trail going off to the right. Instead continue straight along the Forney Ridge Trail. After a slight uphill of perhaps 200ft over 400yd, you'll descend once again. Keep an eye out for patches of blueberry bushes, which typically ripen in August. After another gentle descent, you'll soon arrive at the grassy meadow known as Andrews Bald. The site is named after Anders Thompson, who brought cattle up here to graze in the 1840s.

Assuming fog doesn't cling to the horizon, the views here are outstanding. You can find many fine spots for a picnic, perhaps staking out a place beside some fine flowering plants, including gorgeous flame azaleas – these tend to bloom in late June. Afterwards, retrace your steps to return to your starting point back at Clingmans Dome.

To reach the trailhead, take the road towards Clingmans Dome off Newfound Gap Rd (the turnoff is about 13 miles south of Sugarlands Visitor Center). Park at the lot and walk in the direction of Clingmans Dome. You'll see the trailhead marked 'Forney Ridge' leading down to the left just before you reach the visitor center.

Keep in mind that the road to Clingmans Dome closes from December to late March.

Kephart Prong Trail

Start/End Kephart Prong Trailhead

Duration two hours round-trip

Distance 4.2 miles

Difficulty Easy to moderate

Elevation Gain 860ft

Although it lacks dramatic waterfalls and panoramic views, the **Kephart Prong Trail** (off Newfound Gap Rd) is an intriguing hike, and offers attractions unique to this corner of the park. Instead of knockout views, you'll get a taste of history as you wander past the ruins of an old Civilian Conservation Corps (CCC) camp dating back to 1933. In late spring, it's also a fine spot to see blooming wildflowers.

The trail is named after Horace Kephart, a librarian from St Louis who abandoned his wife and six children to live in a remote part of the Smokies. There he found inspiration, winning acclaim for his honest portrayal of Appalachian peoples in *Our Southern Highlanders*. He also helped plot the Appalachian Trail through the Smokies and was later named one of the fathers of the national park.

Mountain streams play a starring role in this walk, as you'll follow along the Kephart Prong, crossing it several times during your ascent. The trail is fairly easy going, with a bridge crossing over the rushing Oconaluftee River at the outset. Continuing along this wide path (once a road for 4WDs), you'll reach the remnants of the Conservation Corps camp around mile 0.2. Here you'll find a (non-working) stone water pump, moss-covered foundations and a few rather precarious-looking chimneys pointing skyward. This is all that's left of an area that once contained a mess hall, living quarters, a recreation building and various other structures.

The camp was in use for almost a decade during the 1930s and early 1940s. About 200 workers lived here building roads, a water system still used on the Newfound Gap Rd, trails and bridges – including those found on this trail. Afterwards the camp became a barracks for conscientious objectors during WWII. Those sent here continued the work started by the CCC 10 years earlier, as well as assisting with ranger support and other park activities.

Watch out for poison ivy and other hazards as you explore the site (you might also see a trap, which you should steer clear of, that's set up by the national park to capture wild hogs). Continue up the trail as it narrows and winds its way to the first crossing of the Kephart Prong. A slender footbridge with a log railing crosses the churning waterway. Around mile 0.7 you'll see several concrete platforms tucked just off the trail. Although these look like combat bunkers, they're actually the remnants of a fish hatchery run by the Works Progress Administration. These were used to replenish trout and bass in the overfished mountain streams in the park.

As the trail continues, you'll cross the Kephart Prong four more times over the next mile. Surrounded by forest and spanning moss-covered rocks and rushing white water, these log bridges are quite photogenic. However, you'll want to watch your step, especially after rain and during cold weather, as the wood can be slick and icy.

Towards the end of the walk (around mile 1.7), keep an eye out for a few rusting, lichen-covered railroad irons alongside the trail. These were once part of a narrow-gauge railroad used by the Champion Fibre Company. Back in the 1920s, this logging operator left a swath of more than 2000 clear-cut acres in and along the Kephart Prong. The railroad then transported the spruce lumber taken from the site. Luckily this was some of the last logging in the area. In 1931 Champion Fibre sold 90,000 acres of forest land to the government, in what would soon become the Great Smoky Mountains National Park.

Keep heading uphill a bit further, and at mile 2.1 you'll arrive at the Kephart Shelter, a nicely designed wood and stone structure used by overnight hikers. It sits in an area that was once part of the logging camp. From here you'll notice a signboard indicating various other trails that continue onwards. If you're itching to continue onwards, you can reach a junction with the Appalachian Trail in 3.7 miles by taking the Sweat Heifer Creek Trail. Taking the right fork instead leads along the Grassy Branch Trail, where you can connect with Dry Sluice Gap and eventually up to Charlies Bunion (p65) for memorable mountain views. Otherwise it's an easy downhill walk retracing your steps back to the start of the trail.

Parking for the trailhead is along Newfound Gap Rd, located about 7 miles north of the Oconaluftee Visitor Center (right side of the road if coming from the south).

Chimney Tops

Start/End Chimney Tops Parking Area

Duration 1½ to three hours round-trip

Distance 3.5 miles

Difficulty Moderate to hard

Elevation Gain 1460ft

The **Chimney Tops** was once one of the most popular trails in the Smokies. While the views are still impressive, the trail has lost some of its allure following the destructive fires of 2016. You can no longer hike out to the chimneys, which are peaks of bare, metamorphic rock. That final part of the trail will remain closed – likely for years to come – owing to the dangers it poses from its unstable rock face and sheer drop-offs.

That said, it's still a lovely, but strenuous uphill hike taking in a beautiful stretch of the rushing West Prong. Because this area wasn't so heavily logged, you can also find a few old-growth trees rising above the canopy. The trail starts with a fairly gentle ascent for the first mile. You'll pass several bridges, all offering fine vantage points over the churning, boulder-filled stream.

There are also a few spots where you can hike down to the water for idyllic views of moss-covered stones and bountiful thickets of rhododendrons. Wildflowers such as trillium, bee-balm and jewelweed grow in abundance.

After you cross the fourth bridge, you'll have completed the first mile. And now the real fun begins: the next 1300yd is extremely steep, and travels up dozens of steps built into the hillside.

At mile 1.75, you'll arrive at a viewing platform – newly built since the 2016 fires. It provides a vantage point onto the craggy rock faces known as the chimneys, which ironically were the place where the conflagration started. Just below the pinnacles, you'll also see firsthand the devastation of the fires, with blackened trunks and dead trees dotting the scarred, barren hillside. After taking in the view, return to your starting point by retracing your steps along the trail.

The parking area for the trailhead is located along Newfound Gap Rd, about 6 miles northwest of the Rockefeller Memorial, and 7 miles southeast of the Sugarlands Visitor Center (on the right side when driving south).

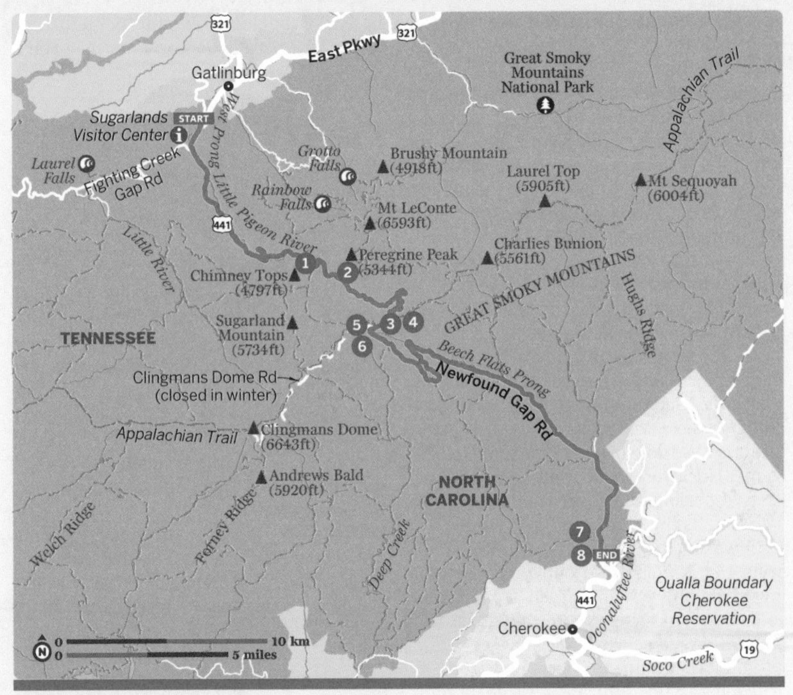

Driving Tour **Newfound Gap Road**

START SUGARLANDS VISITOR CENTER
END OCONALUFTEE VISITOR CENTER
LENGTH 33 MILES; ONE TO THREE HOURS

The park's main artery, Newfound Gap Rd/ Hwy 441, begins just outside Gatlinburg (p92) and heads 33 winding miles to Cherokee, NC, passing many turnouts, picnic areas, nature trails and overlooks along the way.

Between Mile 5.6 and Mile 7.1, you'll have several opportunities to pull over and admire one of the park's best-known geologic features. The Cherokee called them 'Duniskwalgunyi' as they resembled a pair of antlers, while white settlers characterized them as a pair of stone chimneys: **1 Chimney Tops**.

The trailhead and parking area for one of the park's most popular hikes, **2 Alum Cave Bluffs** (p39) is at Mile 8.8. At Mile 12.2 you'll know you've entered the upper elevations of the Smokies as you come to the spruce fir forest that dominates the slopes. The weather is more prickly here – on average it's 10°F to 15°F (5°C to 8°C) cooler than in the lowlands, annual rainfall regularly exceeds 80in and the wind can be fierce.

At **3 Newfound Gap** (p66) travelers pass from Tennessee into North Carolina and the Appalachian Trail crosses the road. In olden days the road passing over the crest of the Smokies did so at Indian Gap, 1.5 miles west of the current site. When this easier passage was discovered in 1850, it was immediately dubbed 'Newfound Gap.' Straddling the state line is the **4 Rockefeller Memorial** (p66), marking the spot where Franklin D Roosevelt formally dedicated the park in 1940.

The turnoff for **5 Clingmans Dome Rd** (p66) is at Mile 13.4. Shortly thereafter, at Mile 13.9, is a large parking area for the **6 Oconaluftee Valley Overlook**, where you'll be treated to impressive views into the valley.

At Mile 28.7, **7 Mingus Mill** (p65) still grinds corn into meal just as it has done for more than a century. The mill operates from early spring through fall, though visitors are welcome any time. It's just a half-mile from the **8 Oconaluftee Visitor Center** (p78), signaling the end of the driving tour.

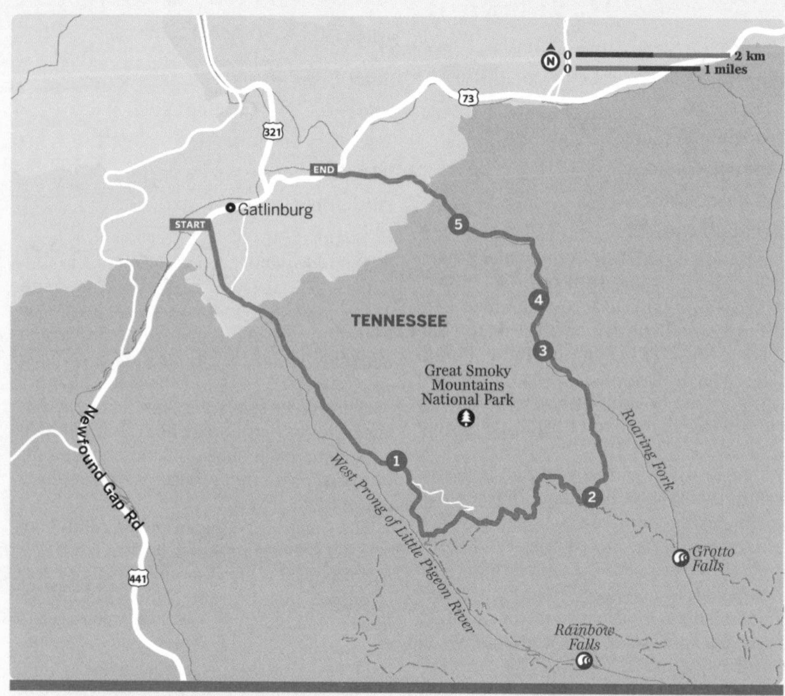

Driving Tour
Roaring Fork Motor Nature Trail

START HISTORIC NATURE TRAIL RD, GATLINBURG
END PLACE OF A THOUSAND DRIPS
LENGTH 8.5 MILES; ONE TO TWO HOURS

The Roaring Fork area is named for one of the park's biggest and most powerful mountain streams and is well loved for its waterfalls, forest and its excellent selection of preserved cabins and other historic structures. If you happen to be in the park during a thunderstorm, don't let it ruin your day – this quick drive is at its best after a particularly hard rain. Keep in mind: the Roaring Fork Motor Nature Trail is closed in winter – it's accessible only from late March to late November.

The 5.5-mile road begins and ends a short distance from downtown Gatlinburg. From Hwy 441 turn onto Airport Rd at the eighth traffic light. Airport becomes Cherokee Orchard Rd, and the Roaring Fork Motor Nature Trail begins 3 miles later.

The first stop on Cherokee Orchard Rd is the 1 **Noah 'Bud' Ogle Nature Trail**, providing an enjoyable jaunt to a mountain farmstead with a streamside tub mill (an improvised contraption built to grind the family corn).

Immediately following the Rainbow Falls Trail you can either turn around and head back to Gatlinburg or continue on Roaring Fork Rd, a narrow, twisting one-way road. The road follows Roaring Fork, one of the park's most tempestuous and beautiful streams. It passes through an impressive stand of old-growth eastern hemlocks, some of which reach heights of more than 100ft and have trunks stretching as much as 5ft across.

From the Trillium Gap Trail the delicate 2 **Grotto Falls** (p51) can be reached via an easy, short hike through forest.

Of considerable historical interest is the hardscrabble cabin at the 3 **Home of Ephraim Bales** and also the more comfortable 'saddlebag' house at the 4 **Alfred Reagan Place** (painted with 'all three colors that Sears and Roebuck had').

A wet-weather waterfall called 5 **Place of a Thousand Drips** provides a wonderful conclusion to your explorations before returning to Gatlinburg.

Sugarlands Valley Nature Trail

Start/End Sugarlands Valley Nature Trail parking area

Duration 30 minutes round-trip

Distance 0.5 miles

Difficulty Easy

Elevation Gain 2ft

The national park's only fully wheelchair-accessible **trail** (off Newfound Gap Rd;) takes visitors on a leisurely half-mile loop through woodland, along the edge of the rushing West Prong of the Little Pigeon River. The trail is wide, fully paved and gently sloped, making it ideal for families with small children and travelers with mobility issues.

If you're in a hurry, you could do this trail in less than half an hour, but it's well worth taking your time. Relatively few visitors stop here, and the peaceful views along the river invite contemplation.

Dappled forest greets you as you begin the walk – a pleasant introduction to the regenerative power of the Smokies. A century ago, this land along the river was completely cleared for timber. Where pine trees now sway in the breeze, there were once farmhouses and fields of corn and wheat.

You'll soon see vestiges of this human-altered landscape as you take the left fork on the trail, stopping beside the stone-walled column sprouting up from the forest floor. This chimney was once part of a summer cottage from the early 1900s.

As you continue further along the trail, the hum of cars along Newfound Gap Rd is replaced by the sound of the gurgling river. Here you can take an unpaved side trail down to the water's edge and look for kingfishers and other birds on the prowl.

As you continue along, take note of the gully that parallels the trail. This started out as a footpath used by Native Americans, and was later transformed by settlers into a road over the mountains that connected this valley with Bryson City to the south.

Pamphlets (50¢) available near the trailhead point out some of the natural and human-made features along the trail.

You'll find the parking area for the trailhead on Newfound Gap Rd, about 0.7 miles south of the Sugarlands Visitor Center (on the left if coming from the north).

Gatlinburg Trail

Start River Rd

End Sugarlands Visitor Center

Duration one hour

Distance 2 miles one way

Difficulty Easy

Elevation Gain 22ft

If you find yourself suddenly allergic to Gatlinburg – it happens – make a beeline south to the edge of downtown. There, just a few steps from the main drag, you'll find a sign marking the start of this pleasant **walk** (River Rd, off Hwy 441 S;) in the woods. With a burbling creek splashing over mossy rocks, a few historic ruins and a photogenic national park sign, you'll shake off those symptoms in a flash. The trail is also open to cyclists and leashed pets.

The trailhead borders a public parking lot on River Rd, near its junction with Hwy 441. If you're in need of any last-minute outdoor gear or apparel, pop into the Nantahala Outdoor Center (NOC; 1138 Parkway) one block away. The trail hugs a creek – the West Prong of the Little Pigeon River – as it breezes through the woods. Next up? A large Great Smoky Mountains National Park sign. Flanked by a stone wall, a split-level fence and soaring trees, it's camera-ready. The path crosses the creek then rolls past old chimneys and other ruins.

You'll also see signs warning passersby that they are walking through a burn area. Here you should watch for hazards such as falling trees and tree limbs. The trail closed for a time after the devastating fires that ripped through parts of the park and Gatlinburg in late November 2016.

Next up is a not-so-photogenic maintenance yard – but hey, at least it's not another Ripley's Museum! Follow the service road and watch for a trail marker telling you to turn right toward Sugarlands Visitor Center. At the visitor center you can pick up information about the park, use the restrooms, catch a ranger program or buy snacks and sodas from the vending machines.

If you don't feel like backtracking to Gatlinburg, hop aboard the Gatlinburg Trolley (p210) for a ride on the tan route, which leaves the Gatlinburg Transit Center every 90 minutes between 9am and 5:30pm. From the Sugarlands Visitor Center, the trolley stops at the Laurel Falls parking lot then Elkmont Campground before returning to downtown.

Roaring Fork Motor Nature Trail, Greenbrier & Around Cosby

Head east from Gatlinburg for some of the finest waterfall hikes in the park.

Ramsey Cascades

Start/End Ramsey Cascades parking area

Duration three to 4½ hours round-trip

Distance 8 miles

Difficulty Moderate to hard

Elevation Gain 2280ft

The hike to Ramsey Cascades takes in some gorgeous forest scenery. Massive old-growth trees, boulder-filled streams and a forest floor sprinkled with wildflowers are among the highlights. The falls themselves are simply magnificent, with rushing white water spilling 100ft down rocky ledges. You'll have to work to enjoy the falls, however, as you ascend more than 2000ft over 4 miles.

The first part of the hike starts out with a fairly easy climb after a long bridge crossing over the rushing Middle Prong of the Little Pigeon River. The wide path initially follows the old road laid out by the logging company, though luckily they didn't get very far into the forest before the national park was created. Even here you'll find a few massive old-growth trees. A few benches are sprinkled along the first mile, where you can sit and contemplate the greenery.

Around mile 1.5, the path loops around a big circle filled with rhododendrons. Just below, the churning Ramsey Prong meets up with Middle Prong. Here a sign announces Ramsey Cascades as 2.5 miles away. This is where the trail narrows and the real climb begins. Watch your step as you make your way over the blackened roots spreading across the path. You'll pass a small stream cascading over moss-covered boulders around mile 2.1, then shortly after, cross over your first log bridge.

Continuing along, you'll pass through old-growth forest with some staggering giants. Around mile 2.6 you'll walk right past two massive tulip trees, with another even larger specimen just beyond.

The trail steepens as you grow nearer to the falls, with the last 400yd requiring some leg work to climb over the big rocks along the path. Finally, at mile 4.0, you've arrived. Take a break and congratulate yourself on reaching one of the prettiest waterfalls in the park. Afterwards, return to the trail's staring point by retracing your steps.

To reach the trailhead, take Hwy 321 for 6 miles east from Gatlinburg and turn right (south) down Greenbrier Rd. Parking for the trail is at the end of this road, 4.5 miles from the turnoff from the highway.

Rainbow Falls

Start/End Rainbow Falls parking area

Duration three to 4½ hours round-trip

Distance 5.4 miles

Difficulty Moderate to hard

Elevation Gain 1600ft

Cascading 80ft down the mountain as the park's highest single-drop waterfall, **Rainbow Falls** (off Cherokee Orchard Rd) is a magnificent sight, particularly after heavy rains. The hike here is fairly challenging, given the 1600ft of elevation gain over just 2.7 miles. Still, this doesn't deter many visitors, so go early to avoid the crowds. The falls are equally captivating in winter, when you can sometimes find them frozen into a spectacular form – though this rare event occurs only during bouts of extremely cold temperatures.

As you start out, you'll pass through the blackened branches and trunks of a scarred landscape – remnants from the Gatlinburg fires that roared through in 2016. You'll make a few stream crossings and around mile 1.5 you'll huff your way uphill, passing some towering old-growth trees just off the path. Thickets of rhododendrons and mountain laurel crowd the path after you pass a log bridge around mile 1.7.

Look for dark-eyed juncos darting about. These sparrow-sized birds have a gray head, neck and wings, with a snow-white underbelly, and they're commonly spotted in the Smokies. Around mile 2.7, you will reach the falls. Find a spot on the rocks to enjoy the view as the foaming spray arcs off in all directions. On sunny days, you may catch sight of rainbows shimmering in the mists – discovering firsthand how these falls earned their name. After a break, retrace your steps along the same trail to return to your starting point.

Roaring Fork Motor Nature Trail, Greenbrier & Around Cosby – Day Hikes

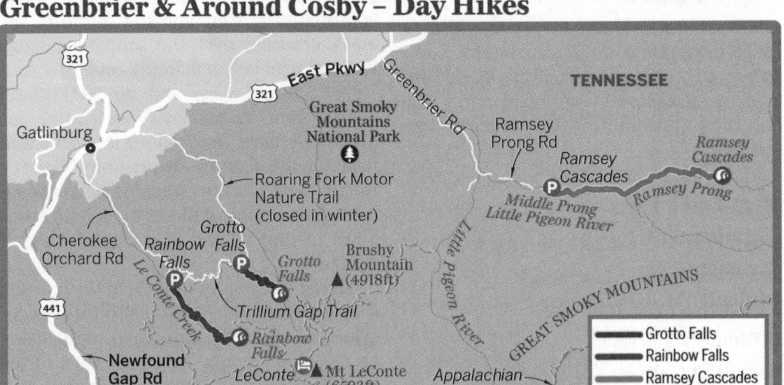

If you're still keen for more hiking, however, you can continue on the trail, which goes across the log bridge and ascends for another 4 miles up to LeConte Lodge (p73). You'll quickly leave behind the masses if you decide to continue onwards. Travelers overnighting at the lodge – or those up for a long hike – can go up via Rainbow Falls and descend via the Trillium Gap Trail for slightly different scenery, including a glimpse of lovely Grotto Falls. However, you'll need to be quite fit and start early to complete this 16-mile loop in one day.

Parking for the trailhead is located along the Cherokee Orchard Rd, a little over 3 miles southeast of Gatlinburg.

Grotto Falls

Start/End Grotto Falls parking area

Duration 1½ to 2½ hours round-trip

Distance 2.6 miles

Difficulty Easy to moderate

Elevation Gain 380ft

This deservedly popular trail leads through lush forest lined with hemlock trees to the lovely **Grotto Falls**, a cascade that tumbles 25ft into a serene moss-fringed pool. It's also the only waterfall in the park that you can walk behind – though take care if doing so, as the slippery, wet stones can lead to some nasty spills.

The hike to the falls is actually part of the longer Trillium Gap Trail, which goes all the way up to the summit of Mt LeConte (a little over 5 miles past Grotto Falls). Set out early if you plan to make it up to the top and back. If you come on Monday, Wednesday or Friday, you might also spy a train of llamas making its way up to the ridge. These animals help resupply the lodge, packing up food and other supplies.

The trail starts off amid sizable American beeches, maples and silverbells (which have gorgeous blooms in the late spring). May and June are particularly lovely times to be here, with a range of blooming wildflowers, including violets, the whimsical Dutchman's breeches and, of course, trillium. Keep an eye out for large black-and-white pileated woodpeckers, which leave their mark (tiny fresh wood chips spattered on the ground from their vigorous tree drillings) all across the forest.

The trail is a fairly continuous uphill climb all the way to the falls, with the loud rush of water (the creek known as Roaring Fork) soon alerting you of your arrival. At the falls, keep an eye out for salamanders. Go early to avoid the crowds, which can pack the place on warm afternoons. After you've had your fill of the pretty setting, retrace your steps to the start of the hike.

The trailhead is located along the one-way Roaring Fork Motor Nature Trail, reachable by taking the Cherokee Orchard Rd from Gatlinburg.

In the winter, when the Roaring Fork road is closed, you'll have the trail all to yourself, though you'll have to hike an extra 5 miles (round-trip) along the Trilium Trail from the nearest parking area.

Cades Cove

The best hikes in **Cades Cove** (Map p70; www.nps.gov/grsm/planyourvisit/cadescove.htm; Cades Cove Loop Rd; P) share a trifecta of charms: awesome scenery, a bit of history and a likelihood of encounters with untamed flora and fauna.

Abrams Falls

Start/End Abrams Falls parking lot

Duration three to four hours

Distance 5 miles round-trip

Difficulty Moderate

Elevation Gain less than 800ft

Not to be effusive, but this **hike** (Map p70; Cades Cove Loop Rd) is darn near perfect: a boisterous creek hugs much of the trail, log bridges keep things adventurous, wildflowers add color in spring, a horseshoe bend snakes into view halfway through and a photogenic waterfall crashes into a wide pool as the final reward. The only drawback is the crowds, which can be quite heavy in summer, during spring-break season in April and on weekends. For solitude get to the trailhead before 9am.

Abrams Falls and Abrams Creek are named for Cherokee Chief Abram, who lived in a village near the mouth of the creek along the Tennessee River in the late 1700s. In the 1920s a descendant of Cades Cove settler John Oliver ran a guest lodge at the trailhead. From the parking lot the well-signed trail enters the woods – filled with oaks, beeches and pines – and immediately crosses a bridge over Abrams Creek. A side trail to the right leads to the Elijah Oliver Place (p69), a half-mile north.

The main trail continues straight and level, tracking the creek. In warmer months look for rhododendron and mountain laurel blooms along the way. At about 1 mile you'll ascend Arbutus Ridge. From the top, after the leaves are down, you can see the horseshoe bend of the creek below. In the spring, as you descend, you might observe wildflower hunters checking the steep sandstone slopes of the ridge for blooms.

From here, in a little over 1 mile, you'll hear the falls before you actually see them. The trail then drops to two creek crossings with log bridges. And then, before the trail bears right, you'll glimpse the crashing cascades through the trees. The falls are only 20ft high, but the force of the water is strong. The view and the sound of the creek crashing over the sandstone ledge into the pool below is impressive.

Obey the signage and do NOT climb on the falls. There have been numerous drownings here. Rocks along the creek and near the falls can be surprisingly slippery. In fact, *Backpacker* magazine once named Abrams Falls one of the 10 most dangerous hikes in the US. But picnics and photos? All good.

The trailhead is at the end of the parking area between stops 10 and 11 on the Cades Cove Loop Rd. The turnoff to the parking area is about 5 miles from the start of the loop. No pets are allowed on this trail.

Gregory Bald

Start/End Forge Rd parking area

Duration six to seven hours

Distance 11 miles round-trip

Difficulty Hard

Elevation Gain 3036ft

As you turn in a slow circle on the high grassy meadow known as **Gregory Bald** (Forge Creek Rd, off Cades Cove Loop Rd), it's easy to appreciate Julie Andrews' joy in the *Sound of Music*. This may not be the Alps, but it's the next best thing in the southern Appalachians, with views of mountains and valleys stretching to the horizon in every direction. And if you arrive in mid-to late June, the orange, pink and fiery-red blooms of the flaming azaleas add one last dab of perfection.

The origins of the high-altitude balds in the park are uncertain. Some of these treeless meadows may have been cleared by white settlers for cattle grazing. Others say natural causes such as wildfires or high winds created small clearings, which were later expanded by cattle owners. Gregory Bald is named for Russell Gregory, a prominent Cades Cove resident whose cows grazed here in the mid-1800s. Today the park service maintains the balds and prevents the forest from encroaching on these broad, open spaces.

In the morning the Gregory Ridge Trail is disarmingly pleasant: birds are chirping, Forge Creek tumbles merrily beside you and sun-dappled leaves frame your views. At 2 miles the trail reaches backcountry

Cades Cove – Day Hikes

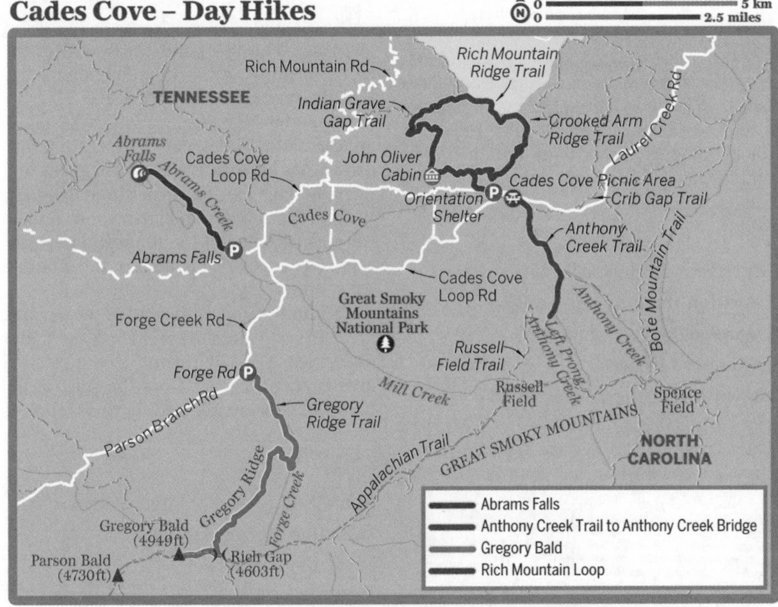

campsite 12, a scenic spot in the shadows of towering old-growth trees. From here the fun ends and the climbing begins. Be sure to pause at the rock outcrop about 1300yd up from the campground – this is your first bird's-eye view of Cades Cove to the north. The trail continues to climb, and climb, finally calling it quits at its junction with the Gregory Bald Trail in Rich Gap, 4.9 miles from the trailhead.

Take a breather here. The 1000yd final push on the Gregory Bald Trail is steep and punishing. Fortunately it's also short and the absence of trees just ahead lets you know that the bald is close. Once you reach its edge, walk right for broad views of Cades Cove then swing up the hill to the survey marker noting that the altitude is 4949ft. You can return to the trail on the path through the azaleas, which typically bloom in mid- to late June. Blueberries make an appearance in August.

From the Cades Cove Loop Rd, turn right onto Forge Creek Rd just beyond the Cades Cove Visitor Center parking lot. Follow Forge Creek Rd south for just over 2 miles. Park at the small parking area beside the trailhead sign for the Gregory Ridge Trail.

Rich Mountain Loop

Start/End Orientation Shelter parking lot

Duration five to six hours

Distance 8.5 miles

Difficulty Hard

Elevation Gain about 1800ft

After a creekside ramble through the forest to the first home built in Cades Cove, this loop climbs the southern slope of Rich Mountain. From the top, pine-framed views of Cades Cove and the town of Townsend shimmer far below. Along the loop keep alert for turkey, deer and the occasional bear. A couple of convenient backcountry campsites can flip this lengthy day hike into a low-key two-day excursion.

The loop – comprised of three trails – begins with a family-friendly walk through a hemlock forest on the 3.4-mile Rich Mountain Loop Trail, which is interrupted by a few easy creek crossings. You'll pass the Crooked Arm Ridge Trail junction after 900yd then reach the John Oliver Cabin (p68) and its split-rail fence at 1.4 miles. John and his wife Lucretia were among the first white settlers in Cades Cove, arriving in 1818. Their log cabin is believed to be the oldest structure in the park.

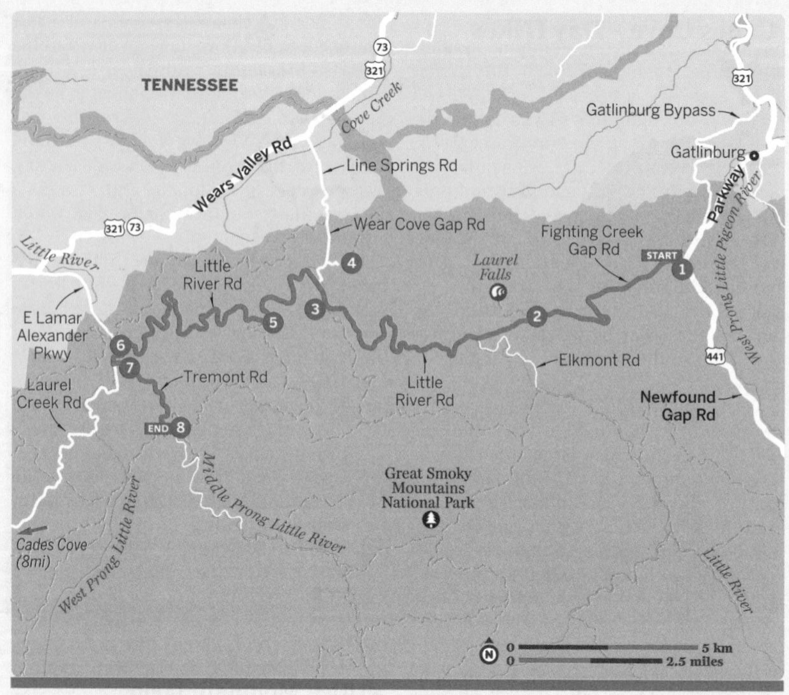

Driving Tour
Little River Road

START SUGARLANDS VISITOR CENTER
END GREAT SMOKY MOUNTAINS INSTITUTE AT TREMONT
LENGTH 18 MILES; ONE TO 1½ HOURS

Formerly an old railroad roadbed serving the timber industry, Little River Rd shadows the snaking Little River to connect 1 **Sugarlands Valley** with Townsend and Cades Cove. The meandering 18-mile route can take as long as 1½ hours to drive.

A short 3.7 miles from Sugarlands is the trailhead for the 2 **Laurel Falls Trail** (p44), one of the most popular hikes in the park.

Ten miles from Sugarlands you'll see a sign for 3 **Metcalf Bottoms Picnic Area** (p66), a large and pretty day-use area on the Little River. Bear sightings are common here. A 1-mile path (walk or drive) leads to the delightful 4 **Little Greenbrier School**, a charming, 19th-century split-log schoolhouse that also served as a church. Original desks, benches and a painted blackboard, still line the room.

Another 1.5 miles down Little River Rd brings you to 5 **The Sinks** (p66), an ominous stretch of water that, according to folklore, once swallowed a logging train whole.

The next major landmark is the 6 **Townsend Wye**, where the West Prong joins Little River and Hwy 73 peels off for Townsend. At this favorite swimming spot you'll find a placid stretch of river with grassy banks. From this point, as you drive into Cades Cove, the road's name changes to Laurel Creek Rd.

Less than a mile past the junction, turn left onto 7 **Tremont Rd**, an uncrowded, 3.2-mile route into a scenic area of the park that once was home to one of the last logging camps in the Smokies.

The 8 **Great Smoky Mountains Institute at Tremont** (p72), a research facility with a visitor center and bookstore, is also worth a visit. Two nearby trails provide pleasant river walks with impressive cascades: the West Prong Trail, on the right just before the institute, and the Middle Prong Trail, at the end of the road.

From here you can chose to continue on to Cades Cove (p52), another 12 miles down an equally appealing and winding road.

You'll ditch the crowds as you leave the homestead and begin climbing. Sounds of wildlife crashing through the underbrush – we saw a few wild turkeys – will keep you on high alert as you follow the creek. Farther along the 2-mile ascent, the bird's-eye views of Cades Cove below are a nice distraction from the huffing and puffing, especially in winter and spring when views are unobstructed through the leafless trees. The Rich Mountain Loop Trail ends at Indian Grave Gap Trail after 3.4 miles. Turn right to follow the latter along the sometimes-narrow ridge, with views of Townsend to the north and Cades Cove to the south.

After 1400yd you'll reach backcountry campsite 5 at the junction with the Rich Mountain Trail (which is not the same as the Rich Mountain Loop Trail). From here continue 1.8 miles on Indian Grave Gap Trail to its junction with Crooked Arm Ridge Trail and the Scott Mountain Trail. If you've packed lunch, turn left on the Scott Mountain Trail for a 500yd detour to backcountry campsite 6, a nice spot for a quiet picnic if no one is here. Don't let the sight of the bear cables – used for food storage – ruin your reverie, but do pack up your trash.

Back at the trail junction, the 2.2-mile Crooked Arm Ridge Trail drops steeply though oaks and maples back to the Rich Mountain Loop Trail, where you'll turn left for the 900yd return to the trailhead.

To access this hike, park in the large lot beside the orientation shelter at the start of the Cades Cove Loop Rd. Since the lot is outside the loop, you don't have to worry about getting stuck on the lengthy one-way drive around the cove. Backcountry campsites 5 and 6 require advance reservation and a permit. To avoid a very steep ascent up Crooked Arm Ridge Trail, hike this loop in a clockwise direction.

Anthony Creek Trail to Anthony Creek Bridge

Start/End Cades Cove picnic area

Duration two hours

Distance 3.2 miles round-trip

Difficulty Easy

Elevation Gain 495ft

For an introduction to the creek-and-forest charms of Cades Cove, take an easy ramble on the kid-friendly Anthony Creek Trail, which doubles as a busy connector to the Appalachian Trail and several notable natural features. With log bridges, burbling creeks, spring wildflowers and soaring trees, the backdrop for the trail is a page from a children's fantasy tale – just watch out for the horse poop!

It gets crowded in summer, but the picnic area beside the trailhead is quite lovely, with tables perched here and there beside the rippling waters of Abrams Creek and its small pools. For younger kids it's a mesmerizing place to explore. And if you're wondering where all those hikers with trekking poles are headed, it's most likely the Anthony Creek Trail, which connects to the Russell Field Trail in 1.6 miles and the Bote Mountain Trail in 3.5 miles. The latter two trails eventually connect with the Appalachian Trail.

The Anthony Creek Trail gets off to a rather uninspiring start, setting out as a utilitarian gravel road carrying park vehicles to places unseen. But the scenery improves after the Crib Gap Trail junction at 400yd, when the horse camp comes into view. Here equestrians tie up their steeds during overnight stays. Beyond the horse camp, the trail morphs from a boring gravel road to a more traditional path through the woods, with hemlock trees and Anthony Creek as the predominant distractions. Keep an eye out for purple iris blooms along the trail in spring – the Tennessee state flower is a beauty. Rhododendrons bloom along the path in July.

A series of small bridges, including two log bridges, soon appear, crossing Abrams Creek three times as the trail begins to ascend. The fourth bridge carries hikers over the Left Prong of Anthony Creek. Just beyond the fourth bridge is a large rock that makes for a nice place to enjoy a snack before turning around.

The gear-wearing hikers you'll see are likely headed up to Rocky Top, the rock outcropping with 360-degree views that inspired the country song of the same name, or they're climbing to Russell Field or Spence Field, two grassy mountaintop meadows. All are on the Appalachian Trail.

Cataloochee Valley

If you like your trails people-free, head to lonely Cataloochee. Old homesteads and prim churches are another highlight. Elk and wild turkeys sightings are likely.

Boogerman Trail

Start/End Cataloochee Rd

Duration four hours

Distance 7.5 miles

Difficulty Moderate to hard

Elevation Gain about 1000ft

Named for a local hermit, this partial loop rolls through a wonderland of soaring old-growth trees. Along the way, moss-covered stone walls flank old homesteads and skinny log bridges ford overgrown creeks. It's all so lonely and wild, you would hardly blink if a hobbit – or maybe a hermit – stepped into view.

The old-growth forest is here thanks to the aforementioned hermit, Robert 'Boogerman' Palmer. He requested that memorable nickname in elementary school, according to community lore. His brother was the legendary hunter and sharpshooter 'Turkey' George Palmer, who killed 106 bears in his lifetime. He was buried in a steel casket, they say, so that the bears still roaming the mountains wouldn't get revenge by mauling his body. The Boogerman's legacy, however, is more lasting – he refused to allow logging on his remote property, so the trees along his namesake trail are huge and sometimes quite unique looking. Keep an eye out for twin-trunk tulip trees, for example, in the higher elevations.

The hike begins at the bridge just west of Cataloochee Campground. From here, follow Caldwell Fork Trail along Caldwell Fork Creek for 1400yd to the marked trailhead for the Boogerman Trail. From here the 4.1-mile path – open to hikers only – begins a rapid ascent through the thick woods, home to young and old Eastern hemlocks as well as maples and oaks. The trail swoops up and down through the forest, passing the site of Palmer's old homestead, where a two-room cabin and various outbuildings once stood. Today not much remains to mark his presence. After a short punishing climb and one long drop, the trail approaches a prominent stone wall. Just beyond look for the big rotted-out tulip tree – a person can stand inside.

The trail rejoins the Caldwell Fork Trail for a 2.8-mile return to the trailhead, crossing Caldwell Creek numerous times. At the time of publication, several log bridges across the creek had gone missing and not been replaced. After a big storm, these crossings may require a knee-high trek in a couple of spots and boot-drenching crossings in the others. These crossings may be unsafe for younger kids, and you will get wet if the water is high. Check the trail status with the camp host or a ranger before setting out and look for warning signs posted at the trailhead.

Rough Fork Trail to Woody Place

Start/End end of Cataloochee Rd

Duration one hour

Distance 2 miles round-trip

Difficulty Easy

Elevation Gain 144ft

With birds singing above, a creek rippling beside you and an old road unfurling through the white pines ahead, it's easy to imagine this place in the late 1860s, when children from the newly combined Woody and Caldwell families would have likely run up and down this path on their way to school or the village. Today the 2-mile hike, which has several fun creek crossings on log bridges, is a great choice for families with younger kids. And if you're hiking alone, never mind those rumors about the Wild Man of Cataloochee...

As you drive down the gravel section of Cataloochee Rd to the trailhead, keep watch for elk in the adjacent meadows. They're particularly active in the early morning and evening. You might also see a few wild turkeys strutting their stuff.

The trail from the parking area crosses Rough Fork Creek several times before pausing at the Woody Place, once a multi-building homestead. Today only the wood-frame home and the springhouse remain. After the Civil War, Jonathan Woody married widow Mary Ann Caldwell and moved into her log cabin, combining their families into an 1860s version of the *Brady Bunch* – with a grand total of 14 children living here. Over the years framed

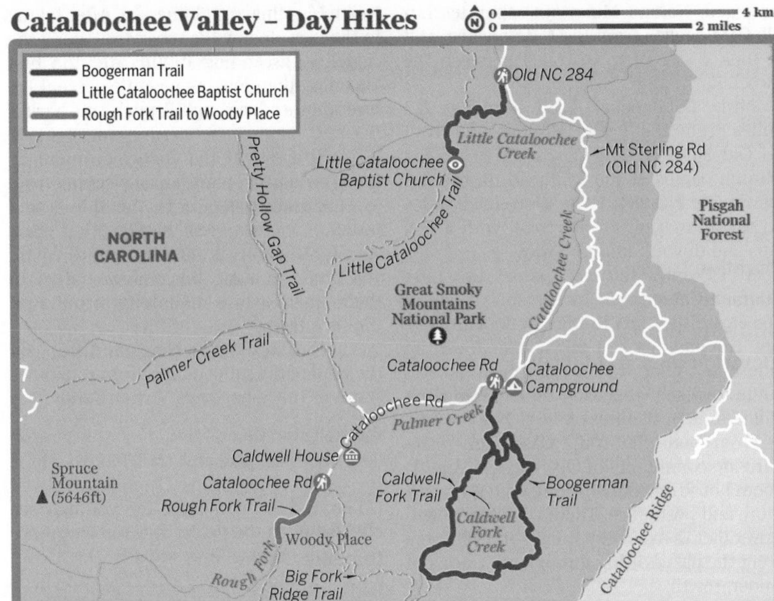

additions subsumed the original log cabin. Porches and a kitchen were also added.

Cataloochee has its own version of Bigfoot and the Loch Ness Monster: the Wild Man of Cataloochee. According to *Hiking Trails of The Smokies,* the Wild Man's legend grew after he was spotted and questioned by a ranger while fishing along Rough Fork in 1976. The man claimed he didn't have a name and that he had lived in the Cataloochee woods all his life. He took off, rangers gave chase, but he eluded capture. Sightings continued over the years and his legend grew, keeping Cataloochee campfire stories a little bit scary over the years.

The trailhead is at the end of the gravel section of Cataloochee Rd, beyond the Caldwell House.

Little Cataloochee Baptist Church

Start/End Old NC 284

Duration two to three hours

Distance 4 miles round-trip

Difficulty Moderate

Elevation Gain 719ft

Hearing the loud peals of a church bell tolling across Little Cataloochee Valley is unnerving, especially if you're hiking alone. The 400lb bell hangs in the steeple above **Little Cataloochee Baptist Church** (off Old NC 284), which sits on a hilltop on a remote stretch of the Little Cataloochee Trail in an already-remote section of the park. How remote is it? Let's just say it's 13.5 miles from the I-40 to the trailhead, and about eight of those miles are unpaved as they bump over a serpentine path through the mountains and forest. The drive is followed by a 2-mile hike through a valley abandoned in the late 1930s.

The church was completed in 1889. Its most noteworthy possession is the aforementioned bell. According to *Top Trails: Great Smoky Mountains National Park,* the church rang the bell every time a local died, ringing it one time for each year of the person's life. Those counting the tolls could then figure out who'd died. Based on our experience, we guarantee you'll be counting the tolls if you hear the bell ring while hiking this lonely valley by yourself!

Little Cataloochee was settled in the mid-1800s by the descendants of families who'd already established themselves in Big Cataloochee Valley, which was growing crowded. Noland Mountain separates Little Cataloochee from Big Cataloochee, and it took a steep trip to travel between the two.

Little Cataloochee Trail stretches 5.2 miles from the Pretty Hollow Gap Trail to Old NC 284. The shortest hike to the church begins at the trailhead on the unpaved Old NC 284. From there it's 2 miles to the church on an old road, with a few ups and downs along the way.

At 1.2 miles the trail passes the 1864 Hannah Cabin, built by the son of one of the earliest settlers in Big Cataloochee Valley. The banging you might hear from the house as you approach could be a ghost... or more likely the back door hitting the doorframe in the breeze.

From here the trail passes the once-thriving community of Ola, where a fine 11-room house once stood along with a general store and post office. There's not much here now other than a rocky stream and whispers from the past drifting through the trees and undergrowth.

A steady climb ends at the white church, which sits on a small bare hilltop. Inside you'll find a pot-bellied stove and white wooden pews. On our visit the rope to the bell could not be found – perhaps tucked behind a hatch door in the ceiling by the mischievous, bell-ringing photographers who'd been hiking a short distance ahead.

It's also possible to hike to the church from Big Cataloochee Valley via the Pretty Hollow Gap and Little Cataloochee Trails, but this 8-mile round-trip hike is the longer and more strenuous option.

To get to the Old NC 284 trailhead, drive 5.5 miles north on Old NC 284 from Little Cataloochee Rd. Along the way, keep right at any forks in the road. Don't block the service-vehicle gate at the tiny parking area.

Additional Hikes

Newfound Gap Road

Charlies Bunion HIKING

(Newfound Gap, Newfound Gap Rd) This oddly named outcropping along the Appalachian Trail offers staggering views. The popular 8-mile (round-trip) trail starts near the Rockefeller Memorial, which straddles North Carolina and Tennessee. After taking in the view, follow the rocky trail along the ridgeline, ascending 1000ft over the first 2.5 miles, then making a gentle descent before another brief uphill push to Charlies Bunion.

You'll arrive at the craggy promontory with its dazzling panorama sweeping from Mt LeConte eastward to the the jagged peaks of the Sawteeth Range. It's a great spot for a picnic, though be careful where you step, as some hikers have fallen to their deaths while scrambling around on the rock face.

The trailhead is at Newfound Gap, on the road of the same name, around 13 miles south of the Sugarlands Visitor Center.

Oconaluftee River Trail HIKING

(family-friendly) This flat, peaceful trail follows along the banks of the pretty Oconaluftee River. Go around dawn or dusk and you may see elk grazing in the fields. The 3-mile, round-trip walk begins just outside the Oconaluftee Visitor Center (p78). You can check out the historic buildings of the Mountain Farm Museum (p65) before setting off.

This is one of only two trails in the park that allows dogs, as long as they're on a leash (the other dog-friendly path is the Gatlinburg Trail; p49). You can also ride a bike along the trail.

Roaring Fork Motor Nature Trail

Baskins Creek Trail HIKING

Near the start of the Roaring Fork Motor Nature Trail, you'll find this trail leading up to pretty Baskins Falls. The fascinating 5.6-mile out-and-back hike draws a fraction of the number of visitors to more popular nearby sites such as Rainbow Falls and Grotto Falls. It's moderately strenuous, with a gain of about 1400ft over the course of the hike.

Along the way, you'll spy white vein quartz, see fire-blackened tree trunks from the 2016 fires and have a few creek crossings.

Around mile 1.2, it's worthwhile taking the 400yd detour to the **Baskins Creek Cemetery**, with its weathered gravestones hidden in a mossy clearing. Another photogenic forest-fringed cemetery lies near the trail's end, which intersects a different stretch of the Roaring Fork Motor Nature Trail.

TOP TIPS

- Get an early start to beat the crowds. Even on the most popular hikes, if you're at the trailhead by 8am, you'll be able to enjoy the forests in peace.
- Don't spend all of your time in Cades Cove and on Newfound Gap Rd. There's so much more to the Smokies, and some of its remote corners can provide the most rewarding travel experiences.
- Bring a cooler and load up on groceries. There are lovely spots for a picnic, and it's a waste of time driving out of the park to lunch spots during the day.
- Don't try to cram too much into one day. Leave time to hang out by streams and linger over mountain views. The magic of the Smokies is in taking it slowly.

OVERNIGHT HIKES

There are scores of options for overnight hikes in the Smokies. You can make a two-day trip that includes park highlights such as Charlies Bunion or Mt LeConte, or hike to less-visited corners of the mountains along routes such as the Lakeshore Trail or the Baxter Ridge. There's also the granddaddy of backpacking trips, the Appalachian Trail, parts of which you can include in many itineraries.

There are few dedicated loop routes in the Smoky Mountains, though the many intersecting trails in the park mean you can plan a loop without having to end far from your starting point. If you are planning on ending at a distant point, however, you can use shuttle services to either take you to the trailhead or pick you up at an arranged time when you finish.

A backcountry permit and a backcountry campsite reservation are required for all backcountry stays in the park. The Backcountry Permit Office is an excellent resource for planning an overnight or multiday hiking trip.

Backcountry Permits

Before heading out, make sure you secure a backcountry permit and reserve a campsite or shelter. It's best to do this in advance online (www.nps.gov/grsm/planyourvisit/backcountry-camping.htm), though you can also do it in person at the **Backcountry Permit Office** (865-436-1297; www.nps.gov/grsm/planyourvisit/backcountry-camping.htm; off Newfound Gap Rd; 8am-5pm). This office can also help you make changes to your itinerary if needed.

You'll get your permit at the same time your backcountry campsite is confirmed. Afterwards, you'll need to print out your reservation and carry it with you throughout your backcountry trip. If you don't have access to a printer, head to the office and they'll print it for you.

Backcountry Campsites & Shelters

The national park has more than 80 backcountry campsites. It also has 15 shelters, most of which are located along the Appalachian Trail. The price to stay at either, including the permit, is $4 per person per night, with a maximum fee of $20. Permits are valid for up to seven nights. Sites have a capacity of anywhere from four people to 14. They can book up on weekends and throughout the busy summer months, so reserve well ahead. Reservations can be made up to 30 days in advance of the first night of your trip.

Keep in mind that some sites also accept horses, mules and other stock. Contact the backcountry permit office if you're planning to travel with your favorite llama.

Emergency Contact

Before departing on an overnight hike in the Great Smoky Mountains, be sure to leave your hiking itinerary, backcountry permit number and date of your return with a contact person who will not be hiking. Pass along to your contact the park's emergency phone number (865-436-9171) as a resource if you do not return as planned.

Shuttle Services

If you're planning a hiking route that doesn't end near your starting point, you'll need to use a shuttle service. These can take you to the trailhead, or pick you up at the end. For something a little more

BACKCOUNTRY REGULATIONS

Bear Cable System All scent-bearing items (food, garbage, toothpaste) must be hung on the bear-cable system at each campsite or shelter. It's wise to cover it with a plastic bag before hanging to protect it from rain. To use the system, detach the clip, pull down the cables and hang your bag from the hook. Then pull it back up and attach the clip back to the eye bolt at the base of the tree. These food-storage cable systems are available at all backcountry campsites. If you don't see it, look around.

Toilet Use If you need to dispose of human waste, bury it in a hole at least 6in deep, and make sure you're at least 100ft from any campsite, trail or water source. Pack out all toilet paper, sanitary napkins, tampons etc. Don't bury these items!

Leave No Trace Pack out all food, trash and gear. Leave nothing behind!

Campfires Fires are allowed only at designated sites and are permitted only in established fire rings. The burning of trash, food items and anything else apart from wood is prohibited. If you can forgo a fire, that's even better.

Washing Up Polluting park waters is prohibited. Do not bathe or wash dishes in streams. Instead, collect water and bathe or wash dishes with it at least 100ft from the water source. Biodegradable soap does not break down in water and is in fact a pollutant.

Group Size The maximum group size is eight people. For bigger groups, you'll have to apply for a special permit from the permit office.

Where to Camp Camping is permitted only at designated campsites and shelters.

Maximum Stay Hikers are not allowed to stay at a campsite for more than three consecutive nights. At shelters, the maximum stay is one night.

creative, you can even book a boat shuttle across Fontana Lake to hike remote western sections of the Lakeshore Trail.

Note that none of these outfits are run by the park service, but all are authorized to operate within the national park.

- ➡ A Walk in the Woods (p78)
- ➡ AAA Hiker Service (p78)
- ➡ Smoky Mountain Guides (p78)
- ➡ Fontana Marina (p31) Provides boat service to trailheads along Fontana Lake.

Newfound Gap Road

Charlies Bunion & Kephart Loop

Start/End Newfound Gap

Duration two days

Distance 14.1 miles

Difficulty Moderate

Elevation Gain 4185ft

The Smoky Mountains are packed with great viewpoints, but the rocky outcropping known as Charlies Bunion offers one of the most memorable panoramas in the park. You'll also get a brief taste of the Appalachian Trail as you walk along the ridgeline. Most visitors do Charlies Bunion (p65) as an out-and-back day hike (8 miles return), but you can leave the day-trippers behind and overnight in a lush valley near the Kephart Prong.

This two-day hike starts near the Rockefeller Memorial, which straddles two states at Newfound Gap (p66), around 13 miles south of the Sugarlands Visitor Center. Check out the views into Tennessee and North Carolina, then find the sign indicating the Appalachian Trail just below. This section of the AT is fairly well traveled (and is busy in springtime with through-hikers), so if you want the scenery to yourself, hit the trail early.

The first 2 miles of the hike follow a fairly steady elevation gain along cool, mixed forest before passing through Fraser fir forest, the bare limbs of the trees evidence of the balsam woolly adelgid wreaking havoc. You'll also see plenty of wildflowers in spring and blackberries in late summer, with views opening up along both sides of the ridge.

Around mile 1.7, you'll pass the junction with the Sweat Heifer Creek Trail, which you'll be coming up the next day. A little further along, around mile 2.7, you'll pass the turnoff to the Boulevard Trail, which leads up to Mt LeConte. A little further along, the Icewater Spring Shelter is a popular overnight stop for through-hikers. The piped spring just beyond does indeed have ice-cold water, though as elsewhere in the park, you'll need to treat it before drinking. From here the path descends through a cool spruce and fir forest before leveling out amid secondary forest of American beech and yellow birch. After a short ascent, you'll see the big rock face just ahead. Then at mile 4.0, a well-weathered signpost announces your arrival at Charlies Bunion.

As you take the narrow spur out to the overlook, keep in mind that careless travelers have fallen to their deaths out on the rocks, so it's best not to scramble around on these ledges.The curious name incidentally comes from Horace Kephart, who was out exploring this section of the Smokies in 1929 with his friend Charlie Connor and photographer George Masa. After spotting the bulbous rock face, he paid homage to his hiking companion (or at least his companion's foot ailment), saying, jovially, that it looked just like Charlie's bunion. Somehow the farcical name stuck – it helped that Kephart was later involved in choosing place names within the park boundaries. If you haven't eaten already, this is a fine place for a long break. With dizzying 1000ft drop-offs, the sweeping panorama spreads from Mt LeConte eastward to the the jagged peaks of the Sawteeth Range.

From Charlies Bunion, you'll continue along the Appalachian Trail for another half-mile before making the right (southward) turn onto the Dry Sluice Gap Trail. You'll likely have this quiet, little-used track all to yourself as you descend through stands of Catawba rhododendrons – at times so thick, they form an enclosed Gothic arch overhead. Around mile 5.8, you'll see the signpost for the Grassy Branch Trail leading off to your right. Take this trail, which keeps descending. You'll pass wind-whipped oak and birch trees, and cross a few small streams, including an offshoot of the Icewater Spring that you traversed far above.

After the long, steady descent, you'll soon hear the rush of the Kephart Prong. Then around mile 8.4, you'll reach a forest of rich secondary growth and arrive at the Kephart Shelter. After dropping your pack (and hoisting up your food items with the bear-proof cable system), you can explore a bit of this former lumber site. If you have the energy, you'll also find remnants of a former CCC corps (p45) further downhill (but it's a bit of a hike back up to the shelter).

Try to get plenty of rest, because you'll have lots of climbing on day two – around 2500ft. The day begins along the Sweat Heifer Creek Trail, which starts a few paces from the shelter. Cross a log bridge over the rushing stream and mossy boulders, then make the slow, steady ascent. Plan a rest stop around mile 1.6 (from the shelter), beside the cooling multi-stage falls of Sweat

Charlies Bunion & Kephart Loop

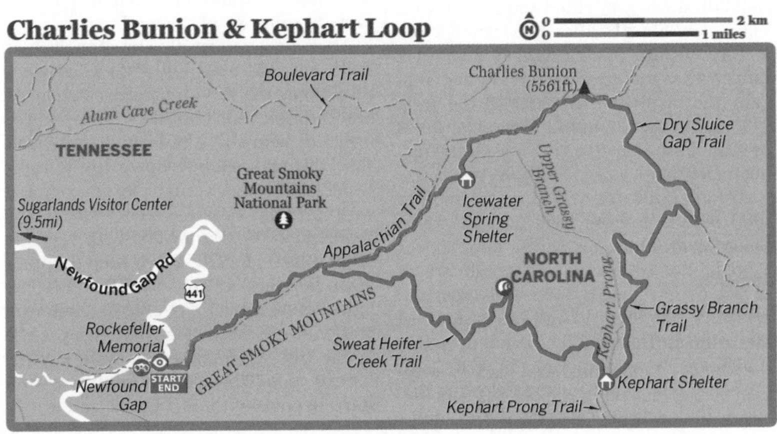

Heifer Cascades. At mile 3.8 you'll meet back up with the Appalachian Trail. Turn left and continue another 1.7 miles to return to your original starting point of the two-day hike.

Around Cosby

Big Creek & Mt Cammerer

Start/End Big Creek Ranger Station

Duration two days

Distance 16.7 miles

Difficulty Moderate to hard

Elevation Gain 3568ft

The eastern side of the Smoky Mountains offers some enchanting landscapes, and on this hike you'll see grand views from a historic watchtower, hike a rolling stretch of the Appalachian Trail and follow beside a cascading, boulder-filled stream that evokes a bit of paradise lost.

A good base for the night before (and perhaps after) the hike is the Big Creek campground (p73), within strolling distance of the trailhead. The walk begins on the **Big Creek Trail**, which follows the scenic, aptly named waterway as it winds its way through lush forest. Around mile 1.4, look for a small side trail leading down to the water and Midnight Hole. This unsigned spot features a 6ft-high cascade of water rushing between huge boulders and filling a large, deep, blue-green pool below. Fringes of rhododendron hang overhead. It's a gorgeous spot for a picnic.

Continuing on, you'll reach Mouse Creek Falls at mile 2.0. Its churning white waters spill 20ft down gray stone and join up with Big Creek. Shortly after this, you'll cross a sturdy bridge (which used to support a railway that was used by the lumber company that exploited this area in the early 1900s). The gentle uphill grade continues as you follow along the river, this time tracing its left bank as you walk westward.

Around mile 5.1 you'll reach another solid bridge to cross back over the river. Before continuing, it's worth stopping for a break along a lovely and serene stretch of Big Creek. Shortly after you cross the bridge, you'll come to the intersection of the Low Gap Trail. You'll be heading up this trail next. However, if you prefer to leave the strenuous ascent for the following day, you'll find several excellent backcountry campsites just south of the turnoff. Campsite 37 is the pick of the two, with sites just a few paces from the rumbling creek. Campsite 36, a few hundred yards further, is for both backpackers and horse riders.

Along the Low Gap Trail, you'll travel 2.5 miles up to the intersection of the Appalachian Trail. Along the way, you'll gain more than 1350ft in elevation, though the first mile is fairly easy going (even downhill in parts). You'll enjoy new perspectives over Big Creek as you wind your way north. Around 1 mile into the trail, you might see signs of former homesteads – piled-up rocks that formed the bases of chimneys, dry-rock bases that supported small spring houses (for keeping food items cool) over trickling springs. Second-growth tulip trees soar high above the cool forest floor.

The last half-mile of the Low Gap Trail gets particularly steep as you make your way past wildflowers and silverbell trees to the Appalachian Trail. Pause here before continuing on – there's more climbing ahead, though the worst of the uphill part is behind you.

The Low Gap, at 4240ft, is indeed a low point on the Appalachian Trail. Over the next 2 miles, you'll ascend another 800ft along a well-used trail with fine views (and refreshing breezes the higher you go). Just after hitting the 2-mile mark, you'll see the turnoff to Mt Cammerer. Although it adds an extra 1.2 miles (round-trip) to your hike, it's well worth taking this spur trail to the rocky overlook. There you'll find a stone fire tower, first built by the CCC in the late 1930s, then, after falling into disrepair, reconstructed in 1995. The 360-degree views from the surrounding circular platform provide a fine lay of the land.

After you return to the Appalachian Trail, it's all downhill. You'll continue east along the AT for another 3.2 miles, descending about 2000ft by the time you meet up with the Chestnut Branch Trail. Take this trail leading down to the right. It passes through verdant forest complete with gurgling streams, mossy stones and a profusion of wildflowers, with very few other hikers in sight. You'll keep dropping down another 1250ft over the next 2.2 miles before returning to Big Creek Ranger Station. Note that when you reach the end of the trail, turn right and walk another 1000yd along the road to return to your starting point at the Big Creek trailhead.

Big Creek & Mt Cammerer

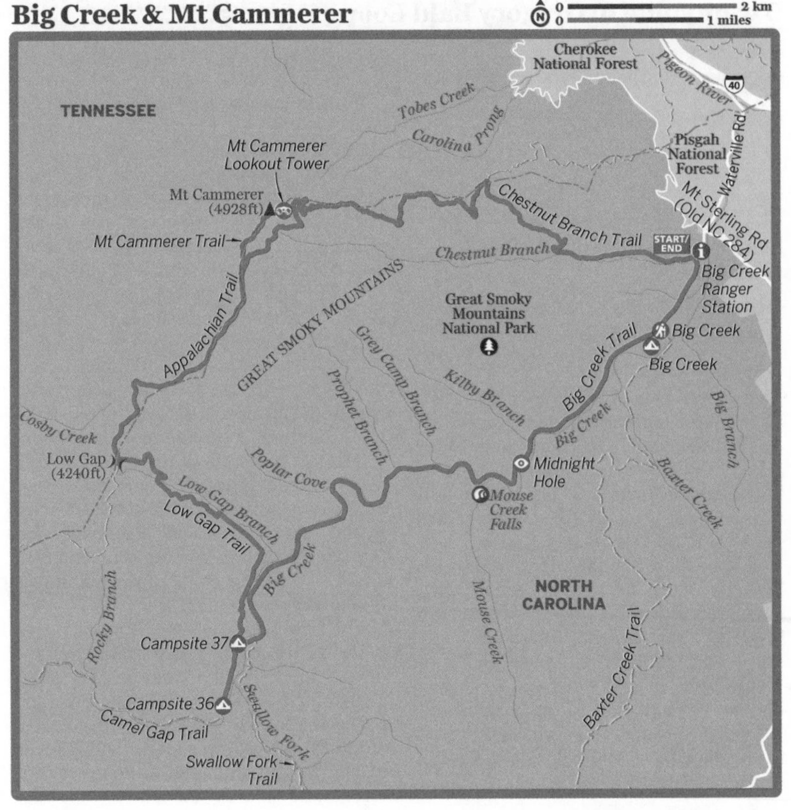

To reach the starting point of the hike, take I-40 to exit 451 and follow Waterville Rd to Big Creek Ranger Station. The trailhead is on the right, just before you reach the campground.

Fontana Dam & Western North Carolina

Solitude and big views are your rewards in the western fringes of the park.

Twentymile to Gregory Bald Loop

Start/End Twentymile Ranger Station

Duration two to three days

Distance 18.3 miles

Difficulty Hard

Elevation Gain 4500ft

In a remote corner of the park, the Twentymile Ranger Station is the starting point for this challenging, uphill **trek** (Twentymile Ranger Station, Hwy 28) to one of the loveliest high-mountain meadows in the Smokies. Along the way, you'll also travel a bit of the Appalachian Trail and have the opportunity to take a detour to an old fire tower with magnificent views over a horizon filled with mountains in all directions.

Twentymile was the sight of the Kitchen Lumber Company, which operated here in the 1920s. The first part of the hike travels along a wide trail, which was once a narrow-gauge railroad used to haul out timber. The grade is fairly gentle for the first 3 miles as you follow along the idyllic Twentymile Creek. Things start to get steeper around mile 3.1 as you follow a south slope of mixed forest up to Sassafras Gap, and the intersection of the Appalachian Trail at mile 5.

Twentymile to Gregory Bald Loop

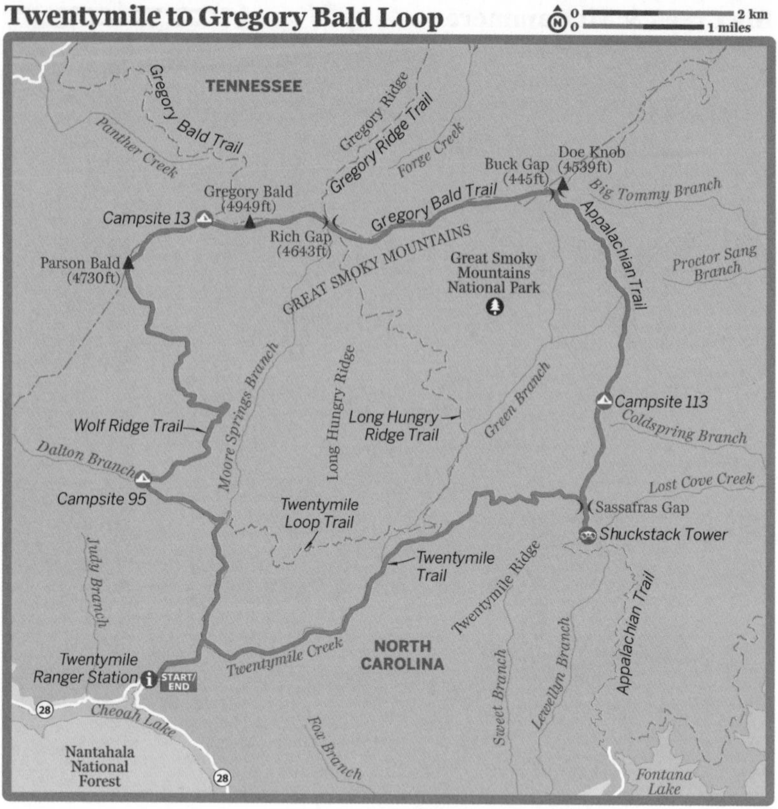

Before continuing north toward the Gregory Bald Trail, it's well worth taking a 500yd detour south along the Appalachian Trail to Shuckstack Tower (p71). This six-story wood and steel fire tower has mesmerizing 360-degree views. The Smoky Mountains undulate off into the distance to the north, while the Unicoi Mountains lie to the west, the Snowbird and Nantahala Mountains to the south and the tail end of the Blue Ridge Mountains to the southeast. You'll want to watch your step on the way up, as the trail is not in the best shape, with a missing handrail and rickety floorboards in places.

After the detour head back north on the Appalachian Trail. If you're making this a two-night trip, you can spend one night at the small campsite 113 located right along the Appalachian Trail. Otherwise, press on up to Doe Knob, 3 miles north of the Twentymile Trail intersection. There you'll turn left along the Gregory Bald Trail and follow this for 3 miles up to the ridge. At the top, you'll reach a grassy meadow, blazing with flame azaleas in the summer, and sweeping views to the north and south. This is Gregory Bald (p52), one of those high-elevation bald patches unique to the southern Appalachia. It was once used by settlers (ones with strong calf muscles, at least) for grazing cattle.

Continue along the same trail, about a half-mile past the bald, to reach campsite 13, which is tucked into a shady patch of yellow birch forest. Congratulations, the worst is over. After hiking up more than 4000ft, you can unwind in one of the loveliest backcountry sites in the park, with ample space and several fire rings – plus the obligatory bear-proof cable system for hanging your food. You'll find water (which needs to be treated) a further 300yd from the campsite along the same Gregory Bald Trail. If you're not too exhausted after the uphill slog, it's worth heading back uphill to watch the sunset from the open meadow.

The next day is an easier, mostly downhill jaunt of just under 7 miles. Follow the Wolf Ridge Trail, located a few paces south of the campsite. Gray wolves once roamed the Smokies and were a bane on livestock-raising settlers, who hunted them to extinction. After about 1300yd, you'll reach Parson Bald, a former grassy bald that the park service is now allowing to return to its native state – with encroaching trees and shrubs, there won't be any views from here. This bald, incidentally, was named after Joshua Parson, an early 1800s-era settler who lived near Abrams Creek (the now-closed Parson Branch Rd is also named after him).

After 4.5 miles you'll pass a side trail leading off to campsite number 95, another fine space to overnight, located in a mixed forest above the rushing Dalton Branch. Continue another half-mile along the Wolf Ridge Trail, where you'll pass the turnoff to Twentymile Loop Trail; just ignore this and keep going south. In another 1.6 miles you'll return to your original starting point.

Twentymile Ranger Station is located on Hwy 28, about 18 miles east of the southern end of Foothills Pkwy.

SIGHTS & ACTIVITIES

Great Smoky sights fall into two rough categories: nature and history. In the nature camp are the park's peaks, waterfalls and forested landscapes, while the history camp includes preserved 19th-century historic settlements scattered around the park. It also has abundant biodiversity, offering unique opportunities for wildlife-watching.

While the park is massive, many of the most popular sights are just off its main artery, Newfound Gap Rd. West of the Sugarlands Visitor Center, the Little River Rd takes you out to other historic areas, including the Elkmont Historic District. Keep heading west to reach the Cades Cove area, which has an excellent assortment of log structures from the early settler days. To the east, remote Cataloochee Valley has several historic buildings to wander through (and is a prime location for elk and black bears).

Newfound Gap Road

Sights are listed here in order of appearance from east to west, beginning at Oconaluftee Visitor Center in North Carolina and ending at Sugarlands Visitor Center in Tennessee. Sights along Clingmans Dome Rd, which heads west from Newfound Gap, and along Little River Rd, which heads west from Sugarlands Visitor Center, are also included.

Mountain Farm Museum MUSEUM

(www.nps.gov/grsm; Newfound Gap Rd, Cherokee; 9am-5pm daily mid-Mar–mid-Nov, plus Thanksgiving weekend) Adjacent to the Oconaluftee Visitor Center (p78), this excellent collection of historic buildings evokes life on a typical farmstead of the late 19th century. Together these structures paint a poignant picture of the mountain people who once eked out their sustenance from this rugged and isolated wilderness.

The wooden buildings are authentic, but were moved here from other parts of the national park in the 1950s. One of the first buildings you come to is the meat house, where a mountain farm's most valuable commodity (usually pork) was butchered, dried and smoked or salted for preservation.

Other structures are dedicated to apples (used for apple sauce, apple butter, cider, vinegar, apple pies and eaten raw), sorghum (used to make molasses) and corn (the most important crop on mountain farms, used for cornmeal and fresh corn, while its shucks were stuffed into mattresses and woven into chair seats, dolls, rugs and brooms). In the summer you can also see live hogs and chickens – a requisite stop for families with small children. A terrific time to visit is in mid-September for the Mountain Life Festival (p21).

Mingus Mill HISTORIC BUILDING

(Mingus Creek Trail, off Newfound Gap Rd, Cherokee; 9am-5pm daily mid-Mar–mid-Nov, plus Thanksgiving weekend) FREE One of the park's most picturesque 19th-century buildings, the Mingus Mill is a turbine-powered mill that still grinds wheat and corn much as it has since its opening back in 1886. You're welcome to explore the multistory structure, checking out its clever engineering mechanisms and walking the length of its 200ft-long flume that brings water from a stream to the mill's turbine. It's located about a mile north of the Oconaluftee Visitor Center (and 4 miles north of Cherokee).

There's usually a park employee on site who can share details about how the whole operation works. There's also a small stand near the entrance where you can purchase ground cornmeal (not milled on-site, but still made the old-fashioned way).

Instagram filters unnecessary for this photogenic timber structure!

Newfound Gap VIEWPOINT

(Newfound Gap Rd) The lowest drivable pass through the Smoky Mountains is located here, at 5046ft. After the pass was discovered in 1872, a new road followed suit, eventually becoming today's Newfound Gap Rd. The site straddles two states and offers fantastic views to the north (Tennessee) and south (North Carolina). The rocky platform is where you'll find the Rockefeller Memorial. It was on this spot on September 2, 1940 that President Franklin Roosevelt formally dedicated the park.

The Appalachian Trail travels right across Newfound Gap (you may see a few hungry hikers trying to hitch a ride up to Gatlinburg for a soft bed and a warm meal). This is also the starting point for the popular 8-mile (return) hike to Charlies Bunion (p65).

Rockefeller Memorial HISTORIC SITE

This two-tiered stone-walled structure overlooking two states commemorates the $5 million contribution John D Rockefeller Jr made to help make the national park a reality. This is also where President Franklin Roosevelt formally dedicated the park on September 2, 1940.

Clingmans Dome VIEWPOINT

(off Clingmans Dome Rd) 'On top of Old Smoky' is Clingmans Dome (elevation 6643ft), the park's highest peak. At the summit a steep, half-mile paved trail leads to an observation tower offering a 360-degree view of the Smokies and beyond. It can be cold and foggy up here, even when the sun is shining in Sugarlands, so bring a jacket. The tower resembles something of a flying saucer, with a gently curving ramp leading up to the top.

Panels around the viewing platform indicate names of the surrounding peaks and distant places of interest.

As one of the must-see sights in the park, Clingmans Dome gets crowded, especially in the summer. Note that the 7-mile access road to Newfound Gap Rd is closed to vehicles from December through March. The viewpoint is open year-round, however, for those willing to hike in – take care on the trails, which can be icy even in March or April.

Carlos C Campbell Overlook VIEWPOINT

(Newfound Gap Rd) This scenic overlook provides a sweeping view of the various types of forests covering the slopes to the east. You'll see spruce-fir forest at the top, northern hardwood below, hemlock forest nestled in the valley and, just to the north, cove hardwood forest. You can also spy pine-oak forest and a small heath bald. A signpost helps show where to look to see the different forest features.

The scene is at its most dramatic in autumn, when golds, reds and oranges blaze across the mountain.

The overlook is located about 2.5 miles south of the Sugarlands Visitor Center. Look for the small parking area to the left as you're driving south.

Elkmont Historic District HISTORIC SITE

(off Little River Rd) Elkmont has much history hidden in its woodlands. Just south of the campground (crossing the bridge over Little River), you'll find a clubhouse and eclectically designed cabins dating back to the early 20th century when the area was a summer retreat for business leaders from Knoxville. One row of cabins, dubbed 'Daisy Town,' has a few dwellings you can wander through, and it's simple to imagine the easy summer living, clubhouse dances and concerts as you explore this abandoned settlement.

Metcalf Bottoms NATURAL FEATURE

(off Little River Gorge Rd) A lovely spot for a picnic, with tables set up along the Little River. Afterwards you can dip your feet in the cool, rushing waters.

The Sinks WATERFALL

A requisite stop when driving Little River Rd is this series of cascades just off the road. Here, the Little River makes a sharp hairpin turn, with water rushing over boulders into deep pools. Although people do swim here, it's extremely dangerous (as is even wading) owing to strong currents and hidden underwater hazards. Drownings and serious injuries have occurred.

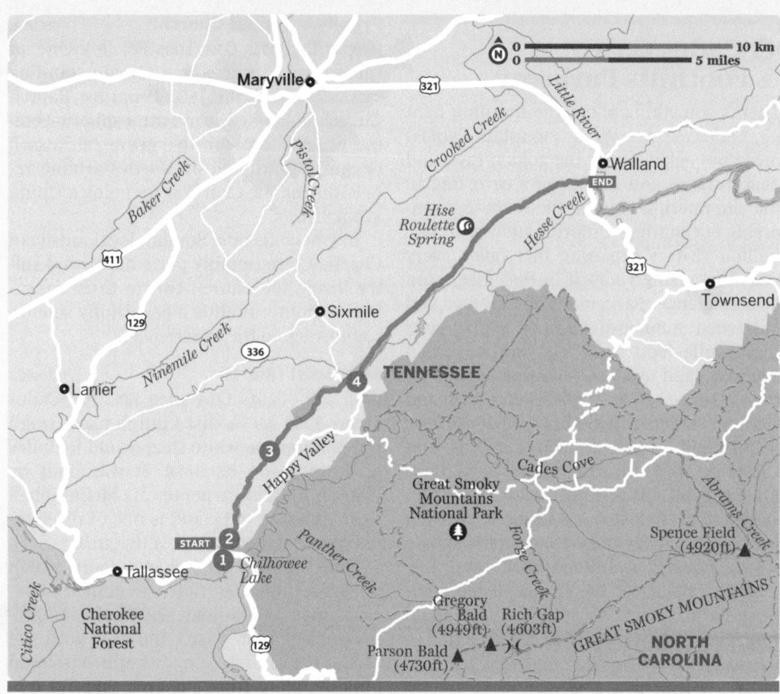

Driving Tour
Foothills Parkway

START CHILHOWEE
END WALLAND
LENGTH 17 MILES; ONE HOUR

Running along the outer boundary of the national park, the Foothills Parkway is a leafy motorway that offers spectacular views of the Smoky Mountains. Consisting of several separate non-contiguous sections, the parkway is best known for its route between Chilhowee and Walland, on the Smokies' western edge.

Though you could zip from one end of this road to the other in as little as 30 minutes, it's well worth slowing down and stopping at the many lookouts along the way. You'll have staggering views across the rolling forests to the east as well as as the fertile lands of the Tennessee River Valley and the distant Cumberland Mountains to the northwest. For the best lighting come early in the morning or late in the afternoon, when the mountain folds are bathed in a golden light.

Driving from south to north, the route starts near a picturesque stretch of **1 Chilhowee Lake**. The first stop is at the **2 vintage sign** about half a mile into the drive. After a few requisite photos of the arching market with its arching triangular backdrop, continue to the **3 first scenic overlook**, located around the 3.5-mile mark. The parking area offers a sweep across the western expanse of the mountains.

Continuing north, you'll pass several more overlooks, each offering slightly different perspectives of the mountain scene. Around 7.2 miles, stop at the unsigned lookout and walk to the viewing platform, which juts out of the valley and affords views of both the west and southwest. Afterwards, cross the road, and take the short but steep trail up to **4 Look Rock Tower** (p69). The half-mile walk leads to a lookout, which is also used as an environmental monitoring station. Once you ascend the ramp to the top, you'll have mesmerizing 360-degree views.

When you reach Walland, you can continue onto the newest section of the Foothills Pkwy. This 16-mile continuation runs southeast to Wear Valley, and opened in November 2018.

⊙ Cades Cove & Foothills Parkway

There's something about the morning light in Cades Cove. With mountain-flanked meadows aglow under the golden rays, and deer, turkeys and black bears cavorting in the shimmering grasses, the scene is memorably enchanting. Unfortunately, with two million visitors exploring this valley every year, immersing yourself in that magic can be a challenge, particularly in summer and fall when bumper-to-bumper traffic jams the 11-mile loop road. The one-way road encircles land used as a hunting ground by the Cherokee before English, Scots-Irish and German settlers arrived in the 1820s. These determined newcomers built cabins and churches while clearing the valley's trees for farmland. Mills, forges and blacksmith shops soon followed, creating a thriving community. Today the creaky cabins, mossy spring houses, weathered barns and tidy cemeteries whisper the stories of the families who made this place their home. You'll hear them best if you arrive before 9am.

Cades Cove Loop Road

There are more than 80 historic structures in the park. Those found along the Cades Cove Loop Rd, from cabins and churches to barns and a gristmill, were built in the 1800s. Look for them at the numbered stops along or near the loop. For details about these historic buildings, pick up the *Cades Cove Tour* booklet ($1) at the **orientation shelter** (Map p70; Cades Cove Loop Rd; ⊙8am-5pm) or the visitor center (p78).

The sights below are listed according to the order they are encountered on the loop drive, beginning at the orientation shelter. If you only have time for a few stops, visit the John Oliver Place, the Methodist Church, the Cable Mill Historic Area and the Tipton Place.

John Oliver Place HISTORIC BUILDING
(Map p70; Cades Cove Loop Rd; P) Built in the early 1820s, this rustic log cabin is the oldest in Cades Cove. Check out the stone chimney, made with mud mortar. The home was built by one of the cove's earliest settlers and remained in the family until the park was founded more than 100 years later.

Primitive Baptist Church CHURCH
(Map p70; Cades Cove Loop Rd; P) One of three rural churches that remain standing in Cades Cove, the 1887 Primitive Baptist Church is flanked by an atmospheric cemetery. Look out for the grave of Russell Gregory, 'murdered by North Carolina rebels' during the Civil War for being a Union sympathizer.

In you come on a Sunday, local musician Charlie Close humbly plays his bowed sultry inside the church two to three mornings a month. It adds a beautifully solemn soundtrack to the experience.

Methodist Church CHURCH
(Map p70; Cades Cove Loop Rd; P) Cades Cove's 1902 Methodist Church has a small but picturesque white steeple and includes gravestones on its lawn. It was built by blacksmith and carpenter JD McCampbell in 115 days for $115, and is one of three remaining rural churches in the area.

Note the two entrance/exit doors, which normally indicates that the church separated men and woman within the congregation, but that wasn't the case with the Methodist Church. It had simply borrowed building plans from a church that did separate its congregation, so two doors were built.

Missionary Baptist Church CHURCH
(Map p70; Cades Cove Loop Rd) The Missionary Baptist Church was formed in 1839 by former Primitive Baptist Church members who were kicked out for advocating missionary work. The building itself dates to 1915.

Rich Mountain Road SCENIC DRIVE
(Map p70; off Cades Cove Loop Rd; ⊙early Apr–mid-Nov) For bird's-eye views of Cades Cove without a strenuous hike, turn right from the Cades Cove loop onto this gravel road across from the Missionary Baptist Church. Just know there's no turning back. Built in the 1920s, this 8-mile adventure takes a serpentine climb up and down Rich Mountain. After leaving the park, it ends in Tuckaleechee Cove to the north.

The road curves past modern mountain homes after leaving the park on the mountainside, when it also opens to two-way traffic. Townsend is 12 miles from the start.

CADES COVE: NEED TO KNOW

➡ Cades Cove Loop Rd is open to motor vehicles from sunrise to sunset.

➡ The road is closed to vehicle traffic until 10am on Wednesday and Saturday between early May and late September. This a great time for cyclists and pedestrians to travel the loop.

➡ The 11-mile loop road is one way. Sparks Lane and Hyatt Lane offer shortcuts if you don't want to drive the full 11 miles.

➡ Use the roadside pullouts if you want to take a long look at the scenery or wildlife. There are also parking spaces at the numbered stops.

➡ There is no overnight parking in the picnic area. If you plan to camp in the nearby backcountry, park in the lot beside the campground store.

➡ The busiest times to visit are summer and the fall foliage season, as well as weekends year-round.

➡ There are restrooms at the visitor center, beside the campground store, at the campground and in the picnic area. You'll find pit toilets at the Abrams Falls trailhead parking lot.

➡ You can buy firewood and ice cream at the campground store.

Elijah Oliver Place HISTORIC BUILDING

(Map p70; Cades Cove Loop Rd; P) The homestead farthest from the Cades Cove Loop Rd, this multi-building property sits at the end of a half-mile stroll through the woods. The cabin was the home of Elijah Wood, son of early settler John Oliver. Don't miss the springhouse and flume by the creek out back. The main house has a 'stranger room' for overnight guests.

Cable Mill Historic Area HISTORIC SITE

(Map p70; Cades Cove Loop Rd; P) To get bread on the table, early residents of Cades Cove first had to mill their grains and corn. Above all other staples, corn was the most important. Every meal included food made from cornmeal, including corn bread, mush, hoecakes and spoon bread. Built in the early 1870s by John Cable, Cable Mill was once one of four or five water-powered gristmills to serve Cades Cove, which reached a peak population of about 700 residents by 1900.

Powered by Mill Creek, the waters of which were routed into the mill via a 235ft-long flume, Cable Mill features a classic overshot waterwheel. The other historic buildings surrounding the mill were brought from other locations in the park to create a living history museum. There's a blacksmith shop, a barn, a smokehouse, a sorghum mill and a homestead, as well as the Cades Cove Visitor Center (p78) and shop – stop by to pick up a bag of corn ground on-site.

Tipton Place HISTORIC BUILDING

(Map p70; Cades Cove Loop Rd; P) The picturesque Tipton homestead was built by Mexican War veteran 'Colonel Hamp' Tipton in the early 1870s. The grounds include a spacious two-floor cabin, blacksmith and carpentry shops, and a replica cantilever barn.

Carter Shields Cabin HISTORIC BUILDING

(Map p70; Cades Cove Loop Rd; P) The last cabin on the loop road is arguably the most photogenic, tucked in a small grassy glade surrounded by the woods. Carter Shields, a Civil War veteran wounded in the Battle of Shiloh, lived here for 11 years in the early 1900s.

Cades Cove Picnic Area PICNIC AREA

(Map p70; off Cades Cove Loop Rd; P 👪) Children enjoy splashing in the shallows of Abrams Creek at this woodsy picnic spot, where a number of tables are perched by the water. You'll find grills, restrooms, 81 picnic sites and the trailhead for the easy and family-friendly Anthony Creek Trail.

Foothills Parkway

Look Rock Tower VIEWPOINT

(Foothills Pkwy) Located along the western section of the Foothills Pkwy (around Mile 7.3 if driving north from Chilhowee), this

Cades Cove

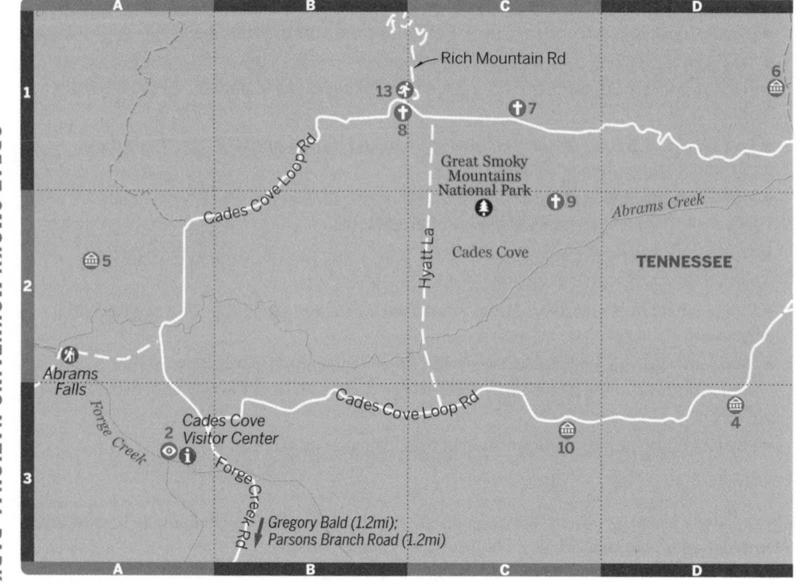

tower is reachable on an easy half-mile trail that starts just north of the parking area. From the top, you'll have 360-degree views of the Smoky Mountains to the west and the surrounding Tennessee River Valley to the east.

The tower is also used to study air quality in the region – you'll notice communication equipment and a control room (closed to the public) on top.

Cataloochee Valley

Tucked in a far-flung corner of the park, deep in the mountains of western North Carolina, Cataloochee feels untamed. It takes an edge-of-your-seat drive to get here, elk and turkey strut around like they own the place and stories of hermits and wild men give the woods a spooky edge. But it wasn't always so. In 1910 the community – comprising Big Cataloochee and Little Cataloochee – was the largest settlement in the Smokies, with 1251 citizens. Farming, apple production and tourism kept the economy buzzing right up until the late 1920s, when folks heard rumors that the park was moving in. Today historic buildings and lush meadows line Cataloochee Rd in Big Cataloochee Valley, which could double as a safari park with all the wildlife roaming between its 6000ft-high peaks. Over Noland Mountain lies Little Cataloochee Valley, where the sights can only be explored by foot or horseback.

Cataloochee Road & Palmer House

There are a half-dozen historic buildings in **Big Cataloochee Valley**, all dating from the late 1800s and early 1900s. Most can be reached on a short auto tour on Cataloochee Rd. A handful of historic buildings line the Little Cataloochee Trail, which can only be traveled by foot or horseback. For more details, buy the the *Day Hike & Auto Tour Cataloochee* booklet ($1.50) at a park visitor center, or get an overview at the **information kiosk** (Cataloochee Rd). Grazing elk are another top sight.

Caldwell House HISTORIC BUILDING
(Cataloochee Rd; P) With its weatherboarding, interior paneling and shingled gables, as well as its white exterior and jaunty blue trim, this frame house, built in 1906, seems almost of the modern era.

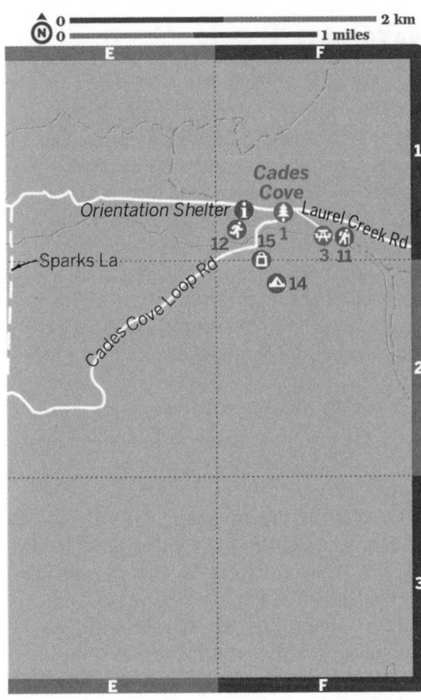

Cades Cove

Top Sights

1 Cades Cove....F1

Sights

2 Cable Mill Historic Area....A3
3 Cades Cove Picnic Area....F1
4 Carter Shields Cabin....D3
5 Elijah Oliver Place....A2
6 John Oliver Place....D1
7 Methodist Church....C1
8 Missionary Baptist Church....B1
9 Primitive Baptist Church....C2
10 Tipton Place....C3

Activities, Courses & Tours

11 Anthony Creek Trail....F1
12 Cades Cove Riding Stables....F1
Cades Cove Trading....(see 15)
13 Rich Mountain Road....B1

Sleeping

14 Cades Cove Campground....F2

Shopping

15 Cades Cove Campground Store & Deli....F1

The L-shaped front porch is a pleasant place to soak up the history and the scenery, which includes a stream rippling out front, a photogenic barn and the sound of birds singing in the background.

Beech Grove School HISTORIC BUILDING
(Cataloochee Rd; P) This 1901 schoolhouse is the one of only three valley schoolhouses still standing. Inside you'll find rows of old desks and a blackboard. School was typically in session from November through January, with an extra two months tacked on if there was enough local funding.

Palmer Chapel CHURCH
(Cataloochee Rd; P) No, this Methodist church isn't turning its back on Cataloochee Rd. Built in 1898 it faces the old road that once ran through the valley. Circuit-riding preachers visited the chapel one Sunday per month. Today the bright-white church hosts the annual **Cataloochee Reunion**, when old timers and the descendants of valley families gather to share memories and news. The reunion was held for the 80th time in 2017, and shows no signs of slowing down.

Palmer House HISTORIC BUILDING
(off Cataloochee Rd; P) The yellow Palmer House is a 'dog-trot' house, meaning it consists of two separate log cabins sitting side by side with a covered breezeway between them. The log cabins were later weatherboarded. Facing the house, the room on the left once served as the Cataloochee Post Office; today it holds a decrepit, but still interesting, collection of exhibits about the lives of the families who resided in Cataloochee.

Fontana Dam & Western North Carolina

Shuckstack Tower VIEWPOINT
It's an uphill slog to get here, but you'll be rewarded with jaw-dropping views once you make it to the historic fire tower and clamber your way to the top. From its 200ft perch you'll have fine views of Fontana Lake and the mountains beyond. It's located just off the Appalachian Trail, about 3.5 (tough uphill) miles from the Fontana Dam, in the southwest corner of the park. Take care climbing up the tower, as some rails are missing and there are loose wooden floorboards up top.

CATALOOCHEE VALLEY: WILDLIFE-WATCHING

The park service released 25 elk into Cataloochee Valley in 2001. Another 27 were released the following year. Elk had once roamed the southern Appalachian Mountains but overhunting and habitat loss caused their decline and eventual disappearance. The last elk in the region was killed in 1850. Some have migrated from the valley to other parts of the park, but a significant number still graze in the meadows and woods of Cataloochee, particularly along Cataloochee Rd. You'll most likely see them grazing in the early morning and late evening. Stay at least 50yd from the elk. Adult males typically weigh 700lb to 800lb, while females clock in at 500lb. They can reach a height of 5ft. Females with calves could charge you if they feel their offspring is threatened. Pick up the free *Return of the Elk* brochure at one of the information kiosks along Cataloochee Rd for more details about elk behavior in various seasons. Frisky males sound their loud bugle calls in the fall.

Wild turkeys and white-tailed deer also roam the valley, so pack your binoculars and a good camera.

COURSES

Great Smoky Mountains Institute at Tremont OUTDOORS

(865-448-6709; www.gsmit.org; Tremont Rd; overnight firefly camp $101, 3-day naturalist course $349, 4-day photography workshop from $668;) This learning center offers a wide range of courses for adults and kids. Among other things, you can go for a guided multiday backpacking trip, attend a photography workshop, or take a naturalist class (dedicated to ecology, birds, plants, mammals, amphibians or developing interpretation and naturalist skills).

There are family camps (with hikes, crafts, swim time and music), discovery camps (for nine to 12 year olds) and wilderness backpacking trips for teens.

Overnight trips and multiday camps include food and lodging. Located 4 miles southeast of Townsend, near the rushing Middle Prong of the Little River, the campus has classrooms and air-conditioned dorms, as well as cabin-style tents, for those staying on-site.

SLEEPING

Great Smoky Mountains National Park provides varied camping options. LeConte Lodge is the only place where you can get a room, however, and you have to hike to the top of a mountain to enjoy the privilege. Gatlinburg has the most sleeping options of any gateway town, though prices are high. Nearby Pigeon Forge, 10 miles north of Sugarlands Visitor Center, and Sevierville, 17 miles north, have cheaper options.

The National Park Service maintains developed campgrounds at nine locations in the park (a 10th remains closed indefinitely). Each campground has restrooms with cold running water and flush toilets, but there are no showers or electrical or water hookups in the park (though some campgrounds do have electricity for emergency situations). Each individual campsite has a fire grate and picnic table. Many sites can be reserved in advance, and several campgrounds (Cataloochee, Abrams Creek, Big Creek and Balsam Mountain) require advance reservations. Reserve through www.recreation.gov.

With nine developed campgrounds offering more than 900 campsites, you'd think finding a place to pitch would be easy. Not so in the busy summer season, so plan ahead. You can make reservations for most sites; others are first-come, first-served. Cades Cove and Smokemont campgrounds are open year-round; others are open March to October.

Backcountry camping is an excellent option, which is only chargeable up to five nights ($4 per night; after that, it's free). A permit is required. You can make reservations online at http://smokiespermits.nps.gov, and get permits at the ranger stations or visitor centers. Be sure to know the campground regulations.

Newfound Gap Road

Camping

Elkmont CAMPGROUND $

(☎865-436-1271; www.recreation.gov; Little River Rd; campsites $21-27; ⊙early Mar-late Nov) The park's largest campground is on Little River Rd, 5 miles west of the Sugarlands Visitor Center. Little River and Jakes Creek run through this wooded campground and the sound of rippling water adds tranquility. There are 200 tent and RV campsites and 20 walk-in sites. All are reservable beginning May 15.

Like other campgrounds in the park, there are no showers, or electrical or water hookups. There are restrooms. Be sure to explore some of the historic sites while you're here. The campground occupies land that was once a logging village, and the abandoned resort cabins of Daisy Town are nearby.

Smokemont CAMPGROUND $

(www.recreation.gov; Newfound Gap Rd; campsite $21-25) The Smokemont Campground's 142 sites are the only North Carolina campsites open year-round. As with most other campgrounds in the park, there isn't much space between sites. At 2200ft elevation, Smokemont is situated beside the rushing mountain stream of Bradley Fork, although no sites directly overlook the water.

The campground is located just off Newfound Gap Rd, about 4 miles north of the Oconaluftee Visitor Center near the park's entrance by Cherokee, NC. This is a good base for hiking, with several trails leading off from the campground.

Lodging

★**LeConte Lodge** CABIN $$

(☎865-429-5704; www.lecontelodge.com; cabins incl breakfast & dinner adult $148, child 4-12yr $85; ⊙mid-Mar–mid-Nov) The only non-camping accommodation in the park is LeConte Lodge. Though the only way to get to the lodge's rustic, electricity-free cabins is on five uphill hiking trails varying in length from 5.5 miles (Alum Cave Trail; p39) to 8.9 miles (Trillium Gap Trail), it's so popular you need to reserve many months in advance.

Reservations for the lodge open on October 1 for the following season, and are booked solid within two days (the most desirable dates fill up within a few hours). However, it's well worth putting your name on a wait list, as openings often become available.

If you score a spot, set out early to make the most of the experience. You can check out photos of past lodge life in the office and lounge, and climb to the very top of the mountain (a further 400yd beyond the cabins). After a hearty meal in the evening, you can sit in rocking chairs and watch the stars come out, or adjourn to the lounge for board games, guitar strumming and browsing old *National Geographic* magazines by lamplight.

Cosby & Big Creek

Both of these campgrounds are in the far eastern fringes of the park. Cosby is in Tennessee while Big Creek is just over the line in North Carolina.

Cosby CAMPGROUND $

(www.recreation.gov; off Hwy 32; campsites $17.50; ⊙late Mar-late Oct) This large, beautifully forested campground is a good alternative to the heavily used campgrounds, as it tends to be slightly less chaotic than Cades Cove or Smokemont. Several loops are lined with more than 100 campsites that afford varying degrees of privacy. The campground lies off Hwy 32, near the Tennessee town of Cosby.

Twenty-six campsites are available for advanced reservations; the other 100 are first-come first-served. During the low season, park rangers might not be around and you'll have to self-pay (so bring appropriate change).

You can access some fine trails here, including the Low Gap Trail, which leads up to the Appalachian Trail, 2.5 miles to the southeast.

Big Creek CAMPGROUND $

(☎reservations 877-444-6777; www.recreation.gov; Big Creek Park Rd; tent sites $17.50; ⊙Apr-late Oct) The smallest of Great Smoky's campgrounds is a tent-only, walk-in affair used mostly by hikers. Five of the 12 sites sit beside the cacophonous Big Creek (sites 10, 11 and 12 are the best). You must haul your gear around 100ft from the car. Advance reservations are essential: there's no self-pay option (and no mobile service) upon arrival.

BETTY4240/GETTY IMAGES ©

1. Laurel Falls (p44)
Rhododendrons blooming are a highlight of visiting Laurel Falls in the early summer. They can also be found throughout the park.

2. Charlies Bunion (p58)
There are breathtaking views to be had from this strangely named outcropping.

3. Clingmans Dome (p66)
The observation tower offers dazzling 360-degree views of the Smokies and beyond.

4. White-tailed deer (p189)
A buck (male deer) in the morning light.

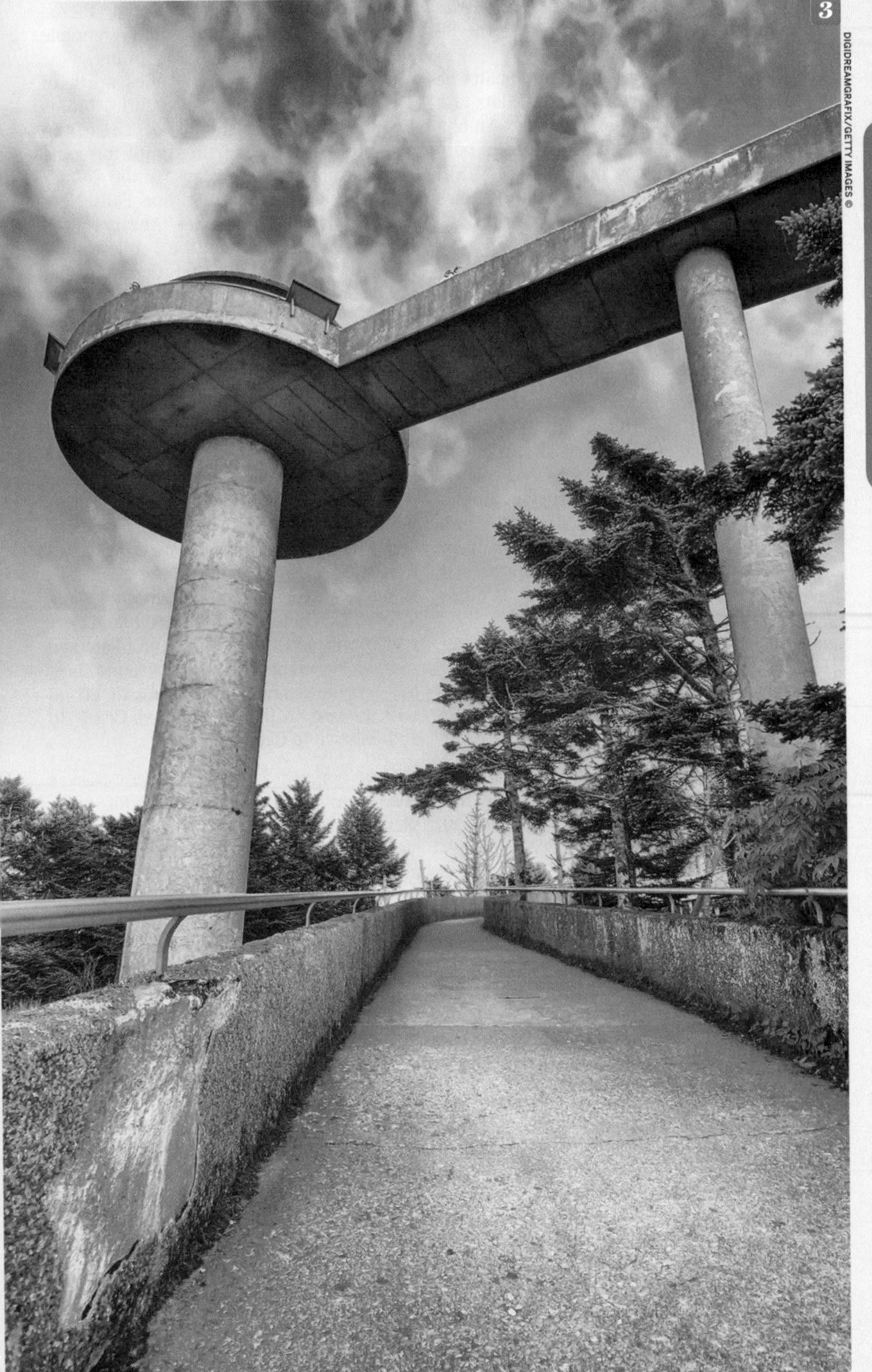

3

DIGIDREAMGRAFIX/GETTY IMAGES ©

To get here, take Tennessee exit 451 off I-40, then proceed upstream beside the Pigeon River to the ranger station.

As with all other campgrounds in the national park, you'll find flush toilets and drinking water, but no showers. Among the excellent trails that start from here is the 5.1-mile (one way) Big Creek Trail (p62), which leads past swimming holes and waterfalls.

Cades Cove, Abrams Creek & Foothills Parkway

There is one developed campground in Cades Cove. A half-dozen backcountry camping locations can be found along trails in the surrounding mountains. Camping at a backcountry site requires a reservation and permit (www.nps.gov/grsm/planyourvisit/backcountry-camping.htm). The campground at Abrams Creek is west of Cades Cove and accessed from the Foothills Pkwy. The closest commercial lodgings are in Townsend, about 9 miles from Cades Cove.

Cades Cove Campground CAMPGROUND $

(Map p70; ☎865-448-2472; www.recreation.gov; campsites $25) This woodsy campground with 159 sites is a great place to sleep if you want to get a jump on visiting Cades Cove. There's a store, drinking water and bathrooms, but no showers. There are 29 tent-only sites. Sites can be reserved in peak season – May 15 through October. The rest of the year, campsites are first-come, first served.

Reservations can be made up to six months in advance. Campsites are $21 during walk-in season. Follow all posted rules for camping in bear country.

Abrams Creek Campground CAMPGROUND $

(☎reservations 877-444-6777; www.recreation.gov; off Happy Valley Rd; campsites $17.50; ⏲late Apr-late Oct) This small, remote campground on the western edge of the park takes a bit of effort to get to, but you'll be well compensated for your journey. Just over half of the 16 sites face pretty Abrams Creek (book sites 01 through 09 for a waterfront view). The others are arranged along the edge of the woods.

You must book before you arrive; there's no pay-upon-arrival option – and no mobile service once you're at the campground.

The campground lies 7 miles north of Hwy 129 along Happy Valley Rd. Abrams Creek is a popular fishing spot. The campground is also the starting point for some scenic trails, including an 11-mile round-trip backcountry trail to Abrams Falls. Note that this trail approaches Abrams Falls from the west and is not the 5-mile round-trip hike to the falls that departs from Cades Cove.

Cataloochee Valley & Balsam Mountain

Cataloochee Campground CAMPGROUND $

(☎877-444-6777; www.recreation.gov; Cataloochee Rd; campsites $25; ⏲late Mar-Oct) This remote campground in a forest of hemlock and white pine has spacious campsites arranged off a loop road. Six of the 27 sites lie along the excellent fishing waters of Cataloochee Creek. Reservations are mandatory year-round, and the campground fills up on summer evenings. The campground host has brochures and maps. Take exit 20 off I-40, go west on Hwy 276 to Cove Creek Rd and follow it to Cataloochee Rd.

Balsam Mountain CAMPGROUND $

(www.recreation.gov; Heintooga Ridge Rd; campsites $25; ⏲mid-May–Oct) This small highlands campground is considered by many to be the park's most lovely, thanks to its privileged placement within an 'island' forest of red spruce and Fraser firs. Though the 46 campsites are somewhat small, the upside is that it discourages behemoth RVs from roosting (though RVs up to 30ft are allowed). The campground is 8 miles from the Blue Ridge Pkwy via Heintooga Ridge Rd.

Fontana Dam & Western North Carolina

Deep Creek CAMPGROUND $

(Deep Creek Rd; campsites $21; ⏲late Mar-late Oct) Near Bryson City this medium-sized family campground with 92 sites offers a good variety of choices and splendid opportunities for hiking and bird-watching. Section C features creekside, tent-only sites; section D, a loop road through the

FIREFLY EVENT

Each year in late spring or early summer, parts of the national park light up with synchronous fireflies (p187), a mesmerizing display where thousands of insects flash their lanterns (aka abdominal light organs) in perfect unison.

The event draws huge crowds of people to the Elkmont Campground, one of the best places in the Smokies to see it. Dates of the event change every year, but it can happen anytime between late May and late June.

Viewing dates are typically announced in April. All those who want to see the event must obtain a parking pass through a lottery system, and then take a shuttle to the site.

Since 2006 the park has limited access using a necessary shuttle service, designed to reduce traffic and minimize any impact on the unique fireflies. The service runs from the Sugarlands Visitor Center for eight days of predicted peak activity during the fireflies' two-week mating period.

The lottery typically opens for three days in late April. It's free to enter the lottery, which uses a randomized computer drawing to ensure fairness. Results are released 10 days after the drawing.

There will be a total of 1800 vehicle passes available, and applicants must apply for either a regular parking pass or large-vehicle parking pass and then can pick two dates to attend the event over the eight-day viewing period. The winners will be charged a $20 reservation fee, which will help cover the park's cost of organizing the logistics. You'll get a parking spot at the visitor center and will get to take the shuttle ($2 per person) to see the event. The shuttle service is the only way that visitors can get there, except for registered campers staying at the Elkmont Campground. People cannot walk the Elkmont entrance road due to safety concerns.

To apply to the lottery, go to www.recreation.gov and search for 'Firefly Event'.

woods, affords more privacy. The waters of Deep Creek give much joy to inner-tubers and anglers (the park, however, discourages inner-tubing here).

Advance reservations are not possible here; it's first-come, first-served. Use the self-pay kiosk (credit cards accepted) upon arrival.

Near the entrance to the campground is the village of Big Creek, with a snack bar and tube rentals. To get there from the depot in Bryson City, turn right onto Depot St, left on Ramseur Rd and then immediately right on Deep Creek Rd.

This is a great base for trout fishing and hiking. Several waterfalls are in easy walking distance from the campground.

Fontana Village Resort LODGE **$$**
(☎828-498-2211; www.fontanavillage.com; 300 Woods Rd, Fontana Dam; d $150-250; 🏊) Near the national park's southern fringe, this old-school resort makes a fine base for a back-to-nature holiday, with miles of cycling and hiking trails right outside the door. Though the facilities are a bit dated, there are loads of activities on offer, including a swimming pool, mini-golf and a marina where you can hire watercraft (kayaks, pontoon boats).

EATING

Nuts and berries notwithstanding, there's nothing to eat in Great Smoky Mountains National Park, save for items from vending machines at Sugarlands Visitor Center (p78) and the meager offerings sold at the Cades Cove Campground store. If you make the hike up to LeConte Lodge (p73), you can purchase cookies, drinks and sack lunches (which means a bagel with cream cheese, beef summer sausage, trail mix and fruit leather). Dinner is included for those staying overnight. Luckily, there are lots of restaurant options in the surrounding towns.

Cades Cove Campground Store & Deli MARKET
(Map p70; ☎865-448-9034; www.cadescovetrading.com; 10035 Campground Dr; ⏰9am-9pm late May-Oct, to 5pm Mar-May, Nov & late Dec) One-stop shopping for campers, hikers and day-trippers, this compact souvenir shop

and market sells T-shirts, hats, camping sundries, snacks, drinks, ibuprofen and firewood. Order burgers, sandwiches and hotdogs at the small deli counter, where you can also buy a soft-serve ice-cream cone after your hike. Also sells cups of coffee.

Information

Blount Memorial Hospital (865-983-7211; 907 E Lamar Alexander Pkwy, Maryville) Located 16 miles northwest of Townsend.

Cades Cove Visitor Center (Map p70; 865-436-7318; www.nps.gov/grsm; Cades Cove Loop Rd; 9am-7pm Apr-Aug, closes earlier Sep-Mar) Halfway up Cades Cove Loop Rd, 24 miles off Hwy 441 from the Gatlinburg entrance.

Clingmans Dome Visitor Station (865-436-1200; Clingmans Dome Rd; 10am-6pm Apr-Oct, 9:30am-5pm Nov) Small, very busy center at the start of the paved path up to the Clingmans Dome lookout.

LeConte Medical Center (865-446-7000; 742 Middle Creek Rd, Sevierville, TN) Located 13 miles north of Gatlinburg.

Oconaluftee Visitor Center (828-497-1904; www.nps.gov/grsm; 1194 Newfound Gap Rd, North Cherokee, NC; 8am-7pm Jun-Aug, to 6pm Apr, May, Sep & Oct, to 4:30pm Nov-Mar;) At the park's southern entrance near Cherokee in North Carolina.

Sugarlands Visitor Center (865-436-1291; www.nps.gov/grsm; 107 Park Headquarters Rd; 8am-7:30pm Jun-Aug, hours vary Sep-May;) At the park's northern entrance near Gatlinburg.

Getting Around

There's no public transportation within the park, and having your own car is ideal, but a handful of shuttle companies offer private transport inside the park. The following outfits can take you to, or pick you up from trailheads, or transport you from lodging outside the park to in-park destinations. You'll need to reserve in advance.

A Walk in the Woods (865-436-8283; www.awalkinthewoods.com)

AAA Hiker Service (423-487-3112; www.aaahikerservice.com)

Smoky Mountain Guides (865-654-4545; www.smokymountainguides.com)

The **Gatlinburg Trolley** (p210) serves downtown Gatlinburg and links to a few outlying areas. The trolley's tan line ($2) goes into the national park June through October, stopping at Sugarlands Visitor Center, the Laurel Falls parking area and Elkmont Campground.

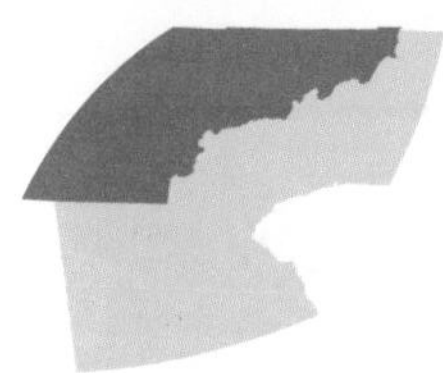

East Tennessee

Includes ➡

Knoxville........................82
Pigeon Forge................88
Gatlinburg.....................92
Chattanooga................97
Cherokee National Forest..........104

Best Places to Eat

- ➡ Stock & Barrel (p85)
- ➡ Crockett's Breakfast Camp (p95)
- ➡ Local Goat (p91)
- ➡ Appalachian Bistro (p92)
- ➡ JC Holdway (p86)
- ➡ St John's Meeting Place (p103)

Best Places to Stay

- ➡ Crash Pad (p101)
- ➡ Inn on the River (p89)
- ➡ Dwell Hotel (p101)
- ➡ Oliver Hotel (p84)
- ➡ DreamMore Resort (p89)
- ➡ Tennessean (p85)

Why Go?

Dolly Parton, East Tennessee's most famous native, loves her home region so much she has made a successful career singing about girls who leave the honeysuckle-scented embrace of the Smoky Mountains for the false glitter of the city. They're always sorry.

Largely a rural region of small towns, rolling hills and river valleys, the eastern third of the state is noteworthy for its friendly folks and pastoral charm. The lush southern Appalachian Mountains are great for hiking, camping and rafting. Pretty waterfalls are a regional specialty. Nearby Great Smoky Mountains National Park lures millions every year, but the crowds are easily ditched in East Tennessee's Cherokee National Forest.

The two main urban areas, Knoxville and Chattanooga, are easygoing riverside cities with lively student populations, great restaurants, fun craft breweries and outdoor adventures galore. For a blast of all things tacky and wacky, Gatlinburg and Pigeon Forge await.

When to Go

In April and May, wildflowers bloom in the mountains and waterfalls gush; festival season starts in the cities.

July and August are the height of rafting season, with numerous trips during Ocoee River dam releases.

Colorful foliage is the backdrop for fall drives in the mountains in October and early November.

East Tennessee

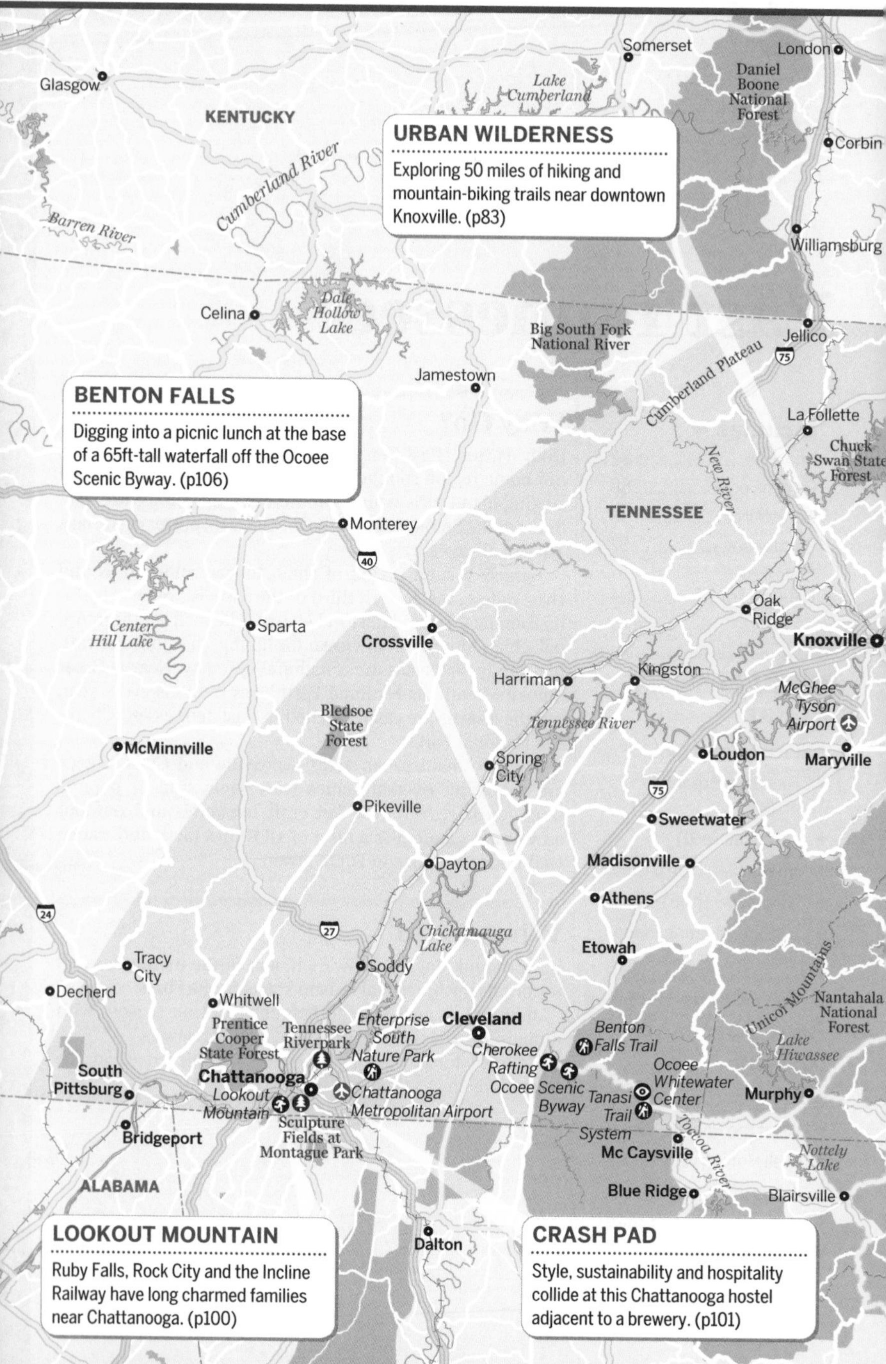

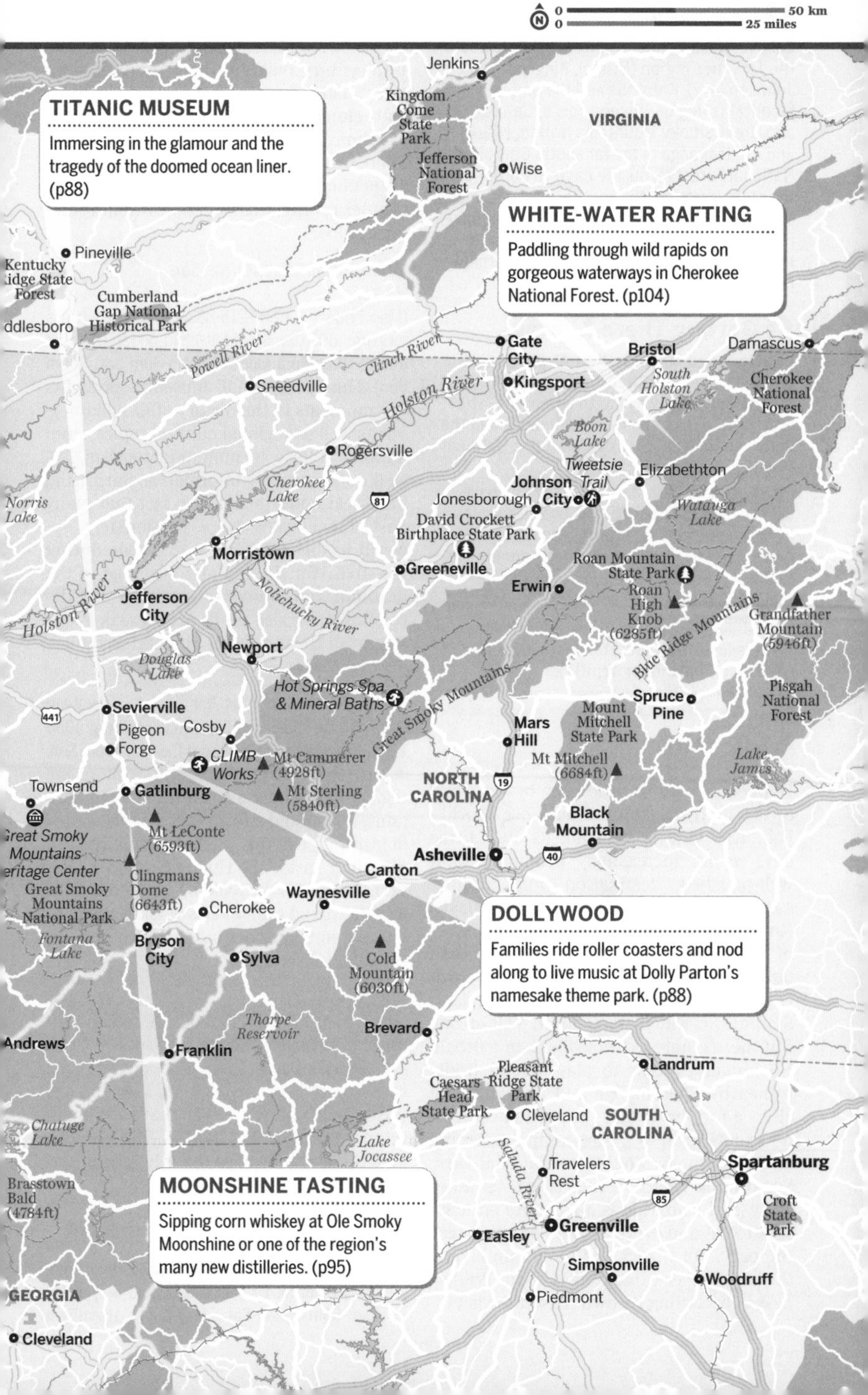

0 50 km
0 25 miles
TITANIC MUSEUM
Immersing in the glamour and the tragedy of the doomed ocean liner. (p88)
WHITE-WATER RAFTING
Paddling through wild rapids on gorgeous waterways in Cherokee National Forest. (p104)
DOLLYWOOD
Families ride roller coasters and nod along to live music at Dolly Parton's namesake theme park. (p88)
MOONSHINE TASTING
Sipping corn whiskey at Ole Smoky Moonshine or one of the region's many new distilleries. (p95)
Jenkins
Kingdom Come State Park
VIRGINIA
Jefferson National Forest
Wise
Pineville
Cumberland Gap National Historical Park
Powell River
Clinch River
Gate City
Bristol
Damascus
Kingsport
South Holston Lake
Cherokee National Forest
Sneedville
Holston River
Boon Lake
Rogersville
Tweetsie Trail
Elizabethton
Cherokee Lake
Norris Lake
Johnson City
Jonesborough
Watauga Lake
David Crockett Birthplace State Park
Morristown
Roan Mountain State Park
Greeneville
Erwin
Roan High Knob (6285ft)
Jefferson City
Nolichucky River
Grandfather Mountain (5946ft)
Blue Ridge Mountains
Newport
Douglas Lake
Hot Springs Spa & Mineral Baths
Great Smoky Mountains
Spruce Pine
Pisgah National Forest
Sevierville
Mount Mitchell State Park
Pigeon Forge
Cosby
Mars Hill
CLIMB Works
Mt Cammerer (4928ft)
Mt Mitchell (6684ft)
Lake James
Townsend
Gatlinburg
Mt Sterling (5840ft)
NORTH CAROLINA
Black Mountain
Mt LeConte (6593ft)
Asheville
Canton
Clingmans Dome (6643ft)
Great Smoky Mountains National Park
Waynesville
Cherokee
Fontana Lake
Bryson City
Sylva
Cold Mountain (6030ft)
Thorpe Reservoir
Brevard
Andrews
Franklin
Landrum
Pleasant Ridge State Park
Caesars Head State Park
Cleveland
SOUTH CAROLINA
Chatuge Lake
Lake Jocassee
Saluda River
Travelers Rest
Spartanburg
Brasstown Bald (4784ft)
Croft State Park
Easley
Greenville
Simpsonville
Woodruff
GEORGIA
Piedmont
Cleveland

Orientation

East Tennessee includes, from north to south, the Tri-Cities region (Bristol, Kingsport and Johnson City), Knoxville and the Smoky Mountalns Region (Pigeon Forge, Gatlinburg and Great Smoky Mountains National Park), and Chattanooga in the far south. Cherokee National Forest forms the eastern border of the state, covering the southern Appalachian Mountains. Great Smoky Mountains National Park divides Cherokee National Forest into two sections – north and south – at its midway point.

Getting There & Away

Chattanooga Metropolitan Airport (p209) and Knoxville's **McGhee Tyson Airport** (p208) are the main gateways to the area; the latter is just 40 miles or so from Gatlinburg and the entrance to Great Smoky Mountains National Park.

The primary interstates passing Knoxville are the I-40 and the I-75. The two interstates overlap southwest of Knoxville for about 20 miles. The latter then veers south, continuing to Chattanooga. Chattanooga can also be reached by I-24.

Amtrak does not stop in East Tennessee.

There are Greyhound stations in **Knoxville** (p88) and **Chattanooga** (p104).

Knoxville

☎865 / POP 186,239

Dubbed a 'scruffy little city' by the *Wall Street Journal* before the 1982 World's Fair, Knoxville is strutting its stuff these days as an increasingly prominent and well-polished destination for outdoor, gastronomy and craft-beer enthusiasts. Knoxville is also home to the University of Tennessee and its rabid college-football fan base. On game days the whole town is painted orange as fans pack Neyland Stadium to watch the beloved Volunteers. But there's more to Knoxville than football. No longer content to play second fiddle to nearby Chattanooga and Asheville, the city – a former textiles production center – now touts itself as a base camp for visitors to Great Smoky Mountains National Park. Sugarlands Visitor Center is just 29 miles away, and Knoxville is a far more enticing spot to eat and drink than other cities near the park. For hikers and mountain bikers, the city's ever-expanding Urban Wilderness is becoming its own reason to visit.

Sights

Downtown's Market Sq is full of ornate 19th-century buildings and lovely outdoor cafes shaded by pear trees, while Old Town and Hundred Block are arty, renovated warehouse districts centered on Gay St. There are a couple of museums and kitschy attractions in town, but Knoxville's best attributes revolve around eating, drinking and the outdoors.

Museum of East Tennessee History — MUSEUM

(Map p84; ☎865-215-8830; www.easttnhistory.org; 601 Gay St; adult/child under 17yr $5/free; ⏲9am-4pm Mon-Fri, 10am-4pm Sat, 1-5pm Sun) This glossy small museum spotlights key moments in the history of East Tennessee as well as regional cultural topics, from 'hillbilly' music to mountain tourism. It's well done and very informative. Surprising historical notes include the fact that many East Tennesseans were passionately opposed to the state's move to secede during the Civil War. There's also coverage of the uranium and plutonium research and development carried on in nearby Oak Ridge as part of the top-secret Manhattan Project during WWII.

Knoxville Museum of Art — MUSEUM

(Map p84; ☎865-525-6101; www.knoxart.org; 1050 World's Fair Park; ⏲10am-5pm Tue-Sat, 1-5pm Sun; P) FREE If you're planning to explore the region, the landscape paintings of mountains, forests and streams are a pretty source of inspiration at this small museum. You can find them inside the Higher Ground exhibition, which covers regional art and artists. Kids like to take an up-close look at the miniature home interiors in the Thorne Rooms diorama collection.

Sunsphere — LANDMARK

(Map p84; ☎865-215-8160; www.worldsfairpark.org/sunsphere; World's Fair Park, 810 Clinch Ave; ⏲9am-10pm) FREE The city's visual centerpiece is the Sunsphere, a golden orb (disco ball!) atop a tower that's the main remnant of the 1982 World's Fair. You can take the elevator up to the 4th-floor observation deck to see the skyline.

Women's Basketball Hall of Fame — MUSEUM

(Map p84; ☎865-633-9000; www.wbhof.com; 700 Hall of Fame Dr; adult $8, child 6-15yr $6; ⏲10am-5pm Mon-Sat May-Aug, 11am-5pm

Tue-Fri, 10am-5pm Sat Sep-Apr; P) You can't miss the massive orange basketball that marks the Women's Basketball Hall of Fame, a nifty look at the sport from the time when women were forced to play in full-length dresses. Interactive features include a half-time locker-room talk by legendary University of Tennessee coach Pat Summitt and a dribbling course to test your skills.

Activities

Just 3 miles from downtown South Knoxville, 50 miles of hiking and cycling trails known as the Urban Wilderness connect historic battlefields, neighborhoods and parks that make up more than 1000 forested acres.

Ijams Nature Center OUTDOORS
(865-577-4717; www.ijams.org; 2915 Island Home Ave; 9am-5pm Mon-Sat, from 11am Sun;) A one-stop shop for enjoying nature in Knoxville, this 300-acre spot is the de facto headquarters for the sprawling Urban Wilderness). Here you can stroll the scenic **River Boardwalk Trail** beside the Tennessee River, enjoy a canopy adventure tour (with a zipline), rent bikes ($20 for four hours) and let the kids roam free in the nature-themed playground.

Hiking and cycling trails here link to connector trails leading to parks, quarries and more trails – all part of the Urban Wilderness. Pick up a trail map ($1) at the information desk. As for pronouncing Ijams, it's 'eye-ams'.

Baker Creek Preserve MOUNTAIN BIKING
(www.outdoorknoxville.com; 3700 Lancaster Ave) Part of the Urban Wilderness, this 100-acre preserve is home to the **Devils Racetrack**, the region's only double-black-diamond mountain-biking trail. One highlight of this 1000yd plunge? A near-vertical 50ft wall ride. But you don't have to be an expert to pedal the preserve. You'll also find a kids-only beginner area with a pump track, plus trails geared to various skill levels.

Mead's Quarry Lake WATER SPORTS
(865-696-0806; www.ijams.org; 2915 Island Home Ave; kayaks, canoes & SUPs per hr $12; 3-7pm Mon-Fri, 10am-6pm Sat, noon-6pm Sun Jun-Aug, reduced hours in fall & spring, closed winter) You can hike around this pink marble quarry, just a short walk from Ijams Nature Center, year-round. In the summer and warmer months, canoes, kayaks and stand-up paddleboards are available for rent to explore the lake. Hikers and cyclists can reach the quarry from other parks in the Urban Wilderness on various trails and greenways. On Saturdays and Sundays in warmer months, **Yee Haw Brewing** sells beer from a hut here.

URBAN WILDERNESS

Highlights within the Urban Wilderness system include **Baker Creek Preserve**, containing the region's only double-black-diamond mountain-bike trail, and **Mead's Quarry Lake**, where you can rent canoes and paddleboards in warmer months. The pretty **Tharp Trace Trail** loops around the quarry, passing an old cemetery and an overlook with a view of Mt LeConte in the Great Smokies. **Ijams Nature Center** doubles as the headquarters of the Urban Wilderness, and it should be your first stop. Here you can pick up a trail map ($1), hike along the Tennessee River on wooden boardwalks, enjoy a nature-themed playground and travel through the treetops on a canopy tour. The **Imerys Trail** and the **Will Skelton Greenway** connect Ijams with other parks and trails in the network. Download the Urban Wilderness mobile map app at www.outdoorknoxville.com for an overview.

Nativat Knoxville ADVENTURE SPORTS
(855-628-4828; www.nativat.com; 2915 Island Home Ave, Ijams Nature Center; adult/child $45/35; 10am-6pm Tue-Thu, to 8pm Fri & Sat, to 4pm Sun Jun-Aug, reduced hours rest of the year;) Lofty trails connect to trees on this self-guided canopy tour, challenging kids with various adventure elements, from rope ladders to swinging bridges to a zipline. Each admission ticket is good for two hours of fun. The registration desk is inside the nature center building.

Festivals & Events

Big Ears Festival MUSIC
(www.bigearsfestival.org; Mar) Avant-garde and experiential festival celebrating music, art and film and the connections between them. Performances are held at various music venues across downtown.

Knoxville

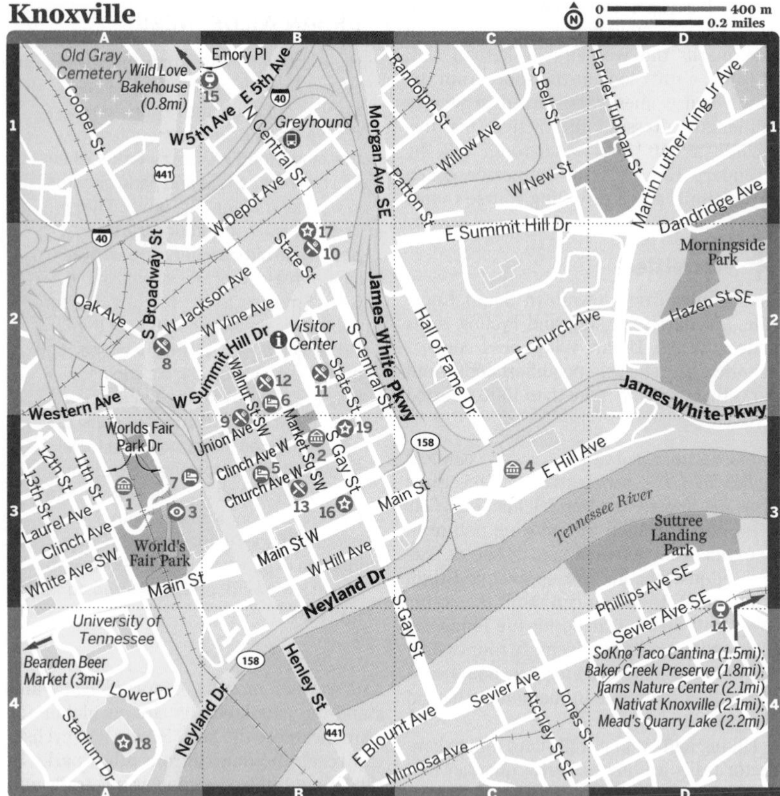

Rhythm & Blooms MUSIC
(http://rhythmnbloomsfest.com; Jackson Ave; ⊙early Apr) East Tennessee musicians and rootsy national acts jam at venues along Jackson Ave in early spring.

Sleeping

With the exception of the Oliver Hotel (p84), midrange business chain hotels have been the best Knoxville could traditionally muster, but that all changed when the city's first luxury hotel, the Tennessean, opened near the Sunsphere in May 2017. Budget chain hotels are scattered along the interstates and around town.

★ **Oliver Hotel** BOUTIQUE HOTEL $$
(Map p84; ☎865-351-0987; www.theoliverhotel.com; 407 Union Ave; r $180-210, ste $255-275; P ❄ @ ☎) Hipster receptionists welcome you to Knoxville's first boutique hotel, boasting 28 modern, stylish rooms with fun subway-tiled showers (with rain-style shower heads), luxe linens, plush throwback furniture and carpets and gorgeous hand-crafted coffee tables. The Peter Kern Library (p87) bar draws craft-cocktail enthusiasts by night. The restaurant, Oliver Royale (mains lunch $10 to $14, dinner $16 to $36), is highly recommended.

Tupelo Honey Cafe, an Asheville-based upscale Southern comfort-food chain, is also here. Complimentary bikes for guests.

Hilton Knoxville HOTEL $$
(Map p84; ☎865-523-2300; www3.hilton.com; 501 W Church Ave; r from $174; P ❄ @ ☎ ≋ 🐾) The sleek color scheme in the guest rooms – white and chocolate brown – is the most exciting thing you can say about this nondescript downtown chain hotel. It is within walking distance of several key attractions, however, and there's a Starbucks on-site. You can sometimes score a great weekday rate – as low as $99 – from third-party travel

Knoxville

Sights

1 Knoxville Museum of Art A3
2 Museum of East Tennessee History .. B3
3 Sunsphere A3
4 Women's Basketball Hall of Fame C3

Sleeping

5 Hilton Knoxville B3
6 Oliver Hotel B2
7 Tennessean A3

Eating

8 Balter Beerworks A2
9 JC Holdway B3
10 Oli Bea B2
11 Phoenix Pharmacy & Fountain B2
12 Stock & Barrel B2
13 Yassin's Falafel House B3

Drinking & Nightlife

14 Alliance Brewing Company D4
15 Crafty Bastard Brewery B1
Peter Kern Library .... (see 6)

Entertainment

16 Bijou Theatre B3
17 Jig & Reel B2
18 Neyland Stadium A4
19 Tennessee Theatre B3

aggregators. Rates decrease on weekends. Self-parking is $14 per night; valet is $20 per night. The pet fee is $50 per visit.

Tennessean BOUTIQUE HOTEL **$$$**
(Map p84; ☎865-232-1800; www.thetennesseanhotel.com; 531 Henley St; r/ste from $239/379; P ❄ @ ≋ 🐾) The Tennessee River is the unifying theme at this posh new hotel across the street from the Sunsphere and the city convention center. Look for maps of the river on guest-room walls, carpets with water-drop designs, and blue accents throughout the building. Southern hospitality is a highlight.

Top amenities include an indoor pool flanked by floor-to-ceiling windows, plus afternoon and evening cocktail service – open to the public – in the stylish Drawing Room (3pm to 11pm Monday to Thursday, to 1am Friday and Saturday, to 10pm Sunday). Self-parking and valet parking are both $20 per day. Pet fee is $100 per stay.

Eating

Pedestrianized Market Sq in downtown Knoxville hosts a wide array of recommended restaurants, while increasingly hip North (NoKno) and South Knoxville (SoKno) are home to many of the city's trendiest coffeehouses and foodie hot spots. Those toting little ones shouldn't miss the Phoenix (p86), a recreated 20th-century soda fountain on Gay St.

★Balter Beerworks GASTROPUB **$**
(Map p84; ☎865-999-5015; www.balterbeerworks.com; 100 S Broadway; mains $9-16; ⌚11am-11pm Mon-Thu, to midnight Fri, 10am-midnight Sat, 10am-11pm Sun) From the communal tables on the patio to the standing-room-only bar to the buzzing dining room, this convivial joint – a former gas station – exudes a welcoming vibe. The pub fare is delicious, and options range from the Gouda-topped burger with sriracha steak sauce to cheesy shrimp and grits with andouille sausage. The easy-drinking house beer is brewed on-site. It may be busy, but solo travelers should feel right at home.

★Stock & Barrel BURGERS **$**
(Map p84; ☎865-766-2075; www.thestockandbarrel.com; 35 Market Sq; burgers $10-16; ⌚11am-10pm Sun-Thu, until 11pm Fri & Sat) Carnivores, welcome to your happy place. The locally sourced and all-natural burgers here groan under decadent toppings such as fried eggs, pimiento cheese and blueberry preserves. The Elvis comes with organic peanut butter, fried bananas and Benton's bacon. The french fries? Crispy and delicious. Craft beer and '80s indie rock round out the fun. It's small, so expect a wait.

Yassin's Falafel House MIDDLE EASTERN **$**
(Map p84; ☎865-219-1462; www.yassinfalafelhouse.com; 706 Walnut St; mains $7-12; ⌚11am-9pm Mon-Sat) Syrian refugee Yassin is a true American success story: he and his wildly popular falafel house have been embraced by Knoxville. The food is fantastic, featuring spicy falafel, hummus and baba ghanoush (don't forget baklava for dessert), among other things. A handful of other Syrian refugees work the kitchen and front counter. Great for a quick and casual lunch.

SoKno Taco Cantina MEXICAN **$**
(☎865-851-8882; www.soknota.co; 3701 Sevierville Pike; tacos $4, mains $8-10; ⌚11am-1am Sun-Wed, to 2am Thu-Sat) After barreling down the Devils Racetrack in the nearby Urban Wilderness, relax and refuel with a slew of flavor-packed street tacos at SoKno. The *pollo* is so good we bet you'll order

WORTH A TRIP

SEVIERVILLE

Sevierville (www.seviervilletn.org), located 35 miles southeast of Knoxville, is the hometown of Dolly Parton, and a **statue** (Map p90; 125 Court Ave) of the country-music star brightens the front lawn of the Sevier County Courthouse, built in 1896. The courthouse square is a pleasant oasis within the ever-growing sprawl that stretches from Sevierville through the ticky-tacky attractions of Pigeon Forge and Gatlinburg right up to the entrance to Great Smoky Mountains National Park, 14 miles south. If sampling artisan whiskey sounds like a good way to escape the craziness, spend an hour at **Sevier Distilling Co** (Map p90; 865-366-1772; www.sevierdistilling.com; 745 Old Douglas Dam Rd; 11am-7pm Mon-Thu, 10am-10pm Fri & Sat, noon-7pm Sun; P) FREE. This intimate place – a contrast to the raucous tasting rooms in Gatlinburg – serves free samples of moonshine, mead and a tequila-inspired whiskey that are all sourced locally. For an outdoor nature walk, pull into the parking lot at the corner of Hwy 441 and Hardin Lane, just west of the courthouse. From here you can stroll on the 2-mile **West Prong Greenway**, part of a riverside park that tracks the Little Pigeon River. There is also a **Tanger Outlets** (Map p90; 865-453-1053; www.tangeroutlet.com; 1645 Parkway; 9am-9pm Mon-Sat, 10am-7pm Sun) discount mall, with several outdoor and adventure-apparel stores. For good budget lodging, try the **Mountain Aire Inn** (Map p90; 865-453-5576; 1008 Parkway; r $79; P ❄ ᯤ)..

another. More than 20 craft beers on tap, too. The $5 lunch special gets you two tacos with a side of chips and salsa. Close to Ijams Nature Center (p83).

Phoenix Pharmacy & Fountain ICE CREAM $
(Map p84; 865-692-1603; www.phoenixpharmacyknoxville.com; 418 S Gay St; ice-cream cone $5; noon-10pm Sun-Thu, 11am-11pm Fri & Sat;) An old-school soda fountain with a 21st-century sense of fun, this kid-friendly spot mixes its sundaes and shakes with modern favorites like Nutella and Rice Krispies. The cherry-topped Great Smoky Mountain builds from a hot fudge base that's topped with a chocolate brownie, vanilla cake, ice cream, caramel, whipped cream and smoked nib brittle. Ice-cream headache? The adjacent pharmacy sells aspirin.

Wild Love Bakehouse BAKERY, COFFEEHOUSE $
(865-200-8078; www.facebook.com/wildlovebakehouse; 1625 N Central St; pastries $3-4, breakfast sandwiches $12; 7am-6pm Mon-Fri, 8am-6pm Sat & Sun;) This scrumptious bakery in happening Happy Holler in North Knoxville sources milk, eggs, cheese and other ingredients from a chalkboard list of local farms. It does incredible sweet and savory croissants, a beautifully delicate lemon olive-oil cake and monstrous Cruze Farm buttermilk breakfast biscuit sandwiches with eggs and maple-glazed sausage that are gone in a blink.

It's also a great craft coffeehouse and there's ample indoor and outdoor patio seating on which to set up a mobile office for a few hours.

Oli Bea BREAKFAST $
(Map p84; 865-200-5450; www.olibeaoldcity.com; 109 S Central St; mains $8-12; 7am-1pm Mon-Fri, 8am-2pm Sat;) It's worth sleeping in Knoxville just to wake to the rich, Mexicanized farm-to-table Southern breakfast fare at this morning stop in Old City. You'll find gussied-up standards (country ham, sage sausage, organic chicken), a sinfully good grilled cheese with buttermilk cheddar, a sunny egg and collard greens and, finally, full-stop-fabulous pork confit *carnitas* tostadas. Several vegetarian options, too.

★ **JC Holdway** AMERICAN $$
(Map p84; 865-312-9050; www.jcholdway.com; 501 Union Ave; mains $20-26; 5:30-9:30pm Tue-Thu, to 10pm Fri & Sat;) You'll want to reserve ahead for the privilege of noshing on James Beard Award–winning chef Joseph Lenn's modern Appalachian comfort cuisine. Lenn, who spent nearly a decade as executive chef at famed Blackberry Farm before returning home to the Knox in 2016, does a ridiculously perfect wood-grilled pork with sweet-potato puree and anything with smoked meat from Benton's Farm.

The space, a former downtown photography studio, calls on stacked firewood as space dividers and there's a large, first-come, first-served bar and open kitchen. One of Knoxville's hottest tables.

Drinking

Knoxville is home to 12 craft-beer breweries (and counting), branded locally as the Ale Trail (www.knoxvillealetrail.com). To visit several in an afternoon or evening, check out Knox Brew Tours (www.knoxbrewtours.com), which will drive you to various breweries for guided tours and beer tastings. You'll find great bars throughout downtown, especially along Gay St and in Old City (a few blocks northeast of Market Sq) as well as North (NoKno) and South Knoxville (SoKno).

Peter Kern Library COCKTAIL BAR

(Map p84; ☎865-351-0987; www.theoliverhotel.com; 407 Union Ave, Oliver Hotel; ⏲4pm-midnight Mon-Fri, 11am-2am Sat & Sun) This marvelous speakeasy, named for a former Knoxville mayor, sits inside a cosy space that served as the library in a former iteration of the Oliver Hotel (p84). Thick-bound books double as drink menus and the craft cocktails are named for literary characters. To enter, look for the red light above the door in the alley beside the hotel.

Alliance Brewing Company MICROBREWERY

(Map p84; ☎865-247-5355; www.alliancebrewing.com; 1130 Sevier Ave; ⏲4-11pm Tue-Fri, noon-11pm Sat, noon-9pm Sun; 📶) Popular with outdoorsy types coming back from the Urban WIlderness, dog-friendly Alliance's SoKno taproom offers 12 taps, some of which are devoted to resurrecting dead styles such as Kottbusser (brewed with oats, honey and molasses) or Grisette (an old German miner's brew). There's a great outdoor patio and a different food truck pulls up nightly.

The Cubana Coffee Brown Ale (made with next door's Three Bears Coffee) and numbered IPA series are especially trip-worthy.

Bearden Beer Market BEER GARDEN

(☎865-851-8922; www.beardenbeermarket.wordpress.com; 4524 Old Kingston Pike; ⏲10am-midnight Mon-Sat, noon-midnight Sun) Part beer garden, part beer store, this no-frills place in western Knoxville epitomizes the best of Scruffy City. The 'garden' – dotted with various tables and chairs on cracked concrete slabs – is tucked tight behind the tiny craft-beer shop. It's all a little downtrodden, but the upbeat folks drinking here on a lazy Saturday afternoon don't mind a lick.

Crafty Bastard Brewery MICROBREWERY

(Map p84; www.craftybastardbrewery.com; 6 Emory Pl; pints from $5; ⏲4pm-midnight Tue-Fri, 2pm-midnight Sat, 2-9pm Sun; 📶) This nano-brewery taproom occupies historic building space in NoKno's Emory Pl district. The rustic, dilapidated, chipped-concrete warehouse vibe augments a defiantly independent mentality that carries over to its 12 IPA-driven taps, which host suds brewed by a former high-school math teacher plus guest brews. It's all very hip and highly recommended by beer snobs (but introverted solo-traveling women may be happier elsewhere).

Try the Big Bastard DIPA. You can check the food-truck schedule and list of current beers on the website.

Entertainment

Tennessee Theatre LIVE PERFORMANCE

(Map p84; ☎865-684-1200; www.tennesseetheatre.com; 604 S Gay St) Re-opening in 2005 after a $25.5-million restoration, this grand 1928 theatre hosts musicians and entertainers – Jason Isbell, the Temptations, John Prine, David Blaine – as well as Broadway plays and the Knoxville Symphony. Even if you can't catch a show, stop in to check out the ornate lobby.

Jig & Reel LIVE MUSIC

(Map p84; ☎865-247-7066; www.jigandreel.com; 101 S Central St; ⏲3pm-3am Tue-Sun) Mountain music and bluegrass bands – which all trace their roots to Appalachia's Scots-Irish settlers – draw appreciative crowds to this exposed-brick Scottish pub in Old City. Nice Scotch list, too.

Bijou Theatre LIVE PERFORMANCE

(Map p84; ☎865-522-0832; www.knoxbijou.org; 803 S Gay St) The fourth-oldest building in Knoxville, this 700-seat venue welcomes indie rockers, comedians and beloved favorites such as the Indigo Girls.

Neyland Stadium STADIUM

(Map p84; ☎865-974-1205; www.utsports.com/facilities/neyland; 1600 Stadium Dr; tours $8) Peyton Manning first made his name here. You can tour the 102,455-capacity football behemoth by calling ahead or emailing utevents@utk.edu.

Information

Besides providing tourism info, the **visitor center** (Visit Knoxville; Map p84; ☎800-727-8045; www.visitknoxville.com; 301 S Gay St; ⏰8:30am-5pm Mon-Fri, 9am-5pm Sat, noon-4pm Sun) also welcomes bands from across the Americana genre for WDVX's **Blue Plate Special**, a free concert series at noon Monday to Saturday.

Getting There & Away

Knoxville's **McGhee Tyson Airport** (p208) is 15 miles south of town and is served by around 20 nonstop domestic flights. The **Greyhound** (Map p84; ☎865-524-0369; www.greyhound.com; 100 E Magnolia Ave) bus station is only about 1 mile north of downtown, making it a convenient option for ground travelers.

Pigeon Forge

☎865 / POP 6092

You can step aboard the *Titanic*, ogle OJ Simpson's white Ford Bronco, and plunge toward the earth on America's first 'wing coaster' in Pigeon Forge, a sprawling cacophony of excess and traffic burning bright in the shadow of the Great Smoky Mountains. With liquor by the drink available since 2013, the city has recently loosened up a bit at night. Pigeon Forge is named in part for the Little Pigeon River, which flows through the action. Its banks were once a roosting spot for passenger pigeons – now extinct. Best known today as the home of Dollywood, Dolly Parton's namesake theme park, the city is packed tight with hotels, restaurants and family-friendly attractions, most of them lining Parkway, the main thoroughfare. Pigeon Forge is just 8 miles from Great Smoky Mountains National Park, but traffic and stoplights can make that 8 miles seem a mighty long way.

Sights

★Titanic Museum MUSEUM

(Map p90; ☎417-334-9500; www.titanicpigeonforge.com; 2134 Parkway; adult $26, child 5-11yr $13; ⏰9am-10pm Jul & early Aug, closes earlier rest of the year; Ⓟ) On April 15, 1912 the steamship *Titanic* sank on her maiden voyage after colliding with an iceberg. The ship's history and the stories of many of her passengers are shared through artifacts, black-and-white photographs, personal histories and thoughtful interactive displays. Highlights include an actual deck chair from the ship, a replica of the grand staircase and a haunting musical tribute to the ship's young musicians, who chose to stay onboard and play, possibly to keep passengers calm. All perished.

Every guest entering the museum is handed a boarding pass linked to a real-life passenger. Will you survive? Check the memorial wall at the end of the tour. If you're assigned to a third-class male passenger, don't get your hopes up!

★Dollywood AMUSEMENT PARK

(Map p90; ☎865-428-9488; www.dollywood.com; 2700 Dollywood Parks Blvd; adult/child $70/57; ⏰mid-Mar–Dec, hours vary seasonally; Ⓟ👪) Dollywood is a self-created ode to the patron saint of East Tennessee: the big-haired, big-bosomed and big-hearted country singer Dolly Parton. A clean and friendly place, the park features Appalachian-themed rides and attractions, the Splash Country water park, mountain crafts, Southern-fried restaurants and the DreamMore Resort. Highlights include nationally acclaimed roller coasters, live-music shows and the Chasing Rainbow Museum, which traces Dolly's fascinating life – her hometown is nearby Sevierville.

Food is surprisingly mediocre, but the 1lb turkey legs are a solid lunch – and an even better photo!

The soaring Wild Eagle 'wing coaster' rises 21 stories, with riders having nothing but air beneath their seats.

Splash Country (adult/child $50/45) is open mid-May to August, and kids go wild for the place. A multi-park ticket costs $80/67 per adult/child.

Alcatraz East Crime Museum MUSEUM

(Map p90; ☎865-453-3278; www.alcatrazeast.com; 2757 Parkway; adult $25, child 8-12yr $15; ⏰10am-9pm Sun-Thu, to 10pm Fri & Sat; Ⓟ) Warning: if you're not in the right frame of mind, the exhibits here can leave you feeling off-kilter. Galleries spotlight different aspects of criminology, beginning with medieval torture and continuing through witch trials, serial killers, famous kidnappings, September 11, capital-punishment techniques and much more. Memorable artifacts include the white Ford Bronco used by OJ Simpson during his infamous 1994 freeway chase, Ted Bundy's typewriter and

DOLLYWOOD TIPS

➡ To avoid the $15 parking fee in the Dollywood lot, hop the red Dollywood route of the Fun Time Trolley (p92) from Patriot Park in Pigeon Forge, where parking is free. One-way fare is 50¢.

➡ Guests of the DreamMore Resort can ride a free shuttle to the park from the resort.

➡ If roller coasters are your main reason for visiting, head left from the entrance to get a jump on the lines for some of the wilder rides.

➡ Many of the coasters do not allow passengers to bring on bags or purses. Be prepared to rent a locker, or to leave bags with someone in your group. Front-gate lockers are $9 to $12 for the day. Ride-to-ride lockers – found beside various attractions – are $7. These are floating lockers, meaning you pay only once but can use lockers in different locations without repaying.

➡ The $35 Timesaver pass allows you expedited access to 10 selected rides across the park.

VW Bug, and John Wayne Gacy's actual Pogo the Clown costume! The stuff of nightmares, truly.

Although children are permitted inside, know your kids. Some of the torture and capital-punishment displays are no-holds-barred and quite disturbing.

Great Smoky Mountain Wheel FERRIS WHEEL
(Map p90; ☎865-286-0119; www.islandpigeonforge.com; 131 Island Dr; adult $14, child 3-11yr $9; ⊙10am-midnight late May-early Aug, varies rest of the year) One ticket gets you three spins inside an all-glass gondola on this 200ft-tall Ferris wheel, which anchors The Island (p91). Views of the Great Smokies are breathtaking.

Sleeping

National and locally owned hotels line Parkway. Many include a complimentary breakfast and most have very welcoming service. A fair number are not pet friendly, so double check before setting out. For unique properties, consider DreamMore Resort, the hotels at The Island, or one of the locally owned mom-and-pops.

Clarion Inn Dollywood Area HOTEL $
(Map p90; ☎865-868-5300; www.choicehotels.com; 124 Waldens Main St; r from $120; P❄️📶🏊) We're not sure what's going on here. Budget prices. Friendly and helpful service. And free perks out the wazoo: popcorn, cookies and specialty coffees in the evening, a generous hot breakfast buffet in the morning, and free coffee and flavored waters throughout the day. The comfy rooms come with a microwave, mini-fridge and balcony. Amazing digs for the price point.

Inn on the River HOTEL $$
(Map p90; ☎800-388-1727; www.myinnontheriver.com; 2492 Parkway; r from $140; P❄️📶🏊) You know what impressed us most? The meeting room that staff can quickly convert into a guest room in a pinch – it's always held for late-night walk-ins who can't find another bed in town on a crowded night. Renovated rooms are comfortably modern with microwaves and mini-fridges. For a nature break, settle into a rocking chair beside the adjacent Little Pigeon River.

Inn at Christmas Place HOTEL $$
(Map p90; ☎888-453-0415; www.christmasplace.com; 119 Christmas Tree Lane; r from $199; P❄️@📶🏊) Every day is Christmas at this delightfully kitsch place, where each room comes with a Christmas tree. Kids will enjoy the indoor and outdoor pools, the Singing Santa and the Glockenspiel clock, which marks the top of the hour in the lobby from 9am to 9pm with joyous holiday cheer.

DreamMore Resort RESORT $$$
(Map p90; ☎865-365-1900; www.dollywood.com/resort; 2525 DreamMore Way; r/ste from $299/345; P❄️📶🏊) Although not as glossy as some resorts, the warm hospitality here is notable and the grounds are impeccably clean and well manicured. The fun starts in the lobby where you're greeted by a big-windowed view of the pool. Rooms were constructed with families in mind, with bunk beds typically ensconced in the wall beside the master bed.

Pigeon Forge

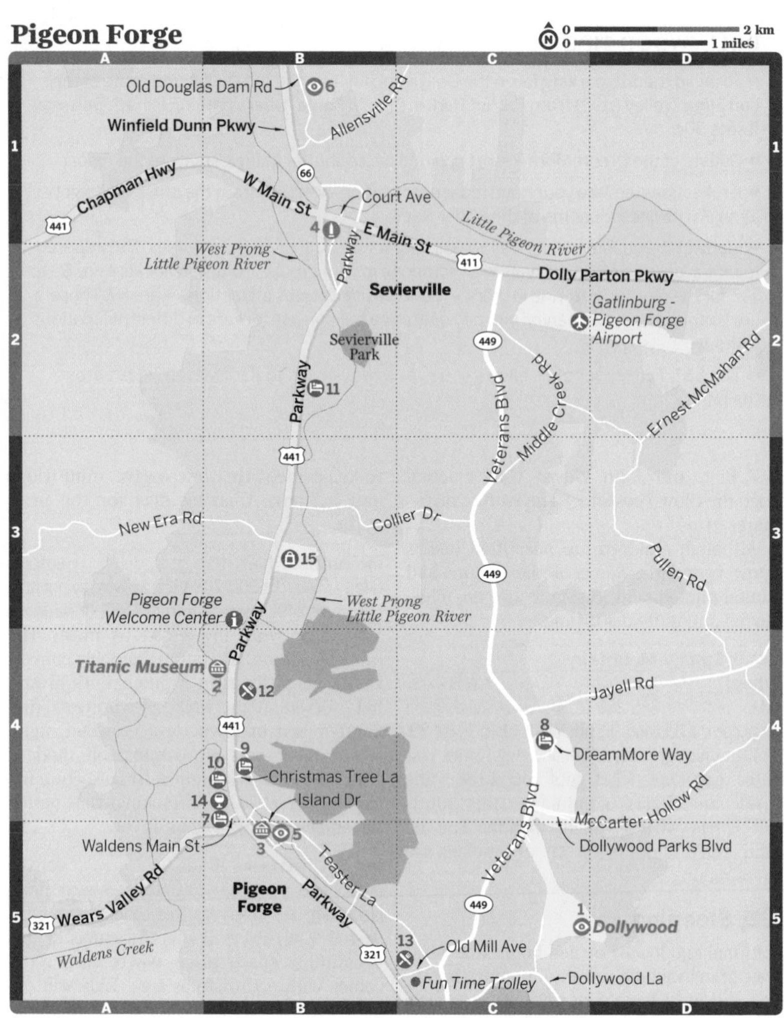

After a day in the adjacent theme parks, unwind with a hot-stone massage at the spa while the kids play air hockey in the game room.

Perks include door-to-door transportation to the theme parks and early Saturday entry to Dollywood. Many overnight and theme-park packages are available on the website.

Margaritaville Island Hotel HOTEL **$$$**
(Map p90; ☎844-434-6787; www.margaritaislandhotel.com; 131 Island Dr; r/ste from $279/329; P ❄ 📶 🏊) Breezy pastels and beach-cottage decor evoke a hip vacation vibe that would make Jimmy Buffett proud. Guests should begin with a drink from the in-room 'Frozen Concoction Maker' then continue the party on the rooftop pool, which is in the sightline of the Great Smoky Mountain Wheel.

Service is a whiff less personable than at other local properties, but who cares after that second concoction?

Eating

National chain restaurants and fast-food outlets are the predominant choice, and they line Parkway and its offshoots. You

Pigeon Forge

Top Sights
1 Dollywood C5
2 Titanic Museum B4

Sights
3 Alcatraz East Crime Museum B5
4 Dolly Parton Statue B1
5 Great Smoky Mountain Wheel B5
6 Sevier Distilling Co B1

Sleeping
7 Clarion Inn Dollywood Area B4
8 DreamMore Resort C4
9 Inn at Christmas Place B4
10 Inn on the River B4
Margaritaville Island Hotel .... (see 5)
11 Mountain Aire Inn B2

Eating
12 Local Goat B4
13 Pottery House Cafe & Grille C5

Drinking & Nightlife
Ole Smoky Barn .... (see 5)
14 Smoky Mountain Brewery B4

Shopping
15 Tanger Outlets B3
The Island .... (see 5)

can find a couple of local options at the Old Mill complex beside Patriot Park, with a few others scattered here and there, but food prepped for mass consumption is the typical choice. There are a handful of grocery stores scattered along Parkway for self-catering.

Pottery House Cafe & Grille AMERICAN $
(Map p90; ☎865-428-0771; www.old-mill.com; 175 Old Mill Ave; mains $9-18; ⏲11am-10pm) Part of the Old Mill shopping and dining complex near Patriot Park, this bustling spot churns out a solid line-up of American fare, with several appealing lighter options: spicy grilled catfish, a grilled chicken sandwich and a strawberry spinach salad.

Across the street, sister restaurant the **Old Mill** (lunch mains $11 to $15, dinner mains $18 to $30) spotlights classic and rib-sticking Southern dishes.

Local Goat AMERICAN $$
(Map p90; ☎865-366-3035; www.localgoatpf.com; 2167 Parkway; lunch mains $9-12, dinner mains $12-28; ⏲11am-11pm Mon-Thu, to midnight Fri & Sat, to 10pm Sun) Don't let the bland corporate exterior fool you. The scratch-made fare inside this busy restaurant is locally sourced and delicious. At lunch burgers get sassy with toppings such as pimiento cheese, bacon jam and crispy onions. Dinner steps up the game with a tenderloin steak salad and shrimp and grits with sriracha. Great craft beer selection on tap. If there's a line and you're traveling by yourself, try snagging a first-come, first-served seat at the bar.

Drinking

Sevier County has long been 'dry' – but there are exemptions for Pigeon Forge, Gatlinburg and Sevierville. Restaurants in Pigeon Forge can serve beer and wine. And in 2013 voters approved an ordinance allowing the sale of liquor by the drink – and within one year 19 liquor licenses had been issued in the city! Today many Pigeon Forge restaurants have bars, but you may find some that don't. Most bars are along Parkway.

Ole Smoky Barn DISTILLERY
(Map p90; www.olesmoky.com; 131 Island Dr; ⏲10am-11pm) Dubbed 'the Barn,' this big-windowed moonshine distillery and tasting room has a front-row seat to the action at The Island, an outdoor retail and entertainment district in the heart of Pigeon Forge. Step up to the counter for quality hooch sippin' and some informative conversation about the many moonshines. The salted caramel is pretty darn good.

Smoky Mountain Brewery BAR
(Map p90; ☎865-868-1400; https://smoky-mtn-brewery.com/; 2530 Parkway; ⏲11am-midnight) The six flagship beers – we like the Helles lager – all pair nicely with the live bluegrass tunes played here almost every night. There's a solid bourbon menu, too.

Shopping

The Island MALL
(Map p90; www.islandinpigeonforge.com; 131 Island Dr; 👪) Shops, restaurants, live music shows and amusement-park thrills keep families busy all day long at The Island, which sprawls beneath the graceful grandeur of the 200ft-high Great Smoky Mountain Wheel (p89). The complex is also home to several hotels, an arcade and a lively show fountain.

Information

On the way into Pigeon Forge from Sevierville, stop by the **welcome center** (Map p90; ☎800-453-8574; www.mypigeonforge.com; 1950 Parkway;

WORTH A TRIP

TOWNSEND

Tucked between Great Smoky Mountains National Park and the Little River, pretty Townsend makes a great base camp for exploring Cades Cove, which is only 9 miles away in the national park. Stylish cabins at **Dancing Bear Lodge** (☎800-369-0111; www.dancingbearlodge.com; 7140 E Lamar Alexander Pkwy; r from $215; P❄📶🐾) are a comfy retreat after a day of hiking, and the delicious mountain-inspired dishes at the lodge's **Appalachian Bistro** (☎865-336-2138; www.dancingbearlodge.com; 7140 E Lamar Alexander Pkwy; mains $18-43; ⊙5-9pm Wed-Sun) are alone worth a drive to Townsend. For an introduction to the region's culture and past, spend an hour exploring the exhibits and historic buildings at the **Great Smoky Mountains Heritage Center** (☎865-448-0044; www.gsmheritagecenter.org; 123 Cromwell Dr; adult/child 6-17yr $8/6; ⊙10am-5pm Mon-Sat, noon-5pm Sun; P). Family-friendly adventures include rafting and tubing the Little River with **River Rat Tubing** (☎865-448-8888; www.smokymtnriverrat.com; 205 Wears Valley Rd; adult/child 6-17yr $15/12; ⊙10am-5pm mid-May–Aug; 👪) or digging into a sundae at **Burger Master Drive-In** (☎865-448-8408; www.burgermaster.net; 8439 Hwy 73; mains $3-6, large ice cream $3; ⊙11am-10pm Jun-Aug, to 8pm Mar-May, to 9pm Thu-Sun Sep & Oct; 👪), around since 1967.

⊙8:30am-5pm Mon-Sat, 1-5pm Sun) for maps, brochures for hotels and attractions, and coupon books galore. Also has information about Great Smoky Mountains National Park.

Getting There & Away

Knoxville is about 30 miles northwest of the city via Hwy 441. Knoxville's **McGhee Tyson Airport** (p208) is 35 miles west of Pigeon Forge.

Getting Around

Departing from Patriot Park, where there is free parking, the **Fun Time Trolley** (Map p90; ☎865-453-6444; www.cityofpigeonforge.com; ⊙all routes 8am-midnight Mar-Oct, 10am-10pm Nov & Dec) travels to many major attractions in Pigeon Forge, as well as to the **Gatlinburg Welcome Center** (p97). The red trolley route runs to Dollywood.

Gatlinburg

☎865 / POP 4138

Wildly kitschy and family-friendly Gatlinburg hunkers at the entrance to Great Smoky Mountains National Park, waiting to stun hikers with the scent of fudge, cotton candy and pancakes, and various odd museums and campy attractions. Boisterous new tasting rooms are drawing thirsty adult crowds to a slew of moonshine distilleries along Parkway, the main drag through town that rolls right into the national park. It's a wild ride of all that's good and bad about the USA, wrapped up in a gaudy explosion of magic shows and whiskey.

With the exception of the Gatlinburg Sky Lift and Anakeesta Mountain, the town emerged from the devastating 2016 wildfires largely unscathed, but memories of the conflagration linger. If you tire of all the flash and bling, you can find a handful of quality cultural and natural attractions in or near the busy downtown.

Sights

Anakeesta AMUSEMENT PARK

(Map p94; ☎865-325-2400; www.anakeesta.com; 576 Parkway; adult/child under 12yr $20/16; ⊙generally 10am-7pm Sun-Thu, to 8pm Fri & Sat; P👪) A chondola whisks visitors from downtown Gatlinburg to this playground in the sky where views of the Great Smokies are superb. Once atop Anakeesta Mountain you can bounce across 16 elevated bridges on the tree canopy walk, hold tight on dueling ziplines (adult/child $30/26), let the kids explore Treehouse Village, or settle into a rocking chair and appreciate the view. The Memorial Walk thoughtfully covers the destructive fires that raged across nearby slopes on November 16, 2016.

Anakeesta is a Cherokee word meaning 'place of the balsams' – and you'll see plenty of them on the canopy walk.

At the time of research, the brand new park had only recently opened, and the grounds were a pleasant and low-key place to explore. An alpine roller coaster along with a dining pavilion and bar should be open by the time you read this.

Gatlinburg Sky Lift CABLE CAR
(Map p94; ☎865-436-4307; www.gatlinburgskylift.com; 765 Parkway; adult/child $16/13; ⏲9am-11pm Jun-Aug, hours vary rest of year) This repurposed ski-resort chairlift lifts you high into the Smokies, providing stellar views. After being damaged in the 2016 wildfires, the lift was completely refurbished. At the time of research, the new Sky Deck was still under construction, with no confirmed completion date. While riding the lift, visitors can expect a smoother ride than before, and seats now hold three instead of two.

Gatlinburg Scenic Overlook VIEWPOINT
(Map p94; Gatlinburg Pkwy Bypass; P) If you don't have time to ride a chairlift from downtown Gatlinburg up to a scenic lookout, you can enjoy a lofty view of downtown and the surrounding mountains from this overlook just a short drive away.

Arrowmont School of Arts & Crafts GALLERY
(Map p94; ☎865-436-5860; www.arrowmont.org; 556 Parkway; ⏲8:30am-5pm Mon-Fri, to 4pm Sat; P) If you're looking for a quality cultural distraction in Gatlinburg, walk to the art galleries and artist studios (viewable from catwalks) at Arrowmont – or take a class! Arts and crafts workshops started here in 1945 and today you can register for weekend, one-week and two-week courses in a vast array of subjects. Take your pick of pottery-making, silk painting, woodworking and more.

Ober Gatlinburg Aerial Tramway CABLE CAR
(Map p94; ☎865-436-5423; www.obergatlinburg.com; 1001 Parkway; adult/child $14/12; ⏲9:30am-9:40pm Mon-Thu, 7:30am-10:40pm Fri & Sat, to 6:20pm Sun with seasonal variations) Ride the scenic 2-mile aerial tramway to the Bavarian-themed Ober Gatlinburg Ski Resort and amusement park.

Ripley's Aquarium of the Smokies AQUARIUM
(Map p94; ☎865-430-8808; www.ripleysaquariums.org; 88 River Rd; ⏲9am-10pm Mon-Thu, to 11pm Fri-Sun Jun-Aug, varies rest of the year; P 👪) One of eight Ripley's attractions in Gatlinburg, the aquarium is a convenient rainy-day destination – just be aware that everyone else downtown will have the same idea and that the exhibit areas can get unpleasantly crowded. Making the aquarium worth the price of admission is the 340ft-long transparent glidepath that tunnels beneath the Shark Lagoon and its mesmerizing inhabitants. Elsewhere, everyone loves the Penguin Playhouse. Learn about Blackbeard, buried treasures and the *Edmund Fitzgerald* in the new Shipwrecks exhibit.

Activities

CLIMB Works ADVENTURE SPORTS
(☎865-325-8116; www.climbworks.com; 155 Branam Hollow Rd, off Hwy 321; mountain biking/ziplining per person from $59/89; ⏲by reservation Mon-Sat) Some 13 miles east of Gatlinburg, this outfitter offers two adventures on its customized courses: ziplining and mountain biking. The 2½-hour ziplining and canopy tour takes you along nine ziplines and over three sky bridges. The views from the treetops are mesmerizing.

Mountain bikers can try their skills on the 2-mile loop trail, which encompasses a bit of singletrack, some climbing and some downhill challenges – there's a fun, corkscrewing wooden boardwalk at the end. As the number of riders allowed on the course is limited, you'll need to call ahead to reserve a space. Price includes bike rental and helmet.

Sleeping

Gatlinburg has thousands upon thousands of hotel rooms, most in the budget to midrange price category. Prices rise in summer, on weekends and during October leaf-peeping season and almost always include some form of breakfast. Many are not pet-friendly.

URBAN ESCAPE: GATLINBURG TRAIL

With the exception of a few ski-lift chairs and chondolas rising from Parkway to nearby mountaintops, you won't find many outdoor adventures in downtown Gatlinburg. If you need to stretch your legs or escape the crowds, follow Parkway south to River Rd, which begins near the entrance to Great Smoky Mountains National Park. Off River Rd you can step onto the Gatlinburg Trail (p49), a 2-mile path through the woods that ends at the park's Sugarlands Visitor Center (p203).

Gatlinburg

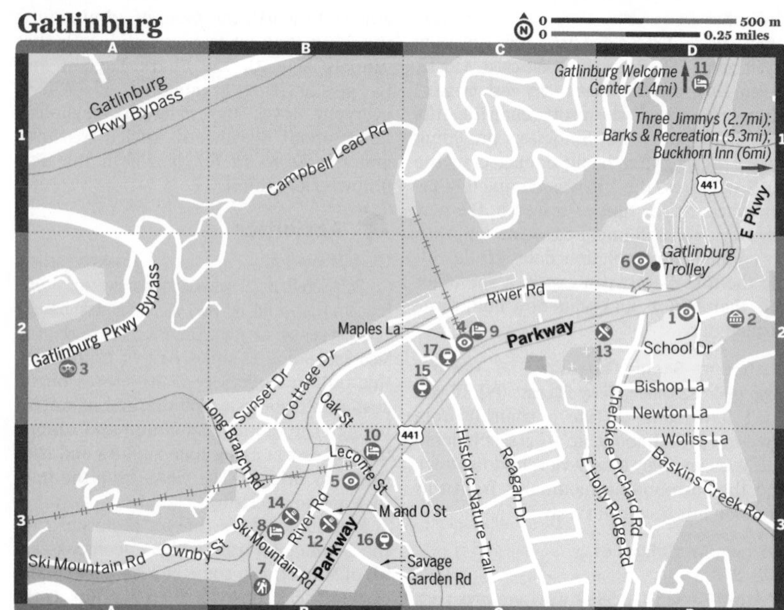

Cabin rentals in the surrounding mountains are also enormously popular. Find a comprehensive list of accommodations at www.gatlinburg.com.

Rocky Waters Motor Inn MOTEL $

(Map p94; ☎865-436-7861; www.rockywatersmotorinn.com; 333 Parkway; r $109-119; ste $129; P ❄ ☎) This pleasantly retro motel has clean, comfy rooms with new hardwood flooring and big walk-in showers and is perched above the river. It's walking distance from downtown, but at a serene remove from the noise and lights. Rooms have a microwave and fridge.

Buckhorn Inn INN $$

(☎865-436-4668; www.buckhorninn.com; 2140 Tudor Mountain Rd; r $125-205, 2-bedroom guesthouse from $240; P ❄ @ ☎) A few minutes' drive and several light years away from the kitsch and crowds of downtown Gatlinburg, the tranquil Buckhorn has nine elegant rooms, seven private cottages and four guesthouses on a property that is a well-manicured private haven. If the unbroken views of Mt LeConte don't relax you enough, have a wander through the fieldstone meditation labyrinth.

Bearskin Lodge LODGE $$

(Map p94; ☎877-795-7546; www.thebearskinlodge.com; 840 River Rd; r/ste from $199/239; P ❄ ☎ ≋) Near the park entrance, this shingled riverside lodge is blessed with timber accents and a bit more panache than other Gatlinburg comers. All of the 96 spacious rooms have flat-screen TVs and some come with gas fireplaces and private balconies jutting over the river. Has an outdoor pool and a lazy river.

Gatlinburg Inn HOTEL $$

(Map p94; ☎865-436-5133; www.gatlinburginn.com; 755 Parkway; r & ste $189-249; P ❄ ☎ ≋) The inviting rocking chairs set a welcoming mood at this downtown classic, which has all the wood paneling, gold rugs and rococo light fixtures you'd expect from an inn open since 1937. An ongoing renovation has introduced new carpet, drapery and bathrooms, and better preserved a series of historic B&W photographs of the park, which are hung in each room. Breakfast included.

Hampton Inn HOTEL $$

(Map p94; ☎865-436-4878; www.hamptoninn3.hilton.com; 967 Parkway; r $179-219; ste $239; P ❄ @ ☎ ≋) Yep, it's part of a chain, but the hotel sits in the thick of the action on

Gatlinburg

Sights
1 Anakeesta D2
2 Arrowmont School of Arts & Crafts D2
3 Gatlinburg Scenic Overlook A2
4 Gatlinburg Sky Lift C2
5 Ober Gatlinburg Aerial Tramway B3
6 Ripley's Aquarium of the Smokies D2

Activities, Courses & Tours
7 Gatlinburg Trail B3

Sleeping
8 Bearskin Lodge B3
9 Gatlinburg Inn C2
10 Hampton Inn B3
11 Rocky Waters Motor Inn D1

Eating
12 Crockett's Breakfast Camp B3
13 Pancake Pantry D2
14 Peddler Steakhouse B3

Drinking & Nightlife
15 Ole Smoky Moonshine C2
16 Smoky Mountain Brewery B3
17 Sugarlands Distilling Co C2

Parkway. Decor is modern, and furnishings include an easy chair and ottoman. Rooms with king beds have a fireplace. Ahhh. Breakfast included.

Eating

Gatlinburg dining is mostly high-volume and middlebrow. Pancake restaurants, steakhouses and ye-olde-country-kitchen-style buffets are all big. But if you're emerging from a day of hiking in the park, you'll be happy enough to tuck into a massive plate of greasy ribs. Expect waits at the more popular restaurants during busy season.

★Crockett's Breakfast Camp BREAKFAST **$**
(Map p94; ☎865-325-1403; www.crockettsbreakfastcamp.com; 1103 Parkway; mains $7-15; ⊙7am-1pm) The hearty breakfasts are fit for mountain men – and flip-flop-wearing tourists – at this faux mountain camp, which is named for Tennessee frontiersman Crockett Maples. The mouthwatering menu includes fully loaded three-egg scrambles, chicken-fried steak with sausage gravy, and French toast stuffed with blueberry cream cheese and served with warm maple syrup, whipped cream and powdered sugar. Hungry yet?

Three Jimmys AMERICAN **$**
(☎865-325-1210; www.threejimmys.com; 1359 E Parkway; mains $9-25; ⊙11am-1am; 📶) Escape the tourist hordes on the main drag and grab a bite at this local's favorite with friendly waitstaff ('Here's your menu, baby...') and a long list of everything: barbecue, turkey Reubens, burgers, champagne chicken, steaks, a great spinach salad and so on. Good bar as well, with a dozen-or-so beers on tap.

Pancake Pantry BREAKFAST **$**
(Map p94; ☎865-436-4724; www.pancakepantry.com; 628 Parkway; breakfast mains $7-12, lunch mains $9-11; ⊙7am-4pm Jun-Oct, to 3pm Nov-May; 👪) Gatlinburg has a thing for pancakes, and this is the place that started it all. The Pantry's secret is simple: real butter, honest-to-goodness fresh-whipped cream and everything made from scratch. We recommend the Swedish pancakes, with lashings of lingonberry jam. At times service and food can seem a little tired, but really, can ya' blame 'em? These crowds!

At lunch there are gourmet sandwiches with funny names such as the Polish Aristocrat, which can be ordered ahead for picnics by the waterfalls of Great Smoky.

Peddler Steakhouse STEAK **$$$**
(Map p94; ☎865-436-5794; www.peddlergatlinburg.com; 820 River Rd; mains $23-40; ⊙5-9pm Sun-Fri, 4:30-10pm Sat; 👪) In a large rustic lodge with exposed timbers and native stone fireplaces, this always-packed spot is loved for its dripping hunks of prime rib, grilled mountain trout and American-sized salad bar. Kids meals are priced by the child's age in dollars, making this a popular family spot.

Drinking

Gatlinburg is home to at least one microbrewery, and Parkway is lined with restaurants and bars that are as good for a drink as anything, but the real fun is to be had at the moonshine distilleries such as Ole Smoky Moonshine and nearby Sugarlands Distilling Co (p96).

★Ole Smoky Moonshine DISTILLERY
(Map p94; ☎865-436-6995; www.olesmoky.com; 903 Parkway; tasting $5; ⊙10am-10pm) At first glance this stone-and-wood moonshine distillery – Tennessee's first licensed

MOONSHINE, BOOTLEGGERS AND AL CAPONE

The Smoky Mountains have deep ties to moonshine – also known in these parts as hooch, white lightning and mountain dew. What is moonshine? If you take away the outlaw reputation, moonshine is nothing more than un-aged whiskey, often sourced from corn. It's also a uniquely American spirit, conjuring visions of hidden copper stills, bearded mountain men and wild car chases with revenuers in hot pursuit of Depression-era bootleggers.

The story of moonshine begins well before the Depression, however, tracing back to the Scots-Irish settlers who followed the Great Wagon Road south from Pennsylvania in the mid-1700s. These hardy pioneers built small farms across the valleys and foothills of the Appalachian mountains, settling the region that now comprises Pennsylvania, West Virginia, Virginia, Tennessee and the Carolinas. Many of these families, particularly in the southern Appalachians, distilled spirits for medicinal purposes. And yes, sometimes 'medicine' included whiskey.

Moonshine earned its modern reputation during Prohibition, when the production and consumption of alcohol in the US was banned by Constitutional amendment in 1920. Enforcement, however, was difficult, and illegal whiskey production became a good source of extra income for Appalachian home distillers. To hide the smoke from their stills, the distillers made their corn liquor at night, under the light of the moon, hence the name moonshine. This primitive un-aged whiskey, also called white whiskey, earned a reputation for its rough taste, or burn.

There are rumors that mobster Al Capone spent time in Johnson City, Tennessee, while running moonshine from the Smokies back to Chicago. The city even earned the nickname "Little Chicago."

Although Prohibition was repealed in 1933, moonshining was a good way for families to make extra cash during the Great Depression, which continued across the 1930s. NASCAR racing is a descendant of the wild automobile chases of the era, when Federal agents chased the souped-up cars used by the bootleggers to deliver their product.

For decades, strict alcohol laws prevented the legal production of distilled spirits across much of southern Appalachia. A recent loosening of these laws – plus the popularity of the Discovery Channel show Moonshiners – has spurred a slew of new distilleries to open, and sales of 'legal' moonshine have sky-rocketed. Ole Smoky Moonshine (p95) was the first distillery to open in Tennessee after the state legislature passed a law in 2009 allowing commercial distilling in 41 counties – an increase from only three.

moonshine maker – appears to have a Disney flair, but it's the real deal. Gathering around the hysterical bartenders, sampling eight to 10 flavors of hooch and taking in colorful commentary is Gatlinburg's best time.

There's live bluegrass on the atrium stage as well from noon to 10pm, and it's usually pretty good – look out for Monroeville, a great progressive bluegrass band from Newport, TN, with a Grammy-nominated producer and engineer on lead vocals.

The moonshine category is growing fast, and so is Ole Smoky. A second, larger location recently opened on Parkway. There's another in Pigeon Forge (p91).

Sugarlands Distilling Co DISTILLERY

(Map p94; ☎865-325-1355; www.sugarlands.com; 805 Parkway; tasting $5; ⏰10am-10:30pm Mon-Sat, noon-6:30pm Sun) The TasteMakers at this cavernous new distillery are akin to carnival barkers as they pour 13 different flavors of moonshine, singing their praises while keeping the counter clean, cracking jokes and asking guests about their hometowns. Peruse the astounding range of flavors with a walk past the colorful, moonshine-filled mason jars lining nearby shelves. Apple pie is a favorite.

Distillery tours with tastings are available ($12), plus there's a day-long distillery workshop ($250). For a $6 cocktail, head to the on-site Cocktail Kitchen.

Smoky Mountain Brewery BREWERY
(Map p94; ☎865-436-4200; https://smoky-mtn-brewery.com; 1004 Parkway; ⏰11:30am-1am; 📶) The microbrewed beer (10 on tap), multiple TV sets and raucous ski-lodge atmosphere really packs in the crowds. The American pub grub on the menu – quesadillas, chicken fingers, pizzas, burgers and pasta – is A-OK, but nothing special.

Shopping

Arts & Crafts Community ARTS & CRAFTS
(www.gatlinburgcrafts.com) More than 100 local artisans sell their creations at shops and galleries dotting an 8-mile driving loop east of downtown. Check the website for a list of artists or pick up a brochure around town. Crafts include pottery, woodworking, paintings and photography. The loop follows Glade Rd, Buckhorn Rd and Hwy 321.

Information

Pop into the **Gatlinburg Welcome Center** (☎865-277-8947; www.gatlinburg.com; 1011 Banner Rd; ⏰8:30am-7pm Jun-Oct, to 5:30pm Nov-May) for official information and maps – including a handy $1 waterfalls map – on both Gatlinburg and Great Smoky Mountains National Park.

Getting There & Away

The vast majority of visitors arrive in Gatlinburg by car. The nearest airport is Knoxville's **McGhee Tyson Airport** (p208), 41 miles away. There's no regular intercity bus service.

Getting Around

Traffic and parking are serious issues in Gatlinburg. The **Gatlinburg Trolley** (Map p94; www.gatlinburgtrolley.org; ⏰generally 8:30am-midnight May-Oct, varies rest of year) serves downtown, and the trolley's tan line ($2) goes into the national park between July and October, with stops at Sugarlands Visitor Center, Laurel Falls and Elkmont Campground. Parking lots around town generally charge $10 for the day. If you get to town very early, you may snag free on-street parking on River Rd.

Chattanooga

☎423 / POP 177,571

Chattanooga is one of the country's greenest cities, with electric buses, miles of well-used waterfront trails, and pedestrian bridges crossing the Tennessee River – all of which makes it hard to credit its reputation in the 1960s as America's dirtiest city. With world-class rock climbing, hiking, cycling and water-sports opportunities, it's one of the South's best cities for outdoorsy types. And it's gorgeous now, too: just check out those views from the Bluff View Art District!

The city was a major railway hub throughout the 19th and 20th centuries, hence the 'Chattanooga Choo-Choo,' which was originally a reference to the Cincinnati Southern Railroad's passenger service from Cincinnati to Chattanooga, and later the title of a 1941 Glen Miller tune. The eminently walkable downtown is a maze of historic stone and brick buildings and has some tasty gourmet kitchens, craft breweries and distilleries. There's a lot to love about the 'Noog.

Sights

★**Songbirds** MUSEUM
(Map p98; ☎423-531-2473; www.songbirdsguitars.com; 35 Station St, Chattanooga Choo Choo Hotel; adult/child under 13yr $16/free, all access $39; ⏰10am-6pm Mon-Wed, to 8pm Thu-Sat, noon-6pm Sun) Opened in 2017 this astonishing guitar collection – the world's largest assemblage of vintage and rare guitars – is Chattanooga's newest world-class attraction. Over 500 guitars, many arranged in timeline fashion from the 1950 Fender Broadcasters (the first mass-produced solid-body electric guitar) to the 1970s, grace this small space, including rock-star axes from Chuck Berry, BB King, Bo Diddly, Roy Orbison and Robbie Krieger of the Doors, among others.

Fender and Gibson make up the bulk of the exhibit, though Rickenbacker and Gretch are in here as well. Notable exhibits include prewar Gibson Arch Tops and an impressive collection of '60s surf guitars. The rarest kickers are housed in the Vault – which requires an all-access admission and guided tour – including every custom-colored Gibson Firebird and an extremely rare 1958 Gibson Explorer.

For guitarists and music fans alike, this is the Holy Grail of guitars. Those with limited knowledge of guitars will get the most out of a visit by taking the guided tour and learning the stories behind some of the more notable guitars in the collection.

Chattanooga

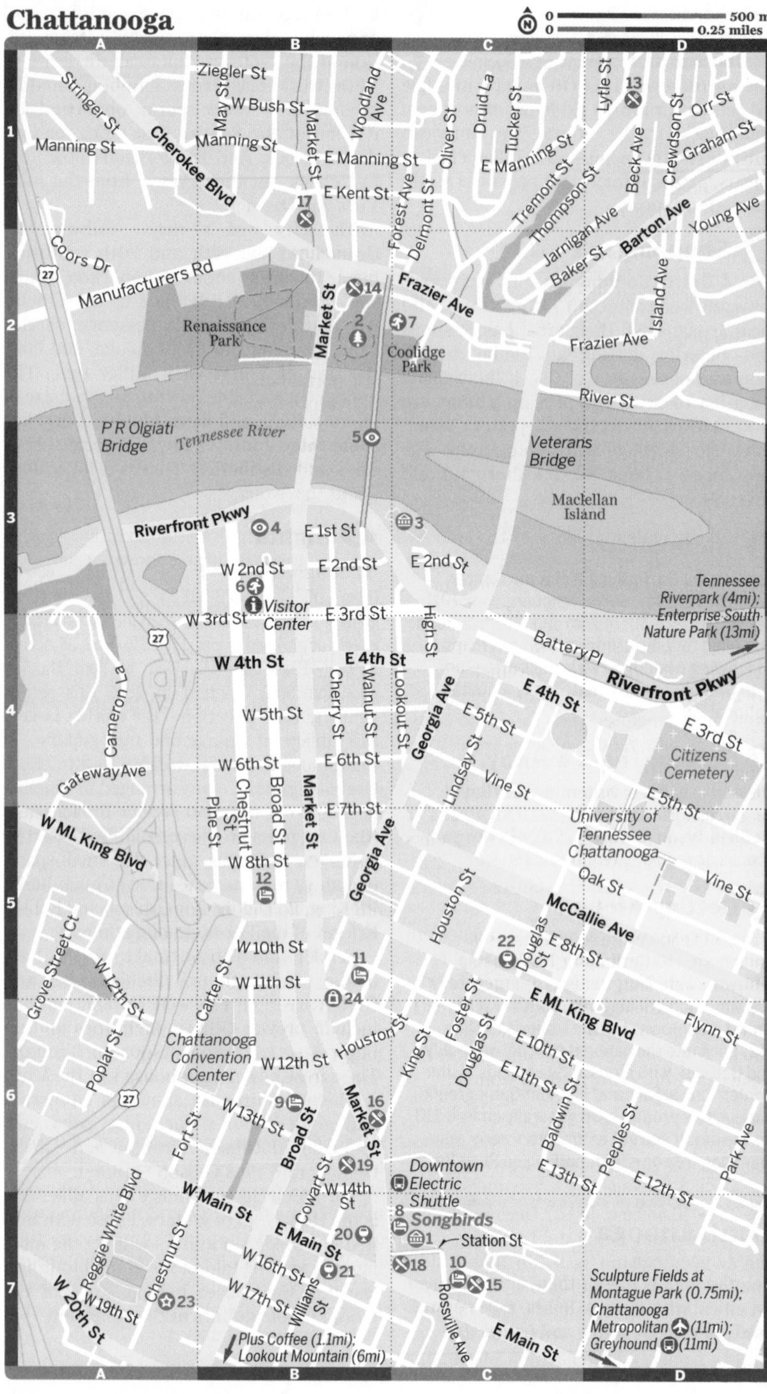

Chattanooga

Top Sights
1 Songbirds ... C7

Sights
2 Coolidge Park ... B2
3 Hunter Museum of American Art ... C3
4 Tennessee Aquarium ... B3
5 Walnut Street Bridge ... B3

Activities, Courses & Tours
6 High Point Climbing ... B3
7 Outdoor Chattanooga ... C2

Sleeping
8 Chattanooga Choo Choo ... C7
9 Chattanoogan ... B6
10 Crash Pad ... C7
11 Dwell Hotel ... B5
12 Read House Hotel ... B5

Eating
13 Aretha Frankenstein's ... D1
14 Clumpies Ice Cream ... B2
15 Flying Squirrel ... C7
16 St John's Meeting Place ... B6
17 Taco Mamacita ... B1
18 Terminal Brewhouse ... C7
19 Urban Stack ... B6

Drinking & Nightlife
20 Chattanooga Whiskey Experimental Distillery ... B7
21 Hi-Fi Clydes ... B7
22 Hutton & Smith Brewing ... C5

Entertainment
23 Signal ... A7

Shopping
24 Warehouse Row ... B5

Check the calendar page of the website for a list of upcoming concerts, which are held on a small stage inside the museum.

Walnut Street Bridge BRIDGE

(Map p98; 1 Walnut St; P) Finished in 1891, this half-mile span carried vehicles from downtown to the North Shore until 1978, when it was closed for safety reasons. In 1993 it was reopened as a pedestrian bridge and park. Since then the bridge has served as a key component in downtown revitalization efforts. The bridge stretches from the Hunter Museum in the Bluff View Arts District downtown to Coolidge Park and nearby shops and restaurants on the North Shore.

A petition was recently launched to change the name of the bridge to the Ed Johnson Memorial Bridge to remember the name of an African American man lynched on the span in 1906. Johnson had been yanked from his jail cell by a mob after being accused of raping a white woman.

Tennessee Aquarium AQUARIUM

(Map p98; 800-262-0695; www.tnaqua.org; 1 Broad St; adult/child 3-12yr $30/19; incl IMAX $38/27; 10am-6pm; P) Occupying two side-by-side but separate buildings, this well-done aquarium is a fun and educational rainy-day destination. The River Journey building spotlights the inhabitants and ecology of the Tennessee River as it flows from the Appalachian Mountains to the Mississippi Delta. Exhibits in the Ocean Journey building showcase salt-water marine life – including piranhas! Crowd-pleasers include the river otters, penguins and lemurs, which swung their way into the aquarium from their island-bound Madagascar habitat in 2017. There's also an IMAX 3D theater on the grounds.

Hunter Museum of American Art GALLERY

(Map p98; 423-267-0968; www.huntermuseum.org; 10 Bluff View; adult/child under 18yr $15/free; 10am-5pm Mon, Tue, Fri & Sat, to 8pm Thu, noon-5pm Wed & Sun; P) Set high on the river bluffs, this striking edifice of melted steel and glass – fronted by an early-20th-century mansion – is easily the most singular architectural achievement in Tennessee. Oh, and its 19th- and 20th-century art collection is fantastic. Permanent exhibits are free the first Thursday of the month between 4pm and 8pm (special exhibits cost $5).

Coolidge Park PARK

(Map p98; www.chattanoogafun.com; 150 River St; P) A good place to start a riverfront stroll. There's a carousel ($1 per ride), well-used playing fields and a 50ft climbing wall attached to one of the columns supporting the Walnut Street Bridge, one of the world's largest pedestrian bridges. The Tennessee Riverpark (p100) greenway rolls through the action along the river.

Abutting the park, the city has installed gabions to restore the wetlands and attract more bird life. Check them out by strolling to the edge of the cool, floating decks that jut over the marsh.

Tennessee Riverpark PARK
(www.hamiltontn.gov/tnriverpark; dawn-dusk; P) A 13-mile, multi-use greenway that runs from downtown through Amincola Marsh and along South Chickamauga Creek. Plans are to expand its reach to a full 22 miles.

Sculpture Fields at Montague Park PARK
(www.sculpturefields.org; 1800 Polk St; dawn-dusk; P) FREE Large-scale sculptures from a global array of artists dot this 33-acre outdoor museum. Open since 2016, the park could benefit from better landscaping and more signage, but it's a pleasant place to stroll on a pretty day, and the art is intriguing.

Activities

Got an outdoor itch you need to scratch? From cycling to hiking to rock climbing, Chattanooga's got you covered. If you prefer your adventures on the water, consider kayaking or stand-up paddleboarding on the Tennessee River. White-water rafting supplies the thrills just east on the wild Ocoee and Nantahala Rivers. Check www.chattanoogafun.com and https://outdoorchattanooga.com for more details about the city's many outdoor opportunities.

★ **Lookout Mountain** OUTDOORS
(800-825-8366; www.lookoutmountain.com; 827 East Brow Rd; adult/child $50/27; hours vary;) Some of Chattanooga's oldest and best-loved attractions are 6 miles outside the city. The combination admission price includes the **Incline Railway**, which chugs up a steep incline to the mountain top; the world's longest underground waterfall, **Ruby Falls**; and **Rock City**, a garden with a dramatic clifftop overlook. You can also purchase a ticket for each of the three attractions individually.

Outdoor Chattanooga OUTDOORS
(Map p98; 423-643-6888; https://outdoorchattanooga.com; 200 River St; 8:30am-5:30pm Mon-Fri) A city-run agency promoting active recreation; the website is a good resource for outdoor information and river and trail suggestions. Check the online events calendar for classes and guided adventures.

While not an outdoor travel outfitter, it does sponsor low-cost canoeing, kayaking, hiking and mountain-biking excursions, as well as outdoor and recreation workshops. Check the website.

Hiking

For an urban stroll, walk the Walnut Street Bridge (p99) to the North Shore then continue along the Tennessee Riverpark. You'll also find trails on Lookout Mountain – in Rock City you'll encounter a few gnomes as you walk toward a lofty viewpoint with a panorama of seven states. Farther afield, Enterprise South Nature Park is home to family-friendly trails that pass historic munitions bunkers. Though it's only open on select days (first and last Saturday December to April, and first and last weekend May through November), the **Lula Lake Land Trust** (www.lulalake.org; $10 per car), offering 6 miles of trails, impresses visitors with scenic cascades and a photogenic punchbowl rock formation around the lake. The **Cumberland Trail** (www.tnstateparks.com), which stretches more than 200 miles along the Cumberland Plateau, passes gorges, waterfalls and hemlock groves. For waterfalls and a historic river trail, drive east to Cherokee National Forest (p104).

Rock Climbing

The city is surrounded by sandstone bluffs well suited for climbing. There are more than 600 climbing routes on the **Tennessee Wall** (www.outdoorchattanooga.com) on the Cumberland Plateau. A popular destination for bouldering is the boulder field at **Stone Fort** (Little Rock City; www.seclimbers.org), located about 13 miles from downtown, with parking and registration at the clubhouse at the Montlake Golf Club.

High Point Climbing CLIMBING
(Map p98; 423-602-7625; www.highpointclimbing.com; 219 Broad St; adult/child under 11yr $17/15; 6am-10pm Mon, Wed, Fri, 10am-10pm Tue, Thu & Sat, 10am-8pm Sun;) With 30,000 sq ft of climbing area, both indoors and outdoors, you won't run out of routes. The facility includes a Kid Zone, bouldering areas, speed zones and a lead-climbing pit. Upping the cool factor? The outdoor area has transparent climbing walls. Classes offered, too.

Road Cycling & Mountain Biking

Cyclists can pedal the 13-mile Riverpark, which tracks the Tennessee River. Bike Chattanooga offers bikes for rent at 38 stations across town. For mountain biking, head to Enterprise South Nature Park. Advanced riders should also check out the singletrack trails at Raccoon Mountain (www.outdoorchattanooga.com).

Enterprise South Nature Park HIKING, MOUNTAIN BIKING
(423-893-3500; www.hamiltontn.gov; 190 Still Hollow Loop; park 7am-7:30pm, vistor center 8am-5pm;) Hiking and mountain-biking trails crisscross this wooded and hilly 2800-acre park about 15 miles northeast of downtown Chattanooga. There are numerous easy cycling trails, making the park a good spot for beginner cyclists and families. The property served as a munitions production facility during WWII and small concrete bunkers eerily dot the park. Bunker 28 is open for exploring. Pick up a free trail map at the visitor center.

Festivals & Events

Chattanooga Nightfall MUSIC
(www.nightfallchattanooga.com; Miller Plaza; May-Aug) A free concert series every Friday.

Sleeping

In addition to the usual suspects, Chattanooga offers some unique sleeping options, including overnighting in a historic railroad sleeper car or at one of the nicest (and greenest) hostels in the world. Modern cabins and breakfast inns also dot the city landscape. Budget chain motels congregate around I-24 and I-75.

★ **Crash Pad** HOSTEL $
(Map p98; 423-648-8393; www.crashpadchattanooga.com; 29 Johnson St; dm, $35, d $85-95, tr $110;) The South's best hostel, run by climbers, is a sustainable den of coolness in Southside, the 'Noog's hippest downtown neighborhood. Co-ed dorms overachieve: built-in lights, power outlets, fans and privacy curtains for each bed. Private rooms feature exposed concrete and bedside tables built into the bed frames. Access throughout is via hi-tech fobs, and linens, padlocks and breakfast supplies are all included.

Up to 95% of the materials were reclaimed from the previous building, and there's solar power to boot. It's the first LEED platinum-certified hostel in the world. Book ahead – it fills with outdoor enthusiasts of all ilks on the weekends. Nice hosts, too.

Chattanoogan HOTEL $$
(Map p98; 423-756-3400; www.chattanoogan hotel.com; 1201 Broad St; r $199-239; ste $269-369;) Newly renovated guest rooms at this luxe property shine with a fresh modern style. The on-site amenities – a day spa and three restaurants – are welcome perks, but our favorite feature is the staff's warm Southern hospitality. In the Southside neighborhood, the hotel is within walking distance of numerous good restaurants, bars and shops.

Dwell Hotel BOUTIQUE HOTEL $$
(Map p98; 423-267-7866; www.thedwellhotel.com; 120 E 10th St; r $225;) It's very hard to improve on excellent, but the former Stone Fort Inn – now the Dwell – has done just that. A new hands-on owner has completely flipped this historic downtown hotel into a design-forward, mid-century modern whirlwind of retro style. The 16 revamped rooms feature painstakingly curated vintage furniture, soothing earth-tone color schemes, rain-style showers and bathtubs.

Each room is unique but all feature exposed brick and hardwood floors – we're partial to the ones with private terraces. The on-site lounge and dining area has an intimate, retro-cool vibe that counts as a current city hot spot. Dubbed the Solarium Cafe (breakfast mains $8 to $14, lunch mains $8 to $12) during the day, it flips into a cocktail bar, Mathilda Midnight (cocktails $9 to $13), in the evening.

Chattanooga Choo Choo HOTEL $$
(Map p98; 423-308-2440; www.choochoo.com; 1400 Market St; r/railcars $159/189;) The city's grand old railway terminal has refocused its mindset from gimmicky train hotel to community entertainment epicenter. Now with 145 newly modernized rooms and 46 authentic Victorian railcar rooms, it remains a kitschy place to sleep, but it's the renovation add-ons that make it a great Southside choice for those who dig being at the center of the action.

A hot new restaurant (Stir), hipster coffeehouse (Frothy Monkey), live music/lounge venue (Track 29/Revelry Room), a comedy club (Comedy Catch), extremely

WORTH A TRIP

JOHNSON CITY & THE TRI-CITIES REGION

Johnson City is more than a catchy reference in Old Crow Medicine Show's popular song *Wagon Wheel*. One of the three municipalities in East Tennessee's Tri-Cities Region – along with Kingsport and Bristol – this former railroad boomtown, now home to Eastern Tennessee State University, is a convenient place to stop for a great meal if you're traveling between Cherokee National Forest and Asheville, NC, on I-26. For a tasty drive-through meal, pull up to the window at **Pal's Sudden Service** (423-854-9536; www.palsweb.com; 3206 Bristol Hwy; burgers $2-5; 6am-10pm Mon-Sat, 7am-10pm Sun; P), a regional fast-food burger chain. Look for the hamburger, hotdog, fries and drink emerging from the turquoise exterior. For a sit-down meal, join locals for a burger and craft beer at **Cootie Brown's** (423-283-4723; www.cootiebrowns.com; 2715 N Roan St; mains $8-22; 11am-10pm; P). **Yee-Haw Brewing** (423-328-9192; www.yeehawbrewing.com; 126 Bufffalo St; 11:30am-9pm Sun-Wed, to midnight Thu-Sat) and **White Duck Taco Shop** (423-328-9193; www.whiteducktacoshop.com; 126 Buffalo St; tacos $4-6; 11:30am-9pm) share space at the old Tweetsie Railroad Depot downtown. If you've brought your bike or your tennis shoes, hop onto the **Tweetsie Trail** (www.tweetsietrail.com; Alabama St at Legion St), a rails-to-trails pathway, for an 8-mile jaunt to Elizabethton. NASCAR fans can drive to the **Bristol Motor Speedway** (423-989-6960; www.bristolmotorspeedway.com; 151 Speedway Blvd, Bristol; adult/senior/child $5/4/3; tours 9am-4pm Mon-Sat year-round, 1-4pm Sun Feb-Oct) to catch a car race and tour 'the world's fastest half-mile.' The speedway is 18 miles north of Johnson City.

cool men's boutique (Refinery 423) and unrivaled vintage guitar museum (p97) have all been added to the complex. Newly pedestrianized Station St, which flanks its northwest side, will now host outdoor events and festivals. The retro Gilded Age bar and stunning grand lobby portico remain, but the future has otherwise arrived for the Choo Choo.

Read House Hotel HISTORIC HOTEL **$$**
(Map p98; 423-266-4121; www.thereadhousehotel.com; 827 Broad St; r $157-166; P) At the time of research, this historic hotel – open continuously since 1872 – was in the middle of a $25-million revamp. The guest rooms that have remained open during construction are very comfortable, if a bit dark, but we hear the new digs will evoke the roaring '20s: grand style with a sense of fun. We suspect the room rates will increase after the remodel, but stay tuned.

Eating

Chattanooga's revitalized downtown is home to quite a few upscale Southern and Modern American kitchens that are worth a visit. Tennessee and Georgia farms help support a vibrant farm-to-table movement in the city. One of the South's most iconic snacks, the MoonPie (two graham crackers stuffed with marshmallow filling and dipped in chocolate), originated in a Chattanooga bakery in 1917.

Urban Stack BURGERS **$**
(Map p98; 423-475-5350; www.urbanstack.com; 12 W 13th St; burgers $7-12; 11am-10pm Sun-Thu, to 11pm Fri & Sat) Perfection? The medium-rare guacamole cheeseburger slathered with a fine chipotle aioli and topped with bacon. And hey, fried chickpeas, why you got to taste so good? Wash it all down with a craft beer and call it a very good day.

Aretha Frankenstein's BREAKFAST **$**
(Map p98; 423-265-7685; www.arethas.com; 518 Tremont St; mains $6-11; 7am-midnight) A skeleton on a skateboard doubles as the chandelier. Old concert posters cover the walls – we see you Sleater Kinney. And you might see old cigarette butts in an ashtray on the porch as you wait. Eww. Still interested? Good. Because the breakfasts are damn good in this cramped cottage of quirk, from three-egg scrambles to the Waffle of Insane Genius. There will be a wait.

Taco Mamacita MEXICAN **$**
(Map p98; 423-648-6262; www.tacomamacita.com; 109 N Market St; tacos $4, mains $10-13; 11am-10pm Sun-Thu, to 11pm Fri & Sat;) This upbeat, longtime favorite keeps 'em coming

in with gourmet tacos, tasty guacamole and an impressive margarita list. The tacos travel the world, coming stuffed with Caribbean jerk chicken, Korean BBQ, gyro-style lamb and shrimp done po'boy style. The slow-cooked beer brisket is always a good idea. Works well for families, too.

Clumpies Ice Cream ICE CREAM $
(Map p98; ☎423-267-5425; www.clumpies.com; 26 Frazier Ave; per scoop about $2.50; ⏰11am-10pm Sun-Thu, to 11pm Fri & Sat; 👪) Spare, welcoming and scooping homemade small-batch ice cream that's oh-so-good. Take your pick of classics such as chocolate and vanilla, or get wild with featured flavors such as burnt sugar brownie, lavender hibiscus or Nutella crunch. Costs 60¢ per ounce. It's near Walnut Street Bridge and Coolidge Park.

Flying Squirrel MODERN AMERICAN $
(Map p98; www.flyingsquirrelbar.com; 55 Johnson St; dishes $8-19; ⏰5pm-midnight Tue-Thu, to 2am Fri & Sat, 10:30am-3pm Sun; 📶) A neighbor to the South's hippest hostel (same owners), Flying Squirrel is at its heart a very cool bar (21 and over only, except for Sunday brunch), but its locally sourced small-plate takes on fusion comfort food make for mighty fine pub grub – pork belly tacos, wild Chilean salmon with baba ghanoush, and chocolate hazel cheesecake, to name a few.

Nineteen taps are devoted to regional craft beer and the cocktails shine as well – try Ms Beauregarde (cucumber-infused gin, creme de violette, lemon and lavender syrup; $9).

Terminal Brewhouse PUB FOOD $
(Map p98; ☎423-752-8090; http://terminalbrewhouse.com; 6 14th St; mains $8-17; ⏰11am-midnight) Looking for a local pint, hearty bar fare and some historic atmosphere? This pub's for you. It's next door to the Chattanooga Choo Choo (p101) hotel.

St John's Meeting Place AMERICAN $$
(Map p98; ☎423-266-4571; www.stjohnsmeetingplace.com; 1274 Market St; mains $14-35; ⏰5-9:30pm Mon-Thu, to 10pm Fri & Sat) The culinary anchor of Chattanooga's Southside is widely considered the city's best night out. It's Johnny Cash black (black granite floor, black-glass chandeliers, black banquettes), lending unorthodox but mod elegance for a foodie habitat. The farm-to-table cuisine features lamb pastrami, pork tenderloin, and nacho burgers with chorizo and pickled jalapeño, tilefish ceviche and so on. Live jazz Thursdays from 6pm to 9pm.

Drinking

Chattanooga is home to several microbreweries, craft-beer pubs and craft-cocktail lounges, many concentrated in the gentrified historic downtown areas of Southside District/Main St and ML King Blvd. The Chattanooga Whiskey Experimental Distillery recently opened across the street from the Choo Choo.

Hi-Fi Clydes BAR
(Map p98; ☎423-362-8335; www.hificlydeschattanooga.com; 122 W Main St; ⏰11am-midnight Sun-Wed, to 1:30am Thu-Sat) The vibe is festive at this corner bar, where you can play ping pong, catch live music on Friday and Saturday nights or just kick it with friends on the couches that anchor the place. The beer list is light on craft brews, but it does serve whiskey sours made with Chattanooga Whiskey and Bloody Marys mixed with moonshine and vodka.

Chattanooga Whiskey Experimental Distillery DISTILLERY
(Map p98; ☎423-760-4333; www.chattanoogawhiskey.com; 1439 Market St; tours $12; ⏰11am-9pm Mon-Wed, to midnight Thu-Sat, noon-7pm Sun) Leading the charge to overturn century-old laws banning the production of whiskey in Chattanooga, the folks behind this new small-batch distillery keep the focus on quality. Tours cover the production and barrel-aging processes and end with a tasting: three spirits and three mini-cocktails. You can stop by in the evening (8pm to midnight Thursday to Saturday) for cocktail service without a tour. A larger production facility recently opened along the riverfront, but no tours are yet offered there.

Hutton & Smith Brewing MICROBREWERY
(Map p98; ☎423-760-3600; www.huttonandsmithbrewing.com; 431 E ML King Blvd; ⏰5-10pm Tue-Thu, noon-midnight Fri & Sat; 📶) 🍃 One of the anchors of the newly hip MLK district, this 20-tap microbrewery ironically added a garage door so that it appears its taproom is housed in a former mechanic's shop (or some such industrial hipster building flip), but alas, it wasn't anything special previously. Nevertheless, the beer – namely the

Good Shist APA, coffee IPA and On-Sight Alt – pleases.

Plus Coffee COFFEE

(☎423-521-2098; www.pluscoffee.co; 3800 St Elmo Ave; ⏰7am-6pm Mon-Fri, 8am-6pm Sat & Sun; 📶) It's easy to drive right by this delightfully minimalist coffeehouse in the up-and-coming neighborhood of St Elmo at the foot of the Incline Railway – the sign disappears a bit into the historic brick building on which it sits. Reclaimed wood tables and vintage furniture dot loft-like space and the menu is simple: brew, pour over and espresso. No need to tip – it actually pays its employees.

☆ Entertainment

Signal LIVE MUSIC

(Map p98; ☎423-498-4700; www.thesignaltn.com; 1810 Chestnut St) Up-and-coming country and indie acts take the stage at this new 1300-person venue. Other than a few cocktail tables in back, it's standing-room only.

Shopping

Warehouse Row MALL

(Map p98; ☎423-267-1127; https://warehouserow.com; 1110 Market St) Restaurants, coffee shops and retailers from big (J. Crew) to small (Onward Reserve) share space in this group of 1800s warehouse buildings.

Information

Located in an outdoor public breezeway beside High Point Climbing, the **visitor center** (Map p98; ☎800-322-3344; www.chattanoogafun.com; 215 Broad St; ⏰10am-5pm) is easy to miss.

Getting There & Away

Chattanooga's modest **airport** (p209) is 9 miles east of the city. The **Greyhound station** (☎423-892-1277; www.greyhound.com; 960 Airport Rd) is just down the road from the airport.

Getting Around

For access to most downtown sites, ride the free **Downtown Electric Shuttle** (Map p98; www.gocarta.org) that plies the center and the North Shore. The visitor center has a route map.

Bike Chattanooga (www.bikechattanooga.com) is Chattanooga's city-sponsored, bicycle-sharing program. Bikes are lined and locked up at 38 stations throughout the city and riders can purchase access passes (starting at $8 for 24 hours) by credit card at any of the station kiosks. Rides under an hour are free.

Cherokee National Forest

Hiding in plain sight along the eastern border of Tennessee, this 650,000-acre national forest is chock-full of outdoor adventures and stunning scenery. Here, white-water rafters careen through class IV rapids on wild rivers, mountain bikers tear through the trees on singletrack trails, and day hikers stop and smell the wildflowers after rock-hopping across burbling streams. As you'll discover, the southern Appalachian Mountains aren't as sleepy as they initially appear. Divided into northern and southern sections, which are separated by Great Smoky Mountains National Park, the forest is home to four ranger districts and 15 recreational zones. The Ocoee District in the southern section is the best known district, impressing visitors with a scenic byway, two vast trail networks and top-tier rafting on the Ocoee River. Across the forest, you'll find waterfalls, wildflowers, picnic areas and scenic overlooks. Many activities are convenient to both eastern Tennessee and western North Carolina.

Sights

North Section & Around

Rhododendron blooms are a pretty sight in June in the Roan Highlands, known for its steep mountains and high-altitude meadows, known as balds.

Roan Mountain State Park STATE PARK

(☎office 423-772-0190, reservations 800-250-8620; http://tnstateparks.com/parks/about/roan-mountain; 1015 Hwy 143, Roan Mountain; ⏰8:30am-4pm; P) FREE This state park encompasses 2006 acres of southern Appalachian forest at the base of 6285ft Roan Mountain. On the top of Roan Mountain, straddling the Tennessee–North Carolina border, are the ruins of the old **Cloudland Hotel** site. The 300-room hotel was built in 1885 by Civil War general John T Wilder.

Legend has it that North Carolinian sheriffs would hang out in the saloon, waiting for drinkers from the Tennessee side to stray across the line, as North Carolina was a dry state back then. There's also a great

HIKING IN THE CHEROKEE NATIONAL FOREST: MARGARETTE FALLS

Start/End Shelton Mission Rd

Duration two hours

Distance 2.7 miles

Difficulty Moderate

Elevation Gain 761ft

Tucked inside the leafy northwestern fringe of Cherokee National Forest, about 12 miles from Greeneville, this waterfall hike might be one of East Tennessee's best half-day adventures. A burbling stream hugs the trail, there's just enough elevation change to make it feel like a workout, and a gorgeous 60ft-high waterfall crashes into a scenic pool at the end. The drawback is the trail's popularity, evidenced by the occasional cigarette butt and empty Bud Light beer can.

The trail starts near an area that was once a busy logging camp. The Pea Vine Railroad carried logs from the forest to Greeneville. From the trailhead, the hike follows a gently ascending forest road. After about a half-mile, you'll come to a a small clearing with an information kiosk. Take the trail to your right and begin climbing. You'll soon take a left at a fork in the trail, about 1200yd ahead. The trail runs parallel to Dry Creek, which burbles photogenically over mossy rocks and downed branches. You'll soon cross the creek on a metal bridge. Up next is a short but very rocky climb, which will slow you down. There's one more stream crossing – you'll be hopping rocks on this one. As you continue, keep an eye out for a large rock formation to your left known as Cathedral Rock. And then, ah, the falls. Named for a local woman who liked to hike to the falls in the 1920s (or so say authorities at the national forest), these striking cascades tumble down a 60ft-high, fan-shaped rock formation into a small pool. There are a few boulders near the base perfect for picnics.

Leashed dogs are allowed on the trail, and you'll likely pass a few dog walkers. You'll also see lots of children darting around. The hike is family-friendly, but watch the kids on the rocks. If you don't trust your balance on rocky climbs, bring a hiking pole.

To reach the trailhead, follow TN 350 south from Greeneville for about 4.5 miles. Cross Hwy 351 and join Greystone Rd. Follow Greystone Rd 1.8 miles to Tabor Rd and turn right. Drive 1.8 miles then turn right onto Shelton Mission Rd. Follow it just over a mile to the parking area.

4.6-mile round-trip hike to **Little Rock Knob** (4918ft) through hardwood forests, with epic clifftop views into Tennessee.

David Crockett Birthplace State Park STATE PARK

(☎423-257-2167; www.tnstateparks.com; 1245 Davy Crockett Park Rd; ⊙museum 8am-noon, 1-4:30pm Mon-Fri, 10am-4:30pm Sat & Sun; P 👪) FREE Mountain men don't leave behind a lot of artifacts, unfortunately, so you won't find any original coonskin caps here, just lots of replicas for sale. Informational displays about the famous frontiersman line the walls – right through someone's office and along the hallway to the bathrooms! Of most interest is the reproduced 1700s cabin and homestead out back beside the pretty Nolichucky River, all in the vicinity of where Crockett was born. The revamped campground has 88 sites (campsites $15 to $35).

South Section

Ocoee Whitewater Center VISITOR CENTER

(☎423-496-0100; www.fs.fed.us/visit/destination/ocoee-whitewater-center; 4400 Hwy 64; day-use per vehicle $3; ⊙Whitewater Center 9am-5pm mid-Mar–mid-Nov, 8:30am-4:40pm Fri-Sun mid-Nov–mid-Mar; grounds sunrise-sunset year-round; P) Site of the canoe and kayak slalom events for the 1996 Summer Olympics, the Ocoee Whitewater Center today doubles as a regional visitor center and a gorgeous place for hiking and cycling. Step inside for maps and outdoor-adventure information or gaze at the Ocoee River from a rocking chair. Out back there's a 1-mile, wheelchair-accessible trail that loops around the boulder-strewn

HIKING IN THE CHEROKEE NATIONAL FOREST: BENTON FALLS

Start/End Chilhowee Recreation Area

Duration two hours

Distance 3 miles round-trip

Difficulty Easy

Elevation Gain 318ft

One of the best waterfall hikes in Cherokee National Forest, this easy adventure in the southern section of the forest starts beside McCamy Lake in Chilhowee Recreation Area. Perched at the end of a 7-mile drive up Forest Road 77 (also known as Oswald Rd), the recreation area is a pretty place to spend the day. There's swimming and fishing in the lake, a campground, restrooms with showers and 25 miles of hiking and mountain-biking trails through the forest. The trails are part of the Chilhowee Trail System, which stretches from the recreation area down Chilhowee Mountain to Parksville Lake.

From the trailhead, the blue-blazed path – also known as Trail No 131 – ribbons past pine trees and hardwoods along a level trail that is also open to mountain bikers. You likely won't have the trail to yourself. The path connects to the Naked Window Loop of the Slickrock Trail and later the Red Leaf Trail. From the Red Leaf Trail junction, you've got about another half-mile to walk.

Anticipation builds as you hear sounds of the creek – hidden behind foliage – rushing toward the falls. At the top of the falls, the trail starts a steep descent on tight switchbacks. Hold onto your kids here; there are lots of roots and rocks. And then Benton Falls appear – a 65ft-high, fan-shaped cascade splashing down layered rocks. There is one rock near the base well suited to a picnic – if you can snag it. It can be a tight squeeze down here when crowded.

On a tragic note, this was the site of a fatal bear attack in 2006 when a black bear attacked a family of three, killing the six-year-old daughter. The bear was euthanized and there have been no problems since. It was also one of only two recorded fatal bear attacks in Tennessee, so odds of harm by a bear are low, but follow all the suggestions on the bear-awareness signs.

There is a $3 day-use fee per vehicle to use the recreation area. Leashed dogs are permitted on the trail. To get to the trailhead, follow Forest Road 77 – part of the **Ocoee Scenic Byway** – 7 miles from Hwy 64 at Parksville Lake. Scenic viewpoints along the way offer photogenic looks at the lake and the Tennessee Valley.

Olympic course. The center anchors the Tanasi Trail System, a 30-mile network of hike-and-cycle trails.

 Activities

There are more than 600 miles of hiking trails crisscrossing the forest. This includes nearly 150 miles of the Appalachian Trail. White-water rafting is an option in both the northern and southern sections of the park. Mountain biking is best on two trail networks in the Ocoee District, in the southern section of the forest.

Hiking

Hundreds of miles of trails are open to hikers. Some of the best day hikes lead to waterfalls. Scenic meadows, called balds, blanket mountain ridges along the Appalachian Trail (AT), which crosses the forest on its run between Georgia and Maine. In the Ocoee District you'll find a network of trails at the Chilhowee Recreation Area and another cluster at the Ocoee Whitewater Center. For solitude head to the Big Frog Mountain Area, home to 35 miles of backcountry trails, including a section of the long-distance Benton MacKaye Trail.

White-water Rafting

A handful of powerful rivers crash through the foothills. Rafting companies guide trips on these rivers in both the north and south sections of the forest. The Nantahala

Outdoor Center (NOC; www.noc.com), which has outposts across eastern Tennessee, western North Carolina and northern Georgia, leads rafting trips on the Ocoee, French Broad and Pigeon Rivers.

In the northern section of Cherokee National Forest, outfitters lead trips down the Pigeon, French Broad and Nolichucky Rivers. Near Gatlinburg and Pigeon Forge, the Pigeon River works well for families looking for a fun half-day on the water, with easy rapids and lots of beautiful scenery. You'll also find family-friendly rapids on the French Broad River, but trips typically start near Asheville, NC. For a wild ride, book a trip on the Nolichucky, which offers a thrilling 8.5-mile run through a steep gorge in the Unaka Mountains. Trips typically start in Erwin, TN.

The Ocoee and Hiwasee Rivers are your best bets for white-water rafting in the southern section of the national forest. Thrill seekers should head directly to the bouncy Ocoee, while families with younger kids may prefer a trip down the low-key Hiwasee. Adventure outfitters for both rivers are generally located within 60 miles of Chattanooga.

Cherokee Rafting RAFTING

(☎800-451-7238; www.cherokeerafting.com; 869 Hwy 64; middle/upper/full river per person $45/45/92; ⏱8:30am-5:30pm Sat & Sun Apr-Aug, additional days vary by trip selected; 👪) Crash through family-friendly rapids on the beloved middle section of the Ocoee River, which bounces through more than 20 class III and IV rapids. Prefer an epic challenge? Ramp it up on the upper section with a plunge through the class III and IV rapids navigated by Olympic paddlers in 1996. Tackling both takes about 6½ hours. Reservations recommended. Children must be at least 12 years old to raft the Ocoee.

Mountain Biking

The best two mountain-biking regions in Cherokee National Forest are in the south section. The **Chilhowee Trail System** stretches from Parksville Lake on the Ocoee River up Chilhowee Mountain to Chilhowee Recreation Area. There are more than 20 miles of trails here, catering to beginners as well as experienced mountain bikers. The Tanasi Trail System is a 30-mile network of trails accessed from the Ocoee Whitewater Center (p105). Pick up a free map of the Tanasi Trails at the Ocoee Whitewater Center. Most trails in both networks are also open to hikers. There is a $3 day-use fee per vehicle at both locations. For more details about the trails in the region, visit www.theblueridgehighlander.com.

Tanasi Trail System HIKING, MOUNTAIN BIKING

(www.fs.usda.gov; off Hwy 64) More than a dozen hiking and mountain-biking trails twist over forested mountains beside the Ocoee River in this trail system in the southern reaches of Cherokee National Forest. Trails range from easy to difficult, and many can be accessed from the Ocoee Whitewater Center (p105), where you can pick up a free trail map.

The 1.7-mile Bear Paw Loop climbs into the woods across from the white-water center, while the adjacent Old Copper Road Trail, a pretty, 4.6-mile out-and-back route, follows a copper-hauling road built by Cherokee laborers in the 1850s.

Scenic Drives

Ocoee Scenic Byway SCENIC DRIVE

(www.fs.usda.gov; Hwy 64 & Forest Rd 77) Prefer wheels to white water? Then check out the mountain-and-river scenery of southeastern Tennessee on this exhilarating 26-mile drive, the first-ever byway in a national forest. Along the way there are there are swimming areas, rocky bluffs and woodsy trails leading to waterfalls. Forest Road 77 passes several scenic viewpoints with bird's-eye views of the river and the Tennessee Valley.

The byway stretches from the western edge of the national forest east along Hwy 64 to Ducktown, with a 7-mile scenic spur up Forest Road 77/Oswald Dome Rd to Chilhowee Recreation Area and the trail to **Benton Falls** (www.fs.usda.gov; Forest Road 77, Chilhowee Recreation Area; day-use fee per vehicle $3).

Sleeping & Eating

North Section & Around

Roan Mountain State Park Lodge LODGE $

(☎800-250-8620; https://tnstateparks.itinio.com/roan-mountain/cabins; 1015 Hwy 143, Roan Mountain; campsites $15-35, cabins $90-160;

year-round, tent camping Apr-Nov; P) Book a campsite or cabin in one of Roan Mountain State Park's most beautiful locations. Cabins have kitchens, full baths and front porches with rocking chairs.

Smokin' Pig BBQ BARBECUE $
(423-638-8227; www.smokinpigbbqtn.com; 708 E Church St, Greenville; mains $4-18; 11am-6pm Mon-Fri, noon-5pm Sat) Go with the pulled pork sandwich with two sides and a drink. It's only $7 and you'll get a delicious sandwich piled high with minced pork BBQ. It will fuel you up just right for a waterfall hike in the nearby Cherokee National Forest (p104).

South Section

Chilhowee Campground CAMPGROUND $
(423-338-3300; www.recreation.gov; Forest Rd 77/Oswald Dome Rd, Chilhowee Recreation Area; campsites $10-20; mid-Apr–early Nov; P) High atop Chilhowee Mountain and just off the Ocoee Scenic Byway, this lovely campground is surrounded by hiking and cycling trails, plus there's a swimming and fishing lake a few steps away. Drinking water, bathrooms and showers are all available.

Information

The **Ocoee Whitewater Center** (p105) is a fantastic source of information for the southern section of the national forest, with maps, brochures and helpful staff. Otherwise, visit the forest service website (www.fs.usda.gov), which provides a fairly helpful overview of activities in Cherokee National Forest and lists contact information for the various ranger district offices.

Getting There & Away

Knoxville's **McGhee Tyson Airport** (p208) is the main gateway to the north section of the park. If you're driving, the north section is flanked by I-81, I-26 and I-40.

The main gateway to the south section of the forest is **Chattanooga Metropolitan Airport** (p209). The junction of I-24 and I-75 is south of the airport. Atlanta is 120 miles southeast of Chattanooga via I-75.

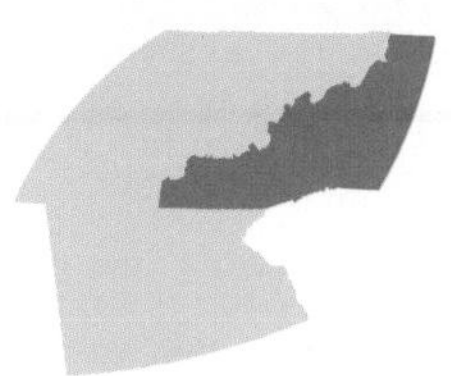

North Carolina Mountains

Includes ➡

Blowing Rock 112
Boone 115
Asheville 117
Cherokee 127
Bryson City 129
Pisgah National Forest 130
Brevard 131
Nantahala National Forest 133

Best Places to Eat

➡ 12 Bones (p122)
➡ Bistro Roca (p114)
➡ Cúrate (p123)
➡ Buxton Hall (p122)

Best Places to Stay

➡ Sweet Peas Hostel (p120)
➡ Everett Hotel (p129)
➡ Lovill House Inn (p116)
➡ Bunn House (p121)

Why Go?

Towering along the skyline of western North Carolina, the mighty Appalachian Mountains hold several distinct subranges, among which the Great Smoky, Blue Ridge, Pisgah and Black Mountain ranges are especially dramatic. Carpeted in blue-green hemlock, pine and oak trees – logged a century ago but now preserved and protected – these cool hills are home to cougars, deer, black bears, wild turkeys and great horned owls. For adventurous travelers, the potential for hiking, camping, climbing and rafting expeditions is all but endless, while yet another photo opportunity lies around every bend.

The Cherokee who hunted on these forested slopes were later joined by 18th-century Scots-Irish immigrants looking for a better life. Lofty towns such as Blowing Rock enticed the sickly, lured by the fresh mountain air. Today, scenic drives, leafy trails and roaring rivers draw visitors from around the world.

When to Go

May is perfect for hiking and biking in the forests and mountains.

Asheville's three-night Mountain Dance & Folk Festival in August showcases the very best traditional music.

October is prime time for fall foliage; the mountains blaze gold, orange and red.

North Carolina Mountains

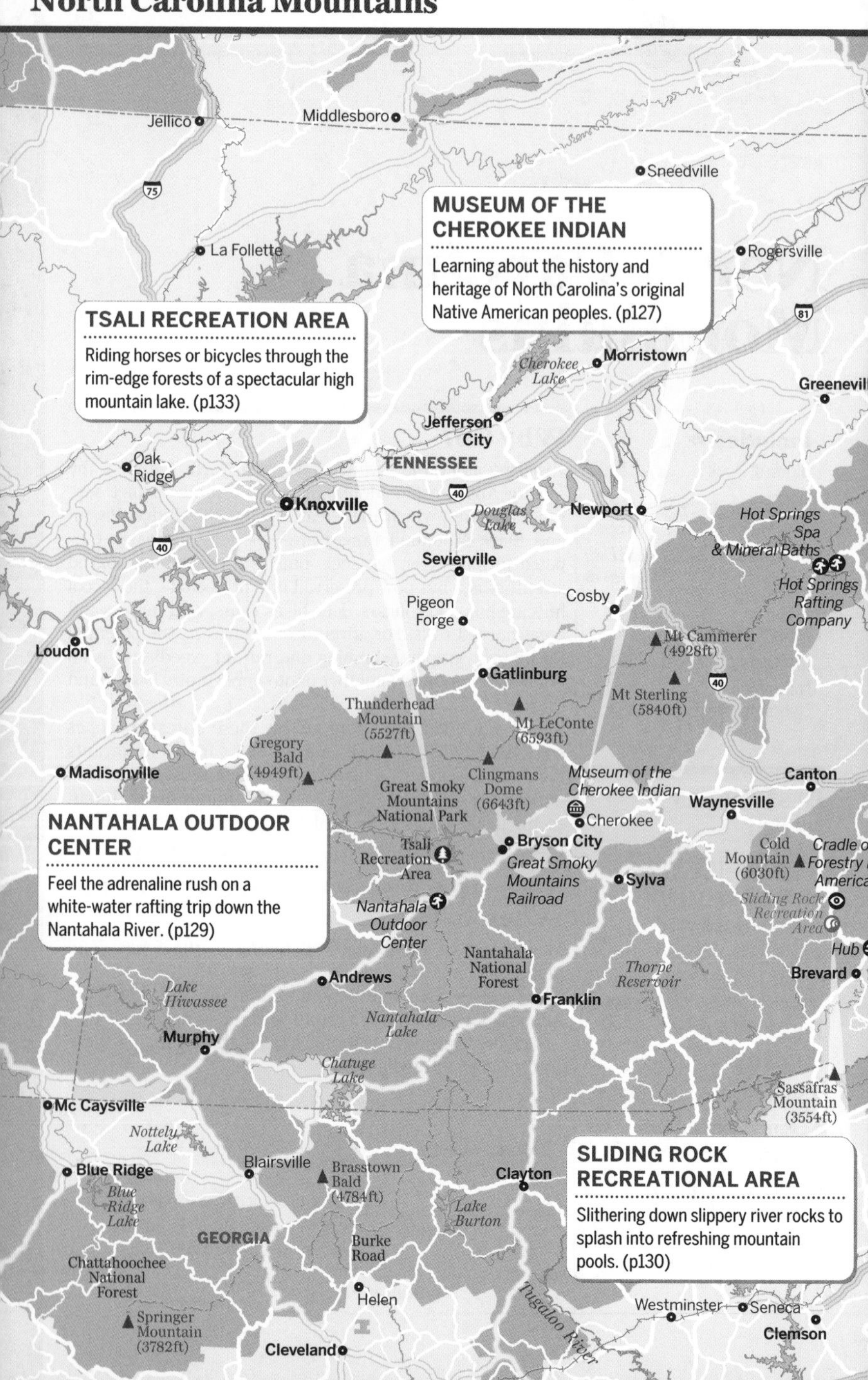

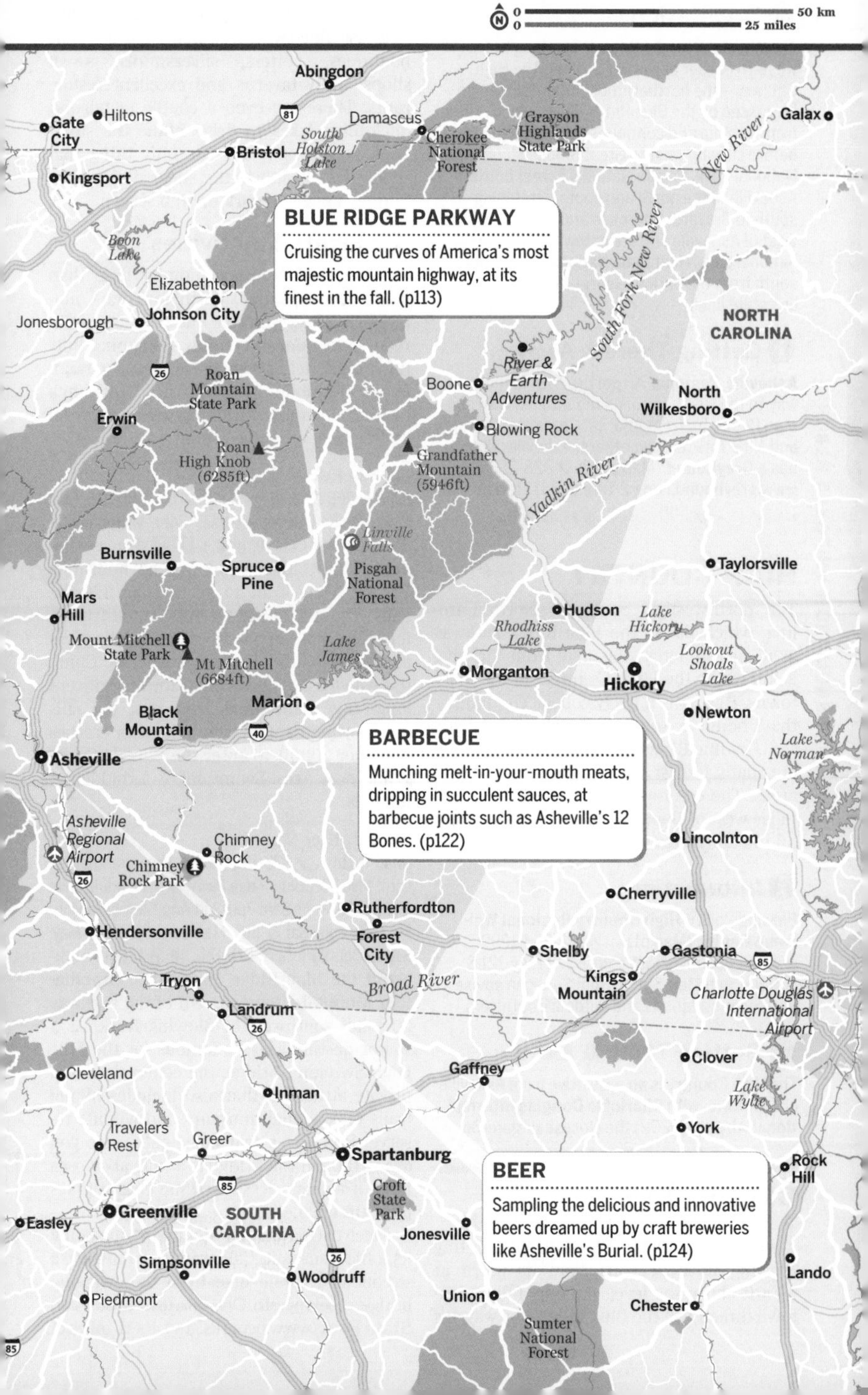

0 — 50 km
0 — 25 miles

BLUE RIDGE PARKWAY

Cruising the curves of America's most majestic mountain highway, at its finest in the fall. (p113)

BARBECUE

Munching melt-in-your-mouth meats, dripping in succulent sauces, at barbecue joints such as Asheville's 12 Bones. (p122)

BEER

Sampling the delicious and innovative beers dreamed up by craft breweries like Asheville's Burial. (p124)

Abingdon
Gate City
Hiltons
Damascus
South Holston Lake
Cherokee National Forest
Grayson Highlands State Park
Galax
New River
Bristol
Kingsport
Boon Lake
South Fork New River
Elizabethton
Johnson City
Jonesborough
NORTH CAROLINA
River & Earth Adventures
Roan Mountain State Park
Boone
North Wilkesboro
Erwin
Blowing Rock
Roan High Knob (6285ft)
Grandfather Mountain (5946ft)
Yadkin River
Linville Falls
Burnsville
Spruce Pine
Pisgah National Forest
Taylorsville
Mars Hill
Hudson
Lake Hickory
Rhodhiss Lake
Mount Mitchell State Park
Mt Mitchell (6684ft)
Lake James
Lookout Shoals Lake
Morganton
Hickory
Black Mountain
Marion
Newton
Asheville
Lake Norman
Asheville Regional Airport
Chimney Rock
Chimney Rock Park
Lincolnton
Cherryville
Rutherfordton
Hendersonville
Forest City
Shelby
Gastonia
Kings Mountain
Tryon
Broad River
Charlotte Douglas International Airport
Landrum
Clover
Cleveland
Gaffney
Lake Wylie
Inman
York
Travelers Rest
Greer
Spartanburg
Rock Hill
Croft State Park
Greenville
SOUTH CAROLINA
Easley
Jonesville
Simpsonville
Woodruff
Lando
Piedmont
Union
Chester
Sumter National Forest

Orientation

The Appalachian Mountains run along the western border of North Carolina. The High Country – the northernmost mountain region – is crossed by the Blue Ridge Pkwy, which rolls in from Virginia and continues south to Asheville before curving west to Great Smoky Mountains National Park. Pisgah National Forest borders Asheville to the north and south, stretching south to Brevard. Cherokee and Bryson City are west of Asheville and are gateway towns to the national park. Nantahala National Forest runs south from the park to Georgia and South Carolina state lines

Getting There & Away

Asheville Regional Airport (p208) is the gateway to the North Carolina mountains, with nonstop flights to/from Atlanta, Charlotte, Chicago and New York, among others. Asheville also has a **Greyhound** (Map p122; ☎828-253-8451; www.greyhound.com; 2 Tunnel Rd) station.

HIGH COUNTRY

The northwestern corner of North Carolina, which flanks the Blue Ridge Parkway as it sets off across the state from Virginia, is known as the High Country. Of the main towns, **Boone** is a lively college community that's home to Appalachian State University (ASU), while **Blowing Rock** and **Banner Elk** are quaint tourist centers near the winter ski areas. The community of **Valle Crucis** is 9 miles west of Boone and home to a wonderful inn and a sprawling outdoor store.

Information

Blowing Rock's **High Country Regional Welcome Center** (Map p114; ☎828-264-1299; www.highcountryhost.com; 6370 Hwy 321 S; ⌚9am-5pm Mon-Sat, to 3pm Sun) can advise on accommodations and outdoors outfitters.

Getting There & Away

The High Country is an easy drive from Asheville or Charlotte, with **Charlotte Douglas International Airport** (p209) the closest air gateway.

Blowing Rock

☎828 / POP 1288

A stately and idyllic mountain village, tiny Blowing Rock beckons from its perch at 4000ft above sea level, the only full-service town directly on the Blue Ridge Parkway. It's easy to be seduced by its postcard-perfect Main St, lined with antique shops, kitschy boutiques, potters, silversmiths, sweet shops, lively taverns and excellent restaurants. There are even a couple of bucolic, duck-filled lakes to drive home the storybook nature of it all. The only thing that spoils the illusion is the sheer difficulty of finding a place to park in high season.

Sights & Activities

Blowing Rock makes a homier base than nearby Boone, 8 miles north, for High Country attractions such as the Tweetsie Railroad, North Carolina's only remaining fully functional steam-engine train, and Grandfather Mountain. As you drive in, pick up a historic downtown walking-tour map from the regional welcome center.

Linville Falls WATERFALL

(☎828-765-1045; www.nps.gov/blri; Mile 316, Blue Ridge Pkwy, Linville; ⌚trails 24hr, visitor center 9am-5pm Apr-Oct; P 👪 🐾) FREE For a wonderful short hike, head up the hour-long Erwin's View Trail to spectacular Linville Falls. This moderate 1.6-mile round-trip offers great close-up views of the Linville River as it sweeps over two separate falls. Climb the wooded hillside beyond for magnificent long-range panoramas back over the falls and, downstream, to where the river crashes a further 2000ft to enter the Linville Gorge Wilderness Area. Swimming is forbidden at the falls.

Grandfather Mountain MOUNTAIN

(Map p114; ☎828-733-4337; www.grandfather.com; Mile 305, Blue Ridge Pkwy, Linville; adult/child 4-12yr $20/9; ⌚8am-7pm Jun-Aug, 9am-5pm Mon-Fri, 9am-6pm Sat & Sun Mar, 9am-6pm Apr, May, Sep & Oct, 9am-5pm Nov-Feb; P 👪) The highest of the Blue Ridge Mountains, Grandfather Mountain, looms north of the parkway 20 miles southwest of Blowing Rock. As a visitor destination, it's famous for the Mile High Swinging Bridge, the centerpiece of a private attraction that also includes hiking trails plus a small museum and wildlife reserve. Don't let a fear of heights scare you away; though the bridge is a mile above sea level, it spans a less fearsome chasm that's just 80ft deep.

Much of Grandfather Mountain – including its loftiest summit, Calloway Peak (5946ft), a strenuous 2.4-mile hike from the swinging bridge – belongs to **Grandfather Mountain State Park** (www.ncparks.gov). Its 12 miles of

DON'T MISS

BLUE RIDGE PARKWAY

You won't find a single stoplight or billboard along the entire Blue Ridge Pkwy, which traverses the southern Appalachians from Virginia's Shenandoah National Park at Mile 0 to North Carolina's Great Smoky Mountains National Park at Mile 469.

Commissioned by President Franklin D Roosevelt as a Great Depression–era public-works project, it's one of America's classic drives. North Carolina's piece of the parkway sweeps and swoops for 262 sinuous miles of sublime mountain vistas. The fall colors, at their finest in October, are out of this world.

The **National Park Service** (☎828-348-3400; www.nps.gov/blri; Mile 384; ⊙9am-5pm) runs campgrounds and visitor centers. Note that restrooms and gas stations are few and far between, and the speed limit never rises above 45mph. For more details about stops, visit www.blueridgeparkway.org.

Parkway highlights and campgrounds include the following, from the Virginia border south:

Cumberland Knob (Mile 217.5) NPS visitor center; easy walk to the knob.

Doughton Park (Mile 241.1) Trails and camping.

Blowing Rock (Mile 291.8) Small town named for a craggy, commercialized cliff that offers great views, occasional updrafts and a Native American love story.

Moses H Cone Memorial Park (Mile 294.1) A lovely old estate with carriage trails and a craft shop.

Julian Price Memorial Park (Mile 296.9) Camping.

Grandfather Mountain (Mile 305.1) Hugely popular for its mile-high pedestrian 'swinging bridge.' Also has a nature center and a small wildlife reserve.

Linville Falls (Mile 316.4) Short hiking trails to stunning falls; campsites.

Little Switzerland (Mile 334) Old-style mountain resort.

Mt Mitchell State Park (Mile 355.5) Highest peak east of the Mississippi (6684ft); hiking and camping.

Craggy Gardens (Mile 364) Hiking trails explode with rhododendron blossoms in summer.

Folk Art Center (Mile 382) High-end Appalachian crafts for sale.

Blue Ridge Parkway Visitor Center (Mile 384) Inspiring film, interactive map, trail information.

Mt Pisgah (Mile 408.8) Hiking, camping, restaurant, inn.

Graveyard Fields (Mile 418) Short hiking trails to waterfalls.

wilderness hiking trails can also be accessed for free at Mile 300 on the parkway.

Tweetsie Railroad AMUSEMENT PARK
(Map p114; ☎828-264-9061; www.tweetsie.com; 300 Tweetsie Railroad Lane; adult/child 3-12yr $45/30; ⊙9am-6pm Jun-late Aug, Fri-Sun mid-Apr–May, late Aug-Oct; 👪) At this much-loved Wild West–themed amusement park, a 1917 coal-fired steam train chugs on a 3-mile loop past heroic cowboys and marauding Indians.

River & Earth Adventures ADVENTURE
(☎828-355-9797; www.raftcavehike.com; 6201 Castle Ford Rd, Todd; half-/full-day rafting $60/100; 👪) Eco-conscious operators offering everything from family-friendly caving trips to rafting class V rapids at Watauga Gorge – plus organic lunches! Canoe ($65), kayak ($35 to $65) and tube ($20) rentals are offered too.

Sleeping

Historic hotels and inns are dotted around the picturesque village, many with expansive mountain views.

Cliff Dwellers Inn MOTEL $
(Map p114; ☎828-414-9596; www.cliffdwellers.com; 116 Lakeview Terrace; r/apt from $124/144; ❄📶🐾) From its perch above town, this aptly named motel entices guests with good service, reasonable prices, stylish rooms and balconies with sweeping vistas.

High Country

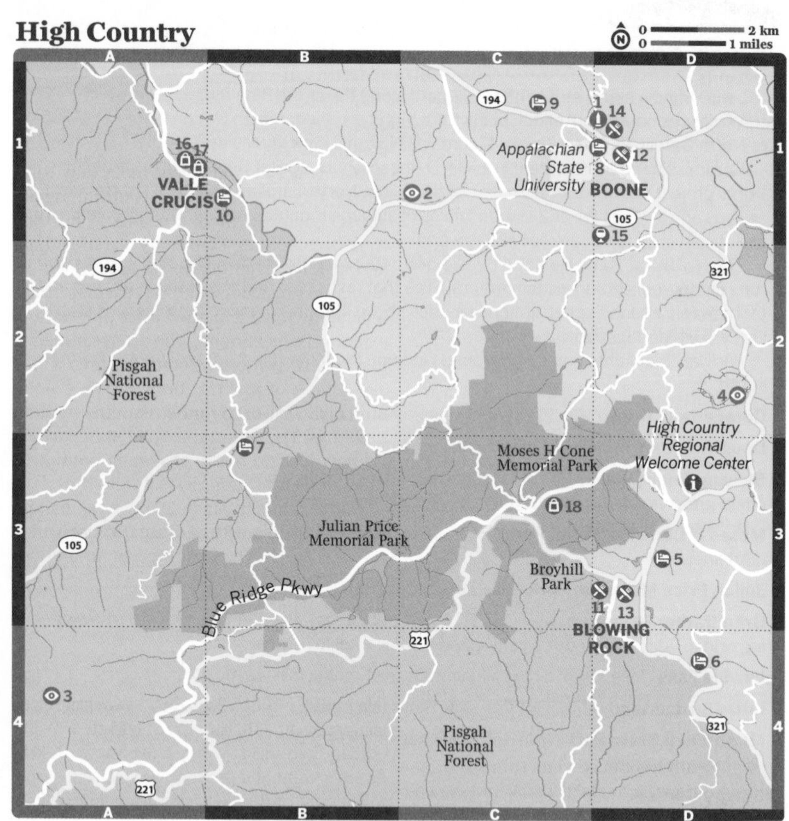

Green Park Inn HISTORIC HOTEL **$$**
(Map p114; ☎828-414-9230; www.greenparkinn.com; 9239 Valley Blvd; r $94-299; P❄📶🐾) This grand white clapboard hotel, 1 mile south of downtown, opened its doors in 1891, and was renovated in 2010 to hold 88 plush rooms and a grill restaurant. The eastern continental divide runs straight through the bar, and Margaret Mitchell stayed here while writing *Gone with the Wind*.

Eating & Drinking

★**Bistro Roca** AMERICAN **$$**
(Map p114; ☎828-295-4008; www.bistroroca.com; 143 Wonderland Trail; lunch mains $9-16, dinner mains $10-32; ⊙11am-3pm & 5-10pm Wed-Mon; 📶) This cozy, lodge-like bistro, in a Prohibition-era building just off Main St, serves upscale New American cuisine – lobster or pork-belly mac and cheese, kicked-up habanero burgers, mountain-trout *banh mi* sandwiches – with an emphasis on local everything. Check out the walls of the atmospheric Antlers Bar, North Carolina's longest continually operating bar, plastered with fantastic B&W pet photos.

Savannah's Oyster House SEAFOOD **$$**
(Map p114; ☎828-414-9354; www.savannahoysterhouse.com; 155 Sunset Dr; mains $10-32; ⊙11am-9pm Tue-Thu & Sun, to 10pm Fri & Sat; 📶) Get over the weirdness of finding a Low Country seafood place in the High Country – let alone the giant shark hanging in the stairwell – and there's much to like about this little cottage restaurant. There's the oysters, obviously, but also the sumptuous, cheesy shrimp 'n' grits, and the varied menu of seafood boils, fish 'n' chips and lobster potpie.

Blowing Rock Ale House MICROBREWERY
(Map p114; ☎828-414-9254; www.blowingrockbrewing.com; 152 Sunset Dr; ⊙11:30am-9pm Mon, Tue & Thu, to 10pm Fri & Sat, noon-9pm Sun; 📶) Blowing Rock's first craft brewery offers 12

High Country

Sights

1 Doc Watson Statue D1
2 Foggy Mountain Gem Mine C1
3 Grandfather Mountain A4
4 Tweetsie Railroad D2

Sleeping

5 Cliff Dwellers Inn D3
6 Green Park Inn D4
7 Hidden Valley Motel B3
8 Horton Hotel D1
9 Lovill House Inn C1
10 Mast Farm Inn B1

Eating

11 Bistro Roca D3
12 Dan'l Boone Inn D1
Melanie's Food Fantasy .... (see 1)
13 Savannah's Oyster House D3
14 Wild Craft Eatery D1

Drinking & Nightlife

Blowing Rock Ale House .... (see 13)
15 Cardinal D1

Shopping

16 Original Mast General Store A1
17 Original Mast General Store Annex A1
18 Parkway Craft Center C3

taps of locally produced suds (pints $5), including a popular pilsner, DIPA and chocolate porter, in a 1940s lodge house. There's food as well as five rooms upstairs ($175), so you don't have to stumble far – though those stairs could be tricky!

Shopping

Parkway Craft Center ARTS & CRAFTS
(Map p114; 828-295-7938; www.southernhighlandguild.org; Mile 294, Blue Ridge Pkwy, Moses H Cone Memorial Park; 9am-5pm mid-Mar–Nov) The Parkway Craft Center, where the Southern Highland Craft Guild sells superb crafts, is housed in a 1901 Colonial Revival mansion that's directly accessible from the parkway and also holds a small museum. The former home of Moses H Cone, who made his fortune in denim, it surveys an estate where hikers and equestrians share 25 miles of carriage roads.

Getting There & Away

Blowing Rock is 8 miles south of Boone via Hwy 321, or more like 25 miles if you detour along the Blue Ridge Parkway. The nearest commercial airport is **Charlotte Douglas International Airport** (p209), 87 miles southeast.

Boone

828 / POP 18,834

Boone is a fun and lively mountain town where the predominantly youthful inhabitants – many of them students at bustling Appalachian State University – share a hankering for the outdoors. Renowned for its bluegrass musicians and Appalachian storytellers, the town is named after pioneer and explorer Daniel Boone, who often camped in the area. Downtown Boone features a fine assortment of low-rise brick-broad, Colonial Revival, art-deco and streamline-modern buildings. Those that line King St in particular now tend to house charming boutiques, cafes, and crafts galleries.

Every summer since 1952, local history has been presented in a dramatization called *Horn in the West,* performed in an outdoor amphitheater above town.

Sights

Foggy Mountain Gem Mine MINE
(Map p114; 828-963-4367; www.foggymountaingems.com; 4416 Hwy 105 S; buckets $30-325; 10am-5pm;) If you're traveling with kids or are a wannabe prospector yourself, stop 3 miles west of Boone to pan for semiprecious stones. Several gem-mining spots are located near the parkway, but this is a smaller operation, run by graduate gemologists who take their craft seriously. Buy rough stones by the bucketload – or even wheelbarrow-load! – and sift them in a flume line.For additional fees, they'll cut and mount your favorite finds.

Doc Watson Statue STATUE
(Map p114; 642 W King St) Bluegrass legend Doc Watson was born 10 miles east of Boone in 1923. He's commemorated by this bronze statue downtown, which depicts him seated and strumming his guitar.

Festivals & Events

Merlefest MUSIC
(www.merlefest.org; 1328 S Collegiate Dr, Wilkesboro; Apr) One of the South's premiere music festivals, this annual event created by Doc Watson has been showcasing the best in bluegrass, folk and Americana since 1988.

Appalachian Summer Festival PERFORMING ARTS
(www.appsummer.org; ⌚ Jul-early Aug) This prestigious month-long arts showcase, staged by Boone's Appalachian State University, uses venues all over campus, and centers on the Schaefer Center for the Performing Arts. Originally rooted in classical music, it now extends across theater, film and the visual arts.

Sleeping

Accommodations in Boone traditionally consisted of standard chain hotels, but the Horton, downtown's first boutique hotel, opened in 2018. You can also find the occasional historic B&B, rental farmhouse or cozy log cabin around town and in the surrounding countryside.

Hidden Valley Motel MOTEL $
(Map p114; ☎828-963-4372; www.hiddenvalleymotel.com; 8725 Hwy 105 S; r from $62; P 📶) A quintessential mom-n-pop motel, set in delightful flower-filled gardens 8 miles southwest of town. The main house is bursting with vintage charm, while the eight guest rooms are cozy but plainer.

Lovill House Inn B&B $$
(Map p114; ☎828-264-4204; www.lovillhouseinn.com; 404 Old Bristol Rd; r from $179; 📶) Boone's finest B&B is a splendid 19th-century farmhouse, a mile west of downtown and surrounded by woods. With its snug rooms, white clapboard walls, and wraparound porch decked out with rocking chairs, it's all wonderfully restful; the breakfast is worth getting up for, though.

Mast Farm Inn B&B $$
(Map p114; ☎828-963-5857; www.themastfarminn.com; 2543 Broadstone Rd, Valle Crucis; r/cottage from $169/299; P ❄ 📶) Featuring worn hardwood floors, claw-foot tubs, and handmade toffees on your bedside table, this restored farmhouse in the beautiful hamlet of Valle Crucis epitomizes rustic chic. Nine cabins and cottages are also available. Settle into the 1806 Loom House log cabin, fire up the wood-burning fireplace and never leave.

As well as breakfast, rates include an evening happy hour with local cheeses and sweets.

Horton Hotel BOUTIQUE HOTEL $$
(Map p114; ☎828-832-8060; www.thehorton.com; 611 W King St; r from $189; ❄ 📶) The 2018 opening of this ultra-central 15-room boutique hotel, in what was once a Studebaker showroom, adds a welcome dash of contemporary style to Boone's lodging options. Its open-air rooftop is a wonderful vantage point overlooking downtown. Check out the website for updated pricing and room information.

Eating

Thanks largely to its many students, Boone holds the High Country's biggest concentration of restaurants. There's plenty of choice, ranging from Southern US to Latin American.

Wild Craft Eatery LATIN AMERICAN $
(Map p114; ☎828-262-5000; www.wildcrafteatery.com; 506 W King St; mains $11-14; ⌚ 11am-10pm Tue-Sun; 🌿) Colorful, quirky downtown cafe, with an outdoor deck on King St, and an emphasis on local ingredients. There's a definite Latin flavor to the menu, with tacos and tamales aplenty, but they also offer Thai noodles and shepherd's pie. Not everything's vegetarian, but most of the standout dishes are, including the Cuzco Cakes, made with smoked quinoa, Gouda and yams.

Melanie's Food Fantasy CAFE $
(Map p114; ☎828-263-0300; www.melaniesfoodfantasy.com; 664 W King St; breakfast mains $6-13, lunch & dinner mains $9-18; ⌚ 8:30am-2pm Sun-Wed, to 9pm Thu-Sat; 🌿) Students and hippie types gather at this farm-to-fork favorite – out on the patio, for much of the year – to gobble serious breakfast dishes (scrambles, eggs Benedict, omelets, pancakes) with a side of home fries. Later on, there's excellent creative Southern cuisine (chipotle-honey salmon and grits, blackened pimiento-cheese burger), with vegetarian options always available (tempeh, soysage etc).

Dan'l Boone Inn SOUTHERN US $$
(Map p114; ☎828-264-8657; www.danlbooneinn.com; 130 Hardin St; breakfast adult $12, child $5-9, lunch & dinner adult $19, child $6-12; ⌚ 11:30am-8:30pm Mon-Thu, from 8am Fri-Sun, dinner only Sat & Sun Nov-May; 📶 👪) Quantity is the name of the game at this restaurant, where the family-style meals are a Boone (sorry) for hungry hikers. Everyone pays the same price, and you can eat as much fried chicken and steak (lunch and dinner) or ham, sausage and bacon (breakfast) as you like. No credit cards.

Drinking

What with Boone being a university town, watering holes are not in short supply, including cheap student dives, microbreweries and mountain saloons.

WORTH A TRIP

MT MITCHELL STATE PARK

A major decision awaits visitors to North Carolina's original **state park** (828-675-4611; www.ncparks.gov; 2388 Hwy 128; park 7am-10pm May-Aug, closes earlier Sep-Apr, office 8am-5pm Apr-Oct, closed Sat & Sun Nov-Mar; P) FREE. Will you drive up Mt Mitchell, at 6684ft the highest peak east of the Mississippi, or will you hike to the top? Make your mind up at the park office, which sits beside a steep 2.2-mile summit trail that typically takes around 1½ hours, one way.

Once up there, you'll see the grave of University of North Carolina professor Elisha Mitchell. He came here in 1857 to prove his previous estimate of the mountain's height, only to fall from a waterfall and die. A circular ramp leads to dramatic views over and beyond the surrounding Black Mountains.

Mt Mitchell State Park is 30 miles northeast of Asheville via the Blue Ridge Pkwy. The entrance is at Blue Ridge Pkwy mile marker 355.5.

Cardinal CRAFT BEER
(Map p114; 828-366-9600; www.thecardinalboone.com; 1711 Hwy 105; 11am-midnight Mon-Thu, to 2am Fri & Sat, noon-midnight Sun;) Locals hunker down in this cozy, barn-like space, 2 miles south of downtown, for Boone's best range of local and regional craft beer (pints $5) – 12 taps in all, as well as $10 craft cocktails. You can also enjoy excellent farm-driven burgers (beef, beet, bison, or game) and pinball or Skee-Ball.

Shopping

Original Mast General Store SPORTS & OUTDOORS
(Map p114; 828-963-6511; www.mastgeneralstore.com; 3565 Hwy 194 S, Valle Crucis; 7am-6:30pm Mon-Sat, noon-6pm Sun;) The first of the many Mast general stores that dot the High Country, this rambling clapboard building still sells many of the same products that it did back in 1883. As well as bacon, axes and hard candy, though, you'll now find hiking shoes, lava lamps and French country hand towels.

Original Mast General Store Annex SPORTS & OUTDOORS
(Map p114; www.mastgeneralstore.com; Hwy 194, Valle Crucis; 10am-6pm Mon-Sat, from noon Sun) The nearby Mast General Store took over this former rival way back when, and now stocks it with outdoor apparel, hiking gear and a whole lot of candy.

Getting There & Away

The closest commercial airport to Boone is **Charlotte Douglas International Airport** (p209), 94 miles southeast.

ASHEVILLE

828 / POP 89,121

The undisputed 'capital' of the North Carolina mountains, Asheville is both a major tourist destination and one of the coolest small cities in the South. Cradled in a sweeping curve of the Blue Ridge Parkway, it offers easy access to outdoor adventures of all kinds, while downtown's historic art deco buildings hold stylish New Southern restaurants, decadent chocolate shops, and the homegrown microbreweries that explain the nickname 'Beer City.'

Despite rapid gentrification, Asheville remains recognizably an overgrown mountain town that holds tight to its traditional roots. It's also a rare liberal enclave in the conservative countryside, home to a sizable population of artists and hard-core hippies. Alternative Asheville life is largely lived in neighborhoods such as the waterfront River Arts District and, across the French Broad River, West Asheville. Remarkably enough, the French Broad River is the world's third-oldest river, its course laid before life on Earth even began.

Sights

Downtown Asheville, which still looks much as it must have in the 1930s, is compact and easy to negotiate on foot. Apart perhaps from its breweries, the city's best-known attraction is the grandiose Biltmore Estate, the largest privately owned home in the country. It luxuriates across a vast green expanse that stretches from Biltmore Village, 2.4 miles south of downtown.

Biltmore Estate HOUSE
(Map p122; 800-411-3812; www.biltmore.com; 1 Approach Rd; adult/child 10-16yr $75/37.50;

Asheville

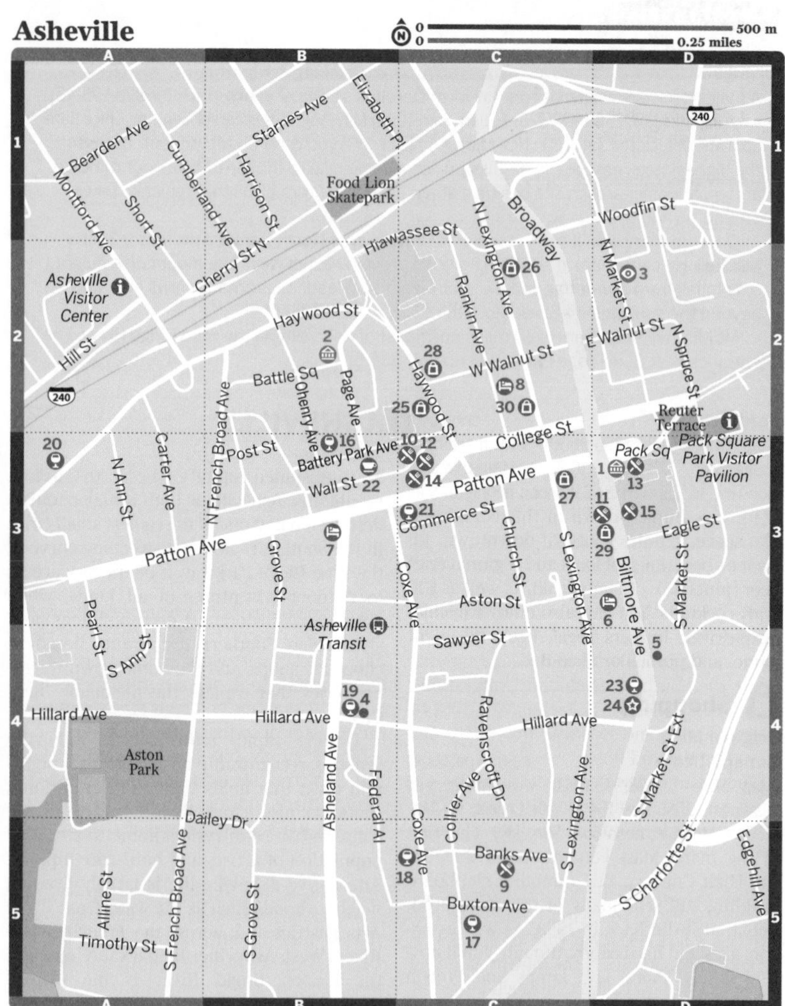

house 9am-4:30pm, with seasonal variations; P) The largest privately owned home in the US, Biltmore House was completed in 1895 for shipping and railroad heir George Washington Vanderbilt II, and modeled after three châteaux that he'd seen in France's Loire Valley. It's extraordinarily expensive to visit, but there's a lot to see; allow several hours to explore the entire 8000-acre estate. Self-guided tours of the house itself take in 39 points of interest, including our favorite, the two-lane bowling alley.

To hear the full story, pay $11 extra for an audio tour, or take the behind-the-scenes Upstairs Downstairs Tour ($20) or the more architecturally focused Rooftop Tour ($20). A 5-mile drive through the impeccably manicured estate, which also holds several cafes and two top-end hotels, leads to the winery and dairy farm in Antler Hill Village.

Folk Art Center CULTURAL CENTER

(Map p122; 828-298-7928; www.southernhighlandguild.org; Mile 382, Blue Ridge Pkwy; 9am-6pm Apr-Dec, to 5pm Jan-Mar; P) FREE Part gallery, part store, and wholly dedicated to Southern craftsmanship, the superb Folk Art Center stands directly off the Blue Ridge

Asheville

Sights

1 Asheville Art Museum D3
2 Asheville Pinball Museum B2
3 Thomas Wolfe Memorial D2

Activities, Courses & Tours

4 BREW-ed B4
5 Lazoom Tours D4

Sleeping

6 Aloft Asheville Downtown D3
7 Downtown Inn & Suites B3
8 Sweet Peas Hostel C2

Eating

9 Buxton Hall C5
10 Chai Pani C3
11 Cúrate D3
12 Early Girl Eatery C3
13 French Broad Chocolate Lounge D3
14 Tupelo Honey C3
15 White Duck Taco Shop D3

Drinking & Nightlife

16 Battery Park Book Exchange & Champagne Bar B3
17 Burial C5
18 Funkatorium C5
19 Hi-Wire B4
20 O. Henry's A3
21 Thirsty Monk C3
22 Trade & Lore B3
23 Wicked Weed D4

Entertainment

24 Orange Peel D4

Shopping

25 Chocolate Fetish C2
26 East Fork Pottery C2
27 Horse & Hero C3
28 Malaprop's Bookstore & Cafe C2
29 Mast General Store D3
30 Tops for Shoes C2

Pkwy, 6 miles east of downtown Asheville. Handcrafted Appalachian chairs hanging above its lobby make an impressive appetizer for the Southern Highland Craft Guild's permanent collection, a treasury of pottery, baskets, quilts and woodcarvings that's displayed on the 2nd floor.

There are daily demonstrations by experts, and the Allanstand Craft Shop on the 1st floor sells high-quality traditional crafts.

Asheville Pinball Museum MUSEUM

(Map p118; ☎828-776-5671; http://ashevillepinball.com; 1 Battle Sq; adult/child 5-10yr $15/12; ⌚1-6pm Mon & Sun, 2-9pm Wed-Fri, noon-9pm Sat) A veritable time machine, this downtown treat transports gamers back to the much-lamented pinball arcades of yesteryear. With stock ranging from vintage cowboy-and-Indian games up to brand-new Game of Thrones editions, something is certain to flip your flippers. Your admission fee covers unlimited plays, though you may have to wait your turn on popular machines.

Chimney Rock Park PARK

(☎800-277-9611; www.chimneyrockpark.com; Hwy 74A; adult/child 5-15yr $13/6; ⌚8:30am-7pm mid-Mar–Oct, 8:30am-6pm Nov, 10am-6pm Dec, 10am-6pm Fri-Tue Jan–mid-Mar; P) The stupendous 315ft monolith known as Chimney Rock towers above the slender, forested valley of the Rocky Broad River, a gorgeous 28-mile drive southeast of Asheville. Protruding in naked splendor from soaring granite walls, its flat top bears the fluttering American flag. Climb there via the 499 steps of the Outcropping Trail, or, assuming it's been repaired by the time you read this, simply ride the elevator deep inside the rock.

The leisurely but less crowded Hickory Nut Falls Trail leads through lush woods for around three quarters of a mile to reach the foot of a 404ft waterfall, high above the river.

Asheville Art Museum MUSEUM

(Map p118; ☎828-253-3227; www.ashevilleart.org; 2 S Pack Sq; ⌚closed for refurbishment) Asheville is waiting with bated breath for the 2019 reopening of its art museum. A huge construction project has been transforming and expanding its Pack Sq home to double the space available for its permanent collection and short-term special exhibitions.

Thomas Wolfe Memorial HOUSE

(Map p118; ☎828-253-8304; www.wolfememorial.com; 52 N Market St; museum free, house tour adult/child 7-17yr $5/2; ⌚9am-5pm Tue-Sat) An incongruous survivor of old Asheville, this downtown clapboard structure was the childhood home of *Look Homeward, Angel* author Thomas Wolfe (1900–38). His autobiographical 1929 novel so offended locals that he didn't return to Asheville (which he fictionalized as 'Altamont') for eight years. Hourly tours, on the half-hour, enter the house itself.

Activities

Smoky Mountain Adventure Center OUTDOORS

(Map p122; ☎828-505-4446; www.smacasheville.com; 173 Amboy Rd; ⊙8am-8pm Mon, to 10pm Tue-Sat, 10am-8pm Sun) One-stop adventure shopping, across the French Broad River 3 miles southwest of downtown. On-site there's an indoor climbing wall, as well as yoga and tai chi classes. They can also arrange bikes for the Blue Ridge Parkway, inner-tubes and paddleboards for the river, plus guided rock climbing, backpacking, day hiking, ice climbing and mountaineering trips.

Tours

BREW-ed BREWERY

(Map p118; ☎828-278-9255; www.brew-ed.com; adults $37-50, nondrinkers $20) Beer-focused historical walking tours, led by Cicerone-certified beer geeks and sampling at two or three different downtown breweries, on Thursdays (5:30pm), Fridays (2pm), Saturdays (11:30am and 2pm) and Sundays (1pm).

Lazoom Tours BUS

(Map p118; ☎828-225-6932; www.lazoomtours.com; $23-29) For a hysterical historical tour of the city, hop on the purple bus, watch out for nuns on bikes – and bring your own booze. Weekend tours feature a live band and stop at breweries.

Festivals & Events

★ **Mountain Dance & Folk Festival** MUSIC

(☎828-258-6101; www.folkheritage.org; AB Tech/Mission Health Conference Center, 340 Victoria Rd; 1/3 nights $25/60; ⊙1st Thu-Sat Aug;) North Carolina's premier showcase for old-time music, this three-day bonanza was founded in 1928 by banjo and fiddle player Bascom Lamar Lansford, as the first folk festival in the entire country.

Craft Fair of the Southern Highlands ART

(☎828-298-7928; www.southernhighlandguild.org; US Cellular Center, 87 Haywood St; ⊙3rd weekend Jul & Oct) At these two three-day annual fairs, craftworkers from all over the South gather to display and sell traditional and contemporary work in all media, including clay, metal, wood, glass and paper.

Sleeping

If you want to be within walking distance of shops, restaurants and South Slope's breweries, downtown is the best place to stay. It holds very few inexpensive options, however. Victorian-style B&Bs are concentrated in the historic Montford neighborhood, a mile north, while chain motels are mostly further out still. The **Asheville Bed & Breakfast Association** (☎828-250-0200; www.ashevillebba.com) handles bookings for a dozen local inns and B&Bs, from gingerbread cottages to alpine lodges.

★ **Sweet Peas Hostel** HOSTEL $

(Map p118; ☎828-285-8488; www.sweetpeashostel.com; 23 Rankin Ave; dm/pod $32/40, r without/with bath $75/105;) This spick-and-span, well-run, contemporary hostel occupies an unbeatable downtown location. The loft-like open-plan space, with its exposed brick walls, steel bunks and blond-wood sleeping 'pods', can get noisy, but at least there's a 10% discount at the Lexington Ave Brewery downstairs. They also warn you if an event coincides with your planned dates.

Downtown Inn & Suites MOTEL $

(Map p118; ☎828-254-9661; www.downtowninnandsuites.com; 120 Patton Ave; r $95;) The Downtown Inn will only suit those who value location and price above amenities and peace. It's an old-style motel on a noisy street, with old-fashioned rooms, but they're reasonably sized and cozy, and you won't find a better price – or free parking, for that matter – elsewhere in the heart of downtown. Rates include a simple buffet breakfast.

Asheville Glamping TENTED CAMP $

(☎828-450-9745; www.ashevilleglamping.com; trailer/yurt/tipi/dome from $100/120/125/135, plus room-cleaning fee per stay $50;) Friendly Joana runs three separate sites: two within 5 miles of downtown, the other 10 miles north towards Hot Springs. Each is peppered with a combination of glammed-up yurts, domes, tipis and vintage Airstream and Spartan trailers, some equipped with hot tubs, deluxe outdoor gas grills and prime Blue Ridge views. There's a minimum stay of two nights. You'll need to be self-sufficient, but for a certain kind of traveler this is a unique getaway.

Bon Paul & Sharky's HOSTEL **$**

(Map p122; ☎828-775-3283; www.bonpauland sharkys.com; 816 Haywood Rd; tent sites per person $21.40, dm/r from $30/78, cottage $105; P@🛜🐾) Bon Paul & Sharky's has been welcoming hostelers into this colorful West Asheville 1920 home, a $10 Uber ride from South Slope, for well over a decade. There's also a separate cottage, while campers in the garden share the bathrooms indoors. Plenty of good bars and restaurants lie within shouting distance (plus an organic market), or you can BYOB.

Campfire Lodgings CAMPGROUND **$$**

(Map p122; ☎828-658-8012; www.campfire lodgings.com; 116 Appalachian Village Rd; tent sites $35-40, RV sites $50-70, yurts $115-135, cabins $160; P❄🛜) All yurts should have flat-screen TVs, don't you think? Sleep like the world's most stylish Mongolian nomad in a furnished multiroom tent, half a mile up a wooded hillside on an unpaved but passable road, 6 miles north of town. Cabins and tent sites are also available. RV sites, higher up, enjoy stunning valley views and the only wi-fi access.

★**Bunn House** BOUTIQUE HOTEL **$$$**

(Map p122; ☎828-333-8700; www.bunnhouse.com; 15 Clayton St; d $249-424; P❄🛜) The six rooms and suites in this meticulously restored 1905 home, in a residential neighborhood half a mile north of downtown, are awash with exposed brick and dark hardwoods. The small rooftop terrace boasts Blue Ridge vistas, while the heated bathroom floors and subway-tiled steam showers are glorious on chilly mountain mornings.

There's no on-site reception – it's like having your own amazing studio apartment. Age 21 and over only.

Omni Grove Park Inn HISTORIC HOTEL **$$$**

(Map p122; ☎828-252-2711; www.omnihotels.com; 290 Macon Ave; r $149-419; P❄@🛜🏊🐾) Commanding sweeping Blue Ridge views, this titanic Arts and Crafts–style stone lodge harks back to a bygone era of mountain glamor. Each of the 36ft-wide lobby fireplaces can hold a standing grown man, and has its own elevator to the chimney. Beyond the spectacular public spaces, though, the guest rooms can seem small by modern standards.

As well as a gargantuan underground spa, with stone pools and indoor waterfalls (day pass $90), the hotel has a golf course, indoor and outdoor tennis courts, and a 'base camp' for the Nantahala Outdoor Center (p129).

Aloft Asheville Downtown HOTEL **$$$**

(Map p118; ☎828-232-2838; www.aloftasheville downtown.com; 51 Biltmore Ave; r from $289; P❄@🛜🏊🐾) With a giant chalkboard in the lobby, groovy young staff, and an outdoor clothing store on the 1st floor, this place looks like the inner circle of hipster. The only thing missing is a wool-cap-wearing bearded guy drinking a hoppy microbrew – oh wait, over there. We jest. Once settled, you'll find the staff knowledgeable and the rooms colorful and spacious.

Not only is the hotel close to several downtown hot spots, its W XYZ bar hosts live music Thursday, Friday and Saturday.

BEER CITY USA

If ever a city was transformed by the craft-beer movement, it's Asheville. A sleepy mountain city when its first brewery, Highland Brewing, opened in 1994, Asheville has become a true destination city for booze-bent hopheads. It now holds almost 30 breweries, catering to a population of around 90,000 locals; were it not for the half-million tourists who join them each year, that's fast approaching a brewery per person (well, almost).

Inevitably, big-name national breweries have been flocking to Asheville too. Both New Belgium and Sierra Nevada, respectively from California and Colorado, have opened major brewing and taproom facilities here. Strolling from brewery to beerhouse in the pub-packed South Slope district – which, yes, slopes south from downtown – it's easy to see why Asheville has been nicknamed Beer City.

Eating

Asheville is a true foodie haven. Downtown and South Slope are bursting with enticing options, including simple (but oh-so-hip!) Southern-fried cafes, ethnic diners and elaborate Modern American and Appalachian kitchens. Farm-to-table is the rule; local, organic and sustainable are mantras. With more alternatives down in the River Arts District and over in West Asheville, you won't starve in these mountains.

Greater Asheville

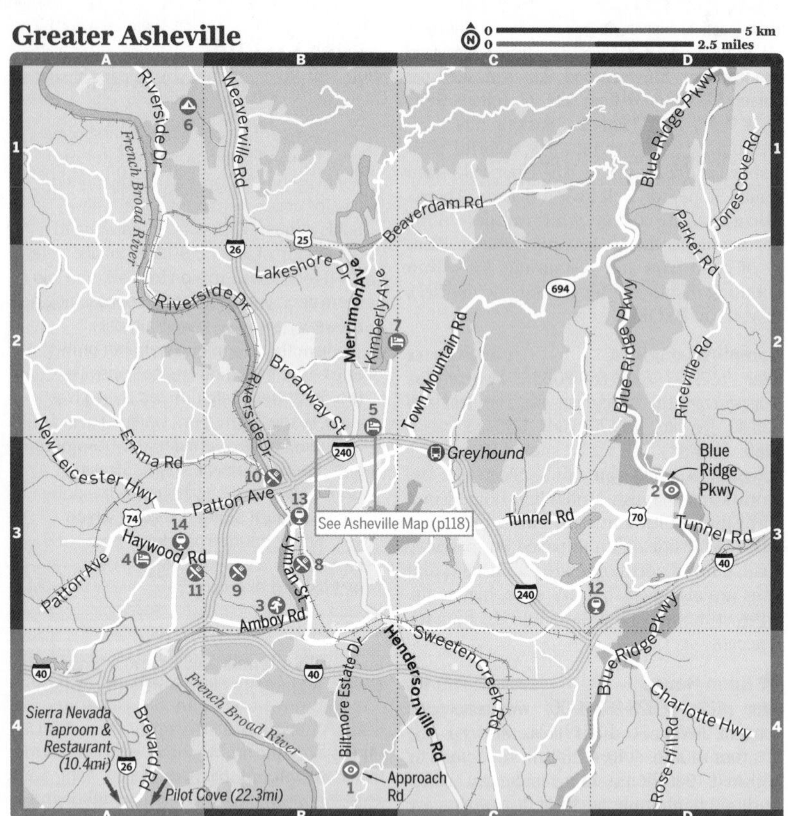

★12 Bones BARBECUE $

(Map p122; ☎828-253-4499; www.12bones.com; 5 Foundy St; dishes $5.50-22.50; ⏰11am-4pm Mon-Fri) How good is the barbecue at 12 Bones? Good enough to lure the vacationing Barack and Michelle Obama back to the River Arts District, a few years back. Expect a long wait, though, before you get to enjoy the slow-cooked, smoky and tender meats, or succulent sides from jalapeño-cheese grits to smoked potato salad.

The warehouse-like space is shared with an outlet of Wedge Brewing (p124); in-the-know regulars skip the line by picking up food from the take-out counter and carrying it around to the pub.

Chai Pani INDIAN $

(Map p118; ☎828-254-4003; www.chaipaniasheville.com; 22 Battery Park Ave; snacks $6.50-10, meals $12; ⏰11:30am-3:30pm & 5-9:30pm; ✎) Literally 'tea and water,' *chai pani* refers more generally to inexpensive snacks. Hence the ever-changing array of irresistible street food at this popular, no-reservations downtown restaurant. Fill up on crunchy *bhel puri* (chickpea noodles and puffed rice) or live it larger with a lamb burger, fish roll, or chicken or vegetarian *thali* (a full meal on a metal tray).

Buxton Hall BARBECUE $

(Map p118; ☎828-232-7216; www.buxtonhall.com; 32 Banks Ave; mains $12-21; ⏰11:30am-3pm & 5:30-10pm; 📶) What happens when two James Beard–nominated chefs, Meherwan Irani and Elliott Moss, open a whole-hog barbecue joint in a cavernous former skating rink on the South Slope? You get the ridiculously good buttermilk-fried-chicken sandwich at Buxton Hall, that's what.

Eastern Carolina–style barbecue here is smoked slow and low – that's the tempo – for 18 hours over hardwood coals, infused with a Moss-family vinegar mop. Everything

Greater Asheville

Sights

1 Biltmore Estate....B4
2 Folk Art Center....D3

Activities, Courses & Tours

3 Smoky Mountain Adventure Center..B3

Sleeping

4 Bon Paul & Sharky's....A3
5 Bunn House....B2
6 Campfire Lodgings....A1
7 Omni Grove Park Inn....B2

Eating

8 12 Bones....B3
9 Admiral....B3
10 Smoky Park Supper Club....B3
11 Sunny Point Cafe....A3

Drinking & Nightlife

12 Asheville Distilling Co....D3
13 Wedge Brewing....B3
14 Westville Pub....A3

is mouthwateringly unforgettable – including the key lime pie, summed up by our server as 'stupid.' No reservations.

Sunny Point Cafe CAFE $
(Map p122; ☎828-252-0055; www.sunnypointcafe.com; 626 Haywood Rd; breakfast dishes $6-12, mains $10-19; ⏰8am-2:30pm Sun & Mon, to 9:30pm Tue-Sat) Loved for its hearty homemade food, this bright West Asheville spot fills up each morning with solos, couples and ladies who breakfast; the little garden out front is the prime spot. Everything, waitstaff included, embraces the organic and fresh. The insanely good huevos rancheros, oozing feta cheese and chorizo sausage, should come with an instruction manual, while the biscuits are divine.

French Broad Chocolate Lounge DESSERTS $
(Map p118; ☎828-252-4181; www.frenchbroadchocolates.com; 10 S Pack Sq; desserts $2.75-7.50; ⏰11am-11pm Sun-Thu, to midnight Fri & Sat) Now happily ensconced in large, glossy premises beside Pack Sq Park, this beloved downtown chocolate shop hasn't lost its chocolate heart. Small-batch, locally produced organic chocolates, chunky chocolate brownies, chocolate-dipped ginger cookies, a sippable 'liquid truffle'...hey, where'd you go?

White Duck Taco Shop MEXICAN $
(Map p118; ☎828-232-9191; www.whiteducktacoshop.com; 12 Biltmore Ave; tacos $3.45-5.25; ⏰11:30am-9pm Mon-Sat, 10:30am-3pm Sun) The chalkboard menu at this downtown taco shop will give you fits. Every single one of these hefty soft tacos sounds like a must-have flavor bomb: spicy buffalo chicken with blue-cheese sauce, crispy pork belly, mole-roasted duck – even shrimp and grits! The margaritas are mighty fine too. In the River Arts District, stop by 1 Roberts St, their original location.

Early Girl Eatery CAFE $
(Map p118; ☎828-259-9292; www.earlygirleatery.com; 8 Wall St; mains $5-16; ⏰7:30am-3pm Mon-Wed, to 9pm Thu & Fri, 8am-9pm Sat & Sun) It's the all-day breakfast menu that draws the crowds to this downtown farm-to-table cafe, where the sunny dining room overlooks a small central square. Go for the house Benny, with tomato, spinach, avocado and poached eggs on grit cakes, or a grilled pimiento-cheese sandwich if it's past your breakfast time.

★ **Cúrate** TAPAS $$
(Map p118; ☎828-239-2946; www.curatetapasbar.com; 13 Biltmore Ave; small plates $6-18; ⏰11:30am-10:30pm Tue-Fri, from 10am Sat & Sun) Owned by hip Ashevillian chef Katie Button and her Catalan husband Félix, this convivial downtown hangout celebrates the simple charms and sensual flavors of Spanish tapas, while adding an occasional Southern twist. Standout dishes run long and wide: *pan con tomate* (grilled bread with tomato), lightly fried eggplant drizzled with honey and rosemary, and a knockout squid-ink 'paella' with vermicelli.

It also features a Barcelona-style *vermuteria* (vermouth bar). Savor the flavors, order another glass of Garnacha and converse with your dinner companions, not your phone. Reservations are a must, especially on weekends, but you can usually snag a bar seat fairly quickly after 9pm.

Smoky Park Supper Club AMERICAN $$
(Map p122; ☎828-350-0315; www.smokypark.com; 350 Riverside Dr; mains $13-36; ⏰5-9pm Tue-Thu, 4-10pm Fri & Sat, 10:30am-9pm Sun;) An anchor of cool in the River Arts District, the largest container-constructed restaurant in the USA is more than the sum of its parts – 19 shipping containers to be exact. Choose between such wood-fired delights as garlic- and lemon-roasted half chicken, cast-iron-seared Carolina fish, or, for vegetarians, roasted local apples stuffed with kale, walnuts and smoked cheddar.

Tupelo Honey SOUTHERN US **$$**
(Map p118; ☎828-255-4863; www.tupelohoneycafe.com; 12 College St; brunch mains $6-17, lunch & dinner mains $9.50-30; ⊙9am-9pm Sun-Thu, to 10pm Fri & Sat) The flagship downtown location of this Asheville-based chain is renowned for New Southern favorites, such as shrimp and grits with goat's cheese – even if the Tupelo-born Elvis himself would surely have gone for the fried-chicken BLT with apple-cider bacon! Brunches are superb, but no matter the meal, say yes to the biscuit. And add a drop of honey.

Admiral AMERICAN **$$$**
(Map p122; ☎828-252-2541; www.theadmiralasheville.com; 400 Haywood Rd; small plates $12-18, large plates $30-38; ⊙5-10pm; 📶) Set in a concrete bunker beside a car junkyard, this low-key West Asheville spot looks divey from the outside. It's inside, though, where the magic happens. One of the state's finest New American restaurants, the Admiral serves wildly creative dishes – saffron tagliatelle with lima beans, zucchini and basil pesto, for example – that taste divine.

Drinking

Asheville is the craft-beer capital of the South, only rivaled in quality and quantity across the entire USA by Portland's Oregon and Maine. The live-music scene is extremely vibrant: you can find music nightly, with bluegrass and old-time aplenty but much more besides; and the Asheville Symphony Orchestra is very progressive, collaborating with hip-hop acts etc.

In South Slope, the de facto brewery district that drops from the southern edge of downtown, 10 highly individual microbreweries lie within stumbling distance of each other, while Buncombe County as a whole has well over 30. In addition, both downtown Asheville and the River Arts District hold diverse arrays of bars and cafes, including frat-boy beer halls, hippie holes-in-the-wall, craft cocktail lounges and live-music venues. West Asheville has a more laid-back townie vibe.

> **ASHEVILLE ALE TRAIL**
>
> Stop by the visitor center (p126) or ask your hotel for the free *Field Guide to Breweries*, which provides key details and maps for the **Asheville Ale Trail** (www.ashevillealetrail.com), an association of local breweries, taprooms and pubs that organizes tours and events.

★**Burial** MICROBREWERY
(Map p118; www.burialbeer.com; 40 Collier Ave; ⊙2-10pm Mon-Thu, from noon Fri-Sun; 📶) This ever-progressive brewery gives experimental batches of Belgian-leaning styles – farmhouse saisons, strong dubbels and tripels – a Southern kick in the pants, using local ingredients such as wildflower honey, chokeberries and juniper branches. Brewers in overalls, a menacing logo, and pitchfork-and-sickle tap and door handles add intrigue. It takes significant willpower to leave the outdoor patio. There's a decent food menu too.

★**Funkatorium** MICROBREWERY
(Map p118; ☎828-552-3203; www.wickedweedbrewing.com/locations/funkatorium; 147 Coxe Ave; ⊙2-10pm Mon-Thu, noon-midnight Fri & Sat, 11am-10pm Sun; 📶) If you need the funk, you gotta have that funk...and you'll find at it at the East Coast's first taproom dedicated to sour, wild ale, Brett and funky beer. For fans, it's pilgrimage-worthy. The rough-and-ready, old world–style taproom holds more than 600 aging barrels, and rotating taps spit 8oz pours for the cause. Get funked up!

★**Battery Park Book Exchange & Champagne Bar** WINE BAR
(Map p118; ☎828-252-0020; www.batteryparkbookexchange.com; 1 Page Ave; ⊙11am-9pm Sun-Thu, to 10pm Fri & Sat) A charming champagne bar, sprawling through several opulent vintage-furnished rooms of a glorious old downtown shopping arcade, with every nook and cranny lined with shelves of neatly cataloged secondhand books covering every imaginable topic. Seriously, who could resist that as a combination? Other wines are also available, along with coffee, cakes, cheese and charcuterie.

Wedge Brewing MICROBREWERY
(Map p122; ☎828-505-2792; www.wedgebrewing.com; 37 Paynes Way; ⊙noon-10pm; 📶) Unlike the spit-shined, well-oiled breweries elsewhere in Asheville, the grungier Wedge in the River Arts District is happy to keep things edgy. The beers are excellent – especially the Iron Rail IPA – but it's the fairy-lit outdoor patio, packed with convivial locals and their dogs, that gives it a one-up on fellow taprooms. Food trucks nightly. Another outlet, nearby and also in the River Arts District, shares a space with 12 Bones (p122).

DON'T MISS

ASHEVILLE DISTILLING CO

With its bags of heirloom grits and photos of crop-dotted fields, the tasting room at **Asheville Distilling Co** (828-575-2000; www.ashevilledistilling.com; 12 Old Charlotte Hwy) evokes the vibe of a cozy Appalachian barn. The rustic look aligns with the goal of founder Troy Ball: to produce an authentic Scots-Irish un-aged whiskey. To replicate the 19th-century taste, Ball uses 1840s heirloom white corn from nearby Crooked Creek Mills. But Ball doesn't just rely on well-credentialed corn. Traditionally, when moonshiners made white whiskey they tossed or sold the bad-tasting heads and tails, which are the batches produced at the beginning and end of a distilling run. They kept the clean middle – the pure heart – for themselves. That's the only part Ball sells.

After the distillery's free tours, which are offered on Fridays and Saturdays at 5pm, visitors sample five whiskeys. They also learn about the inspiring Ball, who moved to Asheville with her husband Charlie in 2004 from Texas, seeking a better climate for her three sons, two of whom have special needs. She took an interest in un-aged whiskey after neighbors from her rural neighborhood brought gifts of moonshine. An energetic entrepreneur, Ball soon realized that there were no quality white whiskeys on the market. She decided to fill that niche with artisan 'moonshine,' becoming the first woman founder of a whiskey distillery in modern times. Celebrate her persistence with a smooth cocktail made from Troy & Sons Platinum American Moonshine.

Wicked Weed MICROBREWERY

(Map p118; 828-575-9599; www.wickedweedbrewing.com; 91 Biltmore Ave; 11:30am-11pm Mon-Thu, to 1am Fri & Sat, noon-11pm Sun;) Henry VIII called hops 'a wicked and pernicious weed' that ruined the taste of beer. His subjects kept quaffing it anyway – just like the lively crowd in this former gas station, which overflows with hoppy brews. Equipped with 58 taps and a broad front patio, it's a big and breezy spot to chill.

Trade & Lore COFFEE

(Map p118; 828-424-7291; www.tradeandlore.com; 37 Wall St; 8am-7pm Tue-Thu, to 10pm Fri-Mon;) Deft baristas dole out serious java in this trendy downtown coffeehouse, drowning in industrial cool but leavened by occasional fits of vintage furniture. Espresso comes courtesy of a top-end La Marzocco machine, and there are four beer taps for lovers of another tipple. The all-gender bathrooms are a tongue-in-cheek dig at state government.

Thirsty Monk CRAFT BEER

(Map p118; 828-254-5470; www.monkpub.com; 92 Patton Ave; 4pm-midnight Mon-Thu, noon-1:30am Fri & Sat, noon-10pm Sun) This scruffy but lovable downtown pub nails a fine drinking trifecta. Downstairs you'll find 16 taps and nearly 200 bottles of Belgian ales; at street level, 20 taps of proprietary, North Carolina and regional craft beers; and on the roof, craft cocktails dating back to before Prohibition.

Hi-Wire MICROBREWERY

(Map p118; 828-738-2448; www.hiwirebrewing.com; 197 Hilliard Ave; 4-11pm Mon-Thu, 2pm-1am Fri, noon-1am Sat, 1-10pm Sun) Set in what used to be a mechanic's garage, this popular South Slope brewery offers a choice array of easy-drinking brews. Its taproom makes a mellow spot to hang with friends on a Saturday afternoon.

Westville Pub CRAFT BEER

(Map p122; 828-225-9782; www.westvillepub.com; 777 Haywood Rd; 10:30am-2am) There's no better spot in West Asheville to bond with local 20- and 30-somethings, over a bottle or two of organic ale, than this veteran neighborhood bar.

O. Henry's GAY

(Map p118; 828-254-1891; www.ohenrysofasheville.com; 237 Haywood St; 4pm-3am) Open since 1976, North Carolina's longest-standing gay men's bar is an Asheville institution, with 'Take the Cake' karaoke on Wednesdays – winners earn a fresh-baked cake – and drag at weekends. Its Underground dance bar, at the back, opens Friday and Saturday only.

☆ Entertainment

For local entertainment and arts listings, pick up the latest edition of alternative news weekly Mountain Xpress (www.mountainx.com).

Orange Peel LIVE MUSIC
(Map p118; ☎828-398-1837; www.theorangepeel.net; 101 Biltmore Ave; tickets $10-35; ⏲shows from 8pm) Asheville's premier live-music venue, downtown's Orange Peel Social Aid & Pleasure Club has been a showcase for big-name indie and punk bands since 2002. A warehouse-sized place, it seats – well, stands – a thousand-strong crowd.

Shopping

An afternoon spent strolling around downtown Asheville is a true delight, with unexpected shopping pleasures around every corner. Along its narrow streets, its century-old buildings hold an intriguing mixture of hip new boutiques and deeply traditional main-street stores.

Horse & Hero ARTS & CRAFTS
(Map p118; ☎828-505-2133; www.facebook.com/horseandhero; 124 Patton Ave; ⏲11am-7pm Sun-Thu, to 9pm Fri & Sat) For a taste of Asheville's contemporary creativity, and a distinctly psychedelic take on Appalachian art, drop into this groovy downtown gallery. As well as graphic design pieces and lithographs, it sells plenty of more affordable craftwork.

Mast General Store SPORTS & OUTDOORS
(Map p118; ☎828-232-1883; www.mastgeneralstore.com; 15 Biltmore Ave; ⏲10am-6pm Mon-Thu, to 9pm Fri & Sat, noon-6pm Sun) This long-standing North Carolina favorite is great for outdoor gear, organic and natural cosmetics, provisions, candy, toys – you name it – much of it produced locally.

Chocolate Fetish CHOCOLATE
(Map p118; ☎828-258-2353; www.chocolatefetish.com; 36 Haywood St; ⏲11am-7pm Mon-Thu, to 9pm Fri & Sat, noon-6pm Sun) With its silky truffles ($2.25) and sinfully good caramels, not to mention 20-minute tasting tours ($10), Chocolate Fetish deserves a flag on any chocolate addict's map. Recommendations? Chai Moon (chai tea and cinnamon), Mocha Magic (almond with espresso) and, our favorite, Habanero Sea Salt, the caramel that hurts so good!

Malaprop's Bookstore & Cafe BOOKS
(Map p118; ☎828-254-6734; www.malaprops.com; 55 Haywood St; ⏲9am-9pm Mon-Sat, to 7pm Sun; 📶) Downtown's best-loved new bookstore is cherished locally for its expert staff, who maintain a carefully curated selection of regional fiction and nonfiction. The cappuccino and wi-fi are very welcome too.

Tops for Shoes SHOES
(Map p118; www.topsforshoes.com; 27 N Lexington Ave; ⏲10am-6pm Mon-Sat, 1-5pm Sun) This may look like a run-of-the-mill, old-school shoe store, but venture inside – it's enormous, with an eye-catching assortment of hiking boots and hip footwear.

East Fork Pottery CERAMICS
(Map p118; ☎828-575-2150; www.eastforkpottery.com; 82 N Lexington Ave; ⏲11am-6pm Mon-Sat, noon-5pm Sun) Beautiful ceramic mugs and plates, made by a collective team of local ceramicists that includes Alex Matisse, the great-grandson of Henri himself. Their shop also sells a few of their favorite things, such as artisanal Japanese cutlery and nail clippers, and wonderful high-end handmade soaps.

Information

Asheville's main **visitor center** (Map p118; ☎828-258-6129; www.exploreasheville.com; 36 Montford Ave; ⏲8:30am-5:30pm Mon-Fri, 9am-5pm Sat & Sun), alongside I-240 exit 4C, sells Biltmore Estate admission tickets at a $10 discount. Downtown holds a satellite **visitor pavilion** (Map p118; ☎828-258-6129; www.exploreasheville.com; 80 Court Pl; ⏲9am-5pm), with restrooms, beside Pack Sq Park.

Getting There & Away

Asheville Regional Airport (p208), 16 miles south of Asheville, is served by a handful of nonstop flights, with destinations including Atlanta, Charlotte, Chicago and New York. **Greyhound** (p112) is 1 mile northeast of downtown.

Getting Around

Although there's very little free parking downtown, public garages are free for the first hour and only cost $1 per hour thereafter. The handy Passport app (https://passportinc.com) facilitates paying for Asheville's parking meters and paid lots.

The 18 local bus routes run by Asheville Transit (ART) typically operate between 5:30am and 10:30pm Monday through Saturday, and shorter hours Sunday. Tickets cost $1, and there are free bike racks. Route S3 connects the **downtown ART station** (Map p118; ☎828-253-5691; www.ashevilletransit.com; 49 Coxe Ave; ⏲6am-9:30pm Mon-Fri, from 7am Sat, 8:30am-5.30pm Sun) with **Asheville Regional Airport** (p208) 10 times daily.

WESTERN NORTH CAROLINA

North Carolina's westernmost tip is blanketed in parkland and sprinkled with tiny mountain towns. The region is rich in Native American history. A large proportion of its Cherokee population were forced off their lands during the 1830s – by their erstwhile ally, Andrew Jackson – and marched to Oklahoma on the Trail of Tears, but many managed to hide in the remote mountains. Their descendants, now known as the Eastern Band of Cherokee Indians, live on the 56,000-acre Qualla Boundary territory, on the southern edge of Great Smoky Mountains National Park (p38).

Rolling across western North Carolina into the mountainous High Country, the contiguous Pisgah and Nantahala national forests hold more than a million acres of dense hardwood trees and windswept mountain balds, as well as some of the country's best white-water rapids – and sections of the Appalachian Trail.

Getting There & Away

Asheville Regional Airport (p208) serves western North Carolina.

Cherokee

☎828 / POP 2136

To most visitors, Cherokee is a typical and rather unlovely gateway town, guarding the southern approaches to Great Smoky Mountains National Park, and lined with tacky souvenir shops and fast-food joints, which culminate in the out-of-place spectacle of Harrah's Cherokee Casino. To the Eastern Band of Cherokee Indians, however – the descendants of those Cherokee who managed to hide in the mountains rather than be expelled from their homeland along the Trail of Tears – this is the headquarters of the Qualla Boundary, an area of tribal-owned land that is not officially a reservation. As such, it holds a major historical museum and a fine traditional crafts gallery.

Sights

★Museum of the Cherokee Indian — MUSEUM

(☎828-497-3481; www.cherokeemuseum.org; 589 Tsali Blvd/Hwy 441, at Drama Rd; adult/child 6-12yr $11/7; ⏲9am-7pm Jun-Aug, to 5pm Sep-May; P) This remarkable modern museum traces Cherokee history from their Paleo-Indian roots onwards. Its villain is the perfidious Andrew Jackson, who made his name fighting alongside the Cherokee, but, as president, condemned them to the heartbreak of the Trail of Tears. One fascinating section follows the progress through 18th-century London of a Cherokee delegation that sailed to England in 1762.

Sleeping

Cherokee holds plenty of motor inns and chain hotels, but the liveliest place to sleep has to be the hotel tower of Harrah's Cherokee Casino. Roadside motels, log cabins and campgrounds also line the scenic, river-hugging Hwy 19 between Cherokee and Bryson City, 10 miles west.

Harrah's Cherokee Hotel — CASINO HOTEL $$

(☎828-497-7777; www.caesars.com/harrahs-cherokee; 777 Casino Dr; r from $179; ❄📶🏊) While it's hardly rural or rustic, this enormous and ever-expanding casino resort holds more than 1000 high-quality hotel rooms, which are larger and more comfortable than anything else you'll find in Cherokee. It also offers indoor and outdoor pools, a spa, and a dozen restaurants.

Eating

It's easy to pick up the usual Great Smoky food – down-home cookin', skyscraper pancake stacks, fudge – in Cherokee. The best place to eat in town, though, has to be Harrah's Cherokee Casino (p128), where options include a buffet, a noodle bar and a pizzeria, along with Ruth's Chris Steakhouse, a high-end chain steakhouse that's the closest Cherokee comes to fine dining.

Sassy Sunflowers — BAKERY $

(☎828-497-2539; www.facebook.com/sassysunflowers; 1655 Acquoni Rd; sandwiches & salads $8-10; ⏲9am-4pm Mon-Fri; 📶🌿) For a wholesome lunch or breakfast, stop to eat a sandwich and salad at the outdoor tables of this cheery roadside bakery-cafe. As well as turkey, chicken and prime rib, the menu includes vegetarian choices such as their signature Sunflower Salad, featuring goat's cheese, apple, cranberries and sunflower seeds. It's south of the river, immediately outside Great Smoky Mountains National Park.

THE CHEROKEE AND THE TRAIL OF TEARS

Under the Treaty of Holston, signed with the United States in 1791, the Cherokee were guaranteed the right to remain in perpetuity in the mountainous regions of northern Georgia and western North Carolina. Within 50 years, they had been rounded up at bayonet point and moved west of the Mississippi, on the forced march remembered as the Trail of Tears.

According to the Cherokee, the villain of the piece was the man they called 'Sharp Knife,' President Andrew Jackson. At the Battle of Horseshoe Bend in 1814, Jackson fought alongside the Cherokee, against a rebellious Creek faction in Alabama. As president, however, he pushed through the Indian Removal Act of 1830, along with 94 separate removal treaties.

Under pressure to become 'civilized,' the Cherokee made huge efforts to adapt to the changing world, adopting Christianity, entering the economy as farmers and blacksmiths, and even holding black slaves. Increasing encroachment upon their lands by white settlers and prospectors, especially in Georgia after gold was discovered in 1828, should have prompted federal support against the states concerned, but Jackson declined to intervene.

The lack of an overall tribal government enabled a small group of Cherokee, the so-called 'Treaty Party,' to sign the Treaty of New Echota in 1835, ceding all Cherokee land east of Mississippi in return for $5 million and land in the west. Although more than 15,000 Cherokee petitioned Congress to be allowed to stay, the treaty was ratified in 1836, obliging them to leave within two years. The Treaty Party faction set off voluntarily, but the remainder stayed put.

In May 1838, 7000 federal troops swept through Cherokee territory, herding men, women and children into makeshift stockades. Some evaded capture, and became the ancestors of what's now the Eastern Band of Cherokee Indians. Of the rest, some traveled by rail and river to Chattanooga, where they met up with those who had walked and continued together, accompanied by a train of 645 wagons. Around 4000 died en route, and the final group reached Indian Territory, in what's now Oklahoma, in March 1839. Their reunion with the Treaty Party provoked bitter conflict, culminating in the execution of several Treaty Party leaders.

Andrew Jackson, meanwhile, had left the presidency. In his Farewell Address of 1837, he congratulated himself that 'the states which had so long been retarded in their development by the Indian tribes residing in the midst of them are at length relieved from the evil.'

Drinking

As Cherokee falls within the Qualla Boundary, there are no bars or alcohol sales anywhere apart from the casino. The closest bars and craft breweries are in nearby Sylva and Bryson City.

Qualla Java Cafe COFFEE
(☎828-497-2882; www.quallajava.com; 938 Tsalagi Rd; ⊙7am-5pm Mon-Fri, from 8am Sat, from 9am Sun; 📶) This welcoming little Cherokee-owned coffee bar, conspicuous for its towering pointed roof alongside the highway, is a good place to kick off the day.

Entertainment

Harrah's Cherokee Casino CASINO
(☎828-497-7777; www.caesars.com/harrahs-cherokee; 777 Casino Dr; ⊙24hr; 📶) As well as all the usual casino games, this high-rise complex holds a towering hotel block (p127), two swimming pools, a spa and restaurants of all kinds. There's also an impressive water-and-video display in the lobby.

Shopping

Qualla Arts & Crafts Mutual ARTS & CRAFTS
(☎828-497-3103; www.quallaartsandcrafts.com; 645 Tsali Blvd/Hwy 441, cnr Drama Rd; ⊙9am-4:30pm, closed Sun Jan & Feb) To pick up authentic Cherokee craftwork, including basketry, stone carving and ceramics, head to this large cooperative gallery.

Getting There & Away

Cherokee's nearest airport is **Asheville Regional Airport** (p208), 55 miles east.

Bryson City

☎828 / POP 1452

This tiny, charming mountain town straddling the Tuckasegee River is not only a cute little base for exploring Great Smoky Mountains National Park (p38), but an adventure destination in its own right. Handily poised for Nantahala National Forest, it's a great spot for water sports such as rafting and kayaking. You might remember it from Cormac McCarthy's 1979 novel, *Suttree* – the title character winds up here after wandering over the mountains from Gatlinburg.

Home to a smattering of good restaurants and breweries, Bryson City is also the starting point for the Great Smoky Mountains Railroad, which leaves from a historic depot downtown.

Activities

Class II and III white-water rafting on the Nantahala River, 12 miles west of Bryson City, draws more than 200,000 paddlers per year, while the Tuckasegee in town is a popular spot for fishing, paddleboarding and kayaking. The Deep Creek Recreation Area, 1.7 miles north of downtown, offers tubing and waterfalls.

Nantahala Outdoor Center RAFTING
(NOC; ☎828-366-7502, 828-785-5082; www.noc.com; 13077 Hwy 19 W; duckie rental per day $35, guided trips $50-200; 8am-8pm Jun & Jul, reduced hours Aug-May) This huge and highly recommended outfitter specializes in wet 'n' wild rafting trips down the Nantahala River. Their 500-acre site, 14 miles southwest of Bryson City, also offers ziplining and mountain biking, and even has its own lodge, a hostel, a mostly year-round restaurant and a seasonal BBQ and beer joint (open May to October). The Appalachian Trail rolls across the property too.

Bryson City Bicycles CYCLING
(☎828-488-1988; www.brysoncitybicycles.com; 157 Everett St; mountain-bike rentals per 24hr from $40; 10am-6pm Tue-Sat) Quite apart from meeting all possible bike needs, including equipment sales, repairs and rentals, this friendly bike shop is worth its weight in saddlebags for the expert and freely given advice on local trail networks.

Road to Nowhere HIKING
(Lakeview Dr;) The so-called Road to Nowhere – officially, Lakeview Dr – leads northwest of Bryson City towards Great Smoky Mountains National Park (p38). It was intended as a scenic drive, but only 6 miles were completed. For a quirky hike, park where the road ends, then keep on walking through the 1200ft tunnel beyond; alternative trails loop back in either 2.2 or 3.2 miles.

Tours

Great Smoky Mountains Railroad RAIL
(☎800-872-4681; www.gsmr.com; 226 Everett St; Nantahala Gorge trip adult/child 2-12yr from $58/34; schedules vary;) These scenic train excursions, lasting around four hours, follow two alternate routes – either east along the Tuckasegee River to Dillsboro, or southwest to the spectacular Nantahala Gorge. Up to four trains run daily on peak summer and fall weekends.

Sleeping

For such a small town, Bryson City is rich with lodging options. The Everett Hotel is the pleasantest spot to sleep, but there are mountain lodges and cabins, budget chain hotels and charming inns as well.

★ **Everett Hotel** BOUTIQUE HOTEL $$
(☎828-488-1976; www.theeverетthotel.com; 24 Everett St; r from $199;) This nine-room boutique hotel occupies a century-old building that once housed western North Carolina's first bank. Beautiful pinewood hallways lead to rooms awash in a mineral-grey palette, with plantation shutters and wonderful dark-stained pinewood ceilings. A fire pit warms the scenic rooftop terrace. Rates include an à la carte breakfast in the excellent house bistro (p130).

Fryemont Inn INN $$
(☎828-488-2159; www.fryemontinn.com; 245 Fryemont St; lodge/ste/cabin from $165/205/260; mid-Apr–late Nov;) The views of the Smokies from this lofty bark-covered mountain lodge are unbeatable. Rooms lack TVs and air-con, but rates include breakfast and dinner in the on-site public restaurant (open 8am to 10am and 6pm to 8pm), which serves trout, steak and lamb. The lodge itself closes in winter, as does its restaurant, but the cottage and balcony suites – the only areas with wi-fi reception – remain open. For nonguests, breakfast in the restaurant costs $10 to $12, while dinner mains are $20 to $31.

Eating

Bryson City is too small to offer a wide range of dining options, but several of the local diners along Everett St serve fresh mountain trout.

Bistro at the Everett Hotel BISTRO **$$**
(☎828-488-1934; www.theeveretthotel.com; 16 Everett St; mains $18-35; ⏲4:30-9pm Mon-Fri, 8:30am-3pm & 4:30-9pm Sat & Sun; 📶) Big windows frame this classy downtown bar-restaurant, where the emphasis is on organic local ingredients, and there are local craft beers on tap. Typical dinner mains include meatloaf, mountain trout and scallops on goat's-cheese grits, while the weekend brunch menu features eggs Benedict and huevos rancheros.

Drinking

Bryson City is home to a couple of craft breweries, and there are a dozen or more en route between here and Asheville, 65 miles east.

Nantahala Brewing Company MICROBREWERY
(☎828-488-2337; www.nantahalabrewing.com; 61 Depot St; ⏲noon-11pm Sun-Thu, to midnight Fri & Sat May-Aug, reduced hours Sep-Apr; 📶) In a massive repurposed WWII military Quonset hut, this Bryson City brewery (pints from $5) counts well over 30 taps in its main taproom. Standouts include the Dirty Girl Blonde Ale, Noon Day IPA, and assorted experimental versions using different hops or production methods.

Getting There & Away

Bryson City is 10 miles west of Cherokee. The closest airport is **Asheville Regional Airport** (p208), 70 miles east of town.

Pisgah National Forest

Pisgah National Forest extends across huge swathes of North Carolina's mountains, curling around Asheville in a convoluted but not quite joined-up circle. To the northeast it includes most of the Blue Ridge Parkway between Blowing Rock and Asheville, extending almost to the summit of Mt Mitchell, while to the north it stretches via Hot Springs to the edge of the Smokies.

The section southwest of Asheville, known as the Pisgah Ranger District and incorporating parts of the original Biltmore Estate (p117), offers wonderful recreational opportunities. It's best approached by leaving the Blue Ridge Parkway at Mile 412. Immediately north of here looms the forested bulk of Cold Mountain, immortalized in Charles Frazier's 1997 book and the subsequent movie. Head south on Hwy 276, and en route to the delightful country town of Brevard, you'll pass several potential stopoffs as well as a helpful ranger station.

Sights

Sliding Rock Recreation Area WATERFALL
(☎828-885-7625; www.fs.usda.gov; Pisgah Hwy/Hwy 276; $2; ⏲staffed 9am-6pm late May-early Sep; 🅿) For a totally exhilarating stop on a journey along the Blue Ridge Parkway, stop off and strip down at Sliding Rock, 7 miles off the parkway. Propelled down this natural 60ft slide of smooth, gently sloping granite by 11,000 gallons of cool stream water per minute, bathers splash into a pool that's up to 8ft deep; swimming skills are essential. If possible, time your visit to avoid the noon-to-4pm crowds.

Lifeguards are present daily in summer, on weekends in fall. When they're not, changing rooms and restrooms are closed, and you should be very wary of entering the water.

Cradle of Forestry in America NATURE CENTER
(☎828-877-3130; www.cradleofforestry.com; 11250 Pisgah Hwy/Hwy 276; adult/child under 13yr $6/3; ⏲9am-5pm early Apr–mid-Nov; 🅿👪) The spot where scientific forestry management was first attempted in the US, financed by George Vanderbilt back in 1895, is now a showcase for the Forest Service. Amid the original log cabins, 4 miles off Blue Ridge Parkway, a visitor center holds interactive exhibits targeted at children, including a scary simulation of a helicopter flying over a forest fire. Paved trails lead through the woods themselves.

Activities

While mountain biking and hiking are the most popular activities in the Pisgah Ranger District, rock climbing is also a big deal, especially on granite domes such as Looking Glass Rock. Several spectacular waterfalls in this ranger district can also be admired from roadside parking lots.

Hiking

Enjoyable and relatively straightforward trails lead to numerous spectacular waterfalls in the Pisgah Ranger District. Among the best are the Twin Falls, accessible on a 4-mile round-trip hike that starts 2.7 miles along Avery Creek Rd, a total of 5 miles up from the intersection of Hwy 276 and Hwy 64.

Biking

Mountain bike trails abound in the Pisgah Ranger District. The Black Mountain trailhead, immediately south of the ranger station, makes an ideal starting point, providing quick access to both the 4-mile Thrift Cove Loop and the 5-mile Sycamore Cove Loop.

Sleeping & Eating

As well as Forest Service campgrounds, including Davidson River Campground (p132), there are plenty of motels and B&Bs in nearby Brevard. For a swanky, modern cabin in the woods, consider the new **Pilot Cove** (☎866-758-2683; www.pilotcove.com; 319 Gateway Junction Dr, Brevard; cabins from $225), which sits on a hill above the Hub and borders the national forest. The property has about 2 miles of private biking trails.

In Brevard you'll also find restaurants to match every taste and budget. Food stores pepper the highway between Brevard and the village of Pisgah Forest, 3.5 miles northeast.

Information

For information and advice on the Pisgah Ranger District, call in at either the **ranger station** (☎828-877-3265; www.cfaia.org; 1600 Pisgah Hwy/Hwy 276; ⏲9am-5pm mid-Apr–mid-Nov, 8:30am-4:30pm mid-Nov–mid-Apr) or Brevard's **Hub**, which also rents out bikes and outdoor equipment.

Getting There & Away

All three districts of Pisgah National Forest are readily accessible from, and connected by, the Blue Ridge Parkway. For the Pisgah Ranger District, head south from the parkway at Mile 412.

WORTH A TRIP

SIERRA NEVADA TAPROOM & RESTAURANT

Asheville isn't limited to small indie brewers anymore. Two West Coast big boys, Colorado-based New Belgium Brewing Co and California-based Sierra Nevada Brewing Co, recently opened their first east coast production facilities and taprooms in the Asheville area. The monstrous **Sierra Nevada Taproom & Restaurant** (☎828-708-6150; www.sierranevada.com; 100 Sierra Nevada Way, Mills River), which opened in 2015, is a bustling pit stop for outdoor adventurers headed back to Asheville from Pisgah National Forest and Brevard. With great food, live music, an outdoor patio, 23 taps and a popular free tour, it's become a destination in its own right. The brewery is 20 miles south of Asheville.

Brevard

☎828 / POP 7822

One of those charming little mountain towns that set travelers daydreaming of putting down roots, Brevard is best known as the home of the prestigious Brevard Music Center. A summer school for music students, the center also stages the Brevard Music Festival (p132), which runs from June through mid-August.

Brevard is also the seat of the ominous-sounding Transylvania County, which more appealingly styles itself as 'Land of Waterfalls.' Visitors flock in year-round to enjoy the surrounding scenery, at its finest in the nearby Pisgah National Forest.

Activities

Brevard makes an ideal base for bikers and hikers, who come to explore the myriad trails, swimming holes and waterfalls hidden away in the slopes of the Pisgah Ranger District of Pisgah National Forest. For advice and equipment, including bike rental, best call in at the Hub, at the foot of Hwy 276.

Hub MOUNTAIN BIKING

(☎828-884-8670; www.thehubpisgah.com; 11 Mama's Place, Pisgah Forest; bike rental per day from $40; ⏲10am-6pm Mon-Fri, from 9am Sat, 10am-5pm Sun) Even if you're traveling with all the right gear and equipment, and don't need to rent from the Hub's extensive array of bikes, be sure to call in at this excellent outfitters for advice and updates on the countless mountain and forest trails nearby. This being North Carolina, it also incorporates its own brewpub, the Pisgah Tavern.

DON'T MISS

HOT SPRINGS

Through-hikers on the Appalachian Trail look forward to their arrival in tiny Hot Springs, famous for its steaming, frothing mineral waters. For a private soak in a riverfront hot tub, visit **Hot Springs Spa & Mineral Baths** (828-622-7676; www.nchotsprings.com; 315 Bridge St; mineral hot tubs from $25, massage $55-150; noon-10pm Mon-Thu, 10am-midnight Fri-Sun). To stretch your legs and experience the best of the AT, tackle the **Short Loop Trail** to the top of **Max Patch Mountain**, a grassy bald with panoramic views. It's 1.6 miles round-trip. For a wilder adventure, sign up for a white-water rafting trip on the French Broad River with **Hot Springs Rafting Company** (877-530-7238; www.hotspringsraftingco.com; 22 Hwy 25; trips adult/child from $45/40; 9am-6pm). At the end of a busy day, catch a few winks at the Mountain Magnolia Inn, built in 1868 and featured on *This Old House*.

Festivals & Events

Brevard Music Festival MUSIC

(828-862-2100; www.brevardmusic.org; Brevard Music Center, 349 Andante Lane; Jun–mid-Aug) The prestigious Brevard Music Center runs this summer-long festival, staging more than 80 concerts, ranging from classical and opera to bluegrass and movie music, in various venues around town.

Sleeping

Brevard offers accommodations to suit all budgets, including campgrounds in the adjoining public lands.

Davidson River Campground CAMPGROUND $

(828-862-5960; www.recreation.gov; 1 Davidson River Circle, Pisgah Forest; tent sites $22-44) At the southern edge of the most spectacular stretch of Pisgah National Forest, 5 miles north of downtown Brevard, this riverside campground – tubing optional! – is better suited to tenters than RVs. The facilities are relatively basic, but the wooded setting is idyllic. Silence is requested, and insisted on, from 10pm to 7am. Hike trails of all levels or just sling a hammock between the trees.

Sunset Motel MOTEL $

(828-884-9106; http://thesunsetmotel.com; 523 S Broad St; r from $99; P) They don't make 'em like the Sunset Motel anymore, so if you've a penchant for vintage motor lodges, and you don't mind every last fixture and fitting looking like it came straight from the 1950s, you won't want to miss it. Choose from cabins, apartments and standard motel rooms, and don't worry – they've got wi-fi and 21st-century TVs too.

Red House Inn B&B $$

(828-884-9349; www.brevardbedandbreakfast.com; 266 W Probart St; r from $160; P) Built as a general store in 1851, the Red House went through various incarnations before becoming a B&B. Set in stately repose five minutes' walk from downtown, it offers superbly quiet, tastefully furnished en suite rooms, plus full cooked breakfasts. The owners also rent out fully equipped vacation homes nearby.

Eating

Browsing the menus as you wander Brevard's simple downtown grid, you're sure to come across something to set your taste buds tingling.

Falls Landing SEAFOOD $$

(828-884-2835; www.thefallslanding.com; 18 E Main St; dinner mains $15-28; 11:30am-3pm Mon, 11:30am-3pm & 5-9pm Tue-Sat) Brevard's favorite fine-dining restaurant works wonders with fish – the owner moved here from the Virgin Islands, and is as happy serving oysters or crab cakes as pan-frying fresh NC trout – but there's plenty more besides, including lamb chops and rib-eye. Burgers ($9) stay on the menu all day, joined by sandwiches at lunchtime.

Drinking & Nightlife

Small Brevard may be, but it still manages to squeeze in no fewer than three breweries downtown.

Brevard Brewing Co MICROBREWERY

(828-885-2101; www.brevard-brewing.com; 63 E Main St; 2-11pm Mon-Thu, noon-midnight Fri & Sat, 2-10pm Sun;) Though it's right in the heart of town, this small local brewery (pints from $3.50) always seems to have a peaceful, welcoming vibe. It specializes in German lagers and pilsners, but also makes an American IPA, as well as seasonal variations including a coriander ale in fall. There's no food.

Getting There & Away

In the absence of public transportation, you'll almost certainly have to drive to Brevard. Ideally, make your way here on the Blue Ridge Parkway, heading south on Hwy 276 from Mile 412.

Nantahala National Forest

The largest of North Carolina's four national forests, Nantahala National Forest covers more than half a million acres of the state's westernmost portion, extending south from Great Smoky Mountains National Park all the way to the South Carolina and Georgia state lines.

The name Nantahala means 'Land of the Noonday Sun' in Cherokee, because only when the sun is at its highest can it penetrate all the way to the floor of the Nantahala Gorge. The gorge itself is in the forest's Nantahala Ranger District, which also holds the tallest waterfall east of the Mississippi. Very close to South Carolina, 26 miles southwest of Brevard, Whitewater Falls can be reached via a steep 1-mile hike from NC 281.

Sights & Activities

Tsali Recreation Area FOREST

(828-479-6431; www.fs.usda.gov; Tsali Rd; 24hr; P) FREE The Tsali Recreation Area has been famed among mountain bikers for so long that local riders rather take it for granted. For out-of-state visitors, though, it offers a great combination of challenging but not overly technical trails, spectacular lake-and-mountain views, and convenient access. All of the four main trails are categorized as moderate, incorporating waterfront stretches beside Fontana Lake plus significant climbs.

They trails are divided into two groups – the Mouse Branch and Thompson Loops, and the longer Left and Right Loops – each of which is reserved for bikers and horse riders on alternate days. The Left Loop is the toughest, with its steep ascents and narrow ledges, while novice riders can opt for a short 5-mile ride by tackling only a segment of the less demanding Right Loop. There are restrooms, showers and bike-washing facilities at the parking lot.

Hiking

Every section of the Nantahala forest holds its fair share of hiking trails. To admire some magnificent – and all too rare – old-growth forest, head to the Joyce Kilmer Memorial Forest, 40 miles west of Bryson City. Easy loop-hikes lead past centuries-old tulip poplars, while the adjoining Slickrock Wilderness Area offers more demanding terrain for backpackers.

Note also that the legendary, long-distance Appalachian Trail (www.appalachiantrail.org) winds across both the Cheoah and Nantahala ranger districts.

Biking

Nantahala National Forest is famous for its mountain biking, with prime destinations including the Tsali Recreation Area (p133), west of Bryson City, and the Jackrabbit Recreation Area, adjoining Lake Chatuge near Hayesville, 100 miles southwest of Asheville.

Sleeping

Both the Tsali and the Jackrabbit recreation areas offer lakeside campgrounds, while Bryson City makes a good overnight base for Tsali in particular.

Tsali Campground CAMPGROUND $

(828-479-6431; www.fs.usda.gov; Tsali Rd; tent sites $15; Apr-Oct; P) This forest-service campground holds around 40 tent sites, some beside a stream and some spreading across a meadow. It has showers and restrooms, but no electric or water hookups.

Getting There & Away

The Tsali Recreation Area is 15 miles west of Bryson City; follow Hwy 74 for 9.6 miles, turn right onto NC 28, and then turn right again onto Tsali Rd (SR 1286) after another 3.4 miles. Follow signs to trailheads and the campground.

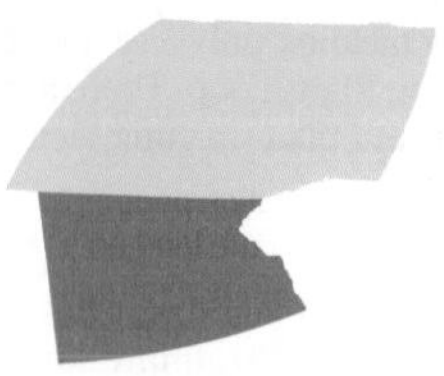

Atlanta & North Georgia

Includes ➡

Atlanta.........................135
Athens.........................154
Dahlonega...................159
Amicalola Falls State Park...................161
Blue Ridge...................162
Helen.......................... 164
Clayton....................... 168
Tallulah Gorge State Park...................169
Toccoa.........................170

Best Places to Eat

- Optimist (p147)
- Staplehouse (p145)
- Dish Dive (p144)
- Octopus Bar (p145)
- Home.made from Scratch (p156)

Best Places to Stay

- Urban Oasis B&B (p140)
- Hotel Clermont (p141)
- Sugar Magnolia B&B (p141)
- Graduate Athens (p154)
- White Birch Inn (p169)

Why Go?

The largest state east of the Mississippi River is a labyrinth of geographic and cultural extremes: right-leaning Republican politics in the countryside rubs against liberal idealism in Atlanta, and small, conservative towns merge with sprawling, progressive, financially flush cities. North Georgia is a wilderness playground for those looking to hike, fish or hunt. The Appalachian Trail ends here amid glorious wooded mountain scenery in this region.

Atlanta, Georgia's culturally rich and multifaceted capital, best illustrates the paradox: on one side it's a bastion of African American enlightenment, a hip-hop hotbed, a film and tech industry upstart and LGBTQ epicenter; on the other, Old South wealth and Fortune 500 investment marry in a city that is an international financial workhorse steeped in conservative Southern values. Together, a sexy metropolis emerges – it's way past *Gone with the Wind*.

When to Go

Georgia's Appalachian Trail through-hikers get moving anytime from late March to mid-April; the region blooms with pretty dogwoods.

College-football season kicks off in September – Athens is a notable good time.

In November, sweltering heat and summer prices retreat; go, before the holidays.

History

Native American culture in Georgia dates beyond pre-Columbian times, but the state began taking shape in the mid-1500s, when the Spanish arrived, followed by the English, who began the first colony at Savannah in 1733. Over its near 300-year history as a territory and state, Georgia has evolved from Old South stalwart to global vanguard, surviving the Civil War wounded but alive, prudently navigating the Civil Rights movement and embracing Hollywood, international business, hip-hop and tech along the way.

Getting There & Away

The main highway that cuts through North Georgia is I-85, but getting between towns usually means long, winding drives on secondary and county roads. On the plus side, the scenery is nice. Atlanta is about 80 miles from both Athens and Dahlonega, and is the most convenient point of air entry for the region. There's also a **Greyhound** (706-549-2255; www.greyhound.com; 4020 Atlanta Hwy, Bogart) station in Athens and an **Amtrak** (p172) station in Toccoa.

ATLANTA

POP 463,878

The South's so-called capital isn't nicknamed Hotlanta for nothing, y'all. Charismatic and lush, Atlanta is an easy-on-the-eyes cavalcade of culture, cuisine and Southern hospitality.

With more than six million residents in the metro and outlying areas, Atlanta continues to experience explosive growth thanks to domestic transplants and international immigrants. Beyond the big-ticket Downtown attractions you will find a constellation of superlative restaurants, a palpable Hollywood influence (Atlanta is a hugely popular film-production center), and iconic African American history. That last point can't be overstated: any nationwide African American intellectual, political and artistic movement you can mention either had its genesis in Atlanta, or found a center of gravity here.

Without natural boundaries to control development, it's fair to say Atlanta is more a region than a city. Yet for all its sprawl and suburbanization, there is a lovely urban core covered with trees – some 36% of the city to be exact, making it one of the most densely forested cities in the US. Distinct neighborhoods are like friendly small towns. The economy is robust, the population is young and creative, and the social scene is diverse.

Orientation

The Atlanta metro area is a sprawling megacity that encompasses an area of 8376 sq miles and is home to more than six million people. It won't be easy to get the lay of the land on a short visit, but the basic terminology you will need to immediately familiarize yourself with is OPT (Outside the Perimeter) and ITP (Inside the Perimeter). These terms refer to the nickname for I-285, the 64-mile loop interstate that encircles the city. Loosely defined, if you are inside the perimeter, it's safe to say you are in the urban core of the city; outside the perimeter is considered the suburbs. Atlantans use these terms constantly when discussing where they live, work and play.

Sights & Activities

Downtown

Centennial Olympic Park, Atlanta's most impressive 1996 Summer Olympics legacy, is the beating heart of the city's compact downtown. Some of the Southeast's biggest attractions – Center for Civil & Human Rights, World of Coca-Cola, Georgia Aquarium, College Football Hall of Fame, CNN Center – all fall within a peach's throw of each other.

★Center for Civil & Human Rights MUSEUM

(Map p142; www.civilandhumanrights.org; 100 Ivan Allen Jr Blvd; adult/senior/child $20/18/16; 10am-5pm Mon-Sat, noon-5pm Sun) This striking 2014 addition to Atlanta's **Centennial Olympic Park** (Map p142; www.centennialpark.com; 265 Park Ave NW; 7am-11pm) is a sobering $68-million memorial to the American Civil Rights and global human-rights movements. Beautifully designed and thoughtfully executed, the indisputable highlight centers on an absolutely harrowing interactive mock Woolworth's lunch-counter sit-in simulation that will leave you speechless and move some to tears.

World of Coca-Cola MUSEUM

(Map p142; 404-676-5151; www.woccatlanta.com; 121 Baker St; adult/senior/child $17/15/13; 10am-5pm Mon-Fri, 9am-5pm Sat & Sun) This self-congratulatory museum might prove entertaining to fans of fizzy beverages and rash commercialization. The climactic moment comes when guests sample Coke products from around the world – a taste-bud-twisting good time. But there are also Andy Warhol pieces on view, a 4D film, company history and promotional materials aplenty.

Atlanta & North Georgia

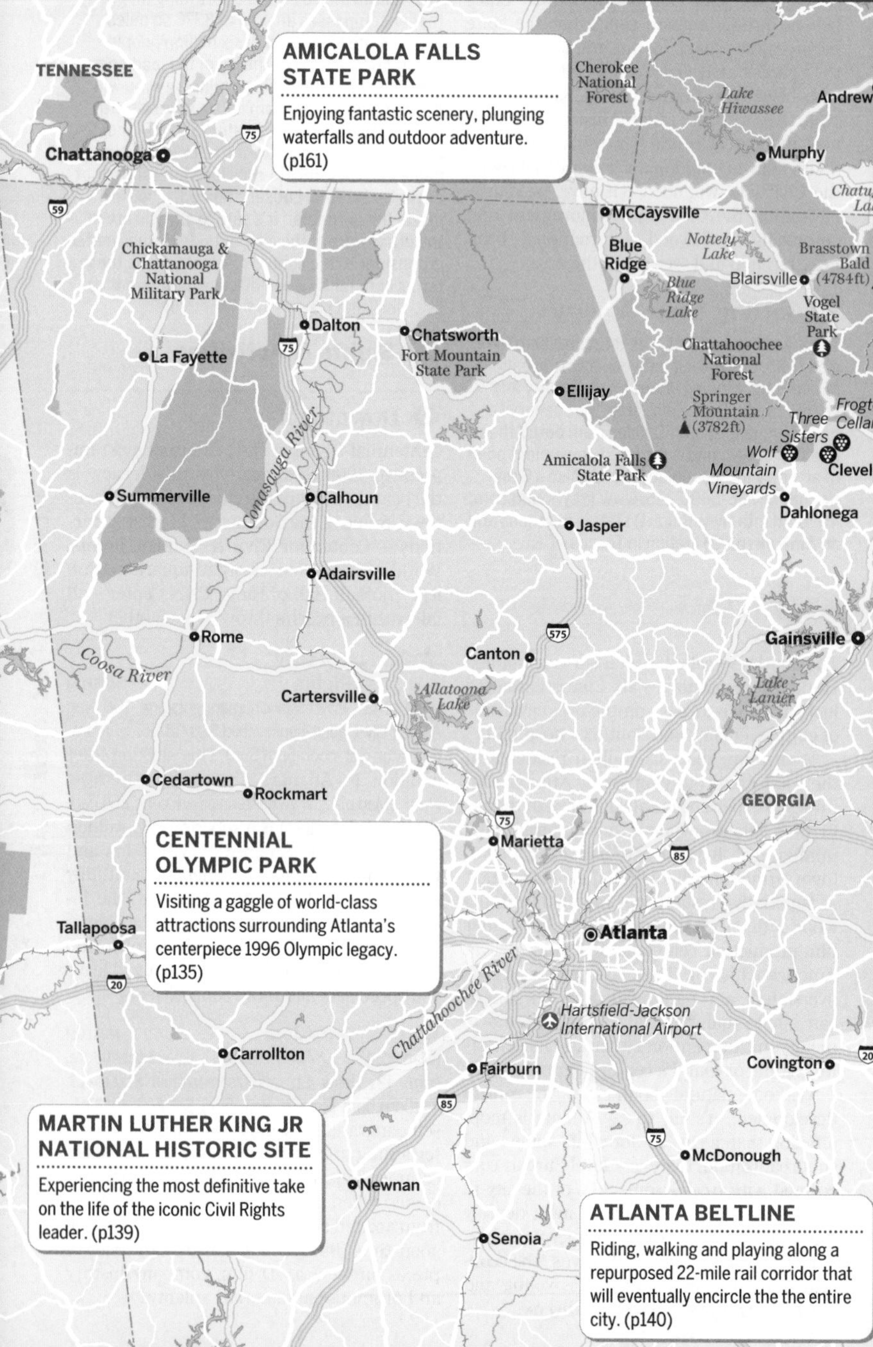

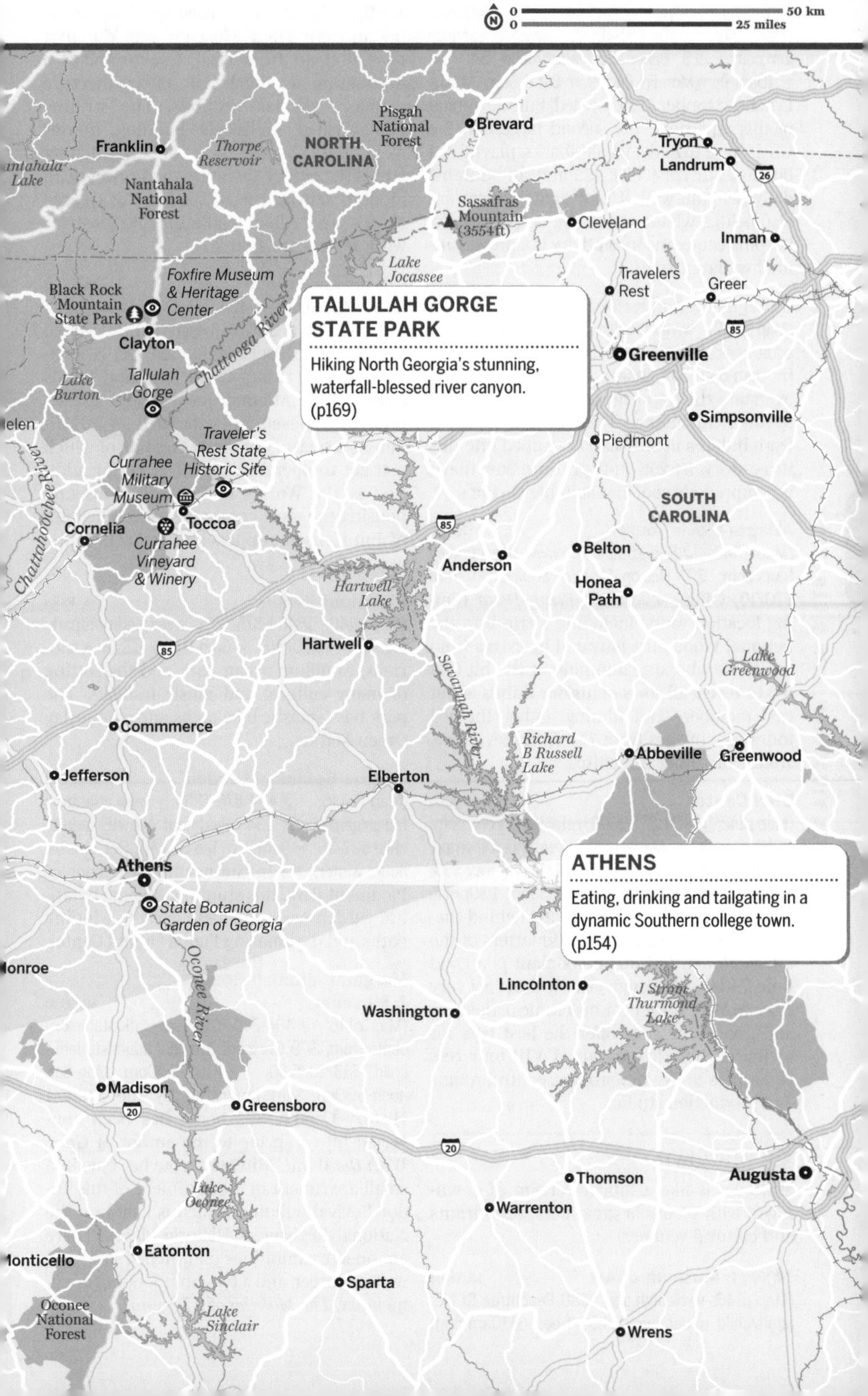

0 — 50 km
0 — 25 miles

TALLULAH GORGE STATE PARK

Hiking North Georgia's stunning, waterfall-blessed river canyon. (p169)

ATHENS

Eating, drinking and tailgating in a dynamic Southern college town. (p154)

Pisgah National Forest
Brevard
NORTH CAROLINA
Franklin
Thorpe Reservoir
Nantahala Lake
Nantahala National Forest
Tryon
Landrum
26
Sassafras Mountain (3554ft)
Cleveland
Inman
Lake Jocassee
Travelers Rest
Greer
Black Rock Mountain State Park
Foxfire Museum & Heritage Center
Clayton
Chattooga River
85
Greenville
Lake Burton
Tallulah Gorge
Simpsonville
Helen
Piedmont
Traveler's Rest State Historic Site
Currahee Military Museum
Chattahoochee River
Toccoa
Cornelia
Currahee Vineyard & Winery
SOUTH CAROLINA
85
Belton
Anderson
Honea Path
Hartwell Lake
Hartwell
85
Savannah River
Lake Greenwood
Commmerce
Richard B Russell Lake
Abbeville
Greenwood
Jefferson
Elberton
Athens
State Botanical Garden of Georgia
Oconee River
Monroe
Lincolnton
J Strom Thurmond Lake
Washington
Madison
Greensboro
20
20
Thomson
Augusta
Warrenton
Lake Oconee
Eatonton
Monticello
Sparta
Oconee National Forest
Lake Sinclair
Wrens

Georgia Aquarium AQUARIUM
(Map p142; ☎404-581-4000; www.georgiaaquarium.com; 225 Baker St; adult/child $40/34; ⏲10am-9pm Mon-Fri, 9am-9pm Sat & Sun) Atlanta's showstopper. It's crowded, but the appeal of this aquarium, the second largest in the US, is hard to deny: whale sharks, playful sea lions at SunTrust Pier 225 and an adorable daily penguin walk. Unfortunately there are also beluga whales and a live dolphin show; keeping cetaceans in captivity is a proven animal-welfare issue.

College Football Hall of Fame MUSEUM
(Map p142; www.cfbhall.com; 250 Marietta St; adult/senior/child $22/19/18; ⏲10am-5pm Sun-Fri, 9am-6pm Sat; P) It is impossible to overstate the importance of college football to American culture. This musem, relocated from Indiana in 2014 and revamped into this three-story, 94,256-sq-ft gridiron sanctuary, is a supremely cool and suitable shrine.

Atlanta Movie Tours TOURS
(Map p142; ☎855-255-3456; www.atlantamovietours.com; 327 Nelson St SW; adult/child from $20/10) Offers several *Walking Dead* filming location tours, including a trip into the fictional Woodbury, narrated by extras from the show who are chomping at the bit (get it?) to reveal all sorts of insider tidbits about cast members and filming. Other themed tours take in sites from *The Hunger Games, Taken* and other franchises.

CNN Center TOURS
(Map p142; ☎404-827-2300; http://tours.cnn.com; 1 CNN Center, cnr Marietta St & Centennial Olympic Park Dr; adult/senior/child $15/14/12, VIP tour $33; ⏲9am-5pm, VIP tours 9:30am, 11:30am, 1:30pm & 3:30pm Mon-Sat) The 55-minute behind-the-scenes tour through the headquarters of the international, 24-hour news giant is a good time for fans. Although visitors don't get very close to Wolf Blitzer (or his cronies), the 9am and noon time slots offer the best bets for seeing anchors live on air. A VIP tour gets you access to live newsrooms, control rooms and production studios.

Midtown

Midtown is like a hipper version of downtown, with plenty of great bars, restaurants and cultural venues.

★High Museum of Art MUSEUM
(Map p146; www.high.org; 1280 Peachtree St NE; adult/child under 5yr $14.50/free; ⏲10am-5pm Tue-Thu & Sat, to 9pm Fri, noon-5pm Sun) Atlanta's modern High Museum was the first to exhibit art from Paris' Louvre and is a destination as much for its architecture as its world-class exhibits. The striking whitewashed multilevel building houses a permanent collection of eye-catching late-19th-century furniture, early American modern canvases from the likes of George Morris and Albert Gallatin, and postwar work from Mark Rothko.

Center for Puppetry Arts MUSEUM
(Map p146; ☎tickets 404-873-3391; www.puppet.org; 1401 Spring St NW; museum $12.50, guided tours $16.50; ⏲9am-5pm Tue-Sun) A wonderland for visitors of all ages and hands down one of Atlanta's most unique attractions, the museum – expanded in 2015 – houses a treasury of puppets, some of which you get to operate yourself. A major addition is the Worlds of Puppetry Museum, housing the most comprehensive collection of Jim Henson puppets and artifacts in the world.

Piedmont Park PARK
(Map p146; ☎404-875-7275; www.piedmontpark.org; 400 Park Dr NE; ⏲6am-11pm) FREE A glorious, rambling urban park and the setting of many cultural and music festivals. The park has fantastic bike paths and a Saturday Green Market.

Atlanta Botanical Garden GARDENS
(Map p146; ☎404-876-5859; www.atlantabotanicalgarden.org; 1345 Piedmont Ave NE; adult/child $22/16; ⏲9am-7pm Tue-Sun Apr-Oct, shorter hours winter; P) In the northwest corner of Piedmont Park, this stunning 30-acre botanical garden has a Japanese garden, winding paths and the amazing Fuqua Orchid Center.

Margaret Mitchell House & Museum MUSEUM
(Map p146; ☎404-249-7015; www.atlantahistorycenter.com; 979 Crescent Ave NE; adult/student/child $13/10/5.50; ⏲10am-5:30pm Mon-Sat, noon-5:30pm Sun) Operated by the Atlanta History Center, this home has been converted into a shrine to the author of *Gone With the Wind*. Mitchell wrote her epic in a small apartment in the basement of this Tudor Revival building, which is listed on the National Register of Historic Places. There are on-site exhibitions on Mitchell's life and writing career, and a two-hour looping documentary, *The Making of a Legend*.

East Side

Atlanta's East Side was the first part of the city to embrace a hip urban living upheaval: Little Five Points has been a bastion of counterculture since the '80s; quality foodie havens started sprouting in bohemian Decatur in the '90s; revitalized urban districts like Inman Park, Candler Park, Old Fourth Ward and East Atlanta Village are now reborn as darling districts for deep-pocketed millennials with a penchant for craft. It's all in stark contrast to Sweet Auburn, the stomping grounds of Martin Luther King Jr and the Civil Rights revolution.

★ Martin Luther King Jr National Historic Site HISTORIC SITE
(Map p150; 404-331-5190; www.nps.gov/malu; 450 Auburn Ave, Sweet Auburn; 9am-5pm; P) FREE The historic site commemorates the life, work and legacy of the Civil Rights leader and one of the great Americans. The site takes up several blocks. Stop by the excellent visitor center to get oriented with a map and brochure of area sites, a 20-minute film, *New Time, New Voice*, and exhibits that elucidate the context – the segregation, systemic oppression and racial violence that inspired and fueled King's work.

Martin Luther King Jr Birthplace LANDMARK
(Map p150; 404-331-5190; www.nps.gov/malu; 501 Auburn Ave, Sweet Auburn; 10am-4pm) FREE Free, first-come, first-served guided tours of King's childhood home take about 30 minutes to complete and require same-day registration, which can be made at the visitor center at the National Historic Site – arrive early, as slots fill fast. The tours can depart anytime between 10am and 4pm, but you are free to visit the rest of the park at your leisure before your designated tour time.

Ebenezer Baptist Church (New) CHURCH
(Map p150; 404-688-7300; www.historicebenezer.org; 101 Jackson St NE, Sweet Auburn; service 9am & 11:30am Sun) The new Ebenezer Baptist Church is the home of the congregation once led by Dr Martin Luther King Jr. As befits one of the most influential church communities in American history, the structure is impressive – light filled, airy and more welcoming than muscular. The church is across the street from the historic Ebenezer Baptist Church, and welcomes visitors to Sunday morning services. Dress nicely.

MARTIN LUTHER KING JUNIOR: A CIVIL RIGHTS GIANT

Martin Luther King Jr, the quintessential figure of the Civil Rights movement and arguably America's greatest leader, was born and raised in Atlanta, the son of a preacher and choir leader. His lineage was significant not only because he followed his father to the pulpit of Atlanta's Ebenezer Baptist Church, but also because his political speeches rang out with a preacher's inflections. King remains one of the most respected figures of the 20th century and is Atlanta's quintessential African American hero, his legacy emblazoned across the city's historic Sweet Auburn district, home to the Martin Luther King Jr National Historic Site.

Fernbank Museum of Natural History MUSEUM
(404-929-6300; www.fernbankmuseum.org; 767 Clifton Rd; adult/child $20/18; 10am-5pm; P) Fernbank is a supremely kid-friendly museum that explores a bunch of subjects (dinosaurs, geology, shells, IMAX-style theater), all attached to a 65-acre old-growth forest and 10-acre Wildwoods outdoor educational area within – reached by elevated walkway from the museum's terrace. While children will have a blast, Fernbank is so well put together and organized that adults will surely enjoy it as well. The museum is northeast of Downtown, near Decatur.

Jimmy Carter Presidential Library & Museum MUSEUM
(Map p150; 404-865-7100; www.jimmycarterlibrary.org; 441 Freedom Pkwy, Poncey-Highland; adult/senior/child $8/6/free; 8am-5pm; P) Located on a hilltop overlooking Downtown, this center features exhibits highlighting Jimmy Carter's presidency (1977–81), including a replica of the Oval Office and his Nobel Prize. Don't miss the tranquil Japanese garden and butterfly garden out back. The 1.5-mile long, landscaped **Freedom Park Trail** leads from here to the Martin Luther King Jr National Historic Site through Freedom Park.

Festivals & Events

★ Peachtree Road Race SPORTS
(919-242-6802; www.atlantatrackclub.org/peachtree; Jul) This July 4 Atlanta tradition is one of the globe's most famous 10km road

ATLANTA BELTLINE

Transforming the way the city moves, lives, works and plays, the **Atlanta BeltLine** (www.beltline.org) is an enormous sustainable redevelopment project. An existing 22-mile rail corridor encircling the city has been repurposed with light-rail transit and 33 miles of connected multiuse trails. It is the most comprehensive transportation and economic development effort ever undertaken in Atlanta and among the largest, most wide-ranging urban redevelopment programs underway in the US. Of most interest to visitors is the 2.2-mile **Eastside Trail** connecting the hip urban neighborhood of Inman Park with Piedmeont Park in Midtown.

races, attracting world-class athletes among its 60,000 annual participants. Started by the Atlanta Track Club in 1970, its coveted official race T-shirt – given only to runners who finish – is designed annually by an *Atlanta Journal-Constitution* contest winner and is an Atlantan status symbol among residents.

★Dragon Con CULTURAL
(☎404-669-0773; www.dragoncon.org; ⏲Aug/Sep) A multigenre convention for freaks and geeks, Dragon Con draws some 80,000 fans of science fiction, fantasy, comic books and other fan-related fantasy genres, who descend on downtown Atlanta often dressed in character over the four-day Labor Day weekend.

★Music Midtown MUSIC
(www.musicmidtown.com; Piedmont Park; from $135; ⏲Sep) Atlanta's biggest and best music festival, a two-day Piedmont Park extravaganza that attracts the biggest names in music. The 2017 lineup included Bruno Mars, Mumford & Sons, Wiz Khalifa, Bastille and Weezer.

Shaky Knees Music Festival MUSIC
(www.shakykneesfestival.com; Centennial Olympic Park; ⏲May) This indie music festival is one of Atlanta's coolest. The 2018 lineup featured LCD Soundsystem, Cage the Elephant, Pixies, the XX and Ryan Adams, among others. Two sister festivals, Shaky Boots (currently on hiatus) and Shaky Beats (May), focus on country and EDM (electronic dance music) genres, respectively.

National Black Arts Festival CULTURAL
(☎404-730-7315; www.nbaf.org; ⏲Sep/Nov) Showcases performing arts, literature and visual arts produced by creative artists of African descent. It is considered one of the most important festivals in the world for art and culture of the African diaspora, and big names like Maya Angelou, Wynton Marsalis and Spike Lee have made appearances.

Sleeping

Atlanta remains short on independent boutique options, long on chains. Rates at Downtown hotels tend to fluctuate depending on whether there is a large convention in town. The least expensive option is to stay in one of the many chain hotels along the MARTA line outside Downtown and take the train into the city for sightseeing.

Aloft Atlanta Downtown BOUTIQUE HOTEL **$**
(Map p142; ☎678-515-0300; www.aloftatlantadowntown.com; 300 Ted Turner Dr NW; r $89-159; P ❄ @ 📶 🏊 🐾) Atlanta's supremely located Aloft hotel is steps from Centennial Olympic Park and peppered with personality (rare for the city's hotels). From the odd but interesting outdoor front patio to a colorful lobby brimming with glittery pop art from a formerly homeless artist and a purple-felt pool table, its playful attitude is refreshing and fun. Rooms are more spacious than most.

Highland Inn INN **$**
(Map p150; ☎404-874-5756; www.thehighlandinn.com; 644 N Highland Ave, Virginia-Highland; s/d from $73/103; P ❄ 📶) This European-style, 65-room independent inn, built in 1927, has appealed to touring musicians over the years. Rooms aren't huge, but it has a great location in the Virginia-Highland area and is as affordably comfortable as being Downtown. It's one of the few accommodations in town with single rooms.

★Urban Oasis B&B B&B **$$**
(Map p150; ☎770-714-8618; www.urbanoasisbandb.com; 130a Krog St NE, Inman Park; r $145-215; P ❄ 📶 🏊) Hidden inside a gated and repurposed 1950s cotton-sorting warehouse, this retro-modern loft B&B is urban dwelling at its best. Enter into a huge and funky common area with natural light streaming through massive windows and make your way to one of three rooms, all discerningly appointed with Haywood Wakefield mid-century modern furnishings. It's like sleeping in a Piet Mondrian painting.

★ Social Goat B&B B&B $$

(☎404-626-4830; www.thesocialgoatbandb.com; 548 Robinson Ave SE, Grant Park; r $125-245; P❄📶) Skirting Grant Park, this wonderfully restored 1900 Queen Anne Victorian mansion has six rooms decorated in country-French-style and is loaded with period antiques. More importantly, however, you'll share the real estate with goats, turkeys, ducks, chickens and cats. A true country escape, plunked into one of the nation's largest urban areas.

Sugar Magnolia B&B B&B $$

(Map p150; ☎404-222-0226; www.sugarmagnoliabb.com; 804 Edgewood Ave NE, Inman Park; r $155-195; P❄@📶) This lovely four-room inn occupies an impeccable 1892 Queen Anne Victorian mansion in Inman Park. Five original working fireplaces, a supremely relaxing back porch and firepit are highlights, as is Debbie, hostess with the mostest who whips up Belgian waffles and Dutch baby pancakes for breakfast. Our favorite room is the blue-curtained Royal Suite with a massive terrace and a tiled bathroom.

Hotel Artmore BOUTIQUE HOTEL $$

(Map p146; ☎404-876-6100; www.artmorehotel.com; 1302 W Peachtree St; r $170-200, ste from $220; P❄@📶) This 1924 Spanish-Mediterranean architectural landmark has been completely revamped into an artistic boutique hotel that's become an urban sanctuary for those who appreciate their trendiness with a dollop of discretion. It wins all sorts of accolades: excellent service, a wonderful courtyard with fire pit and a superb location across the street from Arts Center MARTA station.

Hotel Clermont BOUTIQUE HOTEL $$

(Map p150; ☎470-485-0485; www.hotelclermont.com; 789 Ponce de Leon Ave NE, Poncey-Highland; r $199-319, bunk r $204-314; P❄@📶) With preserved stairwells and unusable original doors, Atlanta's hottest boutique hotel has kept a wink and a nod to this historic 1924 Poncey-Highland building, originally the Bonaventure Arms Apartments. It's decidedly retro and unafraid to be cheeky (the French-American brasserie is named after a former stripper who famously refused to dance with Hitler), and rooms are playful and funky.

Westin Peachtree Plaza HOTEL $$

(Map p142; ☎404-659-1400; www.starwoodhotels.com; 210 Peachtree St NW; r from $163; P@📶🏊) Occupying Atlanta's most iconic and tallest building, the cylindrical, 73-story Peachtree Plaza, the Westin has been featured in film (1981's *Sharky's Machine* starring Burt Reynolds) and on nearly every postcard of Atlanta there ever was. Being a well-regarded chain, rooms and amenities are unsurprising – the appeal here is the view (it's the fourth-tallest hotel in the western hemisphere).

American Hotel BOUTIQUE HOTEL $$

(Map p142; ☎404-688-8600; www.doubletree3.hilton.com; 160 Ted Turner Dr NW; r $129-229; P❄@📶🏊) The original Americana Motor Lodge that once occupied this space opened in 1962 – funded by Martin Luther King's dentist – and was Atlanta's first integrated hotel (these walls have slept such icons as Aretha Franklin and James Brown). This new mid-century modern throwback to the original hotel features design elements around every turn that evoke the hotel's storied past.

Ellis Hotel BOUTIQUE HOTEL $$

(Map p142; ☎877-211-2545; www.ellishotel.com; 176 Peachtree St NW; r $129-249; P❄📶🐾) With business-chic rooms warmly dressed in blue and gray hues and ostrich-skin headboards, the Ellis is contemporary and subtly boutique. You can sleep inside a magnetic field in the Wellness Room; or pick a room on the pet-friendly floor, women's-only floor or 'Fresh Air' floor (with private access and special cleaning rules for allergy sufferers).

Glenn Hotel BOUTIQUE HOTEL $$

(Map p142; ☎404-521-2250; www.glennhotel.com; 110 Marietta St NW; r $189-269; P❄📶) Modern and elegant, the Glenn is housed in a stately 1923 building that was designed by architect Waddy B Wood (fantastic name, by the way). Period films loop over the check-in desk, with wafts of lemongrass filling the lobby. Tranquility rocks line the hallways to the rooms, which are a hybrid of contemporary design and historical accents.

★ Stonehurst Place B&B $$$

(Map p146; ☎404-881-0722; www.stonehurstplace.com; 923 Piedmont Ave NE; r $239-499; P❄@📶) Built in 1896 by the Hinman family, this elegant B&B has all the modern amenities you could ask for and is well located. It's fully updated with ecofriendly water-treatment and heating systems and has original Warhol illustrations on the wall. It's an exceptional choice if you're not on a budget.

Downtown Atlanta

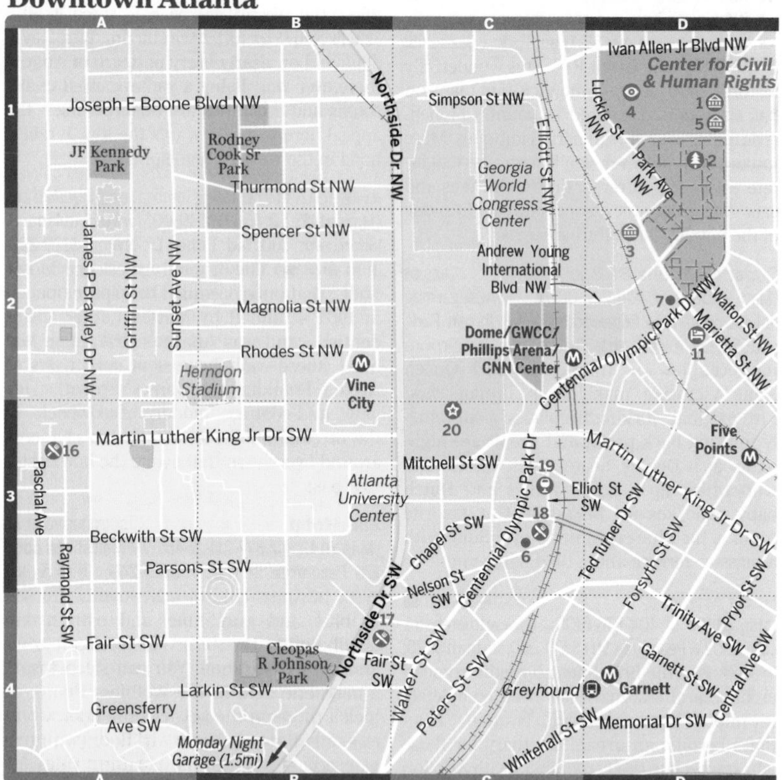

Downtown Atlanta

Top Sights
1 Center for Civil & Human Rights D1

Sights
2 Centennial Olympic Park D1
3 College Football Hall of Fame D2
4 Georgia Aquarium D1
5 World of Coca-Cola D1

Activities, Courses & Tours
6 Atlanta Movie Tours C3
7 CNN Center D2

Sleeping
8 Aloft Atlanta Downtown E1
9 American Hotel E2
10 Ellis Hotel E2
11 Glenn Hotel D2
12 Ritz-Carlton, Atlanta E2
13 Westin Peachtree Plaza E2

Eating
14 Alma Cocina E2
15 Amalfi Pizza E2
16 Busy Bee Café A3
17 Paschal's B4
18 Smoke Ring C3

Drinking & Nightlife
19 Elliott Street Deli & Pub C3
SkyLounge .... (see 11)

Entertainment
20 Mercedes-Benz Stadium C3

Ritz-Carlton, Atlanta LUXURY HOTEL $$$
(Map p142; ☎404-659-0400; www.ritzcarlton.com/en/hotels/georgia/atlanta; 181 Peachtree St NE; r from $489; P❄@🛜) If you told your author during his college days at the University of Georgia that the fiercely independent coffeehouse Jittery Joe's would someday sit inside a Ritz-Carlton Hotel, he would have

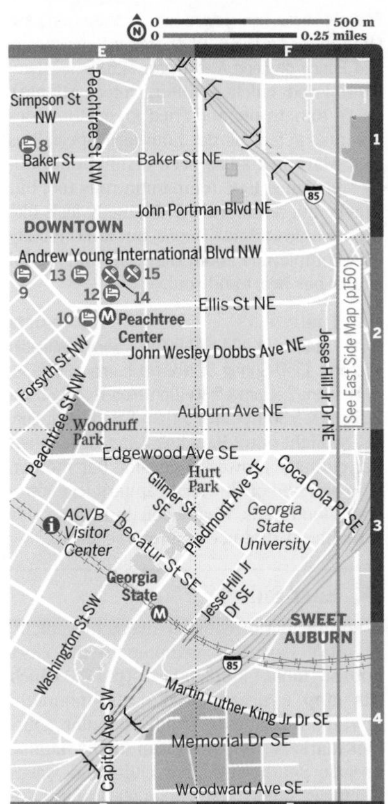

had you committed. But here it sits, one of many positives at this 444-room neoclassical luxury downtown hotel.

Eating

After New Orleans, Atlanta is the best city in the South to eat, and the food culture here is nothing short of obsessive. The Westside Provisions District, Krog Street Market and Ponce City Market are all newish and hip mixed-use residential and restaurant complexes sprinkled among Atlanta's continually transitioning urban neighborhoods.

Downtown & Midtown

Varsity FAST FOOD $

(Map p146; www.thevarsity.com; 61 North Ave NW; combos $6.75-9.50; 10:30am-10pm Sun-Thu, to midnight Fri & Sat) Presidents have dined here (George W Bush, Bill Clinton, Barack Obama), movies have been filmed here *(We Are Marshall)*, millions have eaten here: this iconic greasy spoon (at it since 1928) is the world's largest drive-in. In response to its famous call to order ('What'll Ya Have?'), you can order dishes such as chili dogs and triple-stack bacon cheeseburgers.

Amalfi Pizza PIZZA $

(Map p142; 404-228-7528; www.amalfipizzaatl.com; 17 Andrew Young International Blvd NE; pizzas from $9.50; 11am-10pm Mon-Thu, to 11pm Fri & Sat, noon-10pm Sun;) This new Neapolitan pizzeria makes a for a great Downtown stop for families, with the pies emerging from two dueling, 6000lb wood-burning brick ovens imported from Italy. The way to go here is *carnavale*-style, a star-shaped pizza with a fresh ricotta-stuffed crust – a homage to the original, invented by Pizzeria Attilio in Napoli in the 1930s.

Einstein's BREAKFAST $$

(Map p146; 404-876-7925; www.einsteinsatlanta.com; 1077 Juniper St NE; brunch $9-21; 11am-11pm Mon-Thu, to 1am Fri, 9am-11pm Sat & Sun;) Eclectic Einstein's is a come-one, come-all, free-spirited microcosm of urban living. Gay couples to the left, hip-hop artists to the right, all noshing on Southern-angled, organic-where-possible brunch dishes such as fried-green-tomato eggs Benedict with goat's cheese and a side of pepper-Jack grits or spicy seafood omelets chased with monstrous Bloody Marys (one of Atlanta's best).

Alma Cocina MEXICAN $$

(Map p142; 404-968-9662; www.alma-atlanta.com; 191 Peachtree St NW; tacos $15-30, mains $19-21; 11am-3pm & 5-10pm Mon-Thu, 5-11pm Sat, 5-10pm Sun;) 'Soul Kitchen' cooks contemporary tacos and inventive Mexican fare. There might be tequila-poached pear guacamole to start; small plates such as chili-ash-cured Arctic Char with avocado, Fresno chilies, candied ginger and tequila-ginger *aguachile,* or *huitlacoche* empanadas; and mains such as achiote-rubbed pork chops and seared scallops in cauliflower-hominy puree. Everything is good. You'll fight for a table during the downtown lunch rush.

Paschal's SOUTHERN US $$

(Map p142; 404-525-2023; www.paschalsatlanta.com; 180 Northside Dr SW; mains $11-24; 11am-9pm Sun-Thu, to 11pm Fri & Sat) Slinging old-school Southern soul food, Lowcountry cuisine and Cajun/creole staples for six decades, Paschal's touts bone-in fried-chicken sandwiches, slow-cooked ribs and catfish étouffée among its specialties that have been enjoyed by noteworthy entertainers, politicians and folks about town dating all the way back to the Civil Rights movement.

Herban Fix VEGAN $$
(Map p146; www.herbanfix.com; 565 Peachtree St NW; mains $15-19; ⌚11am-3pm & 5-9:30pm Mon-Thu, 11am-3pm & 5-10:30pm Fri & Sat, 11am-3pm Sun; 📶) 🌿 This contemporary vegan restaurant straddling Midtown and Downtown leans heavily Pan-Asian (the chef is Taiwanese) and will surprise you with its earthy-upscale decor. Dishes are refreshingly creative – grilled eggplant topped with basil and minced garlic, seared pom pom–mushroom steak, soy fish with organic kale simmered in laksa curry – and decidedly tasty.

Smoke Ring BARBECUE $$
(Map p142; www.smokeringatlanta.com; 309 Nelson Street SW, Castleberry Hill; mains $10-15, plates $17-27; ⌚11:30am-10pm Mon-Thu & Sun, to 11pm Fri & Sat; 📶) This sleek Castleberry Hill barbecue restaurant sits in the shadow of Mercedes-Benz Stadium. The pulled pork is divine, especially in the breakfast burrito, but they smoke plenty here beyond the usual suspects, such as ahi tuna, pork belly and lamb belly. The long hardwood bar is ideal for a game-day tipple.

Empire State South SOUTHERN US $$$
(Map p146; ☎404-541-1105; www.empirestatesouth.com; 999 Peachtree St NE; mains $31-46; ⌚7-10:30am & 11:30am-10pm Mon-Thu, to 11pm Fri & Sat, 10am-3pm Sun; 📶) This rustic-hip Midtown bistro serves imaginative New Southern fare and it does not disappoint, be it at breakfast ($7.50 to $11) or throughout the remains of the day. It makes its own bagels, the attention to coffee detail approaches Pacific Northwest levels, and it mixes fried chicken, bacon marmalade *and* pimento cheese on a biscuit!

Federal NEW AMERICAN $$$
(Map p146; ☎404-343-3857; www.thefederalatl.com; 1050 Crescent Ave NE; mains $16-32; ⌚8-10am & 11:30am-2pm Mon, 8-10am, 11:30am-2pm & 5-10pm Tue-Thu, 8-10am, 11:30am-2pm & 5-11pm Fri, 5-11pm Sat, 5-9pm Sun; 📶) Atlanta staple chef Shaun Doty has returned to his kitchen roots at this glam bistro serving everything from a $16 burger to high-end cast-iron steaks ($48 to $62). Doty's Sardinian flatbread is a sought-after Atlanta appetizer. Anything with meat and *frites* (fries) is the way to go here.

Mary Mac's Tea Room SOUTHERN US $$$
(Map p146; ☎404-876-1800; www.marymacs.com; 224 Ponce de Leon Ave; meals $26.95; ⌚11am-9pm) Fried chicken (often voted Atlanta's best), tomato pie and fried green tomatoes are just a few of the Southern specialties that Mary Mac's has been dishing out family-style since 1945 (cinnamon rolls too, but they're not Southern!). It distinctly feels like dining at grandma's house, but ain't nobody ever complained about that! This old-school eatery has heart and soul.

Nan Thai THAI $$$
(Map p146; ☎404-870-9933; www.nanfinedining.com; 1350 Spring St NW, No 1; mains $18-39; ⌚11:30am-2:30pm & 5:30-10pm Mon-Thu, 11:30am-2:30pm & 5:30-11pm Fri, 5-11pm Sat, 5-10pm Sun; 📶) Straight outta Bangkok, Chef Nan honed her culinary prowess alongside her mother, who ran one of the Thai capital's legendary street-food stalls. Wear a collared shirt – this is highbrow dining – and reserve ahead.

East Side

A cornucopia of culinary overachievement, Atlanta's East Side is home to the city's hottest table, Staplehouse (p145), which sits atop a near-biblical gastro-mountain of sought-after eats. Wildly popular gourmet markets, New American foodie haunts, upscale Southern supper clubs and waves of ethnic superstars – Spanish, Italian, Korean fusion, Jamaican, elevated Mexican, old-school Jewish – could fuel your foodie adventures on this side of town for months.

★Ria's Bluebird AMERICAN $
(Map p150; ☎404-521-3737; www.riasbluebird.com; 421 Memorial Dr SE; breakfast $5-13, sandwiches $11.50; ⌚8am-3pm; P 🖊) 🌿 Ria's makes a big deal about being the kind of business that accepts people of all races, religions and sexual orientations, and supports causes that speak to this commitment. It *also* serves one of the most kick-ass breakfasts in greater Atlanta: enormous skillets and delicious soupy brisket and eggs. For lunch, try a pepper turkey melt. Two thumbs up.

★Dish Dive AMERICAN $$
(☎404-957-7918; www.dishdivekitchen.com; 2233 College Ave NE; mains $9-18; ⌚5-10pm Tue-Sat) Located in a teeny house near some railroad tracks, Dish Dive is cooler than you and it doesn't care. Anyone is welcome here, and the food – fresh, seasonal cuisine like turmeric and black-pepper pappardelle, fried

spaghetti squash with poblano-chocolate sauce and the never-off-the-menu masterpiece, braised pork-belly French toast – is high-value, easy-on-the-wallet eating.

★Octopus Bar FUSION **$$**
(Map p150; ☎404-627-9911; www.octopusbaratl.com; 560 Gresham Ave SE, East Atlanta; dishes $6-22; ⏲10:30pm-2:30am Tue-Sat) Leave your hang-ups at the hotel – this is punk-rock dining – and get to know what's good at this unsigned indoor-outdoor patio dive nuanced with graffitied-up walls and ethereal electronica. No reservations, so line up early, and chow down on a Maine lobster roll (drawn butter, tomalley mayo), shoyu ramen (farm egg) or many other innovative executions of fusion excellence.

★Fox Brothers BARBECUE **$$**
(Map p150; www.foxbrosbbq.com; 1238 Dekalb Ave NE, Inman Park; dishes $10-30; ⏲11am-10pm Sun-Thu, to 11pm Fri & Sat; P 📶) At this longtime Atlanta classic, set in Inman Park, ribs are scorched and smoked perfectly with a hint of charcoal crust on the outside and tender on the inside. It's also known for its exceptional Texas-style brisket and Brunswick-stew-smothered tater tots. Always packed.

★BoccaLupo ITALIAN **$$**
(Map p150; ☎404-577-2332; http://boccalupoatl.com; 753 Edgewood Ave NE, Inman Park; mains $16-19; ⏲5:30-10pm Tue-Thu, to 11pm Fri & Sat; 📶) There is so much to love about this dark, candlelit Italian-Southern comfort-food haunt led by Mario Batali–trained chef Bruce Logue, but perhaps none more than his Southern-fried-chicken parma with creamy collards and *strano* pasta. It's hands down a top-five Atlanta dish. This Southern soul food with Italian tweak is made with a lotta love and not to be missed.

★Gunshow MODERN AMERICAN **$$$**
(Map p150; ☎404-380-1886; www.gunshowatl.com; 924 Garrett St SE, Glenwood Park; dishes $10-18; ⏲6-9pm Tue-Sat; 📶) Celebrity chef Kevin Gillespie's innovative and unorthodox Gunshow is an explosively good night out. Guests choose between over a dozen or so smallish dishes, dreamed up by chefs in the open kitchen, who then hawk their blood, sweat and culinary tears dim-sum-style tableside.

★Staplehouse AMERICAN **$$$**
(Map p150; ☎404-524-5005; www.staplehouse.com; 541 Edgewood Ave SE; dishes $5-36; ⏲5:30-10pm Wed & Thu, to 11pm Fri & Sat, noon-4pm Sun; P 📶) The hottest table in Atlanta and the darling du jour of Southern foodies, Staplehouse dishes up innovative, seasonal New American cuisine. Small to medium plates including chicken-liver tart with burnt honey and blood orange are served with such artful precision you kinda feel bad about eating them (except they're delicious, so not *that* bad). The seasonal menu changes often.

Westside

Some of Atlanta best food experiences can be had in the Westside. Quite frankly, you could spend a week eating in the Westside Provisions District and never taste anything that wasn't completely mind-blowing. This is the city's foodie fantasyland.

West Egg Cafe DINER **$**
(Map p146; ☎404-872-3973; www.westeggcafe.com; 1100 Howell Mill Rd, Westside Provisions District; mains $6-15; ⏲7am-4pm Mon-Fri, 8am-5pm Sat & Sun; P 📶 👪) Belly up to the marble breakfast counter or grab a table and dive into black-bean cakes and eggs, turkey-sausage Benedict, pimento-cheese and bacon omelet, or a fried green tomato BLT. It's all reimagined versions of old-school classics, served in a stylish and spare dining room.

Local Pizzaiolo PIZZA **$**
(Map p146; ☎678-705-2672; www.thelocalpizzaiolo.com; 1000 Marietta St NW; pizzas $8-15; ⏲11:30am-9pm Sun-Wed, to 10pm Fri & Sat; 📶) The first of four Atlanta locations for the fiercely traditional (and Associazione Verace Pizza Napoletana–certified) Neapolitan pizza from four-time world pizza-making champion Giulio Adriani. The chef, a native Roman, is said to have received a US Green Card solely based on his signature pizza, the Montanara (flash-fried dough, *ciliegino* tomato sauce, mozzarella, fresh basil and Grana Padano).

Star Provisions Market & Cafe SUPERMARKET **$**
(☎404-365-0410; www.starprovisions.com; 1460 Ellsworth Industrial Blvd NW; mains $8-16; ⏲8am-6pm Mon-Sat, to 4pm Sun; 📶) DIY gourmets will feel at home among the cheese shops and butcher cases, bakeries, organic cafe and kitchen-hardware depots attached to the city's finest dining establishment, Bacchanalia. Excellent picnic and craft-coffee accoutrements. It serves breakfast all day, gourmet sandwiches and pizzas.

Midtown Atlanta

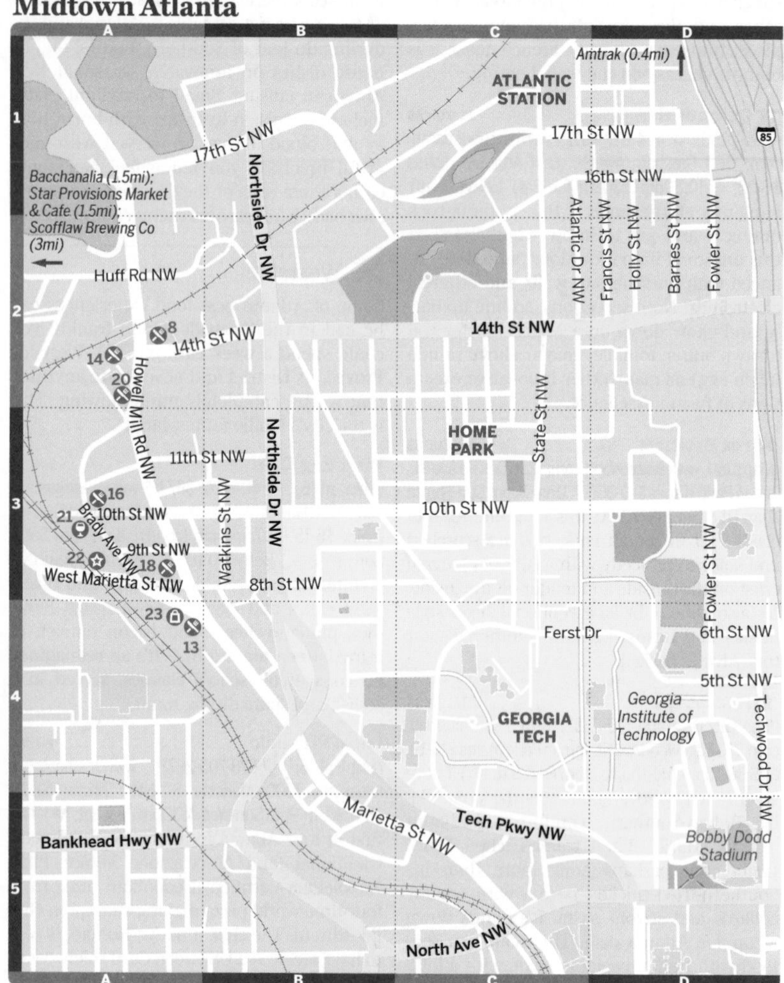

★**Busy Bee Café** SOUTHERN US $$

(Map p142; ☎404-525-9212; www.thebusybeecafe.com; 810 Martin Luther King Jr Dr NW; mains $12-16; ⏰11am-7pm Mon-Fri, noon-7pm Sun) Politicians, police officers, urbanites and hungry miscreants, along with celebrities (it's had pop-ins by MLK Jr, Obama and OutKast) all converge over the city's best fried chicken paired with soul-food sides such as collard greens, candied yams, fried okra and mac 'n' cheese. This Westside classic has been steeped in hospitality and honest-to-goodness food since 1947.

★**Cooks & Soldiers** BASQUE $$

(Map p146; ☎404-996-2623; www.cooksandsoldiers.com; 691 14th St NW; small plates $6-16; ⏰5-10pm Sun-Wed, to 11pm Thu, to 2am Fri & Sat; 📶🍸) A game-changing Westside choice, this Basque-inspired hot spot specializes in *pintxos* (Basque-like tapas) and wood-fired *asadas* (grills) designed to share. Both the food and cocktails are outstanding. Highlights include the house gin and tonics, coal-roasted mushrooms with goat's cheese, crème fraîche and black truffle, and an $84 wood-grilled bone-in rib eye that clocks in at an obviously shareable 2.2lbs (1kg)!

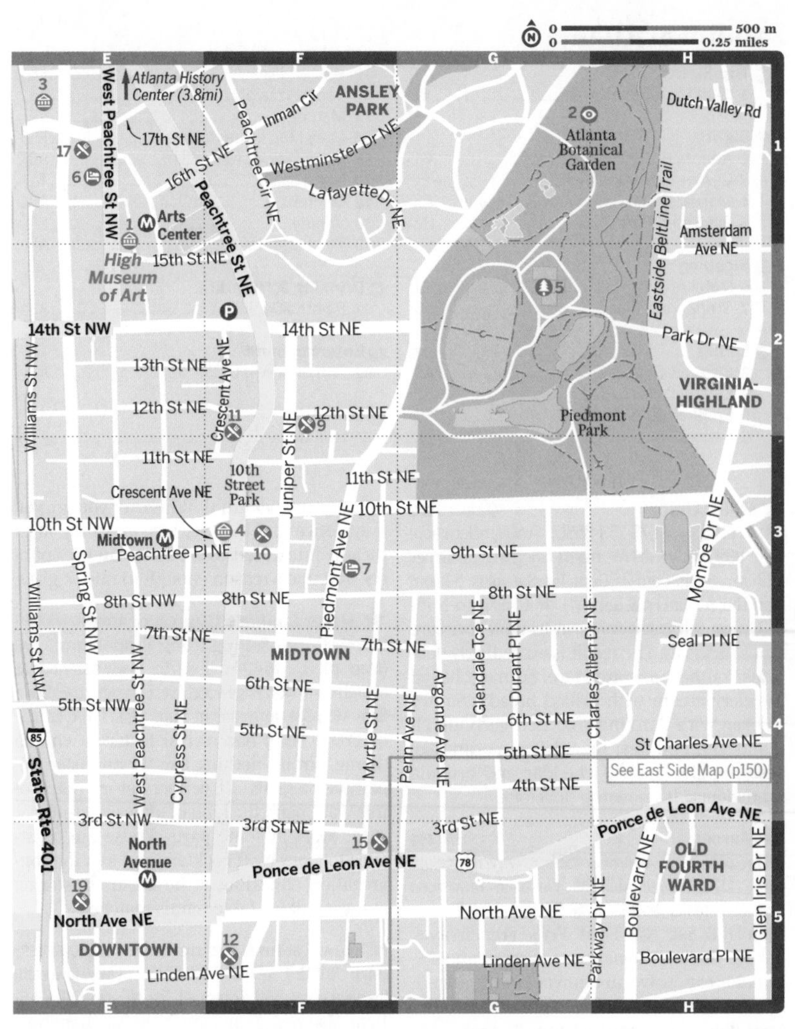

★Bacchanalia MODERN AMERICAN **$$$**
(☎404-365-0410; www.starprovisions.com/bacchanalia; 1460 Ellsworth Industrial Blvd; prix fixe per person $95; ⏰5:30-10pm Mon-Sat; P) Considered one of the top restaurants in the city, Bacchanalia's menu changes daily, and you may choose from multiple dishes for each of the four courses. Start with Maine lobster with fennel, ginger and lemongrass before moving on to Nantucket Bay scallops, lamb with flowing broccoli and ceci-pea *bagna càuda* or Rohan duck with honey and lavender winter citrus.

★Optimist SEAFOOD **$$$**
(Map p146; ☎404-477-6260; www.theoptimistrestaurant.com; 914 Howell Mill Rd; mains $22-68; ⏰11:30am-2:30pm & 5-10pm Mon-Thu, 5-11pm Fri & Sat, 5-10pm Sun; 📶) 🌿 In a short space, we could never do this Westside sustainable-seafood mecca justice. In a word, astonishing! Start with crispy calamari with salsa *matcha* and almonds then move on to a duck-fat-poached swordfish or a daring whole grilled octopus with *aji amarillo* and poblano peppers, and finish with a scoop of house-made salted-caramel ice cream.

Midtown Atlanta

Top Sights
1 High Museum of Art E1

Sights
2 Atlanta Botanical Garden G1
3 Center for Puppetry Arts E1
4 Margaret Mitchell House & Museum F3
5 Piedmont Park G2

Sleeping
6 Hotel Artmore E1
7 Stonehurst Place F3

Eating
8 Cooks & Soldiers A2
9 Einstein's F2
10 Empire State South F3
11 Federal F2
12 Herban Fix F5
13 Local Pizzaiolo A4
14 Marcel A2
15 Mary Mac's Tea Room F5
16 Miller Union A3
17 Nan Thai E1
18 Optimist A3
19 Varsity E5
20 West Egg Cafe A2

Drinking & Nightlife
21 Painted Duck A3

Entertainment
22 Terminal West A3

Shopping
23 Hop City A4

★ Miller Union AMERICAN **$$$**
(Map p146; ☎678-733-8550; www.millerunion.com; 999 Brady Ave NW; mains lunch $12-16, dinner $23-36; ⏰11:30am-2:30pm Tue-Sat, plus 5-10pm Mon-Thu, 5-11pm Fri & Sat; 📶) Credit to Miller Union – it takes its farm-to-table locavore ethos seriously. The result is exceedingly delicious Southern-inspired fare: farm egg baked in celery cream with grilled bread; country chicken with Carolina gold rice, coconut, almond and chutney; or chicken, pecan-sage pesto, apple, smoked cheddar and arugula sandwiches. It's nonstop delicious.

★ Marcel STEAK **$$$**
(Map p146; ☎404-665-4555; www.marcelatl.com; 1170 Howell Mill Rd, Westside Provisions District; steaks $50-130; ⏰5-10pm Mon-Thu, to 11pm Fri & Sat; 📶) Ford Fry's French-style, boxing-themed steakhouse serves unquestionably expensive, unequivocally transcendent cuts of beef from hormone-free, purebred Black Angus cattle from Chicago's Linz Heritage Angus Ranch. Each cut is a labor of love draped over smoldering Georgia hickory wood and finished with salted butter. Perfect order: divinely crusted bone-in filet, brandy *au poivre* sauce, béarnaise fries and burgundy-roasted mushrooms.

Drinking

Downtown & East Side

Atlanta has a busy bar scene, ranging from neighborhood dives to hipster hangouts that want to pass for neighborhood dives to straight-up opulent night haunts for the wealthy and beautiful. Wherever you go, you may notice that this city has one of the most racially integrated social scenes in the country, and that's reason enough to raise a glass.

★ Sister Louisa's Church of the Living Room & Ping Pong Emporium BAR
(Map p150; ☎404-522-8275; www.sisterlouisaschurch.com; 466 Edgewood Ave, Edgewood; ⏰5pm-3am Mon-Sat, to midnight Sun; 📶) This cradle of Edgewood's bar revival fosters a church theme, but it's nothing like Westminster Abbey. Sacrilegious art peppers every patch of free wall space, the kind of offensive stuff that starts wars in some parts. Praise the resistance to fancy craft cocktails and join the congregation, chuckling at the artistry or staring at mesmerizing table-tennis matches.

★ New Realm Brewing Co MICROBREWERY
(Map p150; ☎404-968-2778; www.newrealmbrewing.com; 550 Somerset Tce NE, No 101; ⏰5-11pm Mon-Wed, 11am-1am Fri & Sat, 11am-11pm Sun; 📶) Ex–Stone Brewing Co brewmaster Mitch Steele wrote the book on IPAs. His latest venture, a 20,000-sq-ft restaurant and brewery along the BeltLine's Eastside Trail, is a coup for Southern hopheads. Eight taps (four direct from serving tanks behind the bar) harbor triple IPAs and small-batch brews guzzled by a fun crowd ogling the Atlanta skyline from the upstairs terrace.

★ Porter Beer Bar BAR
(Map p150; ☎404-223-0393; www.theporterbeerbar.com; 1156 Euclid Ave NE, Little Five Points; ⏰11:30am-midnight Mon-Thu, to 2:30am Fri, 11am-2:30am Sat, 11am-midnight Sun; 📶) A bar for the

true suds connoisseur, the Porter has an encyclopedic variety of beers from around the world, including 55 taps and a head-spinning nine-page vintage list with beers dating to 1997 (stored in the drool-inducing cellar) The darkly lit space encompasses a huge bar and an atmosphere perfect for the sampling of a brew or five. There's food.

★Argosy PUB
(Map p150; ☎404-577-0407; www.argosy-east.com; 470 Flat Shoals Ave SE; ⏰5pm-2:30am Mon-Fri, noon-2:30am Sat, to midnight Sun; 📶) This East Atlanta gastropub nails it with an extensive list of rare craft beers (35 taps), elevated bar food – house-cut Kennebec potato fries, miso quinoa burger, wood-fired pizzas – and a vibe that invites you to stay for the rest of the evening. The multi-angled bar snakes its way through a rustic-chic space and living-room-style lounge areas.

★Ladybird Grove & Mess Hall BAR
(Map p150; ☎404-458-6838; www.ladybirdatlanta.com; 684 John Wesley Dobbs Ave NE; ⏰11am-late Tue-Sun, closed Mon) With an enviable location (and enormous patio) overlooking the BeltLine, Ladybird offers its patrons one of the best drinking views in Atlanta. Complement that cocktail or draft beer with some of the classy pub grub on offer from the kitchen. Last call depends on how busy the bar is.

★Brick Store Pub BAR
(☎404-687-0990; www.brickstorepub.com; 125 E Court Sq, Decatur; draft beers $5-12; ⏰11am-1am Mon, to 2am Tue-Sat, noon-1am Sun) Beer hounds geek out on Atlanta's best craft-beer selection at this pub in Decatur, with some 30 meticulously chosen drafts (including those in the more intimate Belgian beer bar upstairs). Nearly 300 beers by the bottle are served from a 15,000-bottle vault, drawing a fun, young crowd every night.

★Golden Eagle Diner's Club COCKTAIL BAR
(Map p150; www.goldeneagleatl.com; 904 Memorial Dr SE, Reynoldstown; 📶) From the owner of Ladybird Grove & Mess Hall comes one of Atlanta's hottest new tables, an impossibly retro step back in time set on plaid carpeting inside a gorgeously renovated 1930s-era train depot. The food is throwback continental classics, but we're here for a cocktail ($10 to $12).

Joystick Gamebar BAR
(Map p150; www.joystickgamebar.com; 427 Edgewood Ave SE; ⏰5pm-2:30am Mon-Fri, noon-2:30am Sat, noon-midnight Sun) Sure, it's a bar, but it's also an arcade full of old-school video games, pinball machines and the folks who love to play them.

★Wrecking Bar Brewpub BAR
(Map p150; ☎404-221-2600; www.wreckingbarbrewpub.com; 292 Moreland Ave NE, Little Five Points; ⏰4-11pm Mon-Thu, noon-midnight Fri & Sat, to 10pm Sun, bar closes later; 📶) In the basement of century-old, heroically restored Victorian-style Kriegshaber House (which was a Methodist Protestant church, a dance school and architectural antiques store in its past lives), western-Carolinian-trained brewmaster Neal Engleman makes magical juicy IPAs, cedar-aged cask IPAs, hoppy sours and so much more at this 16-tap Little Five Points favorite wrapped around original stone pillaring.

Elliott Street Deli & Pub BAR
(Map p142; www.elliottstreet.com; 51 Elliott St SW; ⏰11am-2pm & 4pm-midnight Mon & Wed-Thu, to 2am Tue, Fri & Sat, noon-midnight Sun) Gritty and tiny and sitting defiantly in the shadow of Mercedes-Benz Stadium, the Elliott Street Deli & Pub hangs on as one of Atlanta's best dive bars, tucked off the radar in Castleberry Hill. It also does some of the city's best sandwiches.

Westside

★Monday Night Garage MICROBREWERY
(www.mondaynightbrewing.com; 933 Lee St SW, West End; ⏰4-9pm Mon-Thu, noon-10pm Fri & Sat, 1-6pm Sun; 📶) One of two locations in Atlanta, Monday Night Brewing's barrel-aging and souring facility in the West End is set to become its go-to destination and the anchor of a future craft-beer hub in the city. Fire pits and a BeltLine-facing patio keep things cozy while inside an Airstream trailer and massive mural evoke a trashy-arty feel. Twenty taps.

★Painted Duck BAR
(Map p146; ☎404-352-0048; www.thepaintedduckatl.com; 976 Brady Ave NW; duckpin bowling week/weekend $25/35, shoe rental $4.50; ⏰5pm-midnight Mon-Thu, to 2am Fri, 11am-2am Sat, noon-midnight Sun; 📶) You enter this incredible basement adult playground under a wordless neon green-and-white duck sign and through a graffitied, black-lit hallway that will make you feel like drinking and gaming is an illicit activity. Once inside: jaw drop! Sixteen lanes of chargeable duckpin bowling against a 50ft street-art-mural backdrop of migrating ducks and wildlife.

East Side

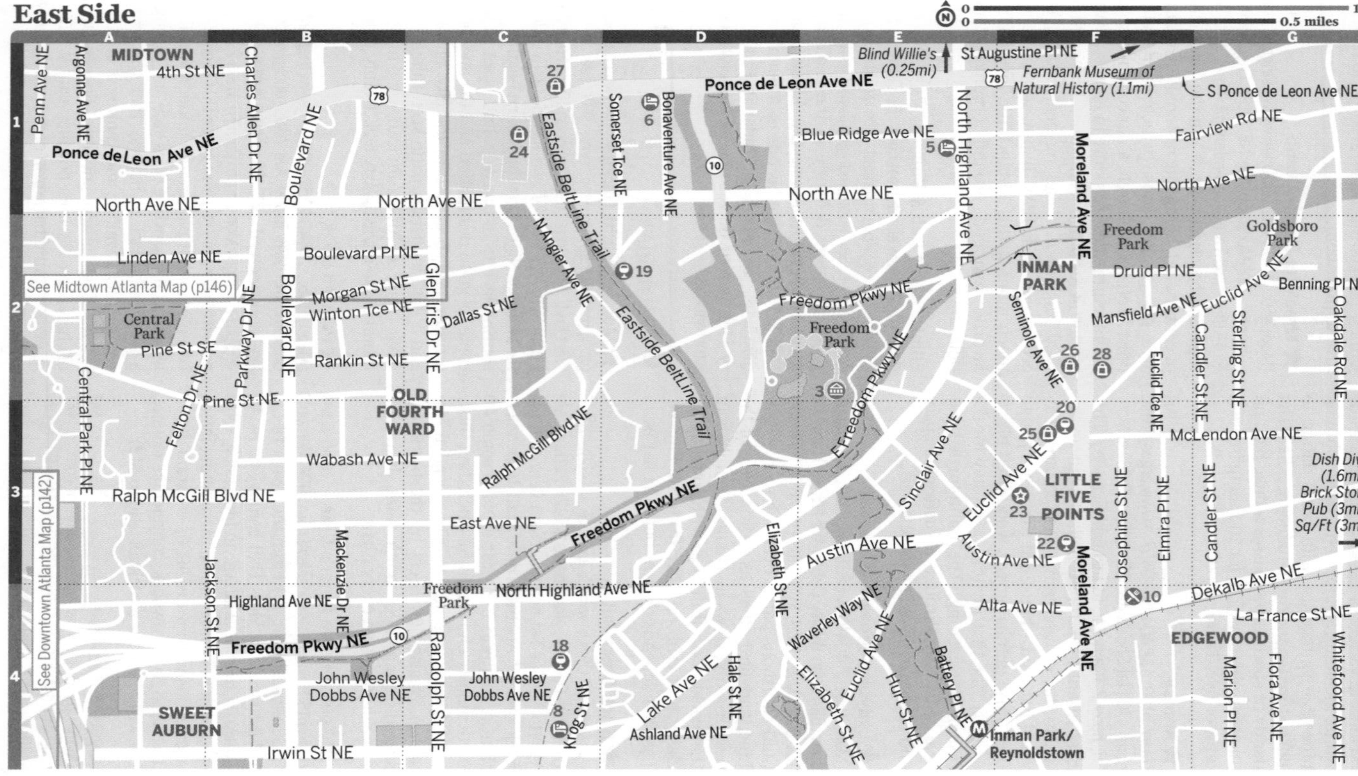
0 1 km
0 0.5 miles
A
B
C
D
E
F
G
1
2
3
4
MIDTOWN
INMAN PARK
LITTLE FIVE POINTS
OLD FOURTH WARD
EDGEWOOD
SWEET AUBURN
Blind Willie's (0.25mi)
Fernbank Museum of Natural History (1.1mi)
Dish Dive (1.6mi); Brick Store Pub (3mi); Sq/Ft (3mi)
See Midtown Atlanta Map (p146)
See Downtown Atlanta Map (p142)
Inman Park/ Reynoldstown
Freedom Park
Goldsboro Park
Central Park
Penn Ave NE
Argonne Ave NE
4th St NE
Charles Allen Dr NE
Boulevard NE
Ponce de Leon Ave NE
S Ponce de Leon Ave NE
St Augustine Pl NE
North Ave NE
Somerset Tce NE
Bonaventure Ave NE
Blue Ridge Ave NE
North Highland Ave NE
Moreland Ave NE
Fairview Rd NE
Eastside BeltLine Trail
N Angier Ave NE
Linden Ave NE
Boulevard Pl NE
Morgan St NE
Winton Tce NE
Glen Iris Dr NE
Dallas St NE
Freedom Pkwy NE
E Freedom Pkwy NE
Druid Pl NE
Euclid Ave NE
Benning Pl NE
Mansfield Ave NE
Seminole Ave NE
Candler St NE
Sterling St NE
Oakdale Rd NE
Euclid Tce NE
Pine St SE
Pine St NE
Parkway Dr NE
Rankin St NE
Felton Dr NE
Central Park Pl NE
Ralph McGill Blvd NE
Wabash Ave NE
Sinclair Ave NE
McLendon Ave NE
Josephine St NE
Elmira Pl NE
East Ave NE
Austin Ave NE
Elizabeth St NE
Jackson St NE
Highland Ave NE
Mackenzie Dr NE
Waverley Way NE
Alta Ave NE
Dekalb Ave NE
La France St NE
John Wesley Dobbs Ave NE
Randolph St NE
Krog St NE
Lake Ave NE
Hale St NE
Ashland Ave NE
Hurt St NE
Battery Pl NE
Marion Pl NE
Flora Ave NE
Whiteford Ave NE
Irwin St NE
78
10
3
5
6
8
10
18
19
20
22
23
24
25
26
27
28

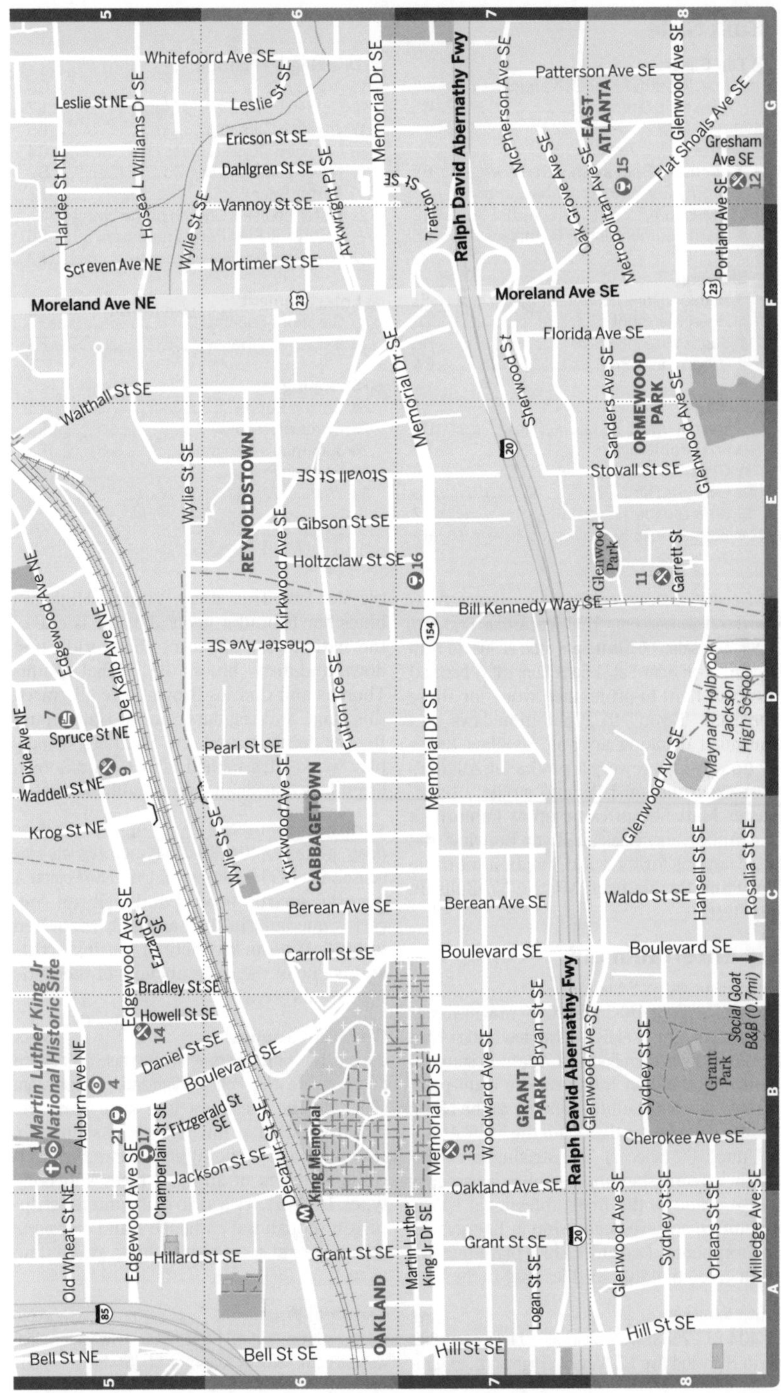
Whiteford Ave SE
Leslie St NE
Leslie St SE
Ericson St SE
Dahlgren St SE
Vannoy St SE
Mortimer St SE
Screven Ave NE
Hardee St NE
Hosea L Williams Dr SE
Wylie St SE
Arkwright Pl SE
Memorial Dr SE
Trenton St SE
Ralph David Abernathy Fwy
McPherson Ave SE
Patterson Ave SE
EAST ATLANTA
Oak Grove Ave SE
Metropolitan Ave SE
Flat Shoals Ave SE
Glenwood Ave SE
Gresham Ave SE
Portland Ave SE
Moreland Ave NE
Moreland Ave SE
Florida Ave SE
Sherwood St
Sanders Ave SE
ORMEWOOD PARK
Walthall St SE
REYNOLDSTOWN
Stovall St SE
Gibson St SE
Holtzclaw St SE
Kirkwood Ave SE
Glenwood Park
Garrett St
Bill Kennedy Way SE
Chester Ave SE
Fulton Tce SE
Edgewood Ave NE
De Kalb Ave NE
Dixie Ave NE
Spruce St NE
Waddell St NE
Pearl St SE
CABBAGETOWN
Maynard Holbrook Jackson High School
Krog St NE
Berean Ave SE
Waldo St SE
Hansell St SE
Rosalia St SE
Carroll St SE
Boulevard SE
Ezzard St SE
Bradley St SE
Howell St SE
Daniel St SE
Martin Luther King Jr National Historic Site
Auburn Ave NE
Chamberlain St SE
Fitzgerald St SE
Jackson St SE
Decatur St SE
King Memorial
Woodward Ave SE
Bryan St SE
GRANT PARK
Sydney St SE
Grant Park
Social Goat B&B (0.7mi)
Cherokee Ave SE
Oakland Ave SE
Old Wheat St NE
Hillard St SE
Grant St SE
Martin Luther King Jr Dr SE
OAKLAND
Logan St SE
Orleans St SE
Milledge Ave SE
Hill St SE
Bell St NE
Bell St SE

East Side

Top Sights
1 Martin Luther King Jr National Historic Site B5

Sights
2 Ebenezer Baptist Church (New) B5
3 Jimmy Carter Presidential Library & Museum E2
4 Martin Luther King Jr Birthplace B5

Sleeping
5 Highland Inn E1
6 Hotel Clermont D1
7 Sugar Magnolia B&B D5
8 Urban Oasis B&B C4

Eating
9 BoccaLupo D5
10 Fox Brothers F4
11 Gunshow E8
12 Octopus Bar G8
13 Ria's Bluebird B7
14 Staplehouse B5

Drinking & Nightlife
15 Argosy G8
16 Golden Eagle Diner's Club E7
17 Joystick Gamebar B5
18 Ladybird Grove & Mess Hall C4
19 New Realm Brewing Co D2
20 Porter Beer Bar F3
21 Sister Louisa's Church of the Living Room & Ping Pong Emporium B5
22 Wrecking Bar Brewpub F3

Entertainment
Clermont Lounge ..... (see 6)
23 Variety Playhouse F3

Shopping
24 Citizen Supply C1
25 Criminal Records F3
26 Junkman's Daughter F2
27 Paris on Ponce C1
28 Wish F2

★**Scofflaw Brewing Co** MICROBREWERY
(www.scofflawbeer.com; 1738 MacArthur Blvd NW, Upper Westside; 10am-5pm Mon & Tue, to 9pm Wed-Fri, noon-8pm Sat, 1-5pm Sun;) Named after the hard-to-pronounce word for those who said, 'F-you!' to Prohibition laws and continued drinking anyway, Scofflaw Brewing Co's 30-tap brewery is producing Atlanta's most experimental IPAs and stouts – brewmaster Matt Shirah came up at California's Lost Abbey and Russian River Brewing, the latter famous for its world-sought-after triple IPA, Pliny the Younger. Motto? 'No Bullshit. Just Beer.'

Entertainment

Mercedes-Benz Stadium STADIUM
(Map p142; 470-341-5000; www.mercedesbenzstadium.com; 1 AMB Dr NW; tours adult/child $25/20; tours 11am-5pm) Atlanta's state-of-the-art, $1.6-billion multipurpose eight-petal retractable-roof stadium is home to the NFL's Atlanta Falcons (football) and the MLS' Atlanta United FC (soccer). The striking, architecturally wowing stadium resembles a camera's aperture and is the first professional sports stadium to achieve Leadership in Energy and Environmental Design (LEED) platinum status (a green building certification) in the US.

Blind Willie's BLUES
(404-873-2583; www.blindwilliesblues.com; 828 North Highland Ave NE, Virginia-Highland; 7pm-late Mon-Sat) This divey Virginia-Highland blues bar behind a neon alligator is one of the nation's top spots for the world's best down-and-dirty blues. Taj Mahal, Rufus Thomas and Charles Brown have all graced this stage and regulars Sandra Hall, House Rocker Johnson and the Shadows usually play weekly. It's named after Georgia's own legendary bluesman, 'Blind' Willie McTell.

Variety Playhouse LIVE MUSIC
(Map p150; 404-524-7354; www.variety-playhouse.com; 1099 Euclid Ave NE, Little Five Points) A historic, smartly booked and well-run concert venue built in 1940 and fully renovated in 2015. It hosts a variety of touring artists and is one of the main anchors of the Little Five Points scene.

Clermont Lounge DANCE
(Map p150; http://clermontlounge.net; 789 Ponce de Leon Ave NE, Poncey-Highland; 5pm-3am Mon-Sat) The Clermont is a strip club, the oldest in Atlanta. But not *just* a strip club. It's a bedrock of the Atlanta scene that welcomes dancers of all ages, races and body types. In short, it's a strip club built for strippers, although the audience – and *everyone* comes here at some point – has a grand time as well.

Terminal West LIVE MUSIC
(Map p146; 404-876-5566; www.terminalwestatl.com; 887 W Marietta St, Westside; box

office 11am-5pm Tue-Fri) One of Atlanta's best live-music venues, this concert space is located inside a beautifully revamped 100-year-old iron and steel foundry on the Westside.

Shopping

★Criminal Records MUSIC
(Map p150; ☎404-215-9511; www.criminalatl.com; 1154 Euclid Ave, Little Five Points; ⏲11am-8pm Mon-Thu, to 9pm Fri & Sat, noon-7pm Sun) This throwback record store is stacked wall to wall with a library's worth of new pop, soul, jazz and metal, on CD or vinyl. It has a fun music-related book section, and a great collection of comic books and graphic novels. Basically, a certain kind of music-lover and genre-loving geek could live here.

Hop City ALCOHOL
(Map p146; ☎404-350-9998; www.hopcitybeer.com; 1000 Marietta St NW, No 302, West Midtown; ⏲10am-9pm Mon-Wed, to 10pm Thu-Sat, 12:30-6pm Sun) Features the largest selection of retail craft beer in the Southeast along with 60 taps to drink from on the premises. The local inventory is obviously extensive, but there are suds from here to Shanghai.

Paris on Ponce VINTAGE, ARTS & CRAFTS
(Map p150; www.parisonponce.com; 716 Ponce de Leon Pl NE; ⏲11am-6pm Mon-Sat, noon-6m Sun) Clocking in at over 46,000-sq-ft and 30-plus vendors, this massively cool vintage shop inside an old mattress factory will floor you with its tragically hip ethos. You'll find anything and everything here, and rummaging through the various sections feels like browsing through a gourmet flea market. Local artists are widely featured.

Citizen Supply CLOTHING
(Map p150; www.citizensupply.com; 675 Ponce de Leon Ave NE, Ponce City Market; ⏲10am-9pm Mon-Sat, noon-8pm Sun) This fiercely curated all-under-one-roof flagship shop stocks a dizzying array of top-quality – some say hipster – brands of products you didn't know you wanted until you saw them: foresty pomades from Mail Room Barber Co, Edison electric bikes, Bradley Mountain canvas and leather bags, Wander North Georgia (p169) T-shirts, Atlanta-centric art, Loyal Stricklin leather-bound Aviator mugs and a whole lot more.

Junkman's Daughter VINTAGE
(Map p150; ☎404-577-3188; www.thejunkmansdaughter.com; 464 Moreland Ave NE, Little Five Points; ⏲11am-7pm Mon-Fri, to 8pm Sat, noon-7pm Sun) A defiant and fiercely independent cradle of counterculture since 1982, this 10,000-sq-ft alternative superstore stocks racks of vintage, ornery bumper stickers, kitschy toys and tchotchkes, *Star Wars* lunch boxes, incense, wigs, offensive coffee mugs and a whole lot more. It put Little Five Points on the map.

Sq/Ft GIFTS & SOUVENIRS
(☎404-373-6607; www.sqftdecatur.com; 149 Sycamore St, Decatur; ⏲11am-7pm Mon, to 8pm Tue-Thu, to 9pm Fri & Sat, to 6pm Sun) It's hard to pin down the shopping genre of Decatur's Sq/Ft – on one visit, you may find graphic-print shower curtains, Phaidon coffee-table books, hip-hop screen-print shirts, macramé wall hangings, Bones&Blooms tea towels and handmade jewelry. Whatever you find, it's going to be awesome.

Wish FASHION & ACCESSORIES
(Map p150; ☎404-880-0402; http://wishatl.com; 447 Moreland Ave, Little Five Points; ⏲noon-8pm Mon-Thu, to 9pm Fri & Sat, 1-7pm Sun) You wouldn't be the first to spy a famous actor or athlete picking up a new pair of graffitied sneakers, blinged-out bomber jacket or distressed jeans at this streetwise street-wear shop, located in a former public library. The shoe section alone is seriously eye-watering in its immensity.

Information

Atlanta Convention & Visitors Bureau (www.atlanta.net) Maps, information about attractions, restaurants, outdoor recreation and accommodations; operates visitor centers at **Underground Atlanta** (Map p142; ☎404-577-2148; www.atlanta.net; 65 Upper Alabama St, ⏲10am-6pm Mon-Sat, noon-6pm Sun) and **Hartsfield-Jackson Atlanta International Airport** (☎404-305-8426; www.atlanta.net; 6000 N Terminal Pkwy, North Terminal; ⏲9am-9pm Mon-Fri, to 6pm Sat, noon-6pm Sun).

Getting There & Away

Atlanta straddles the intersection of three interstates: I-20, I-75 and I-85. **Hartsfield-Jackson International Airport** (p209), 9.5 miles south of Downtown, is the world's busiest airport by passenger traffic. The easiest way into the city from the airport is MARTA, the city's rail system. **Greyhound** (Map p142; ☎404-584-1728; www.greyhound.com; 232 Forsyth St) and **Amtrak** (www.amtrak.com/stations/atl; 1688 Peachtree St NW) both serve the city as well.

Flights, cars and tours can be booked online at www.lonelyplanet.com/bookings.

Getting Around

Despite its sprawling layout and debilitating traffic, Atlanta is fairly easy to navigate both with your own set of wheels or on public transportation. The city is well served by the MARTA bus and rail system and a Downtown tram. And once the groundbreaking Atlanta BeltLine completes its loop by 2030, Atlanta's multiuse trail system will be one of the most progressive in North America, if not the world.

NORTH GEORGIA

Elevation seekers should head to North Georgia, which sits at the southern end of the great Appalachian Range. Those mountains, and their surrounding foothills and upcountry, provide superb mountain scenery, as well as some decent wines and frothing rivers. Fall colors emerge late here, peaking in October. A few days are warranted to see sites such as the 1200ft-deep Tallulah Gorge, and the mountain scenery and hiking trails at Vogel State Park and Unicoi State Park.

Athens

706, 762 / POP 119,980

A beery, artsy and laid-back college town, Athens has an extremely popular football team (the University of Georgia Bulldogs, College Football Playoff National Championship runners-up in 2018), a world-famous music scene, a bona fide restaurant culture and surprisingly diverse nightlife. The university – UGA – drives the culture of Athens and ensures an ever-replenishing supply of young bar-hoppers and concert-goers, some of whom stick around long after graduation and become 'townies.' The pleasant, walkable downtown offers a plethora of funky choices for eating, drinking and shopping.

Sights

★Georgia Museum of Art MUSEUM
(Map p156; 706-542-4662; www.georgiamuseum.org; 90 Carlton St; 10am-5pm Tue, Wed, Fri & Sat, to 9pm Thu, 1-5pm Sun) FREE A smart, modern gallery where brainy, arty types set up in the wired lobby for personal study, while art hounds gawk at modern sculpture in the courtyard garden as well as the tremendous collection from American realists of the 1930s.

State Botanical Garden of Georgia GARDENS
(www.botgarden.uga.edu; 2450 S Milledge Ave; 8am-6pm) FREE Truly gorgeous, with winding outdoor paths and a sociohistorical edge, Athens' gardens are a gift for a city of this size. Signs provide smart context for its amazing collection of plants, which includes rare and threatened species. There are nearly 5 miles of top-notch woodland walking trails too. The visitor center, cafe and gift shop are closed on Mondays but the grounds are open.

University of Georgia UNIVERSITY
(Map p156; UGA visitor center 706-542-0842; www.uga.edu; 405 College Station Rd) Take in a football game at the hallowed grounds of Sanford Stadium, walk around the 160-year-old cast-iron arch (depending on who you are – only UGA grads are supposed to walk *through* the landmark!), or just take in the hip and fun atmosphere around campus and downtown. Whatever you do, it is the 37,000-student University of Georgia, founded in 1781, that keeps Athens' heart beating. The address and phone connect you to the UGA visitor center.

Sleeping

Most hotels in Athens seem to cater to parents visiting young Timmy or Tammy, or alums in town for a Bulldogs game. There are a lot of chain hotels in town and on the outskirts, and most are clean and serviceable. Some cheap motel options can also be found around town, but our research leads us to conclude that you get what you pay for.

★Graduate Athens INN $$
(Map p156; 706-549-7020; www.graduateathens.com; 295 E Dougherty St; r $129-249, ste $280-500; P @) This wonderfully designed boutique hotel, the first of a college-campus chain, is drowning in sexy retro hipness, from potted plants inside old-school, Dewey decimal card-catalog filing cabinets in the lobby to the sweet Crosley turntables and classic video games in the suites.

Local accents, such as chalkboard art of the chemical formula for sweet tea, fortify local allure. Also on-site is a great coffeehouse, bar and grill and live-music venue, all inside an old Confederate iron foundry.

Hotel Indigo BOUTIQUE HOTEL $$
(Map p156; 706-546-0430; www.indigoathens.com; 500 College Ave; r/ste from $179/279; P @) Rooms are spacious, loftlike

pods of cool at this ecochic boutique hotel. Part of the Indigo chain, it's a Leadership in Energy and Environmental Design (LEED) gold-certified sustainable standout. Green elements include regenerative elevators and priority parking for hybrid vehicles – 30% of the building was constructed from recycled content.

Eating

Ideal Bagel Co BREAKFAST $

(Map p156; ☎706-353-0005; 815 W Broad St; bagels $1.25-5; ⏱7am-3pm Mon-Fri, 8am-8pm Sat & Sun; P) They may never allow us past the Hudson River again after writing this, but the bagels here give anything in New York a run for its money. There, we said it! And we stand by it, and dare you, dear reader, to try one of Ideal's onion bagels with schmear and tell us any different. Most popular is the lox, pecan-smoked salmon and smoked mountain-trout extravaganza. It also serves some fine deli sandwiches.

White Tiger BARBECUE $

(www.whitetigergourmet.com; 217 Hiawassee Ave; mains $6.75-11; ⏱11am-3pm Mon-Sat, 6-8pm Thu, 10am-2pm Sun;) The 100-year-old structure doesn't invite confidence, but this off-the-beaten-path local favorite does killer wood-smoked pulled-pork sandwiches – add pimento cheese (and send us a thank-you note!) – plus burgers and even barbecue-smoked tofu and a whole lot more for vegetarians. Chef Ken Manring honed his skills in much higher-brow kitchens before settling in Athens.

Grit VEGETARIAN $

(Map p156; 199 Prince Ave; mains $7.75-8.95; ⏱8am-9:30pm Mon-Wed, to 10pm Thu & Fri, 10am-10pm Sat, 10am-9:30pm Sun;) A Normaltown vegetarian/vegan staple long before it was trendy, this somewhat divey institution is dressed up with the building's original tin-plated ceilings (owned by Michael Stipe, incidentally). The wide-ranging dishes on offer (tofu Reubens, veggie banh mi, noodle bowls, Middle Eastern plates) don't perform culinary miracles, but the vibe makes it a classic city must.

Pouch PIES $

(Map p156; ☎706-395-6696; www.pouchpies.com; 151 E Broad St; pies $5.50; ⏱11am-10pm Mon-Wed, to 11pm Thu-Sat;) In the South, 'pie' usually means something sweet, buttery and served after dinner. For the South African owners of Pouch, 'pie' means savory pastries from around the world: Aussie pies with beef and gravy, Portuguese pies with piripiri white-wine sauce, chorizo and spicy chicken, and even a local offering with pulled pork and peach BBQ sauce! Makes for a great budget meal.

Big City Bread Cafe DELI $

(Map p156; ☎706-353-0029; www.bigcitybreadcafe.com; 393 N Finley St; mains $7.75-12; ⏱7am-9:30pm Mon-Sat, to 3pm Sun;) As you may have gathered, the bread at this restaurant-bakery is awesome, but so are the creations derived from said bread: lamb burgers, grilled cheese and mozzarella, tomato and basil sandwiches etc. Throw in fantastic coffee and a great slate of meal-sized salads and you have a winner.

Ted's Most Best ITALIAN $

(Map p156; www.tedsmostbest.com; 254 W Washington St; mains $8-9; ⏱11am-10pm Mon-Wed, to 11pm Thu-Sat, noon-10pm Sun) This atmospheric eatery occupies a former Michelin tire shop and is a great spot for cheap eats. Pizzas and paninis are what drives it, but the outdoor patio and sandbox/bocce court (when the little ones haven't commandeered it) is the real star of the show.

Ike & Jane CAFE $

(www.ikeandjane.com; 1307 Prince Ave; items $1.55-7; ⏱6:30am-5pm Mon-Fri, 8am-2pm Sat & Sun;) This sunny little shingle in Normaltown

BUCK MANOR

For a glimpse of a classic Athens musical legend, do a drive-by of 748 Cobb St, a Second Empire Victorian home painted 12 different colors. Known as Buck Manor, REM guitarist Peter Buck lived here until his divorce from his wife, Barrie. REM filmed the 'Nightswimming' video here as well as a prerelease promotional video for *Out of Time*. Nirvana spent the night here when they played the 40 Watt Club in 1991. Other REM pilgrimage-worthy sights include the *Murmur* album railroad trestle (Dudley Park); Weaver D's Delicious Fine Foods (1016 E Broad St), whose slogan – 'Automatic for the People!' – spawned the title of the band's 1992 album; and the steeple of the long-demolished St Mary's Episcopal Church, where REM played their first show, at 394 Oconee St.

Athens

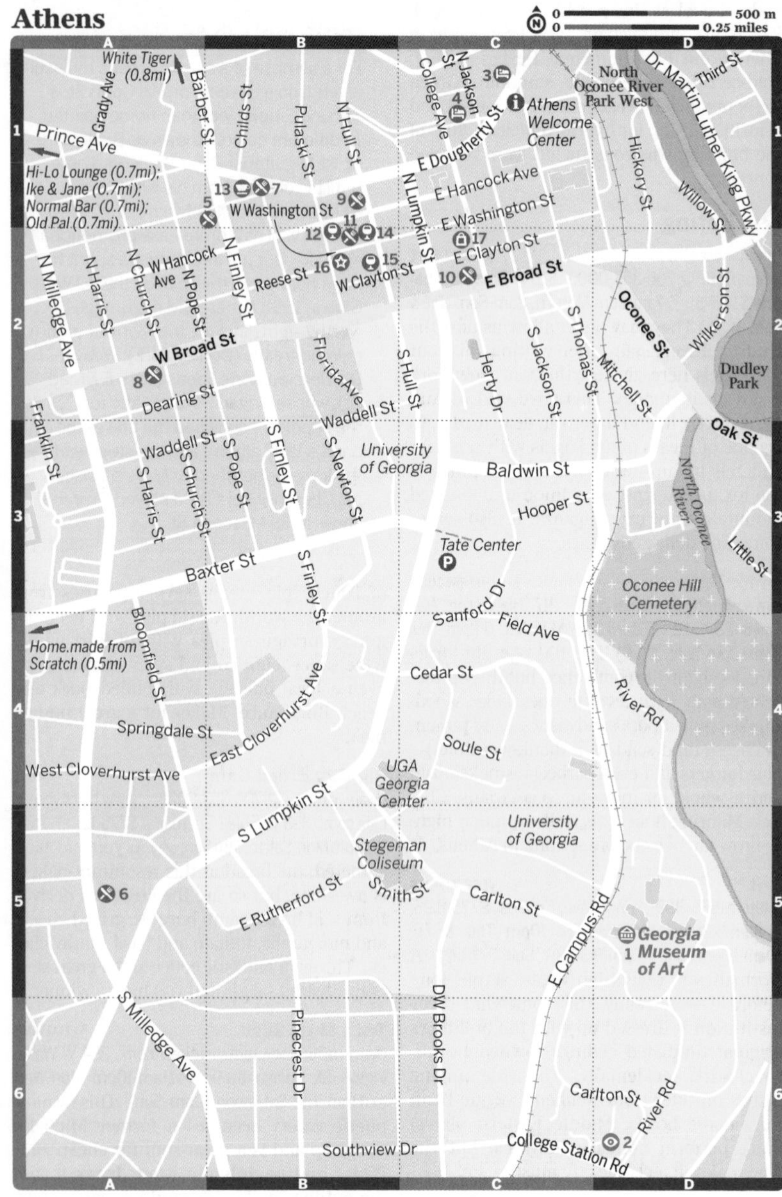

serves decadent doughnuts bedazzled with crazy creative ingredients such as red velvet, cinnamon-toast-crunch cereal and peanut butter, banana and bacon (weekends only). If that's all a bit much for you, the pimento-cheese biscuit or roasted-jalapeño and egg sandwich are both divine.

★ **Home.made from Scratch** SOUTHERN US **$$**

(706-206-9216; www.homemadeathens.com; 1072 Baxter St; mains $16-24; 11am-2pm & 5:30-9:30pm Tue-Sat;) Home.made is upping the game when it comes to nouveau-Southern cuisine. The menu constantly changes based

Athens

Top Sights
1 Georgia Museum of Art ... D5

Sights
2 University of Georgia ... D6

Sleeping
3 Graduate Athens ... C1
4 Hotel Indigo ... C1

Eating
5 Big City Bread Cafe ... B1
6 Five & Ten ... A5
7 Grit ... B1
8 Ideal Bagel Co ... A2
9 National ... B1
10 Pouch ... C2
11 Ted's Most Best ... B2

Drinking & Nightlife
12 Creature Comforts Brewing Co ... B2
13 Hendershots ... B1
14 Manhattan Bar ... B2
15 Trapeze Pub ... B2
World Famous ... (see 14)

Entertainment
16 40 Watt Club ... B2

Shopping
17 Wuxtry Records ... C2

on ingredient availability, but whatever these folks source is always turned into something creative, delicious, rooted in local flavors and often playfully over the top. At lunch, don't miss the fried chicken and pimento-cheese sandwich with a side upgrade to tomato pie.

At dinner, think shrimp and andouille sausage with tomatoes, celery, onions and sweet peppers over grits or boneless chicken thighs with smoked hoppin' John (black-eyed peas, rice, chopped onion and sliced bacon).

National MODERN AMERICAN $$
(Map p156; ☎706-549-3450; www.thenationalrestaurant.com; 232 W Hancock Ave; mains $20-29; ⏲11:30am-10pm Mon-Thu, to late Fri & Sat, 5-10pm Sun;) An effortlessly cool bistro on the downtown outskirts, favored for its daily changing, eclectic menu that jumps from roasted monkfish to roasted chicken on jeweled Carolina Gold rice with dried apricot, pistachio, currants, *schug* hot sauce, yogurt, cucumber, marinated onion and cilantro (got it?). Outstanding vegetarian choices too. Spanish and Middle Eastern accents abound. The bar is one where you may want to sit and sip a while.

Five & Ten AMERICAN $$$
(Map p156; ☎706-546-7300; www.fiveandten.com; 1073 S Milledge Ave; mains $22-48; ⏲5:30-10pm Sun-Thu, to 11pm Fri & Sat, 10:30am-2:30pm Sun;) Sustainably driven, James Beard Award–winning Five & Ten ranks among the South's best restaurants. Its menu is earthy and slightly gamey: Georgia quail with pickled *yacón* and white-miso aioli, and Frogmore stew (stewed corn, sausage and potato). Vegetarians should try baked Crescenza cheese with confit parsnips and blue collard greens or pasta ribbons with grilled tomato sauce, jalapeños and Parmesan. It's tucked away in a restored historic home among UGA's fraternity and sorority row.

Drinking

Nearly 100 bars, restaurants and breweries dot the compact downtown area, so it's not hard to find a good time. To escape students, head to Normaltown, a mile or so west of downtown along Price Ave, where 'townies' and locals tend to hang out.

★Creature Comforts Brewing Co MICROBREWERY
(Map p156; www.creaturecomfortsbeer.com; 271 W Hancock Ave; pints $5.50-7.50; ⏲5-9pm Tue-Thu, to 10pm Fri, 1-6pm Sat & Sun;) Athens' best craft beer emerges from 33 taps at this cutting-edge, dog-friendly former tire shop which excels at staples – Indian Pale Ales (IPAs), amber ales – but isn't afraid to play around with suds (tart blonde ale aged in wine barrels, mixed fermentation ale aged in bourbon barrels with blackberries). Local ingredients often form the backbone of the memorable brews.

There's live music most nights and free tours (hourly 6pm to 9pm). Start with one of Georgia's best IPAs (Tropicália) and then move on to a bevy of innovative pints. The no-sample policy, however, is mighty unorthodox.

Trapeze Pub CRAFT BEER
(Map p156; www.trappezepub.com; 269 N Hull St; ⏲11am-2am Mon-Sat, to midnight Sun;) Downtown's best craft-beer bar installed itself well before the suds revolution. You'll find dozens of taps spanning regional, national and

international brews, and another 100 or so at any given time in bottles. Soak it up with their Belgian-style fries ($3.50), the best in town.

Old Pal BAR

(www.theoldpal.com; 1320 Prince Ave; 4pm-2am Mon-Sat;) This is Normaltown's thinking-person's bar, devoted to seasonal craft cocktails ($9) and a thoughtfully curated bourbon list. It's a beautiful, dark space that has been showered with local preservation awards.

Hi-Lo Lounge BAR

(www.hiloathens.com; 1354 Prince Ave; 4pm-2am Mon-Thu, noon-2am Fri & Sat, 11am-midnight Sun) This chilled-out Normaltown bar and grill has an atmosphere that's somewhere between a dive, a grill and a cool party your friends never told you about. There's an extensive whiskey menu, solid cocktails ($5 to $7), and a good list of craft beers on 14 taps.

Manhattan Bar BAR

(Map p156; 337 N Hull St; 4pm-2am Mon-Sat) This busy little bar is a good spot to soak up some Athens counterculture, find a strong drink and, during winter, sip on some spiked hot chocolate (divine).

World Famous COCKTAIL BAR

(Map p156; www.facebook.com/theworldfamousathens; 351 N Hull; 11am-2am Mon-Sat, 11:30am-midnight Sun;) This bustling spot serves commendable craft cocktails in mason jars amid retro French farmhouse decor. Also hosts intimate comedy and live-music events.

Hendershots COFFEE

(Map p156; www.hendershotscoffee.com; 237 Prince Ave; 6:30am-11pm Mon-Thu, to midnight Fri, 7:30am-midnight Sat, 7am-10pm Sun;) This fantastic coffeehouse pulls triple duty as a great bar and live-music venue. Pick your poison.

Normal Bar BAR

(www.facebook.com/normal.bar.7; 1365 Prince Ave; 4pm-2am Mon-Sat;) This lovable dark storefront bar is not very student-like but still very much Athens. The beer goes from cheap Pabst Blue Ribbon (PBR) to sophisticated local craft IPA. There's a terrific wine list and the crowd is cute, young – but not *too* young; think grad students or even young professors – and laid-back. A cooler version of the quintessential neighborhood bar.

Entertainment

Athens gave us the B-52's and REM, but the live-music scene didn't stop in the '90s – this town both creates and attracts lots of bands. During the fall, football mania takes over the town. Pick up a free copy of *Flagpole* (www.flagpole.com) to find out what's on.

40 Watt Club LIVE MUSIC

(Map p156; 706-549-7871; www.40watt.com; 285 W Washington St; $5-25) Athens' most storied joint has lounges, a tiki bar and $2.50 PBRs. The venue has welcomed indie rock to its stage since REM, the B-52's and Widespread Panic owned this town and today this is still where the big hitters play when they come to town. It has recently embraced comedy as well.

Shopping

Wuxtry Records MUSIC

(Map p156; www.wuxtryrecords.com; 197 E Clayton St; 10am-8pm Mon-Thu, to 9pm Fri & Sat, noon-6pm Sun) REM guitarist Peter Buck once worked these hallowed halls of vinyl and CDs, and it is here where he and singer/customer Michael Stipe first forged the relationship that would become one of the most important alternative music acts in history. The ceiling is peeling, the carpets rotting, the music superb – just the way it should be.

Information

Athens Welcome Center (Map p156; 706-353-1820; www.athenswelcomecenter.com; 280 E Dougherty St; 10am-5pm Mon-Sat, noon-5pm Sun) This visitor center, in a historic antebellum house at the corner of Thomas St, provides maps and information on local tours.

Getting There & Away

This college town is about 70 miles east of Atlanta. There's no main highway that leads here, so traffic can be an issue on secondary state and county roads. The local **Greyhound station** (p135) is actually about 6 miles west of downtown Athens. Buses leave for Atlanta (from $15, 7½ hours, twice daily) and Savannah (from $36, 14 hours, twice daily).

Groome Transportation (706-612-1155; https://groometransportation.com; 3190 Atlanta Hwy, Suite 22) operates 23 shuttles per day year-round between Athens and Hartsfield-Jackson Atlanta International Airport ($39, 2¼ hours). Shuttles leave from the **UGA Georgia Center** (1197 S Lumpkin St) and its Athens office between 2:25am and 9:25pm.

Dahlonega

706, 762 / POP 6050

In 1828 Dahlonega was the site of the first gold rush in the USA (locals are known as 'Nuggets'). These days the boom is in tourism, as it's an easy day excursion from Atlanta and a fantastic mountain destination. Not only is Dahlonega a hotbed of outdoor activities, but downtown in Courthouse Sq is an attractive mélange of wine-tasting rooms, gourmet emporiums, great food, countrified shops and foothill charm. Wine tasting in the surrounding vineyards is on the rise too. There's a vaguely artistic vibe permeating throughout town (especially when it comes to music), often fueled by students at the University of North Georgia, located off the square. Tack on Amicalola Falls State Park just 18 miles west and you have a pretty irresistible bundle of mountain fun.

Sights

★ Wolf Mountain Vineyards WINERY

(706-867-9862; www.wolfmountainvineyards.com; 180 Wolf Mountain Trail; tastings $20, mains $13-15, brunch $35; tastings 11am-5pm Thu-Sat, 12:30-5pm Sun, cafe noon-3pm Thu-Sat, brunch 12:30pm & 2:30pm Sun) Wolf lures a hip and trendy 30-something crowd to its gorgeous, 30-acre winery that frames epic sunsets over Springer Mountain from its tasting-room terrace. Top wines like its *méthode champenoise* 100% chardonnay Blanc de Blanc and crisp and fresh Plentitude (an unoaked chardonnay/Viognier blend) are the way to go. Reservations required for cafe and brunch.

Three Sisters WINERY

(706-865-9463; www.threesistersvineyards.com; 439 Vineyard Way; tastings from $15; 11am-5pm Thu-Sat, 1-5pm Sun; P) A wonderfully unpretentious vineyard where Cheetos, overalls and bluegrass tunes – or fine cheese and great views – pair just fine with the wine.

Frogtown Cellars WINERY

(706-865-0687; www.frogtownwine.com; 700 Ridge Point Dr; tastings $14-24; noon-5pm Mon-Fri, 11-6pm Sat, 12:30-5pm Sun) This beautiful winery has a killer deck where you can sip libations and nibble cheese. It bills itself as the most awarded American winery *not* in California, which we can't confirm, but the wine does go down a treat with a mountain sunset.

Sleeping

Barefoot Hills HOTEL $

(470-788-8043; www.barefoothills.com; 7693 Hwy 19 N; dm $42, r from $115, cabins $150-180; P) On Hwy 19 N, 7 miles or so north of town, this revamped option could be known as the Boutique Hotel Formerly Known as Hiker Hostel. New owners upgraded this former backpackers in 2017, transitioning the converted log cabin to a near boutique-level hotel – but maintaining a hiker focus with a four-bed bunk room, supply store and shuttles to trailheads.

Three stylish shipping-container cabins are built from reclaimed materials found throughout Georgia. They offer mountain, sunset or sunrise views and long-stay amenities (kitchenette, some with washer and dryer). The vibe and traveler camaraderie are gone and the bunk prices have skyrocketed, but it's still a wonderful option. There's a shuttle service from Atlanta for guests.

Cedar House Inn & Yurts B&B $$

(706-867-9446; www.georgiamountaininn.com; 6463 Hwy 19 N; r $135-155, yurts $155; P) Prayer flags, a permaculture farm, bottle trees and, as you may guess, a fairly progressive, environmentally conscious approach to life define the vibe at the Cedar House, on Hwy 19 north of town. Staff can most definitely accommodate gluten-free and vegan breakfast requests. Cozy rooms and two colorful yurts (without air-conditioning) are all inviting places to crash out.

Hall House Hotel INN $$

(Map p160; 706-867-5009; www.hallhousehotel.com; 90 Public Sq; r $165-195; P) A charming historic nest on the square dating to 1881. There are five bright and charming rooms, each uniquely decorated, some with four-poster beds.

Eating

★ Spirits Tavern BURGERS $

(Map p160; 706-482-0580; www.spirits-tavern.com; 19 E Main St; burgers $12-15; 11am-11pm Sun-Thu, to 1am Fri, to midnight Sat;) This full bar dishes up surprisingly creative burgers made from Angus beef or free-range, hormone-free turkey and veggies, including gooey mac 'n' cheese, Greek and Cajun versions. With eight taps and a seasonally changing list of serious cocktails, it's also the best 'bar' in town.

Dahlonega

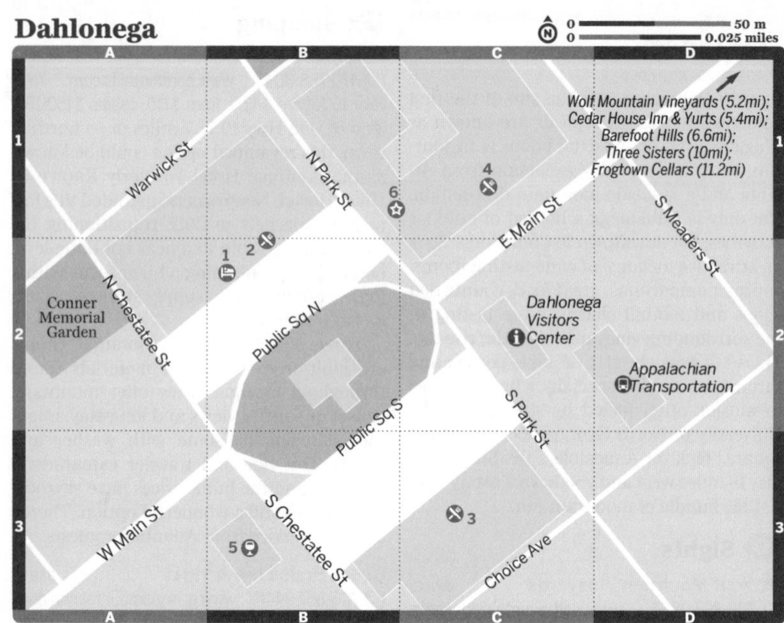

Picnic Cafe & Dessertery CAFE $
(Map p160; https://thepicniccafe.wixsite.com/picniccafe; 30 Public Sq; sandwiches $8.49; ⏲7:30am-7pm Sun-Thu, to 8pm Fri & Sat;) Owned by Dahlonega mayor Sam Norten and the absolute best spot around to mingle with town characters and university students engrossed in local gossip. Picnic does simple and quick biscuit sandwiches for breakfast, and sandwiches such as honey-ham salad, pimento cheese and sweet Georgia peach chicken salad for lunch. Staff is adorable and there are loads of cakes, cookies and other sweet baked love too.

Capers on the Square MEDITERRANEAN $
(Map p160; www.facebook.com/capersonthesquare; 84 Public Sq N; mains $9-20; ⏲11am-9pm Mon, Tue & Thu-Sat, noon-7pm Sun;) This tasty little newcomer on the square leans casual Greek (lamb kabobs, moussaka, shrimp orzo) but each month, it takes on a different Mediterranean country for its specials, almost none of which are otherwise represented in North Georgia other than Italian.

Drinking

Dahlonega bills itself as the Official Wine Tasting Room Capital of Georgia and there are nine wineries in the immediate environs. Additionally, you'll find distilleries (musician Zac Brown, a Dahlonega native, owns one) and a meadery. Otherwise, there are no bars per se in Dahlonega – only restaurants with alcohol. Spirits Tavern (p159) and Crimson Moon Café are your best bets.

Gold City Growlers CRAFT BEER
(Map p160; www.goldcitygrowlers.com; 10 S Chestatee St; ⏲11am-7pm Tue & Wed, to 8pm Thu, to 9pm Fri & Sat, 1-6pm Sun) Dahlonega's best craft-beer destination has 20 taps of mostly Georgia suds but there's a catch: city ordinances only allow growler fill-ups to go, or tastings, which run $6 for four 2oz pours.

But all is not lost. Growlers in 32oz or 64oz sizes can be rented for $1 and a 32oz fill-up (two beers, basically) starts at $6 – so more or less the price of a single pint in many places. So tucking away in your hotel room with a growler and a partner or some friends isn't such a bad deal.

Naturally Georgia WINE BAR
(Map p160; 770-231-5783; www.naturallygeorgia.com; 90 Public Sq N; ⏲noon-6pm Mon & Thu, 11am-8pm Fri & Sat, 12:30-6pm Sun) If you're in need of some wine, head to this tasting room, which pours wines from around the state, from dry whites to robust, Portuguese-style reds.

Dahlonega

Sleeping
1 Hall House Hotel B2

Eating
2 Capers on the Square B2
3 Picnic Cafe & Dessertery C3
4 Spirits Tavern C1

Drinking & Nightlife
5 Gold City Growlers B3
Naturally Georgia .... (see 1)

Entertainment
6 Crimson Moon Café B1

Entertainment

Crimson Moon Café LIVE MUSIC

(Map p160; www.thecrimsonmoon.com; 24 N Park St; 10am-3pm Mon, to 9pm Thu, to 10:30pm Fri & Sat, to 9:30pm Sun;) An organic coffeehouse offering great Southern comfort food (and brunch every day, mains $6.50 to $18) that doubles as an intimate live-music venue. Thursday night is open-mic night and old-time jam sessions take place every second Sunday.

Information

Dahlonega Visitors Center (Map p160; 706-864-3711; www.dahlonega.org; 13 S Park St; 9am-5:30pm Mon-Fri, 10am-5pm Sat & Sun) Has plenty of information on area sights and activities, including hiking, canoeing, kayaking, rafting and mountain biking.

Getting There & Away

Dahlonega is about 70 miles north of Atlanta; the quickest way here is via Hwy 19. There is no public bus service, but folks traveling from Atlanta often take a Metropolitan Atlanta Rapid Transit Authority (MARTA) train to North Springs station in Atlanta and catch an Uber from there ($50 to $75). The nearest Amtrak station is in Gainesville, 21 miles south.

Amicalola Falls State Park

This 829-acre privatized state park, 18 miles west of Dahlonega on Hwy 52, is one of Georgia's most spectacular. It features the mighty 729ft Amicalola Falls. While most folks visit on a day trip from Atlanta or Dahlonega, the park is worth at least an overnight – it offers spectacular scenery, a lodge and excellent hiking and mountain-biking trails.

Sights

Amicalola Falls WATERFALL

(706-265-4703; www.gastateparks.org/amicalolafalls; 280 Amicalola Falls State Park Rd, Dawsonville; per vehicle $5; 7am-10pm; P) The tallest cascading waterfall in the Southeast is a spectacular sight. It tumbles 729ft through protected North Georgia mountain scenery within Amicalola Falls State Park. You can also watch it fall right under foot from the viewpoint bridge on the West Ridge Trail.

Activities

The best option for a quick view of the falls is the **West Ridge Trail**. Drive a half-mile north on Top of the Falls Rd from the visitor center and park in the first parking lot on the right-hand side. From there, the 0.3-mile recycled-rubber (wheelchair-accessible) trail leads to a spectacular viewpoint bridge that traverses the falls. Those more able or with more time can opt for the 2-mile loop to the top of the falls via the first mile of the **Appalachian Approach Trail**, returning via 604 stairs along the **East Ridge Trail**. The aforementioned Appalachian Approach Trail is an 8.5-mile jaunt to **Springer Mountain**.

Sleeping

Len Foote Hike Inn LODGE $$

(800-581-8032; www.hike-inn.com; 280 Amicalola Falls State Park Rd, Dawsonville; s/d $127/180) You will be far, far from the rat race at this hike-in-only lodge, 5 miles from the nearest road and technically outside Amicalola Falls State Park. You'll need to carry in everything, haul out your own trash and reserve in advance. Rooms are comfortable and cozy – a welcome break from the trails – and two hot meals are served each day.

All guests hiking in must check in at the Amicalola Falls State Park Visitor's Center (p162) by 2pm.

Amicalola Falls Lodge LODGE $$

(800-573-9656; www.amicalolafallslodge.com; 418 Amicalola Falls State Park Rd, Dawsonville; campsites $30-40, r from $139, 1-/2-/3-bedroom cabins $159/189/219; P) This lodge is a full-service hotel with beautiful mountain views from every room (though not of the falls); the rustic cottages sleep four to 10. You can eat buffet-style at the on-site Maple Restaurant (p162), and take advantage of local ziplines, archery courses and other adventure activities.

WINE TASTING IN THE DAHLONEGA PLATEAU

Old-world wine enthusiasts may scoff, but North Georgia wine has come a long way in the last decade. When most folks think of wine tasting in Georgia, images of tipsy frat boys and their dates swigging sweet muscadine wines on a Saturday afternoon might spring to mind. We're not saying that never happens, but times have changed. Dahlonega, known as the Heart of Georgia Wine Country, helped secure a Dahlonega Plateau appellation (technically called an American Viticultural Area) from the Alcohol and Tobacco Tax and Trade Bureau for the region's wines in 2018. The town's nine wineries – Frogtown (p159), Three Sisters (p159), Wolf Mountain (p159), Monteluce, Kaya, Cavender Creek, Blue Mountain, the Cottage and Accent Cellars – have won plenty of awards when competing against more famous American wine regions (Frogtown bills itself as the most awarded non-Californian winery in the US). Not only that, but the wineries are gorgeous: blink twice and you might swear you're in Napa Valley or Europe.

To get to the wineries on an organized tour from Dahlonega, **Appalachian Transportation** (Map p160; ☎706-864-0021; www.appalachiantransportation.com; 27 S Park St; per person from $65; ⏲11am-5pm) is your best bet. There are a few companies doing the same from Atlanta but prices are exorbitant – you are better off organizing an Uber for the day.

Eating

Maple Restaurant AMERICAN $
(www.amicalolafallslodge.com; 418 Amicalola Falls State Park Rd, Amicalola Falls Lodge, Dawsonville; buffet $11-17, mains $16-28; ⏲7-11am, 11:30am-3pm & 5:30-9pm; 📶) The Maple Restaurant at Amicalola Falls Lodge (p161) caters both to guests and hungry park visitors and through-hikers. There's a buffet option for all three meals, or à la carte menu of steaks and chops, mountain trout, spaghetti and pizzas (from $12).

Information

Amicalola Falls State Park Visitor's Center (☎706-265-4703; www.amicalolafallslodge.com; 280 Amicalola Falls State Park Rd, Dawsonville; ⏲8:30am-5pm) Through-hikers must register at the park visitor center. Park info, clothing and gear and snacks are also on offer.

Getting There & Away

The park is 18 miles west of Dahlonega on Hwy 52. There is no public transportation, so it's best to have your own wheels.

Blue Ridge

☎706, 762 / POP 1400

Cutesy and wildly popular Blue Ridge was founded in 1866 as a railroad junction (its historic depot, rebuilt in 1906, still sits across from its postcard-perfect Main St). This little town draws hordes of fans in summer for its charming linear downtown rife with restaurants, bars, antique shops and locally owned businesses. While it's hard to believe it was once promoted as the 'Switzerland of the South,' it *is* easy on the eyes and offers more quality distractions than other North Georgia towns. It's known as Georgia's trout capital, and year-round river and stream fly-fishing in the surrounding countryside is a big draw. The town is often considered Atlanta's backyard – a hotbed for wealthy Atlantans to lay down roots with a second home in the mountains.

Activities

Fly-fishing draws serious anglers to Blue Ridge.

Popular day hikes around Blue Ridge include **Falls Branch Falls**, a half-mile round-trip hike that's part of the Benton MacKaye trail system (www.bmta.org), to a double waterfall, and **Long Creek Falls**, a 2.4-mile round-trip hike on the Appalachian Trail.

The 3290-acre, aquamarine **Lake Blue Ridge**,1.5 miles from downtown Blue Ridge, offers kayak and paddleboard rentals at Morganton Point Recreation Area from April through October.

Blue Ridge Fly Fishing FISHING
(Map p164; ☎706-258-4080; www.blueridgeflyfishing.com; 490 E Main St; half-/full-day from $275/375; ⏲8:30am-6pm) Fly-fishing expert Jeff Turner runs half- and full-day fly-fishing outings in Blue Ridge, Ellijay, McCaysville, Suches, Copper Hill and Chattanooga, and float trips on the Toccoa River. Stop by his fly shop smack downtown.

Blue Ridge Scenic Railway RAIL

(Map p164; ☎877-413-8724; www.brscenic.com; 241 Depot St; adult $44-79, child $29; ⊙mid-Mar–Dec) Starting from the historic 1905 downtown depot at 11am on most days (check the schedule online), this scenic-railway ride takes you along 1886-laid tracks to the quaint sister border towns of McCaysville, Georgia and Copperhill, TN, winding along the bank of the Toccoa River, returning at 3pm.

Sleeping

Blue Ridge is home to 1500 mountain homes in addition to B&Bs, motels and chain hotels. While some small and rustic traditional cabins are available, most are luxury mountain homes. To peruse them all in one place, check out www.blueridgemountains.com/wheretostay.html.

Aska Lodge B&B $$

(Map p164; ☎706-632-0178; www.askalodge.net; 178 Calen Dr; r $160-180; P❄📶) This idyllic, two-story pinewood lodge is run by a friendly, well-traveled climber couple. The four rooms all feature highly regarded trade-offs – do you choose the wraparound porch with swing or the in-room Jacuzzi? The wooden sliding bathroom doors and other woodwork throughout the house are produced on-site and there's an outstanding front-yard firepit. It's on wooded grounds 3.5 miles south of downtown and is a nice counter to downtown's touristy madness.

Blue Ridge Inn B&B $$

(Map p164; ☎706-661-7575; www.blueridgeinnbandb.com; 477 W First St; r $175-240; P📶) Bang downtown is this epic three-story Victorian home dating to the 1890s and awash in 12ft ceilings, original hand-carved woodwork and heart-pine flooring. The town's classy choice, it has impeccable rooms with features such as claw-foot tubs or four-poster beds, antique vanities and hardwood bathroom floors. Think quaint, historic and oh so comfortable.

Eating

If Blue Ridge has anything, it's places to eat. Main St is lined with restaurants – everything from down-home country kitchens to sophisticated New American choices and plenty of high-falutin' pub grub in between.

Pink Pig BARBECUE $

(www.budspinkpig.com; 824 Cherry Log St, Cherry Log; mains $7.50-15.50; ⊙11am-9pm Thu-Sun) Pork, ribs and chicken are served in a log cabin with a chimney pumping out smoky essence of pit BBQ. In addition to BBQ, the Pink Pig does soul food such as chicken and dumplings, chicken livers, cured ham and fried green tomatoes. Jimmy Carter is known to be a fan.

Harvest on Main NEW AMERICAN $$

(Map p164; ☎706-946-6164; www.harvestonmain.com; 576 E Main St; mains $18-29; ⊙Mon, Wed & Thu, 11am-4pm Tue, 11am-3pm & 4-9pm Fri & Sat, 11am-3pm & 4-8pm Sun; 📶) With more creative flair than most, this rustic-chic eatery in the heart of the action does hearty mains – seared fish with sesame spinach over chickpea stew, smoked bone-in pork chop with apple BBQ sauce, duck two ways – alongside a hefty wine, craft-beer and bourbon list. Tree-limb chairs, a big fireplace and Southern service keep things cozy. Book ahead, especially on weekends.

Southern Charm SOUTHERN US $$

(Map p164; ☎706-632-9090; www.eatsoutherncharm.com; 224 W Main St; mains $10-17; ⊙11am-8pm Mon-Wed, to 3pm Thu & Sun, to 9pm Fri & Sat; 📶) In a big, bright-yellow house across the railroad tracks from E Main St, this friendly Southern eatery excels at the classics: fried green tomato with a shrimp po'boy, fried chicken, blackened rainbow trout (and don't forget grandma's biscuit chicken potpie).

Drinking & Entertainment

★**Grumpy Old Men** CRAFT BEER

(Map p164; www.grumpyoldmenbrewing.com; 1315 E Main St; pints $5; ⊙1-5pm Thu & Fri, to 6pm Sun; 📶) With cornhole courts, outdoor picnic seating and a DIY ethos, this excellent hop headquarters is a quintessential Southern-brewing good time. There are 18 taps, which often include small-batch or one-off experimental brews (the Grasshoppa Imperial IPA and Hell's Holler Porter are both great). The indoor ski and toilet-seat benches make for fun Instagram moments.

Chester Brunnenmeyer's Bar & Grill BAR

(Map p164; www.chestersblueridge.com; 733 E Main St; ⊙4-11:30pm Mon-Fri, 11:30am-11:30pm Sat, 12:30-11:30pm Sun; 📶) This is one of the town's most popular bars, mainly for its long and social 30-stool bar facing 18 taps of mainly local and regional craft beer. It also does a mean Bloody Mary that drinks like a meal (pepper vodka, Bloody Mary mix,

Blue Ridge

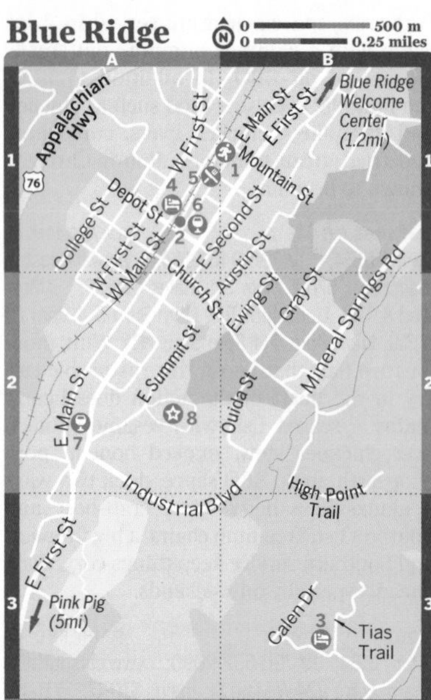

Blue Ridge

Activities, Courses & Tours
1 Blue Ridge Fly Fishing B1
2 Blue Ridge Scenic Railway A1

Sleeping
3 Aska Lodge B3
4 Blue Ridge Inn A1

Eating
5 Harvest on Main A1
Southern Charm .... (see 4)

Drinking & Nightlife
6 Chester Brunnenmeyer's Bar & Grill A1
7 Grumpy Old Men A2

Entertainment
8 Swan Drive In A2

seasoned-salt rim, cheddar cheese, pickled green beans, drunken tomato, stuffed olives, pickled okra, celery, beef stick).

Swan Drive In THEATER
(Map p164; ☎706-632-6690; www.swan-drive-in.com; 651 Summit St; films $8) Dating to 1955, this old-school drive-in theater is one of three still operating in Georgia.

Information

Blue Ridge Welcome Center (☎800-899-6867; www.blueridgemountains.com; 152 Orvin Lance Dr; 8:30am-5pm Mon-Fri, 9am-5pm Sat, 1-5pm Sun) Pick up information on Blue Ridge, Fannin County, the North Georgia Mountains and the Southern Blue Ridge.

Getting There & Away

Just a 90-minute drive north of Atlanta on I-75/I-575, Blue Ridge is probably the most easily accessed of North Georgia's mountain towns.

Helen

☎706, 762 / POP 510

Awash in lederhosen and *fahrvergnügen* (driving pleasure) and lots of other questionable German cliches, gingerbread-trimmed Helen is a little bit of Bavaria in Appalachia (call it 'Alppalachia', if you will). It is certainly a startling, out-of-place sight. In the grand tradition of other touristy German villages such as Colonia Tovar (Venezuela) and Gramado (Brazil), here scores of North Georgians and Atlanta day-trippers (some 1.5 million per year) run amok among German-style architecture fueled by steins of Dunkelweizens, Doppelbocks and Pils like it's Oktoberfest year-round. This kitschy, Epcot-style Alpine playground was dreamed up in the 1960s by a few local businesspeople wanting to revitalize the town. In 1969 local businesses and carpenters got to work – with help from a local artist with German roots – transforming this former mill town into the self-proclaimed best little German town in America.

Sights

Helen's main sight is downtown itself, a small and tiny Bavarian-style village full of confectionery shops; pottery, jewelry, woodworking and leather boutiques, old-time photo studios, and restaurants and pubs. Just outside town, a bevy of interesting and beautiful historic and natural sights abound.

★ **Anna Ruby Falls** WATERFALL
(Map p166; ☎706-878-1448; https://cfaia.org; 3455 Anna Ruby Falls Rd; adult/child $3/free; 9am-5pm Nov-Mar, to 6pm Apr-May, to 7pm Jun-Oct, gate closes 1hr before;) Not to be confused with Tennessee's far more famous Ruby Falls, Georgia's Anna Ruby Falls is tucked away in Unicoi State Park (part of the Chattahoochee-Oconee National Forest) 5.7 miles north of downtown Helen. Here twin

waterfalls spawned by dueling creeks – Curtis Creek and York Creek – drop 153ft and 50ft, respectively. The falls are reached by a gorgeous 0.4-mile paved hiking trail (read: kid- and stroller- friendly, though uphill) from the visitor center.

The falls and the state park have separate entry fees – if you are only visiting the falls, you can drive through the park for free. The recreation area includes picnic facilities.

Unicoi State Park STATE PARK
(Map p166; ☎706-878-2201; www.gastateparks.org/unicoi; 1788 Hwy 356; per vehicle $5; ⏲7am-10pm; P 👪) At this adventure-oriented park, visitors can rent kayaks ($10 per hour), take paddleboard lessons ($25), hike some 12 miles of trails, mountain bike, or take a zipline safari through the local forest canopy ($59).

Vogel State Park STATE PARK
(☎706-745-2628; www.gastateparks.org/vogel; 405 Vogel State Park Rd; per vehicle $5; ⏲7am-10pm; P) Located at the base of the evocatively named Blood Mountain, this is one of Georgia's oldest parks, and constitutes a quilt of wooded mountains surrounding a 22-acre lake. There's a multitude of trails to pick from, catering to beginners and advanced hikers. Many of the on-site facilities were built by the Civilian Conservation Corp; a seasonal museum tells the story of these work teams, who both built the park and rescued the local economy during the Great Depression.

Habersham Vineyards & Winery WINERY
(Map p166; ☎706-878-9463; www.habershamwinery.com; 7025 S Main St; tastings $7.50; ⏲10am-6pm Mon-Sat, 12:30-6pm Sun) One of Georgia's pioneering wineries dating all the way back to 1983. Winemaker Andrew Beaty trained at the University of California, Davis, and wineries in California, and his juice often wins awards. Seek out its Creekstone label, which produces a Viognier, chardonnay, cabernet sauvignon and merlot, among others. Of course, there's a gewürztraminer in the house!

Hardman Farm FARM
(Map p166; http://gastateparks.org/hardmanfarm; 143 Hwy 17, Sautee Nacoochee; adult/child $12/7; ⏲10am-4pm Thu-Sun Mar-Dec) This 1870 Italianate farmhouse set on 173 acres, 2 miles southeast of downtown Helen, is Georgia's newest state historic site. The nearby gazebo-topped Nacoochee Mound and cow pasture hearkens to Cherokee roots. Tours take in the 19th-century parlor with original lighting (check the fascinating telephone and climate-control system), the bedroom of Anna Ruby Nichols (for whom nearby Anna Ruby Falls was named) and the withered dairy barn (there are 19 outbuildings in all).

Activities

Besides eating, drinking and shopping, the number-one activity in Helen – in summer, anyway – is undoubtedly 'shootin' the Hooch' – river tubing on the Chattahoochee River, which winds through the village.

Cool River Tubing Co TUBING
(Map p166; ☎706-878-2665; www.coolrivertubing.com; 590 Edelweiss Strasse; tubing per trip/day $8/12; ⏲9am-6pm) One of two outfitters in Helen that can set you up with 'shootin' the Hooch'. It makes for a damn fine afternoon floating down the river with fellow travelers on a 1½- or 2½-hour trip (alcohol is prohibited but that doesn't mean people aren't buzzed). Cool Tubing also has a booth on Main St.

Festivals & Events

Oktoberfest CULTURAL
(☎706-878-1619; www.helenchamber.com; 1074 Edelweiss Strasse, Helen Festhalle; week/weekend $8/10; ⏲Sep-Oct) Helen goes all out for its annual celebration of German music, food, drinks and dancing (waltzes, polkas, chicken dances), but the dog-friendly *biergarten* is where you want be – nearly 30 breweries pour their wares. The festival starts on weekends in September, switching to a daily party from September 27 to October 28.

Sleeping

As one of North Georgia's most touristy locales, Helen suits all types of lodgings and budgets. Chain motels, B&Bs, cabins, riverside lodges and cottages and German-themed inns are in abundance. Prices increase significantly during Oktoberfest and during fall foliage.

Unicoi State Park & Lodge LODGE $
(Map p166; ☎800-573-9659; www.unicoilodge.com; 1788 Hwy 356 Rd; camping/r/cabins from $15/124/159) Two miles north of the Alpine village, this state-run adventure lodge has something for everyone: 100 cozy rooms, 30 one-, two- and three-bedroom cabins with full kitchen and wood-burning fireplace (our favorite), 82 campsites and 51 RV sites with water, electricity and dump stations.

Helen

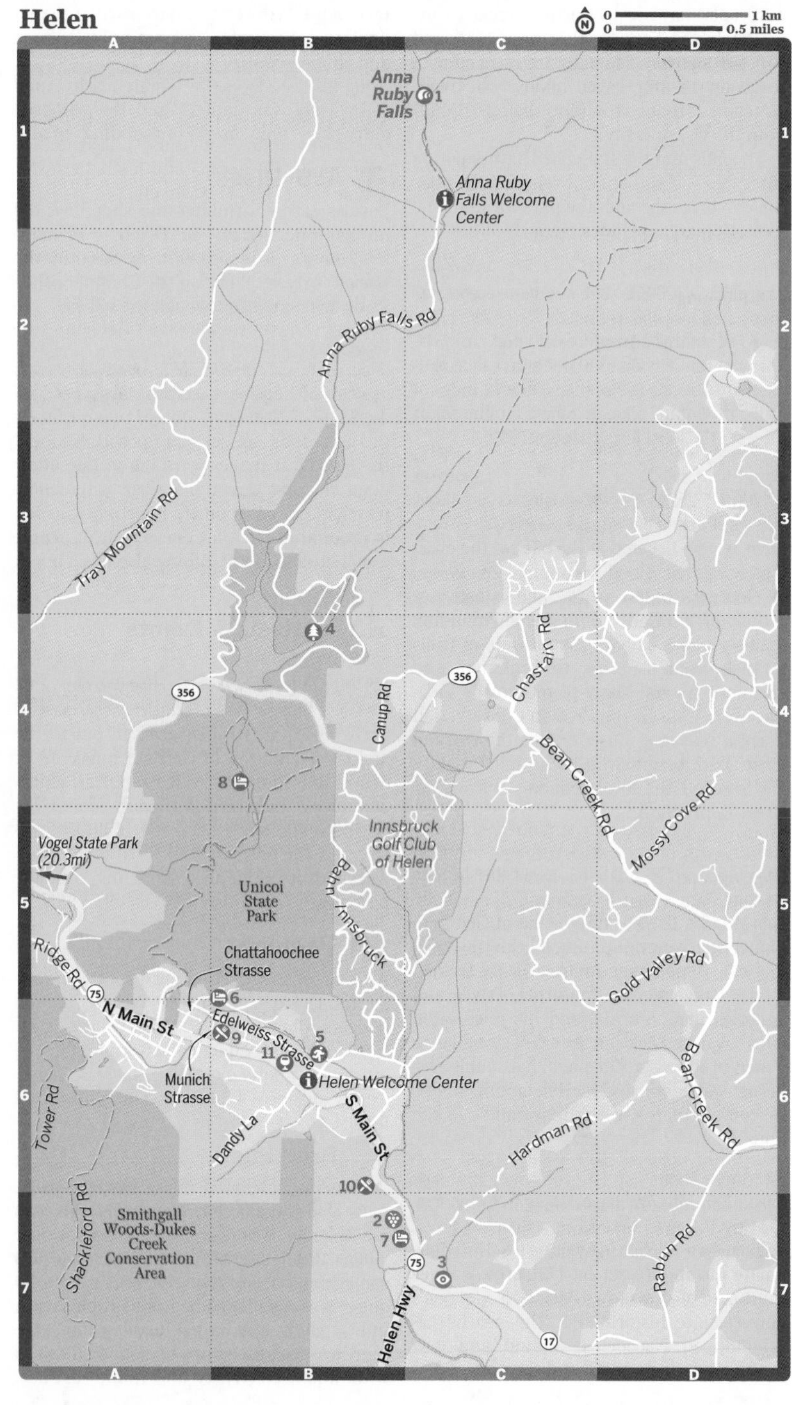
0 1 km
0 0.5 miles
A
B
C
D
1
2
3
4
5
6
7
Anna Ruby Falls
1
Anna Ruby Falls Welcome Center
Anna Ruby Falls Rd
Tray Mountain Rd
4
356
Canup Rd
Chastain Rd
Bean Creek Rd
Mossy Cove Rd
8
Innsbruck Golf Club of Helen
Bahn Innsbruck
Vogel State Park (20.3mi)
Unicoi State Park
Chattahoochee Strasse
Ridge Rd
75
N Main St
6
Edelweiss Strasse
9
5
11
Munich Strasse
Helen Welcome Center
Gold Valley Rd
Tower Rd
Dandy La
S Main St
Hardman Rd
Bean Creek Rd
10
Shackleford Rd
Smithgall Woods-Dukes Creek Conservation Area
2
7
3
Rabun Rd
Helen Hwy
17

Helen

Top Sights
1 Anna Ruby Falls C1

Sights
2 Habersham Vineyards & Winery B7
3 Hardman Farm C7
4 Unicoi State Park B4

Activities, Courses & Tours
5 Cool River Tubing Co B6

Sleeping
6 Alpine Hilltop Haus B5
7 Nacoochee Adventures B7
8 Unicoi State Park & Lodge B4

Eating
9 Bodensee B6
10 Mully's Nacoochee Grill B6

Drinking & Nightlife
11 Catch 22 .... B6

There's a restaurant and tavern on-site and outdoor adventures (paddleboarding, mountain biking etc) from your doorstep. There's a $10 lodging fee, which includes park access.

Nacoochee Adventures TREEHOUSE, CAMPGROUND $
(Map p166; 706-878-9477; www.nacoocheeadventures.com; 7019 S Main St; camping $49) Whether you opt for a treehouse forged from recycled materials, a pioneer-style covered wagon or a gypsy vardo, this primitive campground (no water or electricity) is one of Helen's unique sleeps. Most options are located a half-mile hike into the woods from the office (golf-cart/utility vehicles are available for rent). There is a $95 refundable deposit. You'll need supplies – this is structure and mattress only.

Alpine Hilltop Haus B&B $
(Map p166; 706-878-2388; www.alpinehilltop.com; 362 Chattahoochee Strasse; r from $120; P ❄) Barbara and Frankie are the charming hosts of this B&B tucked away in the woods just behind town, but still close enough to walk. Rooms, in an Alpine-inspired annex, vary from a bit froufrou to more modern and luxurious. There's a fantastic wooden back patio with town views – perfect for morning coffee or a glass of wine.

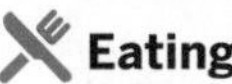

Eating

Helen has carved itself an Alpine niche and the gastronomy on offer here is no exception: hearty German restaurants dominate the culinary landscape. If that's not your thing – or you're all wursted out – there is a handful of gastropubs, BBQ spots and a smattering of ethnic eats (Thai, Mexican etc).

Bodensee GERMAN
(Map p166; 706-878-1026; www.bodenseerestaurant.com; 64 Munich Strasse; mains $16-20; 11am-9pm Sun-Thu, to 10pm Fri & Sat;) Widely considered the best of Helen's German restaurants, Bodensee even boasts a Romanian-trained chef with considerable Bavarian experience. Pork specialties feature aplenty: *hauspfannle* (pork tenderloin with bacon and mushroom-cream sauce, *rouberspiess* (pork loin with paprika, onion and spicy 'Gypsy' sauce) and, of course, schnitzel.

But there are beef (*sauerbraten* with potato dumplings and red cabbage, Hungarian goulash) and veggie choices as well. Get your German on!

Mully's Nacoochee Grill AMERICAN $$
(Map p166; 706-878-1020; www.mullysnacoocheegrill.com; 7277 S Main St; mains $14-34; 4:30-8:30pm Tue, to 9pm Wed & Thu, 11:30am-2:30pm & 4:30-9pm Fri & Sat, 11:30am-2:30pm & 4:30-8pm Sun;) Occupying a relocated rural farmhouse, Helen's foodie find serves a classic menu of globally influenced dishes stereotypically considered fine dining before the New American culinary movement (wedge salads, chicken masala, grilled rib eyes) but ups the ante with slightly more chef-driven, Southern-angled dishes such as peppercorn-crusted pork tenderloin with brandy-cream sauce, and shrimp sautéed with red onions, poblano and red peppers and served with grits.

It's 1.4 miles southeast of the Alpine village. If you are around for Wednesday, Friday, Saturday or Sunday brunch, former Bon Jovi touring guitarist Kent Johnston provides the soundtrack.

Drinking

As you might guess, big steins of German beer and popular German beer brands such as Paulaner, Erdinger, Weihenstephan, Schneider Weisse and Spaten Oktoberfest are big business in Helen. The most atmospheric *biergarten* is probably the one at pretty White Horse Sq. If you're after local and regional craft beer instead, head to Catch 22 (p168).

Catch 22 GASTROPUB
(Map p166; www.catch22gp.com; 8160 S Main St, unit A-1; 11am-9pm Mon, to 10pm Tue-Sat, to 8pm Sun;) The atmosphere is decidedly small-town strip mall, but this is Helen's beer refuge, with 36 taps of regional and national craft beer and a gaggle of friendly staff who feel a beer connoisseur's pain here in German *bierland*. The food is good too (the blackened-tuna tacos are tasty, and you can never go wrong with a burger).

But this is not the place to be chintzy with the tip – there is a 'Shitty Tipper' dry-erase board on the wall!

Information

Anna Ruby Falls Welcome Center (Map p166; 706-878-1448; https://cfaia.org; 3455 Anna Ruby Falls Rd; 9am-4:30pm Nov-Mar, to 5:30pm Apr-May, to 6:30pm Jun-Oct) In addition to gifts and falls information, ask here about May and June nighttime walks to see the rare Orfelia fultoni (known locally as foxfire), a bioluminescent species of fly whose larvae glow spectacularly at night.

Helen Welcome Center (Map p166; 800-858-8027; www.helenga.org; 726 Bruckenstrasse; 9am-5pm Mon-Sat, 10am-4pm Sun) The Alpine Helen/White County Convention & Visitors Bureau runs the town info center. Pick up brochures on restaurants, activities and accommodations as well as tourist info.

Getting There & Away

Helen is tucked away in the North Georgia mountains 86 miles northeast of Atlanta and most easily reached by car via Hwy 19 S.

City parking lots charge $2 (private lots run $5)

Clayton

706, 762 / POP 2270

One of North Georgia's most charming depots, Clayton is on the rise. Founded as Claytonsville by European-American settlers in 1821, today the small town has become somewhat of a Blue Ridge Mountain refuge for outdoor-enthusiast escapees from Atlanta, Athens and beyond. Its adorable downtown and main street are lined with independent businesses and fun restaurants. Clayton's location, surrounded by Rabun County's 20 or so publicly accessible waterfalls and several state parks, makes it a magnet for outdoor distractions. Tallulah Gorge State Park, just 11 miles south, and Georgia's highest state park, Black Rock Mountain State Park (5 miles north), are the big draws in the immediate area.

Sights

Black Rock Mountain State Park STATE PARK
(706-746-2141; www.gastateparks.org/blackrockmountain; per vehicle $5; 7am-10pm Mar 16-Dec 16) Reaching altitudes of 3640ft, Georgia's highest state park is 5 miles north of Clayton. At that height, its obvious draws are the vistas. Like Brasstown Bald (Georgia's highest point), you can see four states from the park's various lookouts on a clear day. There are 11 miles of trails spread over four routes as well as a campground and primitive backcountry camping sites. A picnic from its summit visitor center is the way to go.

Foxfire Museum & Heritage Center CULTURAL CENTER
(www.foxfire.org; 98 Foxfire Lane; adult $8, child 7-10/under 6 $3/free; 8:30am-4:30pm Mon-Sat) Fancy living off the grid? Since 1966, this important, hands-on experiential museum telling the story of Appalachian culture has been solely focused on lost-art-type, back-to-basics Appalachian living skills that have been passed down for generations. There are 10 authentic pioneer log cabins along with artifacts, tools and handcrafted housewares, toys and folk art. It's located on Black Rock Mountain in Mountain City 3.4 miles north of Clayton.

Sleeping

Clayton proper is home to two B&Bs, with another four in Rabun County. The usual chain hotels are here and camping resorts and campgrounds are within 10 to 15 minutes of downtown. Generally speaking, Clayton has some of the top B&Bs in North Georgia.

York House Inn B&B $
(706-746-2068; www.yorkhouseinn.com; 416 York House Rd, Rabun Gap; r $105-190;) Opened in 1896, this is Georgia's oldest B&B and sits on the the National Register of Historic Places. Inviting, rocking-chair-peppered porches lead to 14 spacious rooms with amenities such as Ralph Lauren bedding and original heart-pine floors. Breakfast is serious business: how does baked shaved-ham cups with spinach Parmesan filling, topped with fresh eggs and heavy cream sound? It's 4.8 miles north of Clayton in Rabun Gap.

White Birch Inn B&B $$

(706-782-4444; www.thewhitebirchinn.net; 28 E Savannah St; r week/weekend night from $215/222;) Owned and designed by an architect and interior-designer power couple, this cozy inn is a real stunner, especially where woodwork is concerned. A tree-bark wall forms the backdrop of the fireplace-warmed lounge under tree-limb-wrapped rust-orange lighting. Each of the six rooms is different, but highlights include a copper sink-in bathtub, a tree-branch bed frame and a gorgeous custom wooden vanity.

Eating

Clayton is one of the best small towns in North Georgia for a meal. Along the main drag, there are a couple of fantastic choices, ranging from higher-end New Southern farm-to-table offerings to scrumptious burgers and highbrow pub grub. Further afield you'll find a wide array of choices, including BBQ, Mexican and Italian.

Universal Joint BURGERS $

(www.ujclayton.com; 109 N Main St; burgers $9.50-11.50; 11:30am-10pm Sun-Thu, to midnight Fri & Sat;) Laid-back 'Ujoint' is a local favorite – best outdoor patio in town, 17 taps of local and regional craft beers and perfectly charred burgers adorned in righteously Southern ways. Try the Steinbeck (half pound of Angus beef, house-made pimento cheese, bacon, lettuce, onions, tomato, pickled jalapeño and a pickle). Add a bevy of sassy bartenders and you have yourself an afternoon.

Fortify Kitchen & Bar NEW AMERICAN $$$

(706-782-0050; www.fortifyclayton.com; 69 N Main St; mains $22-35; Tue-Sat;) Clayton's best night out is this stylish farm-to-table supper club from chef Jamie Allred, North Georgia's top kitchen dog. Some of the Southeast's best purveyors form the foundation for incredible fried green tomatoes with blackened Gulf shrimp or cornmeal-crusted Carolina mountain trout with dill pesto. Serious cocktails ($10) and desserts (pecan tart with blood-orange caramel) bookend an evening here.

If you're looking for something more casual, it does gourmet pizza ($12 to $22) next door at Fortify Pi. Dinner reservations essential.

Drinking

White Birch Provisions CAFE

(www.whitebirchprovisions.com; 60 E Savannah St; coffee $1.50-5; 7:30am-5pm Mon, Tue, Thu & Fri, to 2pm Wed, 8am-2pm Sat;) This adorable cafe and gourmet shop serves Clayton's best espresso, and it's a cute and quaint hang space as well. In addition to coffee, you'll find local provisions from around the Southeast, a bakery and a wine cave, all surrounded by local art.

Clark's on Main BAR

(www.clarksonmain.com; 88 N Main St; 11am-midnight Mon & Wed-Sun, 5pm-midnight Tue;) Technically a sports bar and grill (with highly recommended bar food), but with a long bar facing 40 taps of regional and national craft and commercial brews, it's the closest thing Clayton has to a full-on, rowdy bar.

Shopping

★**Wander North Georgia** CLOTHING

(www.wandernorthgeorgia.com; 33 N Main St; 11am-5pm Mon-Thu, to 6pm Fri & Sat, noon-5pm Sun) What started as an outdoorsy mountain blog and Instagram page has turned into one of Georgia's coolest start-ups. The fantastic T-shirts are the main attraction (it's co-owned by a graphic designer), plus the trucker hats, but there are all kinds of meticulously curated woodsmen-type gear here (candles, books like *Cabin Porn* and *Van Life,* beard balm).

Information

Rabun County Welcome Center (706-782-4812; www.explorerabun.com; 232 Hwy 441 N; 8am-5pm Sun-Thu, to noon Fri) Maps, lodging info, brochures on Rabun County.

Getting There & Away

Clayton sits in Georgia's northeast corner, 108 miles northeast of Atlanta and not that far from the Tennessee, North Carolina and South Carolina borders. It's accessed via Hwy 23 N from I-85 and best reached by car.

Tallulah Gorge State Park

This 2739-acre state park is home to a spectacular gorge nearly 1000ft deep and 2 miles long. It protects six endangered plant species, including the persistent trillium (there are at least 22 species in

Georgia) and harbors six waterfalls collectively known as the Tallulah Falls. In the mid-19th century, Tallulah Gorge became a resort area for coastal residents on the run from yellow fever. The introduction of the railroad in 1882 increased access and ushered in the 'Grand Era' of hotels on the rim of the gorge. The damming of the river in the early 1900s to create electricity for Atlanta reduced the flow by 90% or more and killed off a devastating chunk of tourism. Today, it's one of North Georgia's most popular destinations for outdoor adventure, including hiking, biking and climbing. Scenes from 1972's *Deliverance* were filmed here.

Sights & Activities

There are some 20 miles of hiking trails in this gorgeous park, including short, easy walks on the rim of the gorge, passing five waterfalls along the way. In addition to the north- and south-rim trails, the 2-mile **Hurricane Falls Trail** is a moderate, family-friendly hike that will get you deep into the canyon (via 310 steps) to the suspension bridge (from which three waterfalls can be seen), as well as to the base of Hurricane Falls (via a second set of 221 stairs).

To go deeper, you'll require a free gorge-floor permit, limited to 100 per day.

Tallulah Gorge GORGE
(706-754-7981; www.gastateparks.org/tallulahgorge; 338 Jane Hurt Yarn Dr, Tallulah Falls; per vehicle $5; 8am-sunset; P) The 1000ft-deep Tallulah Gorge carves a dark scar across the wooded hills of North Georgia. Walk over the *Indiana Jones*–worthy suspension bridge, and be on the lookout (literally) for rim trails to overlooks. Or get a first-come, first-served permit to hike to the gorge floor – only 100 are given out each day (arrive early, they're usually gone in the morning) and not offered on water-release dates (check schedule online).

Sleeping

The park is home to the **Terrora Campground** (706-754-7979; www.gastateparks.org/tallulahgorge; 300 Jane Hurt Yarn Dr; campsites from $32) as well as three primitive backcountry camping areas with no more than a shelter and a fire ring. There are a handful of private camping and lodge options on either side of Hwy 441 as well as more charming options in Clayton (11 miles), Toccoa (18 miles) and Helen (28 miles).

Information

Jane Hurt Yarn Interpretive Center
(706-754-7981; www.gastateparks.org/tallulahgorge; 338 Jane Hurt Yarn Dr; 8am-5pm) One of the better state-park welcome centers you'll come across, this hosts exhibits on the park, and the people and cultures of the region, and has a small gift and snack shop. Stop here for gorge-floor permits. A 15-minute film, *Tallulah Gorge*, is screened every 30 minutes from 8am to 4pm.

Getting There & Away

Tallulah Gorge State Park sits off Hwy 441, about 97 miles northeast of Atlanta and 65 miles north of Athens. The closest you can get without your own wheels is the **Amtrak** (p172) station in Toccoa, 18 miles south.

Toccoa

706, 762 / POP 8500

Founded shortly after the Civil War, tiny Toccoa – believed to mean 'beautiful' in a Native American dialect – is a small-time North Georgia town with big-time history and hospitality. It's perhaps most famous as the site of WWII's Camp Toccoa at Currahee, the inaugural US Army paratrooper training camp and the inspiration for the miniseries, *Band of Brothers*. The paratroopers' intense training regime involved a daily '3 miles up, 3 miles down' to the top of Currahee Mountain just outside town, which affords a panoramic North Georgia view for those who climb it. Toccoa's historic downtown boasts an epic restored art-deco theater and emblematic low-rise late 19th-century architecture along its main drag, Doyle St. Toccoa Falls, one of the tallest free-falling waterfalls east of the Mississippi River, wows travelers on the campus of Toccoa Falls College. Toccoa is a pleasant surprise.

Sights

★**Toccoa Falls** WATERFALL
(www.cityoftoccoa.com/toccoa-falls.cfm; 77 Azalea Ct, Toccoa Falls College; adult/child $2/free; sunrise-5pm Jan–mid-Feb, to sunset mid-Feb–mid-Dec) This dramatic 186ft-high waterfall, reached along a 500ft path from the visitor center on the campus of Tocca Falls College, is one of the tallest free-falling

waterfalls east of the Mississippi River (it's taller than Niagara – a paltry 167ft). It's a definite wow moment as the falls come into view. But this beauty does not come without tragedy: a dam above the falls failed in 1977 – the resulting flood killed 39 people, Georgia's worst natural disaster in more than 40 years.

Though there is a nominal fee to access the falls, they are free outside visitor-center opening hours (the gate should be open).

Currahee Military Museum MUSEUM

(www.toccoahistory.com; 160 N Alexander St; adult/child $10/free; ⌚10am-4pm Mon-Sat, 1-4pm Sun) Toccoa's pride and joy is this 14,000-sq-ft museum dedicated to the inaugural US Army paratrooper training camp, located here during WWII, and the four Parachute Infantry Regiments who trained here, and went on to be the first American boots on the ground during the Invasion of Normandy. Visitors come from far and wide thanks to Tom Hanks' and Steven Spielberg's Emmy- and Golden Globe–winning war-drama miniseries, *Band of Brothers,* inspired by Camp Toccoa.

The museum not only houses the original 70ft-long Aldbourne stables (disassembled in the UK and reassembled in Toccoa in 2005) and all manner of Camp Toccoa military paraphernalia, but includes a small city museum, which reveals a loaded list of surprising Toccoa-related history: soul-singer James Brown was sent to juvenile detention near Toccoa, where he joined his first R&B group, the Famous Flames; 1956 Olympic weightlifting Gold-medalist Paul Anderson – who still owns a Guinness World Record for the greatest weight ever raised by a human being (6270lb), hails from here. There is also a small exhibit hall dedicated to local veterans and other wars.

Currahee Vineyard & Winery WINERY

(☎706-768-5383; www.curraheevineyards.com; 3301 W Currahee St; tastings $4-10; ⌚noon-6pm Thu, Fri & Sun, 11am-6pm Sat) This small, family-owned and -operated winery does brisk business in the region for its sweet fruit and muscadine wines. While they aren't likely to be fawned over by Robert Parker anytime soon, the Georgia Sunrise peach wine and the Georgia Ole Blue (with blueberries, pomegranate and muscadine) are surprisingly tasty and refreshing, and the 18% alcohol Currahee Apple is a real heart-warmer.

There's often live music on weekends with wine slushies. A BBQ pit-master is brought in on holiday weekends and for other special events throughout the year. Tastings are free with a bottle purchase.

Traveler's Rest State Historic Site HISTORIC SITE

(www.gastateparks.org/travelersrest; 4339 Riverdale Rd; adult/child $5/1; ⌚9am-5pm Sat & Sun) The only surviving travelers' rest along the Unicoi Turnpike (a once-busy thoroughfare over the Appalachian Mountains), this stagecoach inn and plantation was built in 1805. It is extremely well preserved, and you can just imagine exhausted travelers doing everything from tying up their road-weary horses for the night to having gunfights over the last swig of moonshine by the fireplace, à la Quentin Tarantino's *Hateful Eight*. The inn includes numerous original artifacts and furnishings, many crafted by renowned Massachusetts cabinetmaker Caleb Shaw.

Sleeping

Simmons-Bond Inn B&B $

(☎706-282-5183; www.simmons-bond.com; 74 W Tugalo St; r week night $99-129, weekend night $129-149; P 📶) This historic two-story, 1903 mansion is rife with interesting and quirky details, such as a built-in china cabinet that once served as a pie safe, a hidden bathroom in the Colleen room (which is also home to famed journalist Nellie Bly's original oak traveling-writing desk), and late-18th-century heirlooms, ornate woodwork and leaded glass throughout.

The blue-toned Tiffany room (with color-coordinated claw-foot bathtub) is our favorite of the five rooms, but it's hard to go wrong surrounded by this much history.

Eating

X-Factor Grill AMERICAN $

(www.xfactorgrill.com; 27 E Doyle St; mains $6-14; ⌚11am-5pm Mon-Wed, to 9pm Thu-Sat, to 2:30pm Sun; 📶) On historic Doyle St, X-Factor Grill is Toccoa's mainstay bar and grill. It's nothing fancy but it does a decent job with American staples – pecan trout, fish tacos, burgers, catfish, Rueben sandwiches, fettuccine Alfredo – and craft beer (four taps plus a good few dozen in bottles). You even get a fluffy biscuit served before your meal.

Ping's Grill AMERICAN $
(www.facebook.com/pingsgrill; 201 Black Mountain Rd; mains $6.50-10; ⌚11:30am-8pm Tue-Sat, to 4pm Sun; 📶) In a pretty setting on Lake Toccoa, this casual, clubhouse-style restaurant dishes up good burgers, sandwiches and chicken wings over creaky hardwood floors and a roaring fireplace. In summer sit outside on the lakeside patio. It's a convenient option combined with Toccoa Falls (p170) – just 2.5 miles away.

Shopping

All Things Currahee ARTS & CRAFTS
(www.facebook.com/allthingscurrahee; 46 Doyle St; ⌚10am-6pm Mon-Fri, to 4pm Sat) Pop into this charming main-street shop for locally forged arts, crafts and gifts – nearly everything comes from within 100 miles of Toccoa. A few of our favorite things include ceramics, soaps and cosmetics, hand-turned pens and artisanal knives.

Information

Toccoa-Stephens County Welcome Center
(☎706-886-2132; www.visittoccoa.com; 160 N Alexander St; ⌚8:30am-5pm Mon-Fri, 10am-4pm Sat) Run by the Toccoa-Stephens County chamber of commerce. Pop in for info and excellent Southern hospitality.

Getting There & Away

Toccoa is 94 miles southeast of Atlanta and 50 miles north of Athens and reached via the recently expanded Hwy 17 – also known as the Currahee Pkwy.

The town is one of three Georgia stops on the Crescent City **Amtrak** (☎800-872-7245; www.amtrak.com/stations/tca.html; 47 N Alexander St) line from New York to New Orleans.

Understand Great Smoky Mountains National Park

GREAT SMOKY MOUNTAINS NATIONAL PARK TODAY 174

From booming attendance to aging infrastructure to invasive insect infestations, discover the issues affecting the park.

HISTORY 176

The fascinating story of the Great Smoky Mountains and the national park includes ancient seas, Cherokee settlements and Franklin D Roosevelt.

WILDLIFE 185

Keep watch for deer, turkeys and the occasional black bear. The elusive hellbender salamander lives here too.

PEOPLE OF THE SMOKY MOUNTAINS 190

The Cherokee tribe has roots to the region stretching back 1000 years. Descendants of settler John Walker never wanted to leave.

FORESTS OF THE SMOKY MOUNTAINS 194

In the spring, lush woods shimmer in every shade of green in the Great Smokies, which hold an amazing diversity of plant life. Trails lead to old-growth forests and Appalachian balds.

Great Smoky Mountains National Park Today

The Great Smoky Mountains National Park is one of America's great natural treasures. It's also decidedly well loved, drawing more visitors than any other national park in the country. Unfortunately the park faces significant challenges, including tree-felling insects, wildfires and aging infrastructure. The Smokies are also in dire need of funding, which will be essential for the park's success in the years ahead.

Best on Film

A Walk in the Woods (2014) A rollicking, man-vs-nature tale of two aging friends tackling the Appalachian Trail.

A Walk in the Spring Rain (1970) A romantic drama starring Ingrid Bergman and Anthony Quinn, filmed partly in Cades Cove.

Christy (1994–95) Captivating TV series about a young teacher from the city charged with running a rural school in the Smoky Mountains in the early 1900s.

Best in Print

Bear in the Back Seat: Adventures of a Wildlife Ranger in the Great Smoky Mountains National Park (Carolyn Jourdan and Kim DeLozier; 2013) Humorous and engaging accounts of wildlife work.

Our Southern Highlanders (Horace Kephart; 1913) Kephart's fascinating portraits of Appalachian peoples is a classic.

Cold Mountain (Charles Frazier; 1997) Award-winning novel set in the North Carolina mountains during the Civil War.

Cataloochee (Wayne Caldwell; 2007) Epic story following three generations of mountain people.

Loving the Park to Death

The Smokies provides a huge boon to the economies of North Carolina and Tennessee. In 2017 visiting vacationers spent more than $900 million in surrounding communities, supporting nearly 14,000 jobs. From a pure numbers perspective, the park continues to break records, drawing over 11 million visitors during each of 2016 and 2017. Across the country, national park tourism remains a significant driver of the American economy, with every dollar invested by visitors in the National Park Service returning $10 to the economy.

Although the high spending supports local jobs, it doesn't help pay for aging park infrastructure. The park suffers a huge amount of wear and tear, and currently has more than $233 million in deferred maintenance needs. Much of this is related to road repairs needed for some of the park's 200 miles of roads, bridges and tunnels. Other urgent needs include upgrades to the park's headquarters, maintenance along hiking trails and the rehabilitation of historic structures spread across five key areas. Sadly the Smokies aren't unique when it comes to financial struggles: the total deferred maintenance bill for all national parks – nearly $12 billion – is four times the annual appropriation by the US government.

Financial woes have already affected parts of the park. In 2013 Look Rock campground and picnic area, on the west side of the park, was closed owing to a lack of funding to replace its water-treatment system. Five years later it remained shuttered. A high-profile visit to the campground in 2018 by Tennessee Senator Lamar Alexander and US Secretary of the Interior Ryan Zinke, however, brought attention to the park's maintenance backlog with Zinke promising $2 million to reopen Look Rock. Alexander was also there to tout a controversial new bill he was sponsoring in Congress. It would link needed national park funding with revenue earned from energy production on federal lands.

A Plague of Insects

One of the greatest threats to the Smokies comes in the form of a tiny insect: the hemlock woolly adelgid. This invasive species, first detected in the park in the early 1990s, has been devastating the mighty hemlock trees of the Smokies. The aphid, no bigger than a speck of dust, feasts on the sap of the tree and rapidly reproduces. Once infected, a full-grown tree typically dies in less than five years. This ravaging insect is creating an ecological catastrophe since one in five trees in the Smokies is a hemlock.

To combat the infestation, the park is doing its best to treat affected trees by injecting or spraying them with pesticides – not an easy (or inexpensive) option, given the many inaccessible areas where hemlocks grow. The park has also released predator beetles (another non-native species) in hope of wiping out the aphid, though experts say it will be years before the beetles can put a dent in the adelgid population.

The insect devastation is apparent on many popular trails and at viewpoints throughout the park. It also caused the closure of the Parson Branch Rd in 2016. Inspecting park crews spotted more than 1700 dead trees within falling distance of the 8-mile-long roadway. With tree removal estimated at $450,000 and no funds available, the road remains closed to motorists, with no reopening date on the books.

The Chimney Tops Fires

In November, 2016 tragedy stuck Great Smoky Mountains National Park when fire was reported on Chimney Tops, one of the park's most popular trails. The combination of exceptional drought conditions, low humidity and wind gusts that topped 80mph caused the flames to spread over the next few weeks into what would soon become the deadliest wildfire in the eastern USA since the Great Fires of 1947.

Despite the heroic efforts by some 780 firefighters, the park and the nearby towns of Gatlinburg and Pigeon Forge suffered significant damage. Fourteen people died, around 2400 structures were damaged or destroyed, and 14,000 residents were forced to evacuate. The cost in dollars topped $500 million.

Inside the park, more than 15 square miles were scorched, with Chimney Tops taking the brunt of the blow, forcing the closure of one of the park's most beloved trails. It has since reopened, though the final section to the peaks remains closed for the long-term owing to loose rocks and the extreme instability of the rocky soil.

AREA (SQUARE MILES): **816**

ELEVATION RANGE: **875FT TO 6643FT**

VISITORS PER YEAR: **11.3 MILLION**

ECONOMIC IMPACT: **$923 MILLION**

TIME: **EASTERN STANDARD TIME (GMT/UTC MINUS FIVE HOURS)**

if 100 people stayed in GSMNP overnight

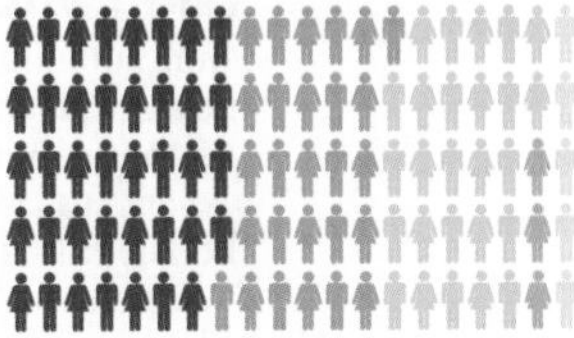

39 would be tent campers
27 would be RV campers
26 would be backcountry campers
3 would be lodgers
5 would be other

seasonal visitation

(% of annual visitors)

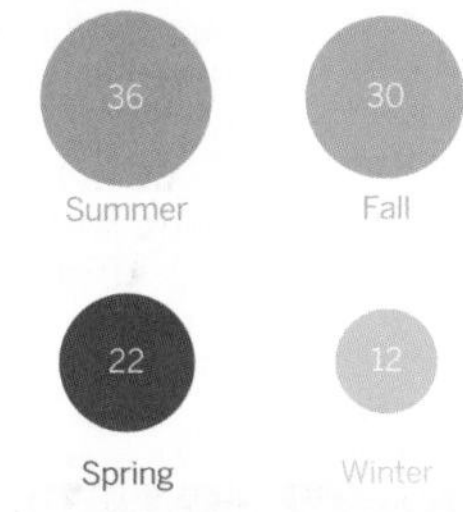

population per sq mile

History

The story of the Smoky Mountains began in primordial times when clashing supersized continents created a chain of mountains that are today among the oldest on the planet. Humans have also left their mark on these ancient Appalachian landscapes. Nomadic tribes were the first to the area, followed by early settlers. In the 1900s lumber companies arrived, nearly wiping out the forests. Luckily, in the 1920s a few visionary locals fought for the park's creation, which finally became a reality in 1934.

The Land

Some 500 million years ago, before the peaks of the Smokies rose into the sky, this area was little more than a shallow marine region along the continental edge. Fossilized remains of burrows and the shells of ancient sea creatures can be found on bedding surfaces of rocks along the Foothills Pkwy in the northwestern reaches of the park. Ancient fossils have also been found in the limestone of Cades Cove, including trilobites (an extinct marine arthropod) and the teeth of 500-million-year-old conodonts (akin to small eels). Some rock formations are even older, dating back more than a billion years, created by the melding of marine deposits and igneous rock in a primordial ocean.

Settler Sites

Cades Cove (p52)

Cataloochee (p56)

Roaring Fork Motor Nature Trail (p48)

Things started to get interesting around 300 million years ago when two massive landmasses collided. Present-day North America, part of the larger landmass of Laurasia (which also included Eurasia), crashed into Gondwana (comprising present-day Africa and South America), becoming part of the single supercontinent of Pangaea. The collision of tectonic plates over millions of years placed tremendous pressure and heat and caused horizontal layers of rock to be thrust upward, thus creating the massive Central Pangaean mountain chain – of which the Appalachian (and Smokies) were a part.

Around 200 million years ago, the supercontinent began to break apart, with massive landmasses peeling off, and the North American and African tectonic plates slowly moved to their current position. After their formation, the Appalachian Mountains were much higher than they are today. Some geologists believe these mountains were

TIMELINE

500 million years ago

Ancient marine creatures inhabit the shallow sea margin that existed in today's Appalachian region. Their fossils are found embedded in rocks along the Foothills Pkwy and elsewhere.

300 million years ago

Two continent-sized landmasses collide, and the tectonic forces push up rocks, slowly forming a vast mountain range with peaks as high as the Himalayas.

200 million years ago

The supercontinent breaks apart, with North American and African tectonic plates drifting to their current positions. The newly formed mountains are subjected to the forces of erosion.

once as high as, or even higher than, the Himalayas. The forces of erosion, caused by wind, water and ice, wore down these soaring peaks over millions of years, with vast quantities of sediment carried toward the Atlantic Ocean and the Gulf of Mexico – even forming some of the beaches on America's southern shores. The erosion process continues even today at the rate of around 2in every 1000 years.

Fast forward a few hundred million years to around 20,000 BC, when vast swaths of North America were covered by glaciers during the ice age. Ice sheets advanced as far south as the Ohio River, but never reached as far as the Smokies. The mountains, however, become a refuge for many species of plants and animals that retreated south from the colder northern climes. This contributed to the great diversity of its forests: there are more tree species in the Smoky Mountains than in all of Europe. The ice age also left its mark in other ways. As the mountains froze and thawed, rocks of all sizes sheered off and tumbled down the slopes and into the valleys below, creating curious boulder fields amid the forests that stand today.

Cades Cove was likely named after the Cherokee chief Kade of Tsiyahi (as the settlement of Cades Cove was called by the Native Americans).

Human Settlement

Native American people lived in the region of the Smoky Mountains since prehistoric times, leaving behind traces of their presence that are still being discovered by archaeologists. Among the finds are 10,000-year-old hunting projectiles used along likely animal migration paths. Ceramics from these early people date back to 700 BC, with primitive agricultural sites dating as far back as 1000 years ago.

When European settlers arrived in the 17th century, they encountered the Cherokee, who lived in settlements along the river valleys. The Smokies lay at the center of their vast territory, and they established seasonal hunting camps, as well as trails through the mountains that connected various settlements. Cades Cove likely once housed a permanent Cherokee village, called Tsiyahi or 'Place of the Otters,' which was located along the banks of Abrams Creek. The other permanent Cherokee settlement within today's park boundaries was Oconaluftee village, set along the river near the present-day Oconaluftee Visitor Center.

Spanish explorer Hernando de Soto was probably the first European to reach the Smokies, when he arrived in the southern Appalachian mountains in 1540. De Soto, who had earned notoriety for his successful invasion of present-day Peru and plunder of Incan riches, launched an expedition from the western panhandle of Florida in hopes of discovering gold in lands to the northeast. De Soto led an expedition of 600 men on a long, wandering journey from which only half of them would return. On their march west along the southern edge of the

The Travels of William Bartram, published in 1791, captures in vivid detail the wildlife, landscapes and native peoples (Creeks, Cherokee, Seminole) of a now vastly different region.

20,000 BC

Vast sheets of glacial ice cover a northern swath of North America. Many plant and animal species migrate into the southern Appalachia region to escape the inhospitable climate.

8000 BC

Early nomadic people hunt game seasonally in the Smoky Mountains and on their periphery. Tools and projectiles made of chert (a non-local lithic stone) are later found within the park.

1200 AD

During the Mississippian period, Native American people create fortified villages in the fertile valleys near the Smokies. They leave behind stamped pottery and platform mounds.

1500

The dominant tribe of central and southern Appalachia, the Cherokee, practice hunting in the mountains and grow crops in the fertile river valleys. They establish villages near the edge of the Smokies.

Smoky Mountains, the Spaniards stopped to camp alongside the Oconaluftee River. There they encountered Cherokee who were collecting mulberries – a delicacy the Spanish would write of extensively during their travels through the region. Although de Soto charted many lands never visited by Europeans, he never did find gold, and he died of a fever along the banks of the Mississippi River two years after setting out.

Perhaps owing to de Soto's failed venture, the wilderness region remained largely unexplored by Europeans for the next two centuries. Then in 1775 the American naturalist and Quaker William Bartram spent several months in southern Appalachia during his four-year journey through the southeast. He became one of the first to accurately write about the region – both about its wildlife and its native people.

The name 'Appalachian' was taken from the Native American tribe Apalachee, based in the Florida panhandle. Following the de Soto expedition, mapmakers used the name 'Apalachen' to denote the name of both the tribe and the region spreading to the north. By 1562 cartographers began applying the name to the mountains themselves.

Toward the end of the 18th century, the first settlers began to appear in the region. The German immigrant John Jacob Mingus and his family were among the first Europeans to set up homesteads in the Oconaluftee River Valley when they arrived in 1798 (their descendants would remain in the region, and later set up the Mingus Mill). Over the next few decades, other homesteaders put down roots in Cades Cove and the Cataloochee Valley.

Life on the Appalachian frontier was a constant struggle for survival in the wilderness. Settlers cut down trees to build log cabins and fences (as well as provide much-needed heat for the bitterly cold winters). They toiled to clear land for farming (not an easy task with boulders often buried in the soil) and built farmhouses, corncribs and smokehouses. The land had rich soil and proved ideal for growing important crops such as corn, wheat, rye, oats, flax and sorghum. In the summer, farmers would hike their sheep or cattle up to the grassy mountain balds where the animals could freely graze. Hogs were left to forage in the thick forests of oak, hickory and chestnut trees surrounding their homes. Homesteaders had to be entirely self-sufficient, although hunting, fishing and trapping supplemented their income and provided goods for bartering, bringing in the likes of coffee, sugar and salt, which the settlers couldn't produce themselves.

Aside from the daily struggles of putting food on the table, there were also the ever-present threats around them: panthers and bears prowled in the forests, and packs of wolves sometimes devastated the pioneers' small herds. Although the settlers were generally on good terms with the Cherokee, renegade bands sometimes raided settlements, carrying off livestock and other goods. By 1819, however, the Cherokee largely disappeared from the area, having been forced to cede all of their lands in the Smoky Mountains in the 1819 Treaty of Calhoun. This formally opened up more areas to settlers.

1540

Spanish explorer Hernando de Soto travels through the southern Appalachian mountains with an expedition of 600 men. He charts new lands and documents his encounters with native people. He never finds gold.

1775

The naturalist William Bartram becomes the first English-speaker to explore the southern Appalachia region. He vividly documents the landscapes and people he encounters along the way.

1790s

John Jacob Mingus, a recently arrived immigrant from Germany, and his family build a homestead along the Oconaluftee River. They become the first European settlers in the Smokies.

1819

In a treaty negotiated with John C Calhoun, the American Secretary of War, the Cherokee are forced to relinquish all claims to a huge swath of lands, including the Smoky Mountains.

THE CIVIL WAR

The Civil War, which erupted in 1861, divided allegiances in the Smokies. Quakers, who were particularly numerous in parts of eastern Tennessee, had long preached abolitionism and vehemently opposed the pro-slavery troops of the Confederates. Fewer than 20% of residents of the three Smoky Mountains counties in Tennessee voted for succession. In North Carolina's Smoky Mountains counties, around 46% of the population favored succession.

Throughout the war, Cades Cove was staunchly pro-Union, and it likely served as a stop on the Underground Railroad for African Americans trying to escape enslavement en route to the free north. Unlike other parts of southern Appalachia, Cataloochee remained pro-Confederate, and sons of early settlers went off to fight for the Confederate Army. Many never returned.

Although no battles ever occurred in the Smoky Mountains, the residents paid a sizable toll during the war. As men went off to battlefields in the north, the farms of the valley lay fallow without able-bodied men to do the work. Soldiers from both sides also raided homesteads, carrying off livestock and other supplies. Sometimes Unionists hunted down Confederate sympathizers, while Confederates sometimes captured men and accused them of draft dodging.

As more settlers arrived, the growing collection of farmsteads turned into tiny villages, with the addition of blacksmith shops, gristmills, churches and later schoolhouses, post offices and dry-goods stores. Communities were tightly knit. Villagers knew each other well, and made a social event out of corn husking, preparing molasses and gathering chestnuts in autumn. They also helped out in times of need. When one settler died, the men would build a coffin, dig a grave and assist with the burial, while the women helped prepare the body. Everyone helped the family of the deceased, assisting around the farm, preparing meals and taking care of the small children. The men were also recruited to help build roads in the area, some of which followed old trails first created by Native Americans.

The population of Cades Cove peaked in the 1850s, when it had 685 residents, with farm sizes averaging between 150 and 300 acres. Cataloochee, however, remained a tiny outpost and wouldn't grow in size or importance for another 50 years.

In Gatlinburg, TN, the town's sole Confederate sympathizer, Radford Gatlin (for whom the town was named), was physically beaten by local Union supporters, and he was forced to move elsewhere.

The Logging Industry

In the decades following the Civil War, a new industry began to emerge: logging. At first, it started out small, with selective timber cutting carried out by local landowners throughout the Smokies. Trees such as ash, poplar and cherry were cut down and sold to lumber mills

1838–39
Around 14,000 Cherokee are removed from their homes and forced to march westwards along what's later called the 'Trail of Tears.' More than 4000 perish from cold, hunger and disease.

1840s
A small group of 800 Cherokee are allowed to stay behind on their ancestral lands. This group and their descendants later purchase land that becomes known as the Qualla Boundary.

1861–65
Residents in the Smokies suffer as the Civil War rages across the country. Soldiers from both sides raid settlements, carrying off food and other supplies.

1870s
John Cable builds his gristmill in Cades Cove. Surrounded by fields, the water-powered mill with its 235ft flume, was one of four or five mills in the area.

ELKMONT: FROM LUMBER TOWN TO LEISURE CENTER

European Americans first settled the valley on the edge of the Little River in the mid-1800s. Back then, a small community of settlers eked out a living raising crops, hunting and cutting down and selling trees from the surrounding forest. All that changed in 1900 when an industrialist named WB Townsend started the Little River Lumber Company and began large-scale logging operations. Townsend acquired more than 80,000 acres, set up sawmills and even ran train tracks to haul the old-growth lumber from Elkmont to the newly created town of Tuckaleechee (later changed to Townsend).

Elkmont boomed as the base for the lumber company, and the surging population saw the creation of a Baptist church, a hotel, a school, a post office, a general goods store and many residences.

In 1909 the railroad was extended all the way to Knoxville. Curiously, an observation car was added to the train, allowing tourists to make the scenic journey into the mountains. As more visitors began arriving, Townsend envisioned a new business opportunity, and he sold 50 acres of lumber company's holdings to the Appalachian Club, a newly formed social club made up of Knoxville businessmen. The club built a hotel and cabins for its members, who came here to escape the heat and bustle of the big city. Soon other members-only clubs opened in the area, including the Wonderland Club, which opened a hotel nearby in 1912.

The 1920s was a time of transition. The logging operations were winding down, mainly because most of the forests here had been clear cut (photos from that period show jaw-dropping devastation). The idea of creating a national park was also slowly beginning to take root.

During the Great Depression, the lumber camp was converted into a camp for the Civilian Conservation Corps, where around 200 men labored at building bridges, roads and other key infrastructure for the new national park. Today, this site is occupied by the Elkmont Campground (p73).

Meanwhile, after the national park became a reality, some cabin-owning club members sold their cabin properties outright; others negotiated multi-year or lifetime leases. A few of these lasted until 2001, when the park finally acquired the remaining properties. In 2012 the Appalachian Clubhouse and the Spence Cabin (a lavish private house built in 1928) were fully restored. Today these are used for private events. Nearby, the 17 cabins of Daisy Village are also slated for restoration, though at present some of them remain closed to the public. Others you can take a peek inside, while wandering down the promenade of this once-lively summer gathering spot – today something of a ghost town (p66) from another era.

in towns outside the Smokies. By 1900, however, industrialists saw enormous financial opportunities in the large stands of old-growth forest in the mountains and began buying up properties and commencing large-scale operations.

1882

A single-room log-cabin schoolhouse is built in the small settlement of Little Greenbrier. Some children travel 9 miles to attend the school, which remains in constant use up until 1936.

1898

Palmer Chapel is completed in Big Cataloochee. Former residents and their descendants continue to hold an annual reunion on the grounds of this pretty white Methodist church.

1900

Following several decades of development, the settlement of Cades Cove reaches its peak population of about 700. Residents grow crops and assist with road building in the area.

Early 1900s

Lumber companies begin buying up tracts of land and start large-scale logging operations. Within 30 years, more than 50% of the forest will be clear cut.

Companies laid down railroad tracks to transport timber, built large mills and created lumber towns that grew into sizable villages. Hundreds of miles of logging roads were blazed through the mountains. Logging boom towns arrived overnight, and the park still bears their place names: Smokemont, Proctor and Tremont. One of the biggest operations was headquartered near present-day Elkmont.

Creation of the National Park

While huge swaths of the forest were being felled by lumber companies, more and more locals were beginning to notice the devastation left by clear-cutting. In the early 1920s a few key figures from Knoxville, TN, and Asheville, NC, began to advocate for the conservation of the Smokies.

Ann Davis was one of the first to put forth the idea of creating a national park in the Smokies. After visiting several national parks out west in 1923, she and her husband, Willis Davis, worked tirelessly to recruit allies towards the goal of creating the park. She even entered politics, and in 1924 became the first woman elected in Knox County to serve in the Tennessee State House of Representatives.

David Carpenter Chapman, the president of a Knoxville drug company, was another outspoken early booster of the park's creation, and is credited with helping to make the park a reality. With his connections in business and politics, he was able to help secure funding for the park and overcome challenges along the way. One of the biggest obstacles was negotiating with timber companies and private property owners to sell their land to the national park. This made the creation of the national park a unique challenge that boosters of western national parks never had to face – since out west, little of the land was privately owned, it was simply a matter of declaring the park's boundaries.

Negotiations began in 1925 and were complex – given there were more than 6000 property owners involved. In 1926 President Calvin Coolidge signed legislation creating Great Smoky Mountains National Park (along with two other national parks). Once signed it was up to the park boosters to secure the funds to purchase the 150,000 acres before the Department of the Interior would assume responsibility.

Then in 1927 the legislatures of Tennessee and North Carolina proffered $2 million each. This fell short of the estimated $10 million required, so park supporters campaigned for funds and received another $1 million from private individuals, groups, and even schoolchildren who sent in spare change they had collected going door to door. The funding still wasn't enough (the price of land had, not surprisingly, risen in the interim). That's when Arno Cammerer, acting director of

Like miners in other parts of America, workers for the Little River Lumber Company bought their food from, and paid rent to, their employer. They worked six days a week, taking Sundays off, which was usually reserved for church-going followed perhaps by a train ride into Townsend.

1910

Cataloochee grows to become the largest settlement in the Smokies, with more than 1200 residents. It's home to a thriving community of farmers, apple growers and moonshiners.

1913

Horace Kephart publishes *Our Southern Highlanders*, describing in fascinating detail the lifestyles and traditions of the Appalachian people. Kephart would become a key supporter in the creation of the national park.

1920

The last mountain lion (cougar) is killed inside the national park. Though no proof of the animal's existence in the park is verified, reports of animal sightings persist into the 21st century.

1924

David Chapman, Ann Davis, Horace Kephart and other leaders advocate for the creation of a national park. Despite initial opposition from landowners and lumber companies, their cause begins to gain traction.

Dolly Parton statue (p86), Sevierville, Tennessee, by artist Jim Gray (www.jimgraygallery.com)

the National Park Service, and David Carpenter Chapman approached the American financier John D Rockefeller Jr and secured a promise of $5 million in funding, which helped bring the final pieces of the puzzle together for the park's creation.

Even with cash in hand, purchases of the small farms and miscellaneous parcels (some of which had yet to be surveyed and appraised) was a cumbersome and lengthy process. Many landowners were reluctant to leave the only home they'd ever known, and some people – such as John Oliver of the Cades Cove community – fought the park commission through the Tennessee court system. But ultimately, he and others would lose their claim to the land. Some people, especially those who were elderly or too sick to move, were granted lifetime leases.

1927

The legislatures of Tennessee and North Carolina each give $2 million for the creation of the national park. Other funds are donated by groups, entrepreneurs and even schoolchildren.

1933

As the Great Depression rages, 22 Civilian Conservation Corps (CCC) are opened in the Smoky Mountains. Around 4000 men receive jobs, helping with reforestation and building bridges, roads and trails.

1934

The Great Smoky Mountains National Park is officially established. Six years later, on September 2, 1940, President Franklin Roosevelt presides over the opening ceremony at Newfound Gap.

1937

The Arts & Crafts Community is created in Gatlinburg. Today there are more than 100 artists demonstrating their skills and selling their products along an 8-mile loop road.

One group of sisters (p191) remained on their 1880s-era homestead well into the second half of the 20th century. Those who stayed had to give up traditional practices, such as hunting, trapping and cutting down timber, but they were allowed to farm and graze their sheep and cattle with special permits. The park viewed this relationship as beneficial, as farmers using the historic fields as pasture prevented reforestation and maintained their scenic, open views.

In 1930 the first superintendent of the park arrived, and he formally oversaw the first transfer of land – 158,876 acres deeded to the US government. At long last the Great Smoky Mountains National Park was a reality, though it wasn't until 1934 that the park was officially established. A few years later, in 1940, President Franklin Roosevelt dedicated the national park for the 'permanent enjoyment of the people' at the newly created Rockefeller Monument at Newfound Gap.

The Great Depression & WWII

As the Great Depression swept across the nation in the early 1930s, President Roosevelt came up with an innovative solution to put people back to work. He created the Civilian Conservation Corps, or CCC, which would serve two purposes: it would create jobs and it would help in the nation's reforestation. CCC camps were set up across the country, with 22 created inside the national park. Around 4000 men, mostly aged 18 to 20, would work for the corps, which ran from 1933 to 1942. The men worked a variety of jobs: planting trees, building bridges and footpaths, erecting fire towers and clearing fire roads. Several groups were also charged with raising trout to replenish fish-depleted streams.

The arrival of WWII brought an end to the CCC camps. Most were closed down and became abandoned ghost towns amid the quickly encroaching forest. One former CCC camp in the park, however, was transformed into a camp for conscientious objectors during the war. Conchies, as they were called, were draftees who objected to the war out of religious, moral or philosophical grounds. They were sent to special Civilian Public Service (CPS) camps around the country.

At CPS 108, located off the present-day Kephart Prong Trail (p45), men lived in military-style barracks and worked nine-hour days, six days a week, undertaking a range of activities. They repaired roads, planted nurseries and continued the world of the CCC, clearing trails and helping to maintain the national park. A few men also volunteered for duty in 'the pest house', an isolated locale in Pinehurst, NC. There the men were infected with pneumonia and influenza as human guinea pigs for research on respiratory diseases. For their labors, none of the men in CPS 108 received any pay, and they were generally

Among the groups in favor of the national park's creation were motorists. Members of newly formed automobile clubs, most of which were branches of AAA, dreamed of driving their shiny vehicles along new roads through the mountain scenery.

1942

Construction begins on the Fontana Dam to help meet soaring electricity demands for manufacturing during WWII. Built in just 36 months, Fontana becomes the largest hydroelectric dam in the east.

1959

Clingmans Dome Observation Tower is completed atop its namesake mountain – the highest peak in the Great Smoky Mountains at 6643ft. The 45ft-tall modern tower is a break from typically rustic 'parkitecture.'

1964

Louisa Walker, the last long-term resident living inside the park's boundaries, dies. The old homestead where she and her 10 sisters and brothers grew up in the 1800s passes to the national park.

1986

Country music legend and East Tennessee native Dolly Parton opens Dollywood theme park on the grounds of the Rebel Railroad steam train attraction, which opened in 1961.

looked down on by locals who called them cowards for avoiding combat service. Yet with the park understaffed as rangers went off to war, the volunteers proved invaluable in keeping things running, and even assisted in the park's administrative duties.

The 2016 Great Smoky Mountain Wildfires

On November 23, 2016 tragedy stuck Great Smoky Mountains National Park when fire was reported on Chimney Tops, one of the park's most popular trails. The combination of exceptional drought conditions, low humidity and wind gusts that topped 80 miles an hour caused the fire to spread quickly in what would soon become the the deadliest wildfire in the eastern USA since the Great Fires of 1947.

Dubbed 'Chimney Tops 2' by firefighters (a smaller fire had burned on Chimney Tops a week earlier), fire suppression was not as speedy as it should have been (several days went by before action was taken). By November 28 a massive firewall was heading toward Gatlinburg with shocking speed. By December 5 a full-on firefighting onslaught was unleashed: 25 hand crews, 61 engines, six helicopters and 780 personnel. But it wouldn't be until late January before containment of the fire reached more than 90%. The town of Gatlinburg was spared due to some heroic firefighting efforts – the only true in-town casualty was the Gatlinburg Sky Lift, which suffered serious damage to its upper section and upper terminal – but the toll otherwise was dreadful: 14 deaths, 175 injuries, more than 2400 structures damaged or destroyed, and the forced evacuation of 14,000 residents. The cost in dollars topped $500 million.

Inside the park, more than 15 sq miles were scorched, with Chimney Tops taking the brunt of the blow, forcing the closure of one of the park's most beloved trails. It has since reopened, though the final section to the peaks remains closed for the long-term owing to loose rocks and the extreme instability of the rocky soil.

Two Tennessee juveniles were arrested and initially charged with aggravated arson in the starting of the fire. However, the charges were later dropped when reports surfaced of downed power lines in the area, and other small fires that might have contributed to the destruction.

Top History Reads

Our Southern Highlanders by Horace Kephart

Bushwhackers: The Civil War in North Carolina by William Trotter

The Wild East: A Biography of the Great Smoky Mountains by Margaret L Brown

2001

The park releases 25 elk from Land Between the Lakes National Recreation Area into Cataloochee Valley. Twenty-seven are released the following year. The last elk in the region was killed in the mid-1800s.

2009

The Tennessee legislature passes a law allowing distilling in 41 counties, an increase from three. Ole Smoky Moonshine Distillery, known as the Holler, opens the following year in Gatlinburg.

2016

Wildfires spread across the north of the park and into Gatlinburg. The fires kill 14 people, destroy more than 10,000 acres inside the Smokies and cause $500 million in damages.

2017

Smoky Mountains welcomes more than 11 million visitors to the park, setting a new record. July is its most visited month, followed by October and June.

Wildlife

The vast wilderness of the Smoky Mountains is home to an astonishing variety of wildlife. Within the boundaries of the national park are 65 mammal species, 240 species of birds, dozens of native fish and 80 types of reptiles and amphibians. Before the creation of the park, humans wiped out a number of species through hunting, trapping and logging. In recent years, however, the park has had success with the reintroduction of several species, including herds of elk.

Black Bears

The most famous resident of the Smokies is the American black bear. Up to 6ft long, and standing 3ft high at the shoulder, the American black bear is the symbol of the national park. Males typically weigh around 250lb (females are smaller and weigh around 100lb), though bears weighing up to 600lb have also been found in the park. Though they look like lumbering creatures when they walk, black bears can run fast, reaching speeds of up to 30mph (faster than 100m world-record holder Usain Bolt). Black bears are omnivores and subsist on wild berries, acorns, grasses, tree buds, flowers and roots, with plant materials providing about 85% of their diet. The other 15% comes from insects, animal carrion and other sources of protein.

Black bears have better eyesight and hearing than humans, though their strongest sense is smell, which is about seven times keener than a dog's. They are most active in the early-morning and late-evening hours during the spring and summer. In the park, bears live an average of 12 to 15 years.

Contrary to common belief, black bears are not true hibernators but do enter long periods of sleep. They may emerge from their winter dens periodically during unusually warm spells or if they are disturbed. Female bears sometimes have a surprise waiting for them when they awaken in the springtime, as their offspring are born during their winter sleep. Females typically give birth to one to four cubs every other year. The cubs arrive in January or February. These tiny newborns weigh just 10oz (less than a can of soda) and will remain close to the mother for about 18 months, or until she mates again. Mating, incidentally, typically takes place in July. Both male and female bears have more than one mate during the summer.

An estimated 1500 bears live in the park – just under two bears per square mile. Indeed, this is the largest protected habitat for bears in the east. Black bears once roamed much of North America, but habitat loss has significantly diminished their range and numbers.

Wildlife Reading

Birds of the Smokies by Peter White

Mammals of the Smokies by Edward Pivorun

Bear in the Backseat by Kim DeLozier and Carolyn Jourdan

Elk

Large herds of elk once roamed vast tracts of wilderness in the eastern United States. Overhunting and a loss of habitat, however, spelled disaster for these great mammals, and large elk were wiped out in North Carolina in the 1700s and in Tennessee by the mid-1800s. Their plight was so severe that by the turn of the 20th century, conservationists believed their species, which once numbered 10 million, was headed for extinction.

In 2001 the park service began to reintroduce elk in the park. Twenty-five animals were taken from the Land Between the Lakes in

Kentucky, with another 27 added the following year; all were placed in Cataloochee. These massive herbivores can weigh up to 700lb and stand 8ft high at the shoulder. Males have antlers, which they grow each spring and shed in the winter. These can span up to 4ft and weigh up to 40lb. Elk grow thick coats of hair in the winter, which they then shed come spring. When elk are spotted rubbing against trees and fences, they are often working to shed this excess hair.

One of the most exciting times to be in the park is during the annual elk rut (aka breeding season). During the fall (September and October) up to 20 female (cow) elk and calves gather into harems, guarded by one or two aggressive mature males, known as bulls. As the bulls watch over their harem, other males compete for the attention of the cows – using tried-and-true methods such as wallowing in their own urine to attract the ladies. They can also let loose a series of shrieking and bellowing calls in what is known as 'bugling.' Sometimes rival bulls face off, charging one another and locking antlers, which can lead to serious injuries or even death.

Elk can often be spotted grazing in the Cataloochee area and on the fields near the Oconaluftee Visitor Center. The best time to see them is around dawn or dusk.

Flying Squirrels

A strong contender for the cutest animal resident of the park, the flying squirrel has big doelike eyes, pink nose, long whiskers and a small furry body, which can glide silently through the air as the animal leaps from treetop to treetop. Although not actually capable of flight, these small rodents have a patagium – a furry, parachute-like membrane stretching from the front paws to the hind legs. This allows them to take dramatic leaps through the branches, soaring across distances of more than 200ft.

There are two species of the animal in the park: the southern flying squirrel and the northern flying squirrel. The southern is the smaller of the two species, stretching about 9in from nose to tail and often weighing just 2oz or 3oz (about as much as a deck of playing cards). The southern is also the more common of the two species, and can live virtually anywhere in the park. The northern flying squirrel, on the other hand, is about 30% larger, but lives only at higher elevations (above 4500ft) in conifer forests. Owing to habitat loss, the northern flying squirrel is now listed as endangered. Both squirrels are nocturnal, and sightings are rare.

Some attempts to reestablish animal species have not been successful. In the 1990s a federal program to reintroduce red wolf colonies to the national park was unsuccessful, and the pack was eventually moved to the northeast coast of North Carolina, where the animals fared better.

Other Mammals

A fine counterpoint to the mighty black bear and massive elk is the pygmy shrew, a rare and diminutive creature so tiny that it weighs less than a penny. It's one of 11 species of mole or shrew found in the park, and isn't often spotted since it spends most of its time underground.

The bobcat is likely the only wild feline living in the national park. Though there are occasional reports of cougar sightings, no concrete evidence of their presence has been found in more than three decades. True to name, bobcats have short, stumpy tails and can weigh up to 70lb. These solitary creatures, with their spotted fur and tufted ears, are quite striking, though rarely spotted owing to their nocturnal habits. Other nocturnal carnivores that inhabit the park include the coyote and the red and gray fox.

More commonly seen mammals are white-tailed deer, eastern chipmunks, red and gray squirrels, raccoons, possums, skunks and bats (of which there are 11 different species in the park). The largest rodent in the Smokies is the beaver, whose handiwork (gnawed-up limbs and dams) you might spot on creeks at lower elevations.

Birds

The wide-ranging topography and varied microclimates of the Smokies create a wide range of habitats for birds. More than 100 bird species breed in the park, while many other birds stopover in the park during their semiannual migrations. On the high ridges where the spruce-fir

SYNCHRONOUS FIREFLIES

One of the great but tiny wonders of the Smoky Mountains is the *Photinus carolinus*, better known as the synchronous firefly. This aptly named insect is famed for its dazzling display of bioluminescence, where thousands of hovering insects flash in perfect harmony.

Some 19 firefly species live in the park, but *Photinus* is the only species to synchronize its flashing patterns. These curious insects are actually beetles, and although they spend one to two years developing from larvae, their short adult lives typically last just 21 days.

Although the light display is related to mating, scientists aren't quite sure why the fireflies synchronize their blinking. One theory is that males will improve their chances of attracting a mate if they all blink together.

The event happens for about two weeks sometime between late May and late June, during the fireflies' short mating season. The exact dates change every year, and are influenced in part by air temperature and soil moisture. One of the best places to see the display is at the Elkmont Campground. During the fireflies' peak activity, you'll need a special permit (p77), given out by lottery, to see it at Elkmont – or you can reserve a campsite (though sites book up months in advance).

forest grows, prevalent species include chestnut-sided warblers, dark-eyed juncos and northern saw-whet owls.

Lower down, the northern hardwood forest and cove hardwood forest are an unusual meeting point for both northern and southern bird species, which reach their extremes on these thickly wooded slopes. Thus you can spot both the black-throated blue warbler, and the southern red-eyed vireo.

The greatest abundance of birds is found in the lower and middle elevations. A few common species include the belted kingfisher, the song sparrow, the eastern screech owl and the downy woodpecker. Even open fields and meadows can be fine places to spot birds, particularly wild turkeys, eastern bluebirds and red-tailed hawks.

Although bird-watchers have been active in the park for nearly 80 years, new birds are continuously being sighted – as was the case in late 2016 and early 2017 when both the Ross goose and the long-eared owl were documented for the first time.

Amphibians

The Great Smoky Mountains are home to more than 40 species of amphibians. You'll find the classic bullfrog, two varieties of dainty tree frogs, the common red-spotted newt and the noxious (to predators) Fowler's toad. The national park, however, is most famous for its salamanders. With 30 species found in the park, this abundant and diverse group of forest dwellers has earned the Smokies the title of 'salamander capital of the world.'

The park has 24 species of lungless salamanders. These creatures have followed an unusual evolutionary path, obtaining oxygen not through their lungs, which they lack, but through the walls of blood vessels lining their skin and the inside of their mouths. They are found throughout the park, in leaf litter and logs in the forests and in and alongside mountain streams.

The rather frighteningly named hellbender is the largest salamander in the park – it can grow up to 29in in length. These elusive aquatic amphibians, endemic to the eastern US, are actually prehistoric animals from the Jurassic period, and have been around for more than 65 million years. They have wide mouths packed with teeth and enjoy feasting on crayfish and other unsuspecting creatures that wander past their underwater hiding spots. Hellbenders have a remarkable lifespan, with one study suggesting some specimens can live up to 50 years in the wild. Yet, hellbenders are quite sensitive to environmental change. Seeing species disappear where once they flourished is an indication of declining quality of river life – hellbenders function somewhat like a canary in the coal mine.

Late April and early May is peak bird migration in the Smokies, and is the best time to spot birds. A skilled bird-watcher exploring various habitats can document as many as 100 different species in a single day.

1. A young bull (male) elk **2.** Young white-tailed deer; their spots will fade as they grow **3.** Pileated woodpecker **4.** A young black bear

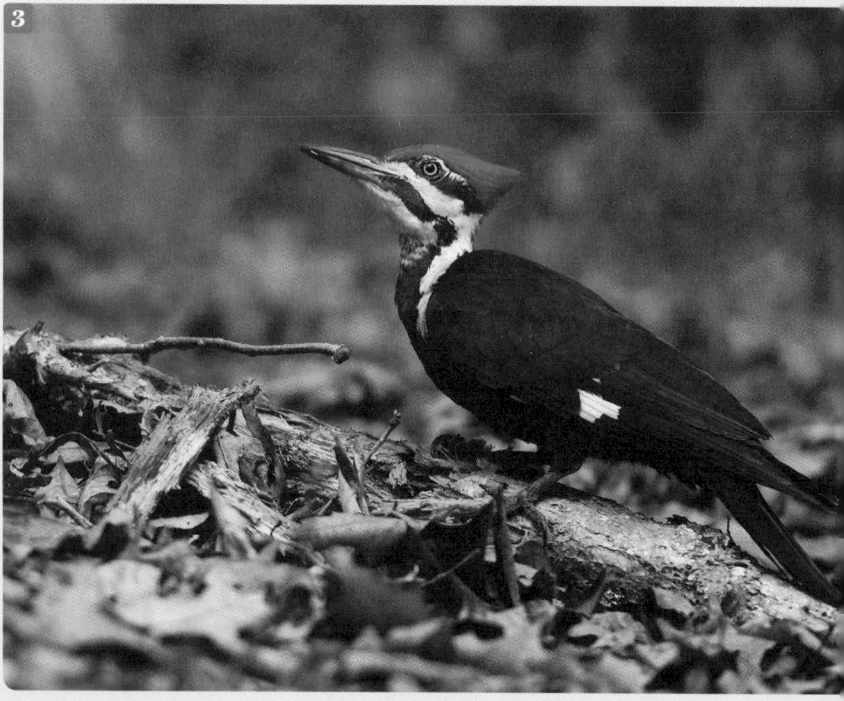

3

CRS PHOTO/SHUTTERSTOCK ©

Wildlife Watching

Wildlife watching is a prime activity across the park, and many times you'll be able to see some of the parks larger mammals from primary roads. If you see cars pulled onto the roadside shoulders, with clusters of pedestrians staring into the trees, it's likely they've spotted something intriguing. Remember that visitors are required to stay at least 50yd from any wildlife.

Elk

Twenty-five elk were released into the park in 2001, and 27 more in 2002. Great viewing spots are the open fields lining Cataloochee Rd and its offshoots, especially in the morning and late afternoon. Another good spot is around the Oconaluftee Visitor Center.

White-Tailed Deer

Deer can be found across the park (there may be more than 6000), but they are easiest to spot in the open fields of Cades Cove and Cataloochee. They are active year-round and typically weigh 100lb to 330 lb.

Birds

Experienced bird-watchers may be able to encounter – by sight or sound – more than 100 bird species in a day during migration season in late April and early May. Look for red-tailed hawks in open fields. At low and mid-level elevations, southern hardwoods are full of birds, and typical species include downy woodpeckers, pileated woodpeckers and eastern screech owls.

Black Bears

Black bears can be found across the park. Campgrounds and trails may close temporarily due to bear activity. Look for them in Cades Cove, Cataloochee Valley and the Roaring Fork Motor Nature Trail.

Wild Turkeys

Wild turkeys can be see walking around the open fields of Cades Cove and Catloochee. You might also see or hear them rustling along trails in Cades Cove.

Frogs

All frog and toad species in the park breed in the water, though they may live in varied habitats. That peeping sound you hear at night may be the Northern Spring Peeper, a vocal tree frog found in the woods near lakes and ponds.

People of the Smoky Mountains

The Smoky Mountains have been shaped not just by forests, rivers and mountains, but also by the people who have lived and toiled in these fertile valleys over the centuries. The Cherokee have deep ties to the land, as these mountains have served as a source of both physical and spiritual sustenance. Sadly many Cherokee would end up being forced to leave and never return. The settlers who came in their wake also developed strong bonds with the land. Old homesteads and other relics from the past can still be found inside the national park.

The Cherokee

One of America's largest indigenous groups, the Cherokee have roots in the Smoky Mountains that date back more than 1000 years. Prior to European contact, the Cherokee lived in fertile river valleys, in small villages set with sturdy wooden-frame houses surrounded by cornfields. There was also a central square and a council house for religious ceremonies and meetings that could hold all of the villagers. Like some other native tribes, the Cherokee recognize seven cardinal directions: north, south, east and west along with up, down and center (or within).

The Cherokee were excellent farmers, and grew corn (the main staple), beans, squash, melons, pumpkins, sunflowers and tobacco. They also supplemented their agrarian ways by hunting and trading with other groups. Society was governed by two ruling authorities – one chief during times of peace, and another who governed when the nation was at war. Despite the hierarchy, tribal councils played an important role at all times in village life.

Some believe the name 'Smoky Mountains' is derived from the Cherokee word *shaconage*, which means 'land of the blue smoke.'

Although only men could serve as chiefs or priests, women could serve as council members when chosen by the village. In fact men and women in Cherokee culture were considered equals, and there were many opportunities for women of the tribe. Some even served as warriors (Warwoman Creek in north Georgia owes its name to one fierce female Cherokee soldier). Marriage was only allowed between members of different clans. Curiously, Cherokee society was originally matrilineal, with bloodlines traced through the mother.

The Cherokee were a dominant presence on the continent prior to European contact. Through warfare and alliances, the Cherokee soon amassed a territory that spread across more than 125,000 sq miles. It covered a huge swath of the present-day South, including Tennessee, the Carolinas, Virginia and Kentucky.

Unfortunately European contact spelled the beginning of the end for the mighty Cherokee nation. Introduced diseases such as smallpox – to which the Cherokee had no natural immunity – left a devastating swath across the continent. One such epidemic in 1738 killed as many as half the tribe. Conflicts flared with the encroaching settlers, and bloody warfare erupted numerous times over the 18th century. After big territorial losses in the late 1700s, the Cherokee went through a period of great change – spurred in part by George Washington, who sought to 'civilize the American Indians.' The Cherokee were encouraged to give up communal farming methods and instead settle in individual farmsteads.

The Cherokee organized a democratic national government, with a chief, vice-chief and 32 council members elected by members of the tribe. They drafted a constitution, with an executive, a legislative and a judicial branch, and ratified a code of law for the newly named Cherokee Nation. Modern farming methods, formal education and Christianity all made inroads into the nation, as mission schools, cotton plantations, gristmills and blacksmithing all opened on Cherokee lands.

One of the pivotal Cherokee figures of this time was Sequoyah, a silversmith and soldier. Although he could neither read nor speak English, Sequoyah became obsessed with the 'talking leaves,' and felt that was somehow key to white settlers' power. After working assiduously for nearly a decade, he invented a writing system for the Cherokee language, which he unveiled in 1821. Consisting of 86 characters, the Cherokee Syllabary became widely adopted by the tribe within a decade. Literacy spread quickly, and five years after the appearance of the syllabary, thousands of Cherokee could read and write – far surpassing the literacy rates of the white settlers around them. Sequoyah became something of a folk hero for the Cherokee, and his achievement is astonishing: it's the only recorded instance of one person single-handedly creating a system of writing.

The Cherokee Council decided the people needed a national newspaper, so they ordered a printing press and began publishing the *Cherokee Phoenix*. The paper, which launched in 1828, soon became a strong voice against the Passage of the Indian Removal Act, one of the most dastardly laws passed by an American president. This 1830 law called for the Cherokee and four other tribes of the southeast (the Choctaw, the Chickasaw, the Seminoles and the Creek) to vacate their lands. The Cherokee lobbied Congress, gathered signatures from around the nation in opposition to the act, and even took their case to the Supreme Court. In the 1832 decision, Worcester vs Georgia, the highest court of the land ruled that the Cherokee were a sovereign nation and that they could not be forcibly moved by the US government.

None of this mattered to President Andrew Jackson. He simply ignored the ruling and ordered the army to invade the Indian lands. Cherokee were forcibly removed from their homes and placed in stockades. In 1838 some 14,000 Cherokee were marched westward towards Oklahoma and Arkansas. During the six-month journey, more than 4000 of them died from hunger, disease and exposure on what became known as the 'Trail of Tears.'

Before the mass exodus, a small group of Cherokee in the western part of North Carolina received special permission to avoid being relocated. Around 1000 Cherokee managed to stay behind, and worked to buy back lands that had been taken from them. Today the Eastern Cherokee number around 15,000, with the majority of them living just outside the national park on the Cherokee Indian Reservation, or Qualla Boundary as it's more commonly called.

The Walker Family

In 1870 John Walker, a former soldier who fought for the Union army during the Civil War, settled with his wife Margaret in a log cabin and rural property in Little Greenbrier Cove. Walker was an industrious man who worked at his farm planting orchards, raising livestock and

Reading the Past

Trail of Tears: the Rise & Fall of the Cherokee Nation by John Ehle

The Walker Sisters: Spirited Women of the Smokies by Bonnie Trentham Myers

Our Southern Highlanders by Horace Kephart

After he lost his job and his wife abandoned him, Horace Kephart (1862–1931) moved to the Smokies and reinvented himself as a naturalist and writer. He authored celebrated books about the Appalachian people and its landscapes, and was a major advocate for the park's creation.

RASCALLY RABBIT

There are numerous Cherokee legends set in the Smoky Mountains, and nearly every mountain, river and valley has a name in Cherokee. Chimney Tops, for instance, is called Duniskwalgunyi, or 'forked antlers' in Cherokee, while Clingmans Dome is known as Kuwahi, or 'mulberry place.' The Cherokee called Gregory Bald Tsitsuyi, or 'rabbit place' and believed this mountain meadow was the where the Great Rabbit lived.

Incidentally the Great Rabbit is quite the trickster in Cherokee mythology. One time this large lagomorph and unrivaled leader of all rabbits schemed to steal one of the loveliest coats of the animal kingdom. The story goes something like this: a council of all the animals was being held to see who possessed the finest pelt. When the Great Rabbit got word of the event, he decided to pay a visit to his friend Otter, who was known to have a particularly fine coat. Upon finding Otter at his favorite creekside locale, he decided to accompany him back to the council to keep him 'safe.'

On their journey, the two camp for the night in a place called Di'tatlaski'yi, 'the place where it rains fire.' Feigning great concern for his friend, Rabbit encourages Otter to remove his coat and hang it from a tree branch while he sleeps. Rabbit meanwhile will graciously keep watch to ensure no fiery particles damage Otter's fine fur. Rabbit waits for Otter to fall asleep, then he flicks embers from their smoldering fire onto his friend, shouting, 'Wake up, Otter! It's raining fire! Make a run for it!' Otter dives into the water, leaving his coat behind in his haste. There Otter remained, where he still lives today (being somewhat mortified, one might imagine, having his clothing stolen from him).

Rabbit, meanwhile, chuckles to himself as he puts on Otter's coat and makes his way to the council. As the sun hangs low over the craggy horizon, a finely dressed creature in a resplendent coat strolls through the meadow. With a paw over his brow and face in shadows, the creature's identity remains a mystery. As he draws nearer, Bear sees through the ruse, rips the coat off Rabbit and swipes at him with his sharp claws. The Great Rabbit, however, dodges out of the way, and loses only his tail to Bear's anger. Rabbit hops off, smiling to himself as he muses over yet another memorable prank played on his unsuspecting mountain colleagues.

making furniture. Over time, he also added on to the property at the homestead.

He and his wife raised a sizable family at Greenbrier. Of the 11 children – seven girls and four boys – all made it to adulthood, a remarkable achievement in the late 19th century when childhood mortality rates were high and medical care was primitive. Strong constitutions must have run in the Walker genes, as many of the children would live well into their 80s.

The children helped out around the farm, and Walker and one of his sons built a log schoolhouse, which also served as a church, for the growing Little Greenbrier community. Education in those days was a privileged escape from the daily chores, and school ran for a few months during the winter. There the children learned the three Rs – reading, 'riting (writing) and 'rithmetic (arithmetic) – and got to spend time with new friends.

When the boys came of age, they married and moved away, as did one of the girls. The other six sisters never married and remained at Little Greenbrier Cove. In fact, after their father died in 1921, they ran every aspect of the 122-acre farm themselves, raising and growing all of their own food and maintaining the farm – churning butter, chopping wood, curing pork in the smokehouse, drying sheepskin and planting vegetables. They also made their own clothes, taking wool from the sheep then spinning and weaving it into fabrics. Cotton and flax, which they also grew, were transformed into textiles, thanks to the skillful work of the sisters. The siblings even kept a herbal garden, and used homemade remedies to treat illnesses.

Following Congressional approval to create the national park in 1926, the legislatures of Tennessee and North Carolina began buying up private properties in the Smokies. This sisters had no intention of leaving their mountain homestead. They held out until the national park was formally created in 1940, at which point they sold their farm and homestead for just under $5000. There was just one condition: the five sisters (one had passed away a decade earlier) would be able to spend the rest of their lives on the farm in a lifetime lease. They remained on the land, but life changed for them, as they had to give up traditional practices such as hunting, fishing, chopping down trees for fuel and grazing livestock.

One lifelong lover of the Smoky Mountains is the singer-songwriter Dolly Parton. Raised 'dirt poor' (as she described it) in a cabin near Greenbrier Valley, she soared to stardom singing about life in the mountains. After the fires of 2016, she raised $9 million for victims.

They became something of a curiosity to early visitors to the national park, particularly after an in-depth article on their anachronistic lifestyle was published in a 1946 issue of *The Saturday Evening Post*. While most of America was enjoying new wonders such as supermarkets and modern appliances – not to mention electricity and indoor plumbing – here was a group of now-elderly sisters living a lifestyle that was straight out of the 19th century. The sisters, however, didn't mind the attention and put up a 'visitors welcome' sign. As travelers passed through 'Five Sisters Cove' (as it was soon called), the Walkers offered for sale their handmade toys, woven tablecloths and baked apple pies.

The sisters lived out the rest of their days on the homestead. After the last Walker sister died in 1964, the property was acquired by the national park and it was added to the National Register of Historic Places in 1976.

Forests of the Smoky Mountains

The Smoky Mountains boast a staggering variety of plant life, with a greater diversity of flora than any other place in North America. The park is home to around 100 native tree species and more than 1500 flowering plants. Much of its diversity is due to its wide variations of elevation (from 875ft to above 6600ft) and geography, with a mix of both southern and northern species. The park's abundant rainfall and high humidity in the warmer months also provides ideal growing conditions.

Forest Varieties

You can see very different types of vegetation depending on where you are in the park. Dry, sunny, south-facing ridges will have different species from those on cooler, wetter, north-facing slopes. Elevation plays an even bigger role in defining what grows where.

Top Field Guides

Trees of the Smokies by Steve Kemp

Wildflowers of the Smokies by Peter White

Native Trees of the Southeast by L Katherine Kirkman et al

Hemlock Forest

Hemlock forests dominate at lower elevations (below 4000ft) in moist areas, across shaded slopes and along streams. Around 87,000 acres of the park are covered by hemlock forests. These evergreen trees were saved from felling, as they weren't commercially valued by lumber companies. As a result some of the oldest and largest trees in the park are eastern hemlocks. They've been called the 'redwoods of the east,' and they can grow to more than 150ft tall, reaching up to 10ft in diameter. Some specimens in the park are more than 500 years old.

Sadly the non-native woolly adelgid (uh-DEL-jid) has wreaked havoc on the hemlocks. Many infested trees have died, and without intervention nearly all will be wiped out. This is having a devastating effect on the surrounding microclimate as they provide a cooling habitat for many other species. Without the towering, shade-providing hemlocks, stream temperatures will increase, endangering the survival of trout and other cold-water animal and plant species. The forest floor will also receive dramatic increases in sunlight, which could in turn wipe out native ferns and other plants reliant on cool, moist shade. The huge gaps in the canopy could also promote other invasive plant species. Compounding the problem is the lack of other shade-tolerant species to take the place of the hemlocks.

After heavy logging in the early 20th century, only pockets of primary forest survive in the Smoky Mountains. Biologists estimate that about 100,000 acres (or 20%) of the national park contains old-growth forest.

Pine & Oak Forest

In the mountains up to about 4500ft, where the slopes are dry and exposed, you can expect to find forests dominated by pine and oak trees. These types of forests are more common on the west side of the park. Thickets of mountain laurel and stands of rhododendron grow well here, as do flowering dogwood trees, galax, yellow poplars and hickory. Of the park's 11 species of oak and five species of pine, the most commonly found trees are scarlet oak, chestnut oak, black oak, Table Mountain pine, Virginia pine and pitch pine. Forest fires are not uncommon in these habitats and can be necessary for some species' reproduction and forest regeneration.

Cove Hardwood Forest

In Appalachian parlance, coves are sheltered valleys with deep, fertile soils. These are the most botanically diverse forests of the Smoky Mountains, and grow on slopes of up to 4500ft. You'll find tulip tree, yellow buckeye, sugar maple, black cherry, magnolia, yellow birch and Carolina silverbell among dozens of other species. Wildflowers are also profuse in these forests, and autumn colors are dazzling. Those regions passed over by loggers boast trees of record sizes. One of the best places to see these forests firsthand is along the Ramsey Cascades Trail, or the shorter Cove Hardwood Nature Trail at Chimneys Picnic Area off Newfound Gap Rd.

Northern Hardwood Forest

Growing at elevations of 4500ft to 6000ft, these broad-leaved forests have a decidedly northern feel, akin to the wooded areas of New England and the Great Lakes region. Here you find predominantly American beech and yellow birch dominating the canopy, along with mountain maple, white basswood, yellow buckeye and pin cherry. Around 28,000 acres of northern hardwood forest is old-growth. The Smokies are also known for their beech gaps, when stands of American beech trees take over and monopolize high mountain gaps. Look for them on south-facing slopes along the high ridges, such as along the road up Clingmans Dome, where the gaps interrupt spruce-fir forest at regular intervals.

Top Trails for Old-Growth Forest

- *Boogerman (p56)*
- *Cove Hardwood Nature*
- *Gregory Ridge (p52)*
- *Laurel Falls (p44)*
- *Ramsey Cascades (p50)*

Spruce & Fir Forest

Dominating the high peaks of the Smoky Mountains are these iconic evergreen forests. Also called boreal or Canadian zone forests, the spruce-fir forest grows at elevations above 4500ft and shares characteristics of habitats in eastern Canada. They are a legacy of the ice age, when northern plants migrated south to escape the continental glaciers. When the weather warmed, these northern species remained, continuing to thrive on the cool mountain ridges of the Smokies. Today, two coniferous species rule the ridges: Fraser firs and red spruce. Unfortunately these forests are being decimated by a non-native insect, with the balsam woolly adelgid wiping out the Fraser fir population. Atop Clingmans Dome, you'll see large stands of dead Fraser firs stretching in all directions.

THE LOSS OF THE AMERICAN CHESTNUT

American chestnut trees once made up about one-third of the Smokies' tree species. In springtime their blossoms were so thick that the mountains appeared as if they were covered in snow. Then in the first half of the 20th century, a fungus from Asia swept across the country, killing every American chestnut in its path. By 1950 an estimated four billion trees had died, and the American chestnut forest had been wiped forever from the planet. Botanists describe the chestnut blight as the largest ecological catastrophe in North America during the 20th century.

American chestnuts were once lords of the forest, with their treetops stretching up to 120ft high. You can still see their stumps in the park, some of which even sprout. These young saplings don't reach very high before they too are felled by the blight, which continues to live deep in the trees' roots.

Some naturalists, however, haven't given up hope that the chestnut may some day make a comeback. A group of researchers from West Virginia University have discovered a virus that attacks the blight-causing fungus. If they can replicate the virus and move it from tree to tree, the American chestnut may be able to grow and thrive once again. Yet another group is cross-breeding American chestnuts with blight-resistant Chinese chestnuts, in hopes of creating a new strain of tree that can someday return to the American forests.

Appalachian Balds

In some places at high elevations, there are patches of land entirely devoid of trees. These include grassy balds, which are not unlike highland meadows (more commonly observed in lowland prairies), and heath balds, covered in thickets of mountain laurel and rhododendrons. How these unique Appalachian land features formed remains something of a mystery. Grassy balds were used by early settlers to graze their livestock, though scientists have determined through soil samples that these tree-free areas existed even before the sheep and cattle arrived. Another theory is that megafauna – herbivorous mastodons and woolly mammoths – grazed here some 10,000 years ago. Two fine grassy balds where you can contemplate the distant past (and enjoy the magnificent views) are Gregory Bald (p52) and Andrews Bald (p45).

One of the best places to see a wide variety of ecosystems laid out in one scenic panorama is at the Carlos C Campbell Overlook on Newfound Gap Rd.

Invasive Species

Over the last century, a number of non-native insects and fungi have been discovered in Great Smoky Mountains National Park. As these typically have arrived from Europe or Asia, the native species have no natural defenses and have quickly succumbed to the devastating blights.

The hemlock woolly adelgid was first detected in the national park back in 1992. Within a few years the aphid-like insect spread to other parts of the Smokies, and it now threatens the survival of all eastern hemlocks in the park. Because of the importance of hemlocks, the Smokies face one of the greatest ecological challenges since the blight that wiped out the American chestnut tree. Scientists believe the sap-sucking insect originally came from Japan. Having no predators, it spreads quickly and can kill a fully grown tree in just three to five years. The national park is doing its best to fight the adelgid, using pesticides where possible, though they've only been able to treat 15% of the park's hemlock trees at the time of writing. The park has also released non-native predator beetles (again taken from Japan), which feed exclusively on adelgids, though this has shown limited success.

The Smokies harbor various species of carnivorous plants. Among the most unusual is the sundew, which exudes a glistening, sticky fluid that attracts insects. When the insect becomes ensnared, the leaves then surround it, and the plant's digestive juices go to work, slowly consuming the hapless creature.

The lovely flowering dogwood is under attack from dogwood anthracnose, a fungus whose origins are unknown. It has killed thousands of trees in the Smokies, and the park has found no effective treatment for the disease.

Another insect that has left a swath of destruction in its path is the balsam woolly adelgid. First spotted in the park back in 1962, this tiny creature has attacked and killed 90% of the mature fir trees in the park. The Fraser fir, endemic to the southern Appalachian, has been a particularly devastating loss for the park.

The park's beech trees are also suffering from a combination of non-native beech scale and and a species of invasive fungus.

It isn't just the tiny creatures that are damaging the park's delicate ecosystems. Wild hogs are another hugely destructive species the park has had to contend with. European wild boar were brought to a private game reserve in the early 1900s. Less than a decade later, they escaped and their population exploded. Today the descendants of those first hairy ungulates can weigh well over 100lb. They're adaptable, they breed quickly and often successfully compete with native animals for food sources. They also damage native plants and eat other animals, including one species of salamander found only in the Smoky Mountains. You might see hog traps off in the woods on some hiking trails.

Survival Guide

CLOTHING & EQUIPMENT.......198
What to Wear 198
What to Take...........199

DIRECTORY A–Z....202
Accessible Travel 202
Accommodations....... 202
Electricity 203
Etiquette 203
Food.................. 203
Internet Access......... 203
Legal Matters 204
LGBTIQ+ Travelers...... 204
Money................. 204
Opening Hours 204
Post................... 204
Public Holidays......... 204
Safe Travel............ 205
Telephone 206
Time.................. 206
Toilets................ 206
Tourist Information............ 206
Travel with Pets 206
Visas.................. 207

TRANSPORTATION..208
GETTING THERE & AWAY 208
Entering the Country............ 208
Air.................... 208
Land.................. 209
GETTING AROUND.......209
Bicycle................ 209
Boat.................. 209
Bus & Shuttle.......... 209
Car & Motorcycle........210
Local Transportation 210

HEALTH & SAFETY.......... 211
BEFORE YOU GO......... 211
Health Insurance.............211
IN THE PARK 211
Medical Assistance 211
Common Ailments....... 211
Environmental Hazards 212
Safe Hiking 214

Clothing & Equipment

What to Wear

Take time to plan your clothing well before you hit the road. Don't wait until the last minute to realize that your waterproof jacket isn't warm enough, or that you need a new pair of hiking boots and won't have time to break them in. The main things to keep in mind when planning your wardrobe are to choose garments that are moisture-wicking, breathable, waterproof (and windproof), insulating and, of course, comfortable.

You'll need to strategize carefully, especially if you plan to camp in the backcountry. First-time visitors are often surprised by the weather, which can get quite cold at higher elevations, particularly if the rains arrive. Spring comes late to the mountains, and nighttime temperatures can dip below freezing even in April. At higher elevations snow is possible from November to April, and rain falls year-round – not surprising for a region that receives 55 to 85 inches of rain per year.

Come prepared for dramatic shifts in weather regardless of the season.

Clothing

Modern outdoor garments made from synthetic fabrics (which are breathable and actively wick moisture away from your skin) are better for hiking than anything made of cotton. Cotton T-shirts are particularly ill-suited to outdoor activities, as cotton holds water, meaning as you sweat you'll feel chilly if the weather turns cold and wet. Jeans (which are made of cotton denim) are also a bad choice for hiking as they'll make you feel sweaty and uncomfortable on hot days, and can chafe your skin as you perspire. Denim is also very slow to dry and becomes heavy when wet. In cold weather denim can pull heat from your body, increasing the risk of hypothermia.

Insulation is another key consideration to keep in mind. In cooler temperatures wool shirts, socks and sweaters are preferred. Gone are the days of old-school scratchy wool garments. Merino wool, in particular, is an excellent fabric, as it's warm, breathable and moisture-wicking – plus it's not as prone to retaining odors (a fact sure to be appreciated by your hiking companions). Synthetic fabrics such as nylon and polyester are generally more affordable than wool and some are created with recycled materials. On the downside, these tend to trap odors, though some manufacturers incorporate antimicrobial properties, which helps neutralize odor-causing bacteria.

Your clothing should also be fairly rugged so it can stand up to unexpected scrapes with boulders, tree stumps and slashing branches. Tights and yoga pants, while comfortable, might not last under the rigors of mountain hiking. Cargo pants have the added advantage of allowing you to stash essentials (snacks, pocketknife, sunscreen) without having to dig around in your pack when you need something.

You'll also want a hat to provide sun protection in the summer (one that's rainproof serves double duty) and a warm hat as well as gloves for those chilly days (and colder nights) from fall through early spring.

Layering

To cope with changing temperatures and exertion, layer your clothing.

Upper body: Start with a base layer made of synthetic thermal fabric or merino wool; second layer is a long-sleeved shirt; third layer can be a fleece sweater or jacket that wicks away moisture. Outer shell consists of a waterproof and breathable jacket. If it's cold, you might want to pack a puffy jacket. Choose one with synthetic rather than down insulation, since down loses its warmth-retaining properties when wet.

Lower body: Shorts will be most comfortable in

midsummer, though some people prefer long pants – light, quick-drying fabric is best. If you want options, go with convertible pants with zip-off trouser legs that can be converted into shorts on warm days. Waterproof over-pants form the outer layer, and in winter wear a wool base layer.

Undergarments: Again it's wise to avoid cotton and chose moisture-wicking fabrics. Make sure your underwear is non-chafing; seamless designs are best for hiking. On cold days you may want to add an extra layer of long underwear.

Waterproof Shell

Smoky Mountains hikers should always carry a wind-proof, waterproof rain jacket, headwear and, in the cooler months, pants. Gore-Tex or similar breathable fabrics work best.

Footwear, Socks & Gaiters

Regardless of style, water-proof boots are essential given the wet weather and abundant stream crossings along many of the trails.

Some hikers prefer the greater agility allowed by lightweight boots, while others insist on heavier designs that give firm ankle support and protect feet in rough terrain. Hiking boots should have a flexible (preferably polyurethane) midsole and an insole that supports the arch and heel. Nonslip soles (such as Vibram) provide the best grip.

When considering what type and style of footwear to bring, weigh the advantages of heavier hiking boots with the burden of the added weight – a couple extra pounds on your feet can make a noticeable difference when you're hiking up several thousand feet for the day.

Ideally purchase shoes in person rather than online so you can try on several options to see what works best with your feet. Preferably try on hiking boots in the afternoon or evening to accommodate for foot swell. Try boots on with whatever socks you plan on wearing; they should still offer plenty of toe room.

Many hikers carry a pair of river sandals to wear when crossing streams, creeks and rivers. They're also handy for wearing around camp when you want to give your feet some extra breathing room. Alternatively some hikers use gaiters, which are worn atop your boots and can keep your feet dry during shallow water crossings or when hiking through snow. They also keep twigs, pebbles and other trail debris out of your shoes, while also protecting against pests (like ticks) from climbing into your boot tops.

Merino-wool socks that draw moisture away from your feet are another must; synthetic options can also work. It's wise to pack an extra pair in case your feet get wet during a stream crossing – they can also add extra insulation if you develop a blister on the trail.

Do not wait until the day before your hike to purchase footwear, as you'll want at least a week or so to break them in.

PRE-DEPARTURE CHECKLIST

- ☐ Print backcountry permits for campsites and shelters if overnighting on the trails.
- ☐ Leave details of your hiking itinerary with a friend or family member not traveling with you.
- ☐ Inform your debit-/credit-card company that you're going away.
- ☐ Arrange for appropriate travel insurance.
- ☐ Bring cash for the camping fee if you plan to camp in the off-season. Pay at the self-pay kiosks.

What to Take

Clothing aside, you'll want to make sure you're properly outfitted for your trip to the Smoky Mountains. Even if you're only planning to undertake short hikes, it's worth the time and investment assembling gear that serves you well.

Backpack & Daypack

Look for a comfortable backpack that effectively distributes the weight between shoulders, spine and hips. Take plenty of time to try on backpacks and find one that fits to your body and is comfortable. Of all your gear, this is one item that is best purchased in person. Carefully consider the length of your trip before selecting a backpack. Internal-frame backpacks fit snugly against your back, keeping the weight close to your center of gravity. Look for one with good ventilation.

Even if the manufacturer claims your pack is waterproof, use a super-lightweight rain cover.

For day hikes, consider using a daypack that doubles as a hydration system (such as a Camelbak); if using a reservoir system, you'll still want to bring a water bottle as a backup.

Tent

A three-season tent will suffice for most camping and backpacking trips in the Smokies. Winter overnight trips will necessitate a four-season tent for protection from the elements. The floor and the outer shell, or rainfly, should have taped or sealed seams and covered zips to stop leaks. Be sure to consider the weight if you're going to be backpacking.

Sleeping Bag & Mat

Three-season sleeping bags will serve the needs of most campers. Down fillings are warmer than synthetic for the same weight and bulk but, unlike synthetic fillings, do not retain warmth when wet. Mummy bags are the best shape for weight and warmth. Third-party European Norm (EN) temperature ratings (20°F/-7°C, for instance) show the coldest temperatures at which a typical man or woman should feel comfortable in the bag. During summer, nights at most park campgrounds can be hot and humid, though the odd 50-degree low is also a possibility.

If you're coming in the early spring or in the fall, you'll want a sleeping bag that rates below freezing (to 15°F/-9°C or even 0°F/-18°C, depending on your tolerance for the cold). You'll also want a sleeping pad for insulation from the cold ground. Inflatable sleeping pads work best; foam mats are a low-cost but less comfortable alternative.

Another extra worth considering is an inner sleeping-bag liner. This helps keep your sleeping bag clean, and it also adds an insulating layer. Silk liners are lightest.

Water Filtration

The water in the park looks lovely and clear, but it is not safe to drink untreated. The protozoan Giardia lamblia may be present. Before drinking, you'll need to boil for one minute, chemically treat the water, or use a filter capable of removing particles as small as 1 micron.

Most travelers prefer a filter for its convenience (boiling is cumbersome in the backcountry, and chemical treatment requires long wait times given the cold temperatures of mountain waters). Inexpensive, lightweight options such as the Sawyer Squeeze Water Filter System are quite popular.

Stove & Fuel

If you're heading into the backcountry, and plan to do some cooking, you'll need a stove. Note that if you're front-country camping, a stove is not necessary, as you can cook over the grated fire pits at every campsite.

The type of fuel you'll use most often will help determine what kind of camp stove is best for you. The following types of fuel can be found in the US, and local outdoors stores can help you choose an appropriate camp stove if you aren't traveling with your own.

White gas Inexpensive, efficient and readily available throughout the country, reliable in all temperatures and clean-burning. More volatile than other types of fuel.

Butane, propane and isobutane These clean-burning fuels come in nonrecyclable canisters and tend to be more expensive. Best for camping in warmer conditions, as their performance markedly decreases in below-freezing temperatures.

Denatured alcohol Renewable; the most sustainable alternative. Burns slowly but also extremely quietly.

Hiking Gear

Make sure you have good rain gear (and waterproof boots) before hitting the trail. Precipitation is always a possibility, no matter when you come.

A good walking stick or two lightweight ski poles will come in handy while hiking the challenging uphill and downhill trails in the Smokies.

Even if you intend to complete your hike before nightfall, bring along a flashlight just in case something happens and you can't make it back before sunset.

There are no toilets out on the trails, so you'll need to be prepared. Be sure to bring toilet paper and a lightweight trowel for digging a hole and burying your waste (in a hole no less than 6in deep that's at least 100ft from any trail, waterway or campground). Pack out toilet paper, sanitary napkins and tampons – bring sealable bags so you can carry these out.

Emergency Supplies

Pack a first-aid kit – and know what's in it. At a minimum, you'll want antiseptic wipes, bandages, gauze pads, medical tape and antibacterial ointment to treat cuts, scrapes and blisters. It should also include pain-relief medication (such as ibuprofen), insect sting relief, antihistamine, tweezers and a pocket knife (or other multi-tool). Don't forget to pack epinephrine if you're allergic to insect stings, and bring other meds you might need (an inhaler if you have asthma, pre-filled insulin pens if you have diabetes etc).

Other useful items to have include an emergency Mylar blanket, a whistle and signal mirror for attracting attention and a fire starter (for an emergency survival fire).

Some hikers also travel with bear pepper spray, which is permitted in the park. If you choose to bring it, make sure you know how to use it, and keep it handy (in arm's reach, not stuffed in the bottom of your backpack) in case you need it.

PACKING LIST

Clothing

- ☐ Hiking boots with sturdy soles and good ankle support
- ☐ Wide-brimmed hat in the summer
- ☐ Fleece or sweater, plus long underwear (merino wool or synthetic)
- ☐ Lightweight trousers
- ☐ Waterproof jacket and pants
- ☐ Warm hat, scarf and gloves in the winter
- ☐ Gaiters or spare shoes (river sandals) for over-the-ankle creek crossings
- ☐ Moisture-wicking socks

Equipment

- ☐ Water bottle and reservoir (such as a Camelbak)
- ☐ Water filtration system (pump or chemical disinfectants)
- ☐ Trail map and compass
- ☐ Pocket knife
- ☐ Safety mirror and whistle to attract attention in emergencies
- ☐ Walking stick or trekking poles
- ☐ Sunscreen and lip balm
- ☐ DEET insect repellent
- ☐ Backpack with a rain cover
- ☐ First-aid kit
- ☐ Crampons (for winter hiking)
- ☐ High-energy food and snacks
- ☐ LED headlamp and flashlight with spare batteries
- ☐ Survival bag or blanket

Overnight Hikes

- ☐ Sleeping bag and sleeping mat
- ☐ Lightweight tent, tarp and rainfly
- ☐ Garbage bags for protecting suspended food bag in the rain
- ☐ Toilet paper, trowel and sealable plastic bags for packing out trash. Note that human waste must be disposed of at least 100 feet from any campsite
- ☐ Biodegradable soap, toiletries and towel
- ☐ Cooking, eating and drinking utensils, including a stove, fuel and dehydrated food
- ☐ Matches and lighter
- ☐ Sewing/repair kit (duct tape for patching jackets and tents)

Optional Gear

- ☐ Binoculars
- ☐ Camera and/or cell (mobile) phone plus a portable power supply (such as a solar charger)
- ☐ GPS receiver and/or altimeter

Directory A–Z

Accessible Travel

Although most hiking trails are not wheelchair accessible, the national park does its best to accommodate travelers with disabilities. And all visitors can partake in the park's spectacular scenic drives.

The park's main visitor centers at Sugarlands, Oconaluftee and Cades Cove are all accessible, with dedicated accessible parking spots and accessible restrooms.

The park also has one excellent trail that is accessible: **Sugarlands Valley Nature Trail** (off Newfound Gap Rd; 🚻). This half-mile trail is smooth and level with a wide paved path that skirts along a pretty river and past remnants from the early 20th century.

Other places worth exploring include historic sites in Cades Cove, which has hard-packed gravel paths running around the area. Buildings can be viewed only from the exterior, though the Cable Mill and the Becky Cable House are both accessible via a ramp.

The path to Clingmans Dome is paved, but owing to its steepness, it is not ADA approved. However, with assistance, many travelers with disabilities have made the trip up.

Accommodations

Great Smoky Mountains National Park provides varied camping options. **LeConte Lodge** (☎865-429-5704; www.lecontelodge.com; cabins incl breakfast & dinner adult $148, child 4-12yr $85; ⊙mid-Mar–mid-Nov) is the only place where you can get a room, however, and you have to hike to the top of a mountain to enjoy the privilege. Gatlinburg (p93) has the most sleeping options of any gateway town, though prices are high. Nearby Pigeon Forge (p89), 10 miles north of Sugarlands Visitor Center, and Sevierville (p86), 17 miles north, have cheaper options.

Camping & Campground Regulations

FOOD PREP & STORAGE

Bears and other wildlife are a real concern when it comes to proper food handling. All food, preparation and storage items (including pots, coolers and utensils) must be kept sealed in a vehicle (preferably the trunk) when not in use. If you're traveling by motorbike or other means without proper storage, the following campgrounds have food storage lockers: Balsam Mountain, Big Creek, Cades Cove, Cataloochee, Cosby, Deep Creek, Elkmont and Smokemont. Unattended or improperly stored coolers and food may be impounded by campground staff and stored at the campground office. The park takes the issue very seriously, and violators are subject to fines.

GARBAGE & WASTE WATER

Dispose of garbage promptly in the animal-proof dumpsters provided. Put waste water in sinks or in dump stations; don't pour it on the ground.

REGISTRATION

For first-come, first-served campsites, you'll need to register and pay a fee either at the staffed campground office or at a self-pay kiosk. If faced with the latter, be sure to bring a wide variety of bills (plenty of single dollars, fives and 10s) as you may have to put the payment into an envelope and slide it into a box. Currently only Deep Creek Campground has a self-pay credit-card kiosk.

BOOK YOUR STAY ONLINE

For more accommodations reviews by Lonely Planet authors, check out http://lonelyplanet.com/hotels/. You'll find independent reviews, as well as recommendations on the best places to stay. Best of all, you can book online.

RESERVATIONS

Rules regarding reservations vary from campground to campground. At Abrams Creek, Balsam Mountain, Big Creek and Cataloochee, advance reservations are required for the entire season – ie you won't be able to just show up and use a self-pay option. Campsites at Cades Cove, Cosby, Elkmont and Smokemont can be reserved in advance for the period May 15 through October 31. For Deep Creek (and at other times for the above campgrounds), it's first-come, first-served.

LENGTH OF STAY

You can stay a maximum of 14 days at each campground. If you want to stay longer, you'll need to move to another campground.

PEOPLE PER SITE

No more than six people at a time can use one campsite.

CAMPFIRES & WOOD

Fires are only permitted in the fire grates. Do not bring firewood into the park, as you can unwittingly bring devastating pests with it. Only heat-treated firewood that is bundled and certified by the USDA is allowed in the park. Campers are allowed to collect firewood from the ground.

BATHROOMS

All of the campgrounds have running water and flush toilets. None have showers, so prepare to rough it a bit.

PETS

Pets are permitted in campgrounds, but must always remain on a leash. Excessive barking is not allowed (pipe down, Rover!).

BACKCOUNTRY

There are specific regulations (p60) for hiking and camping in the backcountry (see p59).

Electricity

Type A
120V/60Hz

Type B
120V/60Hz

Etiquette

Etiquette in the Smoky Mountains largely relates to respectfully navigating the sometimes vast crowds at overlooks and on popular trails.

PHOTOGRAPHY

When looking for that perfect spot to snap that panoramic or waterfall view, be cognizant of fellow visitors taking photographs. Try to stay out of frame of photographs and don't hog the best spot.

SHARE THE TRAIL

Step to the right to allow faster hikers to pass. Uphill travelers have the right-of-way.

NOISE

Keeping quiet is the best way to enjoy the sounds of the Smokies – its gurgling streams, twittering birds and leaves rustling in the breeze. Do not yell up (or down) a trail to a friend, and keep conversation levels low, especially after dark.

Food

Nuts and berries notwithstanding, there's nothing to eat in Great Smoky Mountains National Park, save for items from vending machines at **Sugarlands Visitor Center** (☎865-436-1291; www.nps.gov/grsm; 107 Park Headquarters Rd; ⊙8am-7:30pm Jun-Aug, hours vary Sep-May; 📶) and the meager offerings sold at the **Cades Cove Campground store** (☎865-448-9034; www.cadescovetrading.com; 10035 Campground Dr; ⊙9am-9pm late May-Oct, to 5pm Mar-May, Nov & late Dec). If you make the hike up to LeConte Lodge, you can purchase cookies, drinks and sack lunches (which means a bagel with cream cheese, beef summer sausage, trail mix and fruit leather). Dinner is included for those staying overnight.

Luckily, there are lots of restaurant options in the surrounding towns.

Internet Access

Wi-fi is generally available at visitor centers (but only

SLEEPING PRICE RANGES

The following price ranges refer to a double room with bathroom in high season. Unless otherwise stated, tax is included in the price.

$ less than $150

$$ $150–250

$$$ more than $250

inside). Elsewhere in the park, internet is non-existent. Indeed, it's very difficult to get even cell-phone reception in the park. Hotels and lodges outside of the park generally offer free wi-fi.

Legal Matters

If arrested, you have a right to an attorney. If you cannot afford an attorney, one will be provided. US law presumes innocence until proven guilty.

LGBTIQ+ Travelers

The Smoky Mountains welcomes gay and lesbian travelers, but there are no particular services or entertainment geared towards LGBTIQ+ visitors.

Money

You'll find plenty of ATMs in Gatlinburg, but if camping in the off-season, bring small bills (dollars, fives, 10s) to pay at the self-pay kiosks upon arrival.

Tipping

Hotels $1 to $2 per bag is standard; gratuity for cleaning staff is generally $2 to $5 per day.

Restaurants and bars 15% to 20% from the before-tax total is expected.

Guided trips Customary to tip trip leader, at your discretion.

Consider the length, party details and itinerary of your trip.

Opening Hours

The park is open 24 hours a day, year-round. However, many secondary roads maintain seasonal closures, and only two of the park's campgrounds are open year-round. Backcountry campsites are open year-round, but some close periodically owing to bear activity. Visitor centers are open year-round (closing only on Christmas Day), but the hours change seasonally. Other park sites, such as LeConte Lodge and the Mingus Mill, open seasonally (typically mid-March to mid-November).

Visitor Centers 8am or 9am–7pm April to August; to 6:30pm March, September and October; to 5:30pm November; to 4:30pm December to February

Riding Stables (Sugarlands, Smokemont, Cades Cove) 9am–5pm

Road Opening Dates

Primary roads such as Newfound Gap Rd are open year-round, weather permitting. After a big snowstorm, however, even these roads may be closed. For the latest info on road closures check the National Park Service website (www.nps.gov/grsm/planyourvisit/temproad-close.htm), its Twitter feed (www.twitter.com/smokies-roadsnps), or call 865-436-1200, extension 631.

Balsam Mountain Rd Late May to late October

Cades Cove Loop Rd Sunrise to sunset year-round, but closed to vehicles sunrise to 10am Monday and Wednesday from early May to late September

Clingmans Dome Rd April through November

Forge Creek Rd Mid-March to late December

Newfound Gap Rd (Hwy 441) Year-round

Heintooga Ridge Rd Mid-May to October

Little Greenbrier Rd Early April to late November

Little River Rd Year-round

Parson Branch Rd Permanently closed owning to hazardous trees

Rich Mountain Rd Early April to early November

Roaring Fork Motor Nature Trail Early April to late November

Roundbottom/Straight Fork April to October

Campground Opening Dates

Abrams Creek Late April to mid-October

Balsam Mountain Mid-May to early October

Big Creek April to late October

Cades Cove Year-round

Cataloochee Late March to late October

Cosby Late March to late October

Deep Creek Late March to late October

Elkmont Early March to late November

Look Rock Closed for repairs

Smokemont Year-round

Post

The US Postal Service (www.usps.com) is inexpensive and reliable. Standard letters up to 1oz cost 50¢ within the US. Postcards and letters to destinations outside the US cost a universal $1.20.

Public Holidays

Public holidays do not affect park opening hours. Visitor centers are open every day of the year except Christmas Day.

New Year's Day January 1

Martin Luther King, Jr Day 3rd Monday in January

Presidents Day 3rd Monday in February

Easter Late March or early April

Memorial Day Last Monday in May

Independence Day July 4

Labor Day 1st Monday in September

Columbus Day 2nd Monday in October

Veterans Day November 11

Thanksgiving Day 4th Thursday in November

Christmas Day December 25

Safe Travel

The mountain wilderness of the Smokies poses many dangers, but you can minimize risks by traveling sensibly and being prepared. You'll always want to account for adverse weather, as conditions can change rapidly in the mountains.

Although there are plenty of bears, as well as venomous snakes, the far greater threat to park visitors is an accident involving motor vehicles, falls (while hiking, horseback riding or cycling) and swimming.

A few other hazards in the park to keep in mind are slippery or icy trails, various poisonous plants (poison ivy among them) and stinging insects.

Insects

Mosquitos can be a problem in the Smoky Mountains, depending on where and when you go. In the height of summer at lower elevations, you'll need to liberally apply repellent to avoid getting devoured. At other times of year (and at higher elevations), the nefarious insects are less of an issue.

Ticks can also be present in the region, so you'll want to check yourself carefully after visiting the park. Since some ticks can carry Lyme disease, you'll want to avoid them if possible. Repellent with DEET and appropriate dress (long pants, a hat) will minimize the risks.

Watch out for yellowjacket wasps, which can be aggressive and deliver painful stings. Their nests are sometimes found on trails and alongside streams. If you have allergies to bee or other insect stings, be sure to travel with an epinephrine kit.

Other insects you may encounter on the trail include gnats and biting flies. DEET and protective clothing will help.

Wildlife

Remember the cardinal rule: stay at least 50yd (150ft) away from all wildlife in the park. Never approach an animal, and make sure you dispose of food scraps and other waste in the animal-proof receptacles at campgrounds and some trailheads.

Some animals, including skunks and raccoons, carry rabies, so be sure to report any unusual animal behavior to a ranger.

Trail Safety

Even short hikes can become treacherous after heavy rain. At any time of year you might encounter moss-covered rocks, wet leaves and slick roots. These can lead to bad falls, and the consequences can be significant on trails that traverse steep, narrow cliff faces. Always travel with appropriate footwear: wear ankle-supporting boots with good soles, and use crampons or some other winter traction device during icy conditions – which can persist into May on some trails.

A good walking stick is also useful. If you lack one, shops in Gatlinburg sell them, as do the **Sugarlands Visitor Center** (☎865-436-1291; www.nps.gov/grsm; 107 Park Headquarters Rd; ⏰8am-7:30pm Jun-Aug, hours vary Sep-May; 📶) and the **Oconaluftee Visitor Center** (☎828-497-1904; www.nps.gov/grsm; 1194 Newfound Gap Rd, North Cherokee, NC; ⏰8am-7pm Jun-Aug, to 6pm Apr, May, Sep & Oct, to 4:30pm Nov-Mar; 📶) 🌿.

Waterfalls & Rivers

The park's numerous waterfalls are among its most outstanding attractions, but take care when visiting them as slippery rocks can lead to some bad falls. Along those lines, don't ever try to climb up the waterfalls – you might see rocky, muddy paths going up – but this is never a good idea as there have been dozens of falling deaths over the years (including one as recently as 2017).

You'll need to be cautious around mountain rivers and streams. Drowning is one of the leading causes of death in the park, and unfortunate hikers have suffered serious injuries from falls along riverbanks. Streams can become swollen after heavy rainfall, making passage across dangerous. Some log bridges can be slippery, so watch your step. On stream crossings where there are no bridges – or the bridges have washed away (not uncommon after heavy storms) – you'll have to use your best judgment; when in doubt, don't do it! In general, if the water is flowing rapidly, don't cross if it's above your knees.

There are no lifeguard-surveyed swimming areas in the Smokies. Rangers advise against swimming and riding inner tubes anywhere inside of park boundaries.

EATING PRICE RANGES

The following price ranges are for a main course, not including tip.

$ less than $15

$$ $15–25

$$$ more than $25

Cold & Heat

Hypothermia is a life-threatening condition that occurs when prolonged exposure to cold thwarts the body's ability to maintain its core temperature. Hypothermia is an all-season danger and can even occur during the summer at higher elevations due to wind, rain and cold. Remember to dress in layers and always carry rain gear.

During the summer, you'll also need to prepare for the heat, when the Smokies can be very hot and humid. Carry plenty of water to avoid dehydration, wear a wide-brimmed hat and use sunscreen. Know your hiking limits: hikes along the challenging uphill trails can lead to heat exhaustion.

Trees & Limbs

Have a look around before resting on the trail or setting up camp for the night. Move away from any trees or limbs that might fall or pose a hazard.

Telephone

Dialing Codes

US phone numbers begin with a three-digit area code, followed by a seven-digit local number. When dialing a number within the same area code, simply dial the seven-digit number; for long-distance calls, dial the entire 10-digit number preceded by 1. For direct international calls, dial 011 plus the country code plus the area code plus the local number. If you're calling from abroad, the US country code is 1.

Cell Phones

You might be able to get cell phone service at high points near the edge of the Great Smoky Mountains National Park, but coverage is typically not available across the park.

You'll need a multiband GSM phone to make calls in the US. Installing a US prepaid rechargeable SIM card is usually cheaper than using your own network. They're available at major telecommunications or electronics stores (such as Radio Shack) in Gatlinburg. If your phone doesn't work in the US, these stores, as well as superstores, also sell inexpensive prepaid phones.

Time

The national park, East Tennessee, North Carolina and Georgia are on US Eastern Standard Time (GMT/UTC minus five hours)

Toilets

You'll find public toilets at the visitor centers, in campgrounds and in picnic areas, as well as at sites such as Clingmans Dome, Newfound Gap, the Mingus Mill and atop Mt LeConte. There are pit toilets near the parking areas at several popular trailheads (including Rainbow Falls and Abrams Falls), but no drinking water is available at any of the trailheads.

If you're in the backcountry and nature calls, the rule is to bury waste in a hole at least 6in deep, and ensure that you're at least 100ft from any campsite, trail or water source. You should also pack out your used toilet paper and other objects – carry sealable plastic bags, just in case.

Tourist Information

The park's four interior visitor centers:

Sugarlands Visitor Center (☎865-436-1291; www.nps.gov/grsm; 107 Park Headquarters Rd; ⏰8am-7:30pm Jun-Aug, hours vary Sep-May; 📶) At the park's northern entrance near Gatlinburg.

Cades Cove Visitor Center (☎865-436-7318; www.nps.gov/grsm; Cades Cove Loop Rd; ⏰9am-7pm Apr-Aug, closes earlier Sep-Mar) Halfway up Cades Cove Loop Rd, 24 miles off Hwy 441 from the Gatlinburg entrance.

Oconaluftee Visitor Center (☎828-497-1904; www.nps.gov/grsm; 1194 Newfound Gap Rd, North Cherokee, NC; ⏰8am-7pm Jun-Aug, to 6pm Apr, May, Sep & Oct, to 4:30pm Nov-Mar; 📶) 🍃 At the park's southern entrance near Cherokee in North Carolina.

Clingmans Dome Visitor Station (☎865-436-1200; Clingmans Dome Rd; ⏰10am-6pm Apr-Oct, 9:30am-5pm Nov) Small, very busy center at the start of the paved path up to the Clingmans Dome lookout.

Travel with Pets

The national park isn't the best place to travel with your dog, though it is possible to bring along the furry friend if you don't mind making some sacrifices. Inside the national park, pets are allowed in campgrounds, in picnic areas and along the road, though they must be kept on

> **PRACTICALITIES**
>
> **Smokies Guide** Free park newspaper issued quarterly covering campgrounds, things to do and news. Available at park visitor centers.
>
> **Smokies Trip Planner** (www.nps.gov/grsm/planyourvisit/trip-planner.htm) Online planning guide with information about favorite destinations and top activities within the park.

a leash (no longer than 6ft) at all times.

Pets are permitted on only two hiking trails: the Oconaluftee River Trail and the Gatlinburg Trail. These smooth, flat walking trails provide a fine introduction to the Smokies, but if this is all you'll see, you're rather limiting yourself. Pets are also not allowed to be left unattended in a vehicle – meaning you can't leave Goldie in the rental car while you go off for a long hike.

Wherever you go, be sure to collect and properly dispose of any pet waste.

Some other natural parks in the region have a more lenient policy with pets. Check out Cherokee National Forest, Nantahala National Forest and the Chattahoochee National Forest.

SMOKING

Smoking is forbidden in all restaurants, bars, hotel rooms and indoor public areas in North Carolina. In Tennessee smoking is still allowed in many bars. Fire restrictions often include smoking bans on all trails. Call park headquarters (865-436-9171) for current restrictions.

Pet Boarding

If you decide you'd rather be canine-free for a few hours or days, you'll find boarding centers outside the park, including in Cherokee and Gatlinburg. One recommended Gatlinburg boarding facility is the cheekily named **Barks & Recreation** (☎865-325-8245; www.barksandrecgatlinburg.com; 2159 East Pkwy, Gatlinburg; boarding per 24hr $35-42; ⌚8am-8pm Mon-Sat, 10am-6pm Sun), which receives positive reviews. Be sure you bring along your veterinarian records. Most places cannot accept dogs (for daycare or boarding) without them.

Visas

Visitors from Canada, the UK, Australia, New Zealand, Japan and many EU countries don't need visas for stays shorter than 90 days. Citizens of other nations should check http://travel.state.gov.

Transportation

GETTING THERE & AWAY

Most visitors to the Great Smoky Mountains National Park will fly in to one of the surrounding cities. After you fly in, you'll need a car as there's no public transportation to the park. There's a wide variety of car-rental outfits at each of the airports.

Flights, cars and tours can be booked online at lonelyplanet.com/bookings.

Entering the Country

Passports

Your passport should be valid for at least another six months after you leave the US.

Visa Waiver Program (VWP)

Though most foreign visitors to the US need a visa, the VWP allows citizens of 38 countries to enter the country for stays of 90 days or less without first obtaining a visa. Go to the website (www.dhs.gov/visa-waiver-program-requirements) for a list of participating countries and detailed information.

Electronic System for Travel (ESTA)

Visitors eligible for the VWP must apply for entry approval via ESTA. While it is recommended travelers apply at least 72 hours before travel, you may apply any time before boarding your flight and in most cases the process takes no more than half an hour. See the website fore more information: https://esta.cbp.dhs.gov/esta

Resources

US Department of State (www.travel.state.gov) Up-to-date visa and immigration information.

US Department of Homeland Security (www.dhs.gov) Clear details on requirements for travel to the US; follow the How Do I?/For Travelers/Visit the US links.

Air

Airports & Airlines

The main airports nearest to the park are at Knoxville, TN; Asheville, NC; Chattanooga, TN; Charlotte, NC; and Atlanta, GA.

McGhee Tyson Airport (☎865-342-3000; www.flyknoxville.com; 2055 Alcoa Hwy, Alcoa) Located 15 miles south of downtown Knoxville in Alcoa, TN (and 40 miles northwest of the Sugarlands Visitor Center). It is served by Allegiant, American, Delta, Frontier and United airlines, with around 20 nonstop flights, including to Chicago, Dallas and Washington, DC.

Asheville Regional Airport (AVL; ☎828-684-2226; www.flyavl.com; 61 Terminal Dr, Fletcher) Outside Fletcher, 16 miles south of Asheville. Served by a handful of nonstop flights, with routes including

CLIMATE CHANGE & TRAVEL

Every form of transport that relies on carbon-based fuel generates CO_2, the main cause of human-induced climate change. Modern travel is dependent on airplanes, which might use less fuel per mile per person than most cars but travel much greater distances. The altitude at which aircraft emit gases (including CO_2) and particles also contributes to their climate change impact. Many websites offer 'carbon calculators' that allow people to estimate the carbon emissions generated by their journey and, for those who wish to do so, to offset the impact of the greenhouse gases emitted with contributions to portfolios of climate-friendly initiatives throughout the world. Lonely Planet offsets the carbon footprint of all staff and author travel.

Atlanta, Charlotte, Chicago and New York. It's located 58 miles east of the Oconaluftee Visitor Center.

Chattanooga Metropolitan Airport (CHA; ☎423-855-2202; www.chattairport.com; 1001 Airport Rd) Chattanooga's modest airport is just east of the city and is served by direct flights from Charlotte, Chicago, Dallas and New York, among a few others. It's about 140 miles southwest of the park.

Charlotte Douglas International Airport (CLT; ☎704-359-4013; www.cltairport.com; 5501 Josh Birmingham Pkwy) Located 7 miles west of Uptown, Charlotte's airport is an American Airlines hub that welcomes nonstop flights from continental Europe and the UK. This airport is 170 east of the park.

Hartsfield-Jackson International Airport (ATL, Atlanta; ☎800-897-1910; www.atl.com) Atlanta's huge airport, 12 miles south of downtown, is a major regional hub and an international gateway. It's 175 miles south of the park.

Land

The vast majority of visitors to the park arrive by car. Buses serve nearby cities, though you'll still need to hire a car from there to reach the park.

Bus

Greyhound (www.greyhound.com) operates direct bus routes between main towns in the US. It serves Knoxville, Asheville, Chattanooga, Charlotte and Atlanta, but unfortunately there are no bus services to Gatlinburg or other towns close to the park.

Car & Motorcycle

From Knoxville, TN, it's an easy drive to the north part of the park. If you're heading to Cades Cove, take Hwy 321 to Townsend, then take the Laurel Creek Rd. To reach Sugarlands Visitor Center and the start of the Newfound Gap Rd, stay on Hwy 321 past Townsend to Wear Valley, then turn south onto Line Springs Rd. This eventually turns into Little River Rd as it takes you straight into the park. Total driving time from Knoxville to either Cades Cove or the start of Newfound Gap Rd is around 70 minutes.

From Asheville, NC, take I-26 north to I-40 west. Exit onto Hwy 74 toward Clyde, then take Hwy 19 toward Cherokee. Follow this road past Maggie Valley, then turn onto the Blue Ridge Pkwy, a scenic route that will lead you to the edge of the national park. As the parkway ends, turn right onto Hwy 441 (aka Newfound Gap Rd). The Oconaluftee Visitor Center is less than a mile from the Blue Ridge Pkwy. Total driving time is about 75 minutes from Asheville to the Smokies.

If you're coming from Altanta, take I-85 north and merge (left lane) onto I-985 east, following signs towards Gainesville. Stay on this route as it turns into Hwy 23 north. Continue to Dillsville, then follow signs onto Hwy 74 heading west. Shortly you'll see signs for Cherokee and the national park; turn onto Hwy 441, which will lead you straight into the park and the Oconaluftee Visitor Center (a 3½-hour drive from Atlanta).

GETTING AROUND

Bicycle

Unfortunately, options are lacking for cyclists in the Smokies. There are no mountain-biking tracks in the park, and bikes are not allowed on most trails. The exception are these three short, flat trails: the Gatlinburg Trail, the Oconaluftee River Trail and the lower Deep Creek Trail.

> **DEPARTURE TAX**
>
> Departure tax is included in the price of a ticket.

Cycling on the park roads is permitted but not recommended – even if you're a big fan of hills. The roads through the park are narrow, and with often heavy traffic to contend with, it's simply too dangerous to realistically consider.

One notable exception is the 11-mile Cades Cove Loop Rd, which closes to motor vehicles from sunrise to 10am on Wednesday and Saturday mornings from early May until late September. Bikes are available for hire from the Cades Cove Campground store.

Boat

The landlocked Smoky Mountains are a challenging destination for boaters. About the only waterside transport near the park is at **Fontana Village Resort** (☎828-498-2211; www.fontanavillage.com; 300 Woods Rd, Fontana Dam), which offers one-way and round-trip boat transport across the lake for those seeking pristine trout-fishing spots and remote hiking trails. Contact the marina.

Bus & Shuttle

There's no public transportation within the park. A handful of shuttle companies offer private transport inside the park. The following outfits can take you to, or pick you up from, trailheads or transport you from lodging outside the park to in-park destinations. You'll need to reserve in advance.

A Walk in the Woods (☎865-436-8283; www.awalkinthewoods.com)

AAA Hiker Service (☎423-487-3112; www.aaahikerservice.com)

Smoky Mountain Guides (☎865-654-4545; www.smokymountainguides.com)

Car & Motorcycle

Automobile Associations

American Automobile Association (www.aaa.com) Along with maps and trip-planning information, AAA members also receive discounts on car rentals, air tickets, hotels and attractions, plus emergency roadside service and towing. It has reciprocal agreements with international automobile associations such as CAA in Canada – be sure to bring your membership card from your country of origin.

Better World Club (www.betterworldclub.com) This ecofriendly association supports environmental causes in addition to offering emergency roadside assistance for drivers and cyclists, discounts on vehicle rentals (including hybrids and biodiesels) and auto insurance.

Driver's License

Tennessee and North Carolina recognize foreign drivers' licenses and do not require an International Driving Permit (IDP). However, an IDP, obtained in your home country, is recommended if your country of origin is a non-English-speaking one.

Some car-rental agencies require an IDP, so be sure to ask in advance.

Insurance

Liability insurance covers people and property that you might hit. For damage to the rental vehicle, a collision damage waiver is available for about $20 per day. Collision coverage on your vehicle at home may also cover damage to rental cars – check your policy before leaving home. Some credit cards offer reimbursement coverage for collision damage if you rent the car with that credit card.

Most rental companies stipulate that damage a car sustains while driven on unpaved roads is not covered by the insurance they offer. Check with the agent when you make your reservation.

Parking

You'll find ample parking at visitor centers and at popular trailheads. However, these often overflow in the summertime, so go early to get a spot.

Road Rules

Throughout the US, cars drive on the right side of the road. Apart from that, road rules differ slightly from state to state, but all require the use of safety belts as well as the proper use of child safety seats for children under the age of five.

Speed limits vary. The maximum interstate speed limit in Tennessee and North Carolina is 70mph, although interstate speeds can drop to 55mph in urban areas. On two-lane highways, the speed limit is 55mph unless otherwise posted; on mountain roads it's 45mph unless otherwise posted. If you are pulled over by the police, do not get out of your car. Collect your license and other documents and wait for the officer to come to you.

Pay attention to livestock- or deer-crossing signs – tangle with a deer, cow or elk and you'll total your car in addition to killing the critter. You can incur stiff fines, jail time and other penalties if caught driving under the influence of alcohol.

Local Transportation

Gatlinburg Trolley

The **Gatlinburg Trolley** (www.gatlinburgtrolley.org; ⌚generally 8:30am-midnight May-Oct, varies rest of year) serves downtown Gatlinburg on various routes. The service's tan line ($2) goes into the national park from June through October and stops at Sugarlands Visitor Center, the Laurel Falls parking area and Elkmont Campground.

Health & Safety

BEFORE YOU GO

Health Insurance

No matter how long or short your trip, make sure you have adequate travel insurance, purchased before departure. At a minimum, you need coverage for medical emergencies and treatment, including hospital stays and an emergency flight home if necessary. Medical treatment in the US is of the highest caliber, but the expense could very well bankrupt you.

You should also consider getting coverage for luggage theft or loss and trip cancellation. If you already have a home-owner's or renter's policy, investigate what it will cover and consider getting supplemental insurance to cover the rest. If you have prepaid a large portion of your trip, cancellation insurance is a worthwhile expense. A comprehensive travel-insurance policy that covers all these things can cost up to 10% of the total outlay of your trip.

Worldwide travel insurance is available at www.lonelyplanet.com/travel-insurance. You can buy, extend and claim online anytime – even if you're already on the road.

IN THE PARK

Medical Assistance

If you have an emergency in the park and you have cell service, dial 911; be sure you note your location (trail, campground etc).

For long-distance and toll-free calls, dial 1 followed by three-digit area code and seven-digit local number.

Park Headquarters & Park Emergency Number	☎865-436-9171
General Park Information	☎865-436-1200
Backcountry Information	☎865-436-1297
Gatlinburg Police	☎865-436-5181
Cherokee Police	☎828-497-4131

There are several hospitals near the park, including **Blount Memorial Hospital** (☎865-983-7211; 907 E Lamar Alexander Pkwy, Maryville), 16 miles northwest of Townsend, and **LeConte Medical Center** (☎865-446-7000; 742 Middle Creek Rd, Sevierville, TN), 13 miles north of Gatlinburg.

Emergency rooms are required to treat all patients regardless of ability to pay, but clinics will require proof of insurance or immediate payment.

Common Ailments

Some of the more common ailments include blisters, fatigue and sore joints. Be sure to break in your hiking boots (and build up your stamina) before you arrive, and bring along a first-aid kit to treat any minor scrapes.

Blisters

To avoid blisters, make sure your walking boots or shoes are well worn in before you hit the trail. Boots should fit comfortably, with enough room to move your toes. Wear specialized walking socks that fit properly; be sure there are no seams across the widest part of your foot. Wet and muddy socks can cause blisters, so pack a spare pair. If you feel a blister coming on, treat it sooner rather then later by applying a bit of moleskin or duct tape.

Fatigue

More injuries happen toward the end of the day rather than early, when you're fresher. Although tiredness can simply be a nuisance on an easy hike, it can be life-threatening on narrow, exposed ridges or in bad

RECOMMENDED VACCINATIONS

No vaccinations are currently recommended or required when visiting the national park. For the most up-to-date information, see the Centers for Disease Control website (www.cdc.gov).

weather. Never set out on a hike that is beyond your capabilities on the day. If you feel below par, have a day off.

Don't push yourself too hard – take rests every hour or two and build in a good half-hour lunch break. Toward the end of the day, take the pace down and concentrate harder. Drink plenty of water and eat properly throughout the day – nuts, dried fruit and chocolate are all good energy-rich snacks.

Giardiasis

This parasitic infection of the small intestine, commonly called giardia, may cause nausea, bloating, cramps and diarrhea, and can last for weeks. Giardia is easily diagnosed by a stool test and readily treated with antibiotics.

To protect yourself from giardia, do not drink water from springs or streams without filtering, boiling or chemically treating it first, as the water may be contaminated. Most hikers prefer using a filter (one that has a pore size of 1 micron or less to remove giardia).

Giardia can also be transmitted from person to person if proper hand washing is not performed.

Knee Strain

Although climbs are more challenging, your legs may feel the burn on long, steep descents. You can't eliminate strain on the knee joints when dropping steeply, but you can reduce it by taking shorter steps that leave your legs slightly bent and ensuring that your heel hits the ground before the rest of your foot. Some walkers find that compression bandages help, and trekking poles are very effective in taking some of the weight off the knees.

Environmental Hazards

Preparation and responsibility for your own safety are key to a safe adventure.

Bites & Stings

Take precautions to avoid bites and stings. Young children and the elderly are particularly vulnerable to extreme reactions.

SNAKES

Copperheads and timber rattlesnakes are the two species of venomous snake found inside the park. These snakes are not aggressive and prefer to avoid humans. Most bites occur from people stepping on an unnoticed snake. Those bitten will experience local pain and swelling. Death is rare even without treatment (no fatality from a snakebite has ever been recorded in the Smokies).

To treat a snakebite, place a light constricting bandage over the bite (wrapping as you would for a sprain or fracture), keep the wounded part of the body below the level of the heart and move it as little as possible. Attempting to suck out the venom and/or applying a tourniquet is not recommended. Stay calm, send for help and avoid unnecessary activity. If walking out is necessary, do so slowly, with frequent rest stops.

TICKS

Wear long sleeves and pants to protect from ticks. Always check your body for ticks after walking through high grass or thickly forested areas. If ticks are found unattached, they can simply be brushed off. If a tick is found attached, press down around the tick's head with tweezers, grab the head and gently pull upward – do not twist it. (If no tweezers are available, use your fingers.) Don't douse an attached tick with oil, alcohol or petroleum jelly.

Diseases transmitted by ticks such as Rocky Mountain spotted fever and Lyme disease are not common in the park. However, if you become ill after receiving the bite, seek medical treatment immediately.

Tick bites can occur any time of year, though infections are more common in the warm-weather months from May to September.

YELLOWJACKETS, BEES & WASPS

A sting from a yellowjacket, bee or wasp can cause minor local swelling, though it can lead to life-threatening anaphylactic shock for those allergic to stings. Those with allergies should always carry an EpiPen.

If stung, over-the-counter antihistamines such as Benadryl can help reduce swelling. If bitten on the hand, remove rings immediately.

Cold & Wet Weather

The wintertime brings wet and icy weather to the park. Be sure to dress properly for the elements and be prepared for changing weather conditions.

HYPOTHERMIA

This life-threatening condition occurs when prolonged exposure to cold thwarts the body's ability to maintain its core temperature. Hypothermia is a real danger, regardless of the season. Cold, wet and wind can form a deadly combination, even with temperatures in the 50°Fs (10°C to 15°C). At higher elevations, hypothermia can even occur in the summer.

Symptoms include uncontrolled shivering, poor

muscle control and irrational behavior. Treat symptoms by putting on dry clothing, giving warm fluids and warming the victim through direct body contact with another person.

Prevention is the best strategy: Remember to dress in layers and wear a waterproof, windproof outer jacket.

Heat

Summer days can bring high heat and humidity to the park. Take it slowly and don't underestimate your water requirements before setting out on a hike.

DEHYDRATION & EXHAUSTION

Lack of water can cause dehydration, which can lead to heat exhaustion. To prevent dehydration, make sure to drink plenty of fluids. Hikers should drink a gallon of water per day, and anyone overnight hiking should bring a water treatment system (p200).

Take note if you haven't had to urinate as often as usual, or if your urine is dark yellow or amber colored. These are indicators of dehydration, which can rapidly spiral into more dire health concerns. Loss of appetite and thirst may be early symptoms of heat exhaustion, so even if you don't feel thirsty, drink water often and have a salty snack while you're at it. Add a little electrolyte-replacement powder to your water. Err on the side of caution and bring more water and food than you think you'll need.

Characterized by fatigue, nausea, headaches, cramps and cool, clammy skin, heat exhaustion should be treated by drinking water, eating high-energy foods, resting in the shade and cooling the skin with a wet cloth. Heat exhaustion can lead to heatstroke if not addressed promptly.

HEATSTROKE

Long, continuous exposure to high temperatures can lead to heatstroke, a serious, sometimes fatal condition that occurs when the body's heat-regulating mechanism breaks down and one's body temperature rises to dangerous levels.

Symptoms of heatstroke include flushed, dry skin, a weak and rapid pulse, poor judgment, inability to focus and delirium. Move the victim to shade, and use whatever means possible to cool the victim, such as drenching their clothing with creek water. Send for help, as this is a medical emergency.

Lightning Strikes

Lightning strikes can sometimes lead to respiratory and cardiac arrest. Victims may be saved through the prompt administration of CPR – even without medical equipment available.

When seeking shelter, avoid high trees, solitary trees and rocky outcroppings and overhangs.

Poisonous Plants

Poison ivy is widely present in the park. Learn to recognize its three-leaf pattern. Vines may not be easy to identify, and should be avoided.

Standing Trees

Remember to look up before setting up your camp. Don't camp under dead tree limbs or near standing dead trees – and with virulent insect infestations, the park has a lot of dead trees.

Streams & Waterfalls

Heavy rain can sometimes lead to dangerously swollen streams and washed-out bridges. Don't attempt to make a stream crossing unless you're sure you can make it. When in doubt, turn back. Use a walking stick or hiking poles for added balance while crossing.

Avoid camping next to swollen streams.

Don't ever attempt to climb to the top of a waterfall. Several visitors have fallen or been swept to their deaths while clambering around on top of falls.

TAP WATER & NATIONAL PARK WATER SOURCES

Visitors are strongly advised to treat all water before drinking from any of the natural water sources in the Smoky Mountains. Those rushing streams look crisp, clean and clear, but the protozoan Giardia lamblia may be present in those waters. Before drinking you'll need to boil the water for one minute, chemically treat the water (ie with water purification tablets) or use a filter capable of removing particles as small as 1 micron.

Tap water from the towns and cities near the park is generally safe to drink. The exception is during occasional cases of burst pipes and water outages, which lead utility companies to issue 'boil advisories.' During such times, pathogens could be present in the water, and consumers are urged not to use tap water for drinking, brushing teeth or bathing, unless it has been boiled for a full minute.

Outside of the park, some cabins available for hire use well water, which can have a strong smell of sulfur. Inquire with the lodge before booking, or come prepared with your own high-quality filtration device.

Safe Hiking

It's easy to become complacent when hiking in the Smokies, given the clearly marked signage and generally well-maintained quality of the trails. But hiking here can be serious business. There are numerous medical emergencies each year on the trails, and several people have died.

The best way to ensure a rewarding hike is proper planning. Learn about the trails, honestly assess your limitations and respect them.

Before You Go

Before departing for an overnight backcountry hike, give a contact person your itinerary, including your destination after the hike, the date of your return, and the permit holder's name. Upon completion of your hike, call your contact – if you do not return on schedule, that person should call the park headquarters at 865-436-9171.

Hike Smart

➡ Stay on marked trails, both for your safety and to control erosion. It's extremely difficult for rescuers to find a hiker who has wandered off-trail.

➡ Don't hike alone. Most of those who get in trouble are solo hikers, for whom the risks are multiplied. Backcountry hikes are safer (and more enjoyable) with a companion.

➡ Go slow to avoid overexertion. Ideally you should be able to speak easily while hiking, regardless of the grade. Be sure to take a five- to 10-minute break every hour to recharge.

➡ Pay close attention to your intake of food and fluids to prevent dehydration and hyponatremia (low blood sodium level). One good strategy is to have a salty snack and a long drink of water every 20 to 30 minutes. In summer months each hiker should drink 3 to 4 quarts of water per day, sipping constantly. Eat before you're hungry and drink before you're thirsty.

➡ In addition to sturdy, comfortable, broken-in boots and medium-weight socks, bring moleskin for blisters and make sure your toenails are trimmed.

➡ Don't be overly ambitious. Particularly for novice hikers, it's a good idea to spend the first day or two gauging your ability and response to the climate and terrain. Work your way up to more difficult trails.

➡ Hike during the cooler early morning and late-afternoon hours, especially in summer.

Rescue & Evacuation

Hikers should take responsibility for their own safety and aim to prevent emergency situations, but even the most safety-conscious hiker may have a serious accident requiring urgent medical attention.

If a person in your group is injured, leave someone with them while others seek help. If there are only two of you, leave the injured person with as much warm clothing, food and water as it's sensible to spare, plus a whistle and flashlight. Mark their position with something conspicuous.

Sprains

Ankle and knee sprains are common injuries among hikers, particularly when crossing streams and slippery rocks. To help prevent ankle sprains, wear boots that have adequate ankle support. If you suffer a sprain, immobilize the joint with a firm bandage, and if possible, immerse the foot in cold water. Relieve pain and swelling by resting and icing the joint, and keeping it elevated as much as possible for the first 24 hours. Take over-the-counter painkillers to ease discomfort. If the sprain is mild, you may be able to continue your hike after a couple of days.

Behind the Scenes

SEND US YOUR FEEDBACK

We love to hear from travelers – your comments keep us on our toes and help make our books better. Our well-traveled team reads every word on what you loved or loathed about this book. Although we cannot reply individually to your submissions, we always guarantee that your feedback goes straight to the appropriate authors, in time for the next edition. Each person who sends us information is thanked in the next edition – the most useful submissions are rewarded with a selection of digital PDF chapters.

Visit **lonelyplanet.com/contact** to submit your updates and suggestions or to ask for help. Our award-winning website also features inspirational travel stories, news and discussions.

Note: We may edit, reproduce and incorporate your comments in Lonely Planet products such as guidebooks, websites and digital products, so let us know if you don't want your comments reproduced or your name acknowledged. For a copy of our privacy policy visit lonelyplanet.com/privacy.

WRITER THANKS

Amy C Balfour

Thank you to Tennessee locals Melissa Peeler and Lauren Batte for joining me on this adventure for a few days and sharing their expertise. Thanks also to Katie Lane, Teddy Colocotronis, Scooter Colocotronis, Stephanie Baker Jones, Chad Graddy, Jim Hester, Deborah Stacy Gebhardt, Jimmy Surface, Marjorie Joyce, Buck the Cataloochee camp host, the Cades Cove campfire and moonshine crew, and Lane and Beth Lastinger – Pilot Cove hosts extraordinaire. Many, many thanks to co-writer Regis St Louis and Destination Editor Trisha Ping.

Kevin Raub

Thanks to my wife, Adriana Schmidt Raub, Destination Editor Trisha Ping and my fellow Georgian in crime, MaSovaida Morgan and Jade Bremner. On the road, thanks to: Jason and Jennifer Hatfield, David and Aynsley Corbett, Jeff Fenn, Sharon Crenshaw, Jerry Brown, Tobie Chandler, Teka Earnhardt, Jode Mull, David Junker, Travis Currie, Hannah Amick, Mary Reynolds, Jenny Odom, Mary Reynolds, Sarah Horten and Keaton Thurmond.

Regis St Louis

Many thanks to Trisha Ping for inviting me on board, and to Amy Balfour for sharing tips. I'm grateful for the insight shared by the many park rangers, backpackers and AT through-hikers I met along the way. Special thanks to my wife Cassandra and our daughters Magdalena and Genevieve who joined me for frosty nights of camping and some magnificent hikes throughout the park.

Greg Ward

Thanks to the many wonderful people who helped me on the road, especially at Historic Stagville Plantation, Price's Chicken Coop, Bryson City Bicycles, and the Orange County Visitor Center. Thanks too to my editor Trisha Ping for giving me this opportunity, and to my dear wife Sam for everything else.

ACKNOWLEDGEMENTS

Climate map data adapted from Peel MC, Finlayson BL & McMahon TA (2007) 'Updated World Map of the Köppen-Geiger Climate Classification', Hydrology and Earth System Sciences, 11, 163344.

Cover photograph: The Great Smoky Mountains on Sunny Autumn Day. Marje/Getty Images©

THIS BOOK

This 2nd edition of Lonely Planet's *Great Smoky Mountains National Park* guidebook was researched and written by Amy C Balfour, Kevin Raub, Regis St Louis and Greg Ward, as was the previous edition. This guidebook was produced by the following:

Destination Editor Trisha Ping

Senior Product Editors Kate Mathews, Vicky Smith, Grace Dobell

Product Editor Rachel Rawling

Senior Cartographer Alison Lyall

Book Designer Lauren Egan

Assisting Editors Andrew Bain, James Bainbridge, Katie Connolly, Helen Koehne, Kellie Langdon, Gabrielle Stefanos

Assisting Cartographers Corey Hutchison, Julie Sheridan, Diana Von Holdt

Cover Researcher Fergal Condon

Thanks to Alicia Johnson, Sandie Kestell, Mazzy Prinsep

Index

A

Abrams Creek 76
Abrams Falls 52, **53**
accessible travel 202
  Sugarlands Valley Nature Trail 49, 202, **44**
accommodations 202-3, 204, *see also individual locations*
activities 17, 19-21, 26-31, 33 *see also individual locations, activities*
adventure sports
  Gatlinburg 93
  Knoxville 83
air travel 208-9
alcohol 15
Alum Cave Bluffs 12, 39, **44**, **12**, **24**
Amicalola Falls State Park 161-2
amphibians 187
amusement parks
  Anakeesta 92
  Dollywood 88, 89
  Tweetsie Railroad 113
Andrews Bald 45
animals 15, 72, 185-7, 189, *see also individual animals*
Anthony Creek Trail to Anthony Creek Bridge 55, **53**
Apalachee people 178
Appalachian balds 196
Appalachian Summer Festival 116
Appalachian Trail 9, 31, **9**
aquariums
  Georgia Aquarium 138
  Ripley's Aquarium of the Smokies 93
  Tennessee Aquarium 99
area codes 15, 206
Asheville 117-26, **118**, **122**
  accommodations 120-1
  activities 120
  drinking 121, 124-5
  food 121-4
  entertainment 125
  festivals & events 120
  shopping 126
  sights 117-19
  tours 120
  travel to/from 126
  travel within 126
Asheville Ale Trail 124
Asheville Distilling Co 125
Athens 154-8, **156**
Atlanta 135-54, **136-7**
  accommodations 134, 140-3
  activities 135-9
  climate 134
  Downtown 135-9, 143-4, 148-9, **142**
  drinking 148-52
  East Side 139, 144-5, 148-9, **150-1**
  entertainment 152-3
  festivals & events 139-40
  food 134, 143-8
  highlights 136-7
  Midtown 138, 143-4, **146-7**
  shopping 153
  sights 135-54
  tours 138
  travel seasons 134
  travel to/from 153
  travel within 154
  Westside 145-8, 149-52
Atlanta BeltLine 140
ATMs 204

B

Balsam Mountain 76
Baskins Creek Trail 58
bathrooms 206
beer 125, *see also* breweries
bicycling 15, 28-9, 209, *see also* mountain biking
  Bryson City 129
  Cades Cove 28
  Chattanooga 101
  Parson Branch Road 28-9
Big Creek 62-3, 73-6, **63**
Biltmore Estate 117-18
birds 186-7, 189
black bears 185, 189, **189**
Black Rock Mountain State Park 168
blisters 211
Blowing Rock 112-15
Blue Ridge 162-4
Blue Ridge Parkway 113
boat travel 209
bobcats 186
Boogerman Trail 56, **57**
books 174, 177, 184, 185, 191, 194
Boone 115-17
Brevard 131-3
breweries
  Asheville 120, 125-6, 131
  Athens 157
  Atlanta 149, 152
  Blue Ridge 163
  Chattanooga 103
  Gatlinburg 97
  Johnson City 102
  Knoxville 85, 87
  Pigeon Forge 91
Bryson City 129-30
Buck Manor 155
Buck, Peter 155
budget 15
bus travel 209-10
bushwalking, *see* hiking
business hours 204

C

cable cars
  Gatlinburg Sky Lift 93
  Ober Gatlinburg Aerial Tramway 93
Cades Cove 12, 69, 177, **53**, **70-1**, **12**
  accommodations 76
  activities 68-70
  day hikes 52-5, **53**
  sights 68-70
Cades Cove gristmill 12, **12**
campfires 60
campsite reservations 16
canoeing 31
Capone, Al 96
car travel 209, 210, *see also* drives
  driver's licenses 210
  insurance 210
  organizations 210
  road rules 210
  safety 14
Carlos C Campbell Overlook 66, 196
Cataloochee Valley 13, **57**
  accommodations 76
  activities 70-1
  day hikes 56-8, **57**
  sights 70-1
  wildlife 13, 72, **13**
cell phones 14, 206
cemeteries 58
Charlies Bunion 58, 60-2, **61**, **74**

Map Pages **000**
Photo Pages **000**

Chattanooga 97-104, **98**
Cherokee (town) 127-8
Cherokee mythology 128, 192
Cherokee National Forest 104-8
Cherokee people 128, 190-1, 192
chestnut trees 195
children, travel with 32-6, **32**
Chimney Tops 16, 46, **44**
churches
  Ebenezer Baptist Church (New) 139
  Little Cataloochee Baptist Church 57
  Methodist Church 68
  Missionary Baptist Church 68
  Palmer Chapel 71
  Primitive Baptist Church 68
Civil War 179
Clayton 168-9
climate 14, 19-21, *see also individual regions*
Clingmans Dome 9, 66, **8-9**, **29**, **74**
clothing 198-9
Cosby
  accommodations 73-6
  day hikes 50-1, **51**
  overnight hikes 62-3, **63**
costs 15
courses 72
craft beer 121
Crockett, David 105
cultural centers
  Folk Art Center 118-19
  Foxfire Museum & Heritage Center 168
currency 15
cycling, *see* bicycling

D
Dahlonega 159-61, **160**
dangers, *see* safety
day hikes 39-58
  Abrams Falls 52, **53**
  Alum Cave Bluffs 12, 39, **44**, **12**, **24**
  Andrews Bald 45, **44**
  Anthony Creek Trail to Anthony Creek Bridge 55, **53**
  Baskins Creek Trail 58
  Boogerman Trail 56, **57**
  Cades Cove 52-5, **53**
  Cataloochee Valley 56-8, **57**
  Charlies Bunion 58
  Chimney Tops 16, 46, **44**
  Cosby 50-1, **51**
  Gatlinburg Trail 49, 93, **44**
  Greenbrier 50-1, **51**
  Gregory Bald 52-3, **53**
  Grotto Falls 51, **51**, **18**
  Kephart Prong Trail 45-6, **44**
  Laurel Falls 44, **44**, **74**
  Little Cataloochee Baptist Church 57-8, **57**, **18**
  Newfound Gap Road 39-49, 58, **44**
  Oconaluftee River Trail 58
  Rainbow Falls 11, 16, 50-1, **51**, **11**
  Ramsey Cascades 50, **51**, **28**
  Rich Mountain Loop 53-5, **53**
  Roaring Fork Motor Nature Trail 50, 58, **51**
  Rough Fork Trail to Woody Place 56-7, **57**
  Sugarlands Valley Nature Trail 49, 202, **44**
deer 186, **2**, **34**, **74**
dehydration 213
disabilities, travelers with 202
distilleries
  Asheville 125
  Chattanooga 103
  Gatlinburg 95-6
  Pigeon Forge 91
  Sevierville 86
Dolly Parton 88, 89, 193, **182**
Dollywood 88, 89
drinks 121, 162
drives
  Blue Ridge Parkway 113
  Cherokee National Forest 107
  Foothills Parkway 67, **67**
  Little River Road 54, **54**
  Newfound Gap Rd 47, **47**
  Ocoee Scenic Byway 107
  Rich Mountain Road 68
  Roaring Fork Motor Nature Trail 48, **48**
driver's licenses 210
driving, *see* car travel
drones 15

E
East Tennessee 79-108, **80-1**
  accommodations 79
  climate 79
  food 79
  highlights 80-1
  travel seasons 79
economy 174-5
electricity 203
elk 15, 72, 185-6, 186, 189, **13**, **188**
Elkmont 16, 66, 180
emergencies 15, 59, 200
environmental issues 175, 186, 195
equipment 199-201
etiquette 203
events, *see* festivals & events, music festivals
exchange rates 15

F
farms 165
fatigue 211-12
ferris wheels 89
festivals & events 19-21, *see also* music festivals
  Appalachian Summer Festival 116
  Craft Fair of the Southern Highlands 120
  Dragon Con 140
  Festival of Christmas Past 21
  Independence Day Midnight Parade 20
  Mountain Life Festival 21
  National Black Arts Festival 140
  Oktoberfest 165
  Peachtree Road Race 139-40
  Wildflower Pilgrimage 16, 19
films 174
fireflies 16, 20, 77, 187, **20**
fishing 162
flying squirrels 186
Fontana Dam
  accommodations 76-7
  activities 71
  overnight hikes 63-5, **64**
  sights 71
food 203, 205, *see also individual locations*
Foothills Parkway 16, **67**
  accommodations 76
  activities 68-70
  drives 67, **67**
  sights 68-70
frogs 189

G
galleries, *see* museums & galleries
gardens, *see* parks & gardens
Gatlin, Radford 179
Gatlinburg 16, 92-7, **94**
Gatlinburg Trail 49, 93, **44**
Gatlinburg Trolley 210
gay travelers 204
giardia 212
Grandfather Mountain 112-13
Great Depression 183
Great Rabbit 192
Great Smoky Mountains Institute at Tremont 16, 72
Great Smoky Mountains National Park 38-78, **40-1**
  accommodations 38, 72-7
  activities 65-71
  courses 72
  driving distances 38
  food 77-8
  highlights 40-1

Map Pages **000**
Photo Pages **000**

hiking 39-65
sights 65-71
tourist information 78
travel to/from 208-9
travel within 78, 209-10
viewpoints 38
Great Smoky Mountain Wildfires 184
Greenbrier 50-1, **51**
Gregory Bald 52-3, **53**
gristmills (Cades Cove) 12, **12**
Grotto Falls 51, **51**, **18**

H

hardwood forests 195
health 211-14
heat exhaustion 213
heatstroke 213
Helen 164-8, **166**
hellbenders (salamander) 187
hemlock forests 194
hemlock woolly adelgids 175, 196
High Country 112-17, **114**
hiking 17, 27-8, 39-65, **26**, *see also* day hikes, overnight hikes, waterfall hikes
Appalachian Trail 9, 31, **9**
Bryson City 129
Chattanooga 100
Cherokee National Forest 105, 106
clothing 198-9
equipment 198-201
Great Smoky Mountains National Park 39-65
health 214
maps 28
Nantahala National Forest 133
Pisgah National Forest 130
regulations 60
safety 205, 214
tips 59
trail difficulty ratings 39
weather 27
historic sites
Beech Grove School 71
Cable Mill Historic Area 69
Caldwell House 70-1
Carter Shields Cabin 69
Elijah Oliver Place 69
Elkmont Historic District 66
John Oliver Place 68
Mingus Mill 65-6
Palmer House 71
Rockefeller Memorial 66
Tipton Place 69
history 18, 176-84
books 177, 184, 191
Civil War 179
Great Depression 183
Great Smoky Mountain Wildfires 184
logging 179-81
Martin Luther King Jr National Historic Site 139
North Georgia 135
Trail of Tears 128
WWII 183
holidays 204-5
horseback riding 29, 31, **30**
Hot Springs 132
hypothermia 206, 212-13

I

immigration 208
Independence Day Midnight Parade 20
insurance 210, 211
internet access 203
internet resources 15, 206
invasive species 196
itineraries
northern explorer 25, **25**
park highlights 22, **22**
Smoky Mountains 23, **23**

J

Johnson City 102

K

kayaking 31, **30**
Kephart, Horace 191
Kephart Loop 60-2, **61**
Kephart Prong Trail 45-6, **44**
King Jr, Martin Luther 139
Knoxville 82-8, **84**
accommodations 84-5
activities 83
drinking 87
entertainment 87-8
festivals & events 83-4
food 85-7
sights 82-3
travel to/from 88

L

Laurel Falls 44, 74, **44**, **74**
legal matters 204
LGBTIQ+ travelers 204
lightning strikes 213
literature, *see* books
Little Cataloochee Baptist Church 57-8, **57**, **18**
Little Pigeon River 13, **13**
Little River Road 54, **54**
logging 179-81
Lookout Mountain 100
lungless salamanders 187

M

medical services 78, 211
Merlefest 115
mines 115
mobile phones 14, 206
money 14, 204
moonshine 96
mosquitos 205
motorcycle travel, *see* car travel
mountain biking 16, 28-9
Baker Creek Preserve 83
Brevard 131
Chattanooga 101
Cherokee National Forest 107
Gatlinburg 93
Knoxville 83
Nantahala National Forest 133
Pisgah National Forest 130
Mountain Life Festival 21
Mt Cammerer 62-3, **63**
Mt LeConte 10, **10**
Mt Mitchell State Park 117
museums
Alcatraz East Crime Museum 88-9
Arrowmont School of Arts & Crafts 93
Asheville Art Museum 119
Asheville Pinball Museum 119
Center for Civil & Human Rights 135
Center for Puppetry Arts 138
College Football Hall of Fame 138
Currahee Military Museum 171
Fernbank Museum of Natural History 139
Georgia Museum of Art 154
High Museum of Art 138
Hunter Museum of American Art 99
Jimmy Carter Presidential Library & Museum 139
Knoxville Museum of Art 82
Margaret Mitchell House & Museum 138
Mountain Farm Museum 65, **35**
Museum of East Tennessee History 82
Museum of the Cherokee Indian 127
Songbirds 97-9
Titanic Museum 88
Women's Basketball Hall of Fame 82-3
World of Coca-Cola 135
music festivals
Big Ears Festival 83
Brevard Music Festival 132
Chattanooga Nightfall 101
Merlefest 115
Mountain Dance & Folk Festival 120
Music Midtown 140
Rhythm & Blooms 84
Shaky Knees Music Festival 140

N

national forests, *see also* state parks
Cherokee National Forest 104-8
Nantahala National Forest 133

national forests *continued*
Pisgah National Forest 130-1
nature centers
Cradle of Forestry in America 130
Ijams Nature Center 83
nature trails
Roaring Fork Motor Nature Trail 12, 48, 50-1, 58, **48**, **51**, 3, 12
Sugarlands Valley Nature Trail 49, 202, **44**
Newfound Gap Rd 10, **44**, **47**, 11, 24
accommodations 73
activities 65-6
day hikes 39-49, 58, **44**
drives 47, **47**
overnight hikes 60-2, **61**
safety 14
sights 65-6
newspapers 206
North Carolina Mountains 109-33, **110-11**
accommodations 109
climate 109
food 109
highlights 110-11
travel seasons 109
North Georgia 154-72, **136-7**
accommodations 134
climate 134
food 134
highlights 137-8
history 135
travel seasons 134

O

oak forests 194
Ocoee Scenic Byway 107
Oconaluftee River Trail 58
Oconaluftee Valley Overlook 47, 5
opening hours 204
overnight hikes 59-65
Big Creek 62-3, **63**
Charlies Bunion 60-2, **61**, 74
Cosby 62-3, **63**
Fontana Dam 63-5, **64**
Kephart Loop 60-2, **61**
Mt Cammerer 62-3, **63**
Newfound Gap Road 60-2, **61**
permits 59
Twentymile to Gregory Bald Loop 63-5, **64**
western North Carolina 63-5, **64**

P

parks & gardens
Atlanta Botanical Garden 138
Chimney Rock Park 119
Coolidge Park 99-100
Piedmont Park 138
Sculpture Fields at Montague Park 100
State Botanical Garden of Georgia 154
Tennessee Riverpark 100
Parson Branch Road 28-9
Parton, Dolly 88, 89, 193, 182
passports 208
people 190-3
permits 59
pets, travel with 206-7
Pigeon Forge 88-92, **90**
Pigeon River 13, 13
pine forest 194
Pisgah National Forest 130-1
planning
budgeting 15
calendar of events 19-21
entrance fees 14
family travel 32-6
internet resources 15, 206
itineraries 22-5, **22**, **23**, **25**
opening dates 15
park basics 14
park rules 15
repeat visitors 16
travel seasons 14, 19-21
plants 15, 194-6, *see also individual species*
pleated woodpeckers 188
poison ivy 213
population 175
postal services 204
public holidays 204-5
pygmy shrews 186

R

Rainbow Falls 11, 16, 50-1, **51**, 11
Ramsey Cascades 50, **51**, 28
ranger programs 33
regulations 60
religion 175
REM 155
Rich Mountain Loop 53-5, **53**
Roan Mountain State Park 104-5
Roaring Fork Motor Nature Trail 12, 48, 50-1, 58, **48**, **51**, 3, 12
rock climbing
Chattanooga 100
Rough Fork Trail to Woody Place 56-7, **57**

S

safety 205-6, 212-14
Sevierville 86
Sliding Rock Recreation Area 130
smoking 207
snakes 212
sprains 214
spruce-fir forests 195
state parks, *see also* national forests
Amicalola Falls State Park 161-2
Black Rock Mountain State Park 168
David Crockett Birthplace State Park 105
Grandfather Mountain State Park 112-13
Mt Mitchell State Park 117
Roan Mountain State Park 104-5
Tallulah Gorge State Park 169-70
Unicoi State Park 165
Vogel State Park 165
Sugarlands Valley Nature Trail 49, 202, **44**
swimming 31
synchronous fireflies 16, 20, 77, 187, 20

T

Tallulah Gorge 170
Tallulah Gorge State Park 169-70
telephone services 14, 206
ticks 212
time 206
tipping 204
Toccoa 170-2
toilets 206
tourist information 78, 206
Townsend 92
Trail of Tears 128
travel to/from Great Smoky Mountains National Park 208-9
travel within Great Smoky Mountains National Park 78, 209-10
Tri-Cities Region 102
Tsali Recreation Area 133
tubing 165
Twentymile to Gregory Bald Loop 63-5, **64**

U

Unicoi State Park 165
University of Georgia 154
Urban Wilderness 83

V

vacations 204-5
viewpoints 17, 38
Carlos C Campbell Overlook 66, 196
Clingmans Dome 9, 66, 8-9, 29, 74
Look Rock Tower 69-70
Newfound Gap 66
Shuckstack Tower 71
visas 207, 208
Vogel State Park 165

W

Walker Family 191-3
Walker, John 191-3
walking, *see* hiking
water 213

Map Pages **000**
Photo Pages 000

water sports 83, 129, *see also individual water sports*
waterfall hikes 28
  Abrams Falls 52, **53**
  Benton Falls 106
  Grotto Falls 51, **51**, **18**
  Hurricane Falls Trail 170
  Laurel Falls 44, **44**, **74**
  Margarette Falls 105
  Rainbow Falls 11, 16, 50-1, **51**, **11**
  Ramsey Cascades 28, 50, **51**, **28**
waterfalls 11
  Abrams Falls 52
  Amicalola Falls 161
  Anna Ruby Falls 164-5
  Benton Falls 106
  Grotto Falls 51, **18**
  Laurel Falls 44, 74, **74**
  Linville Falls 112
  Margarette Falls 105
  Rainbow Falls 11, 16, 50, **11**
  Ramsey Cascades 28, 50, **28**
  safety 205-6
  Sinks, the 66
  Sliding Rock Recreation Area 130
  Toccoa Falls 170-1
weather 14, 19-21, *see also individual regions*
websites 15, 206
western North Carolina 127-33, **64**
  accommodations 76-7
  overnight hikes 63-5, **64**
  sights 71
white-tailed deer 186, **2**, **34**, **74**, **188-9**
white-water rafting 31, **2**
  Bryson City 129
  Cherokee National Forest 106-7
  Pigeon River 13, **13**
wild turkeys 189
Wildflower Pilgrimage 16, 19
wildflowers 15, 16, **20**
wildlife 16, 72, 185-9
  Cataloochee 13, 72, **13**
  safety 205
wineries
  Currahee Vineyard & Winery 171
  Dahlonega 162
  Frogtown Cellars 159
  Habersham Vineyards & Winery 165
  Three Sisters 159
  Wolf Mountain Vineyards 159
Wolfe, Thomas 119
WWII 183

Z

ziplining
  Bryson City 129
  Gatlinburg 92, 93
  Knoxville 83

Map Legend

Sights
- Beach
- Bird Sanctuary
- Buddhist
- Castle/Palace
- Christian
- Confucian
- Hindu
- Islamic
- Jain
- Jewish
- Monument
- Museum/Gallery/Historic Building
- Ruin
- Shinto
- Sikh
- Taoist
- Winery/Vineyard
- Zoo/Wildlife Sanctuary
- Other Sight

Activities, Courses & Tours
- Bodysurfing
- Diving
- Canoeing/Kayaking
- Course/Tour
- Sento Hot Baths/Onsen
- Skiing
- Snorkeling
- Surfing
- Swimming/Pool
- Walking
- Windsurfing
- Other Activity

Sleeping
- Sleeping
- Camping
- Hut/Shelter

Eating
- Eating

Drinking & Nightlife
- Drinking & Nightlife
- Cafe

Entertainment
- Entertainment

Shopping
- Shopping

Information
- Bank
- Embassy/Consulate
- Hospital/Medical
- Internet
- Police
- Post Office
- Telephone
- Toilet
- Tourist Information
- Other Information

Geographic
- Beach
- Gate
- Hut/Shelter
- Lighthouse
- Lookout
- Mountain/Volcano
- Oasis
- Park
- Pass
- Picnic Area
- Waterfall

Population
- Capital (National)
- Capital (State/Province)
- City/Large Town
- Town/Village

Transport
- Airport
- BART station
- Border crossing
- Boston T station
- Bus
- Cable car/Funicular
- Cycling
- Ferry
- Metro/Muni station
- Monorail
- Parking
- Petrol station
- Subway/SkyTrain station
- Taxi
- Train station/Railway
- Tram
- Underground station
- Other Transport

Routes
- Tollway
- Freeway
- Primary
- Secondary
- Tertiary
- Lane
- Unsealed road
- Road under construction
- Plaza/Mall
- Steps
- Tunnel
- Pedestrian overpass
- Walking Tour
- Walking Tour detour
- Path/Walking Trail

Boundaries
- International
- State/Province
- Disputed
- Regional/Suburb
- Marine Park
- Cliff
- Wall

Hydrography
- River, Creek
- Intermittent River
- Canal
- Water
- Dry/Salt/Intermittent Lake
- Reef

Areas
- Airport/Runway
- Beach/Desert
- Cemetery (Christian)
- Cemetery (Other)
- Glacier
- Mudflat
- Park/Forest
- Sight (Building)
- Sportsground
- Swamp/Mangrove

Note: Not all symbols displayed above appear on the maps in this book

OUR STORY

A beat-up old car, a few dollars in the pocket and a sense of adventure. In 1972 that's all Tony and Maureen Wheeler needed for the trip of a lifetime – across Europe and Asia overland to Australia. It took several months, and at the end – broke but inspired – they sat at their kitchen table writing and stapling together their first travel guide, *Across Asia on the Cheap*. Within a week they'd sold 1500 copies. Lonely Planet was born.

Today, Lonely Planet has offices in Franklin, Dublin, Beijing and Delhi, with more than 600 staff and writers. We share Tony's belief that 'a great guidebook should do three things: inform, educate and amuse'.

OUR WRITERS

Amy C Balfour

Great Smoky Mountains National Park; East Tennessee Amy lives in the Shenandoah Valley in the foothills of the Blue Ridge Mountains in Virginia. After a backpacking trip through the Smokies on the Appalachian Trail, she fell hard for the national park. Her favorite places in the Great Smoky Mountains and East Tennessee include the summit of Gregory Bald, Abrams Falls, the meadows of Cataloochee Valley and just about everywhere in Chattanooga. Amy has authored or coauthored more than 40 books for Lonely Planet, including *USA*, *Eastern USA* and *Florida & the South's Best Trips*. Her stories have appeared in *Backpacker*, *Sierra*, *Southern Living* and *Women's Health*.

Kevin Raub

Atlanta & North Georgia Atlanta native Kevin Raub started his career as a music journalist in New York, working for *Men's Journal* and *Rolling Stone* magazines. He ditched the rock 'n' roll lifestyle for travel writing and has written nearly 50 Lonely Planet guides, focused mainly on Brazil, Chile, Colombia, USA, India, the Caribbean and Portugal. Raub also contributes to a variety of travel magazines in both the USA and UK. Along the way, the self-confessed hophead is in constant search of wildly high IBUs in local beers. Follow him on Twitter and Instagram (@RaubOnTheRoad).

Regis St Louis

Great Smoky Mountains National Park Regis grew up in a small town in the American Midwest – the kind of place that fuels big dreams of travel – and he developed an early fascination with foreign dialects and world cultures. He spent his formative years learning Russian and a handful of Romance languages, which served him well on journeys across much of the globe. Regis has contributed to more than 50 Lonely Planet titles, covering destinations across six continents. His travels have taken him from the mountains of Kamchatka to remote island villages in Melanesia, and to many grand urban landscapes. When not on the road, he lives in New Orleans.

Greg Ward

North Carolina Mountains Since whetting his appetite for travel by following the hippy trail to India, and later living in northern Spain, Greg Ward has written guides to destinations all over the world. As well as covering the USA from the Southwest to Hawaii, he has ranged on recent assignments from Corsica to the Cotswolds, and Japan to Corfu. See his website, www.gregward.info, for his favorite photos and memories.

Published by Lonely Planet Global Limited
CRN 554153
2nd edition – Mar 2021
ISBN 978 1 78868 094 3

10 9 8 7 6 5 4 3 2 1
Printed in Singapore